George Frederick Root

The New Choir and Congregation

A Collection of Hymns, Tunes, Anthems and Chants

George Frederick Root

The New Choir and Congregation
A Collection of Hymns, Tunes, Anthems and Chants

ISBN/EAN: 9783337296537

Printed in Europe, USA, Canada, Australia, Japan

Cover: Foto ©Thomas Meinert / pixelio.de

More available books at **www.hansebooks.com**

THE NEW

CHOIR AND CONGREGATION:

A COLLECTION OF

HYMNS, TUNES, ANTHEMS, CHANTS,

AND

RESPONSIVE SERVICES

FOR

The Choir and "All The People."

BY

GEO. F. ROOT.

PUBLISHED BY

| JOHN CHURCH & CO. | ROOT & SONS MUSIC CO. |
| CINCINNATI. | CHICAGO. |

EXPLANATORY.

Worship or praise is an individual matter. The attempt to have either done for us by others, must in the nature of the case be futile, and choirs that assume either to worship or praise for their congregations undertake the impossible, and usually find themselves simply performers, and their congregations audiences, listening, as at a concert, to their musical performances.

All that choirs can do for congregations, beyond entertaining them musically, is in the way of preparing them for musical worship, and in leading them in it—the worshiping each must do for himself.

This does not imply that it is wrong to enjoy the music of God's house, for it is no more wrong to enjoy the music of the choir than it is the eloquence of the minister or the beautiful or grand architecture of the edifice in which the worship takes place. The disorder comes from allowing the enjoyment to center and end in the music, the eloquence or the architecture.

The old hymn says:—

> " Rise from transitory things
> Toward heaven, thy native place."

Transitory things are not necessarily bad things. The tune is transitory, the edifice is transitory, all the beautiful things of nature are transitory; yet they are all lawfully ours for the fullest enjoyment they are capable of giving, even in divine worship, if while using them we rise, in our thoughts and affections, above the earthly tones or forms—if we look "through nature up to nature's God." Since "the greater includes the less," he who worships God in song keeps all the earthly pleasure of the music, while he adds to it the higher enjoyments of the heaven toward which he rises.

But this task of "rising" must not be made too difficult. We are all so inclined to let our enjoyments center and end in the senses, that small hindrances keep us down. The choir who feel that they must please the people musically or be dismissed, are bound by iron chains to their music; and in exclusively choir music, if the congregation do not hear distinctly the words that the choir sing, or hearing, do not see any special appropriateness in them or in the music, they will hardly find it possible to listen otherwise than for mere musical enjoyment. Especially is this true if they feel that
(ii)

the choir are there to "perform" the music for them. Still, in every religious society there are, and will continue to be, those who cultivate music, and those who, however fond of it, pay no attention to its cultivation ; and from the former will come choirs and music lovers who will not willingly be confined to the familiar tunes that all can sing. Any true statement of the musical problem must include these facts, and of course any plan for its solution must have regard to them also.

The effort long and earnestly made by Dr. Lowell Mason and his followers (among whom the author of this work is glad to enroll himself), to have singers give up on Sunday all music excepting that in which all the people could join, has not succeeded. With higher musical culture comes so strongly the desire to make use of higher musical powers than the old tunes require that it can not be resisted. Still, tunes are "old" only because they are good. Thousands of competitors for public favor that started in the race with them have dropped away and are forgotten ; and the "old tunes," so rich in hallowed memories and associations, are, and ever must be, indispensable to public worship.

It is well known, however, that exclusive choir performances have a tendency to place the "old tunes" and the singing of them lowest in the musical services of the church, which is a rank as unjust to their merits as it is hurtful to their influence.

Moreover, the thought of choirs, as "performers" is not a right one, for that implies an "audience," and performers and an audience are not the true elements of a worshiping assembly. There should be neither "lookers on " to see others worship, nor persons to be merely entertained by what is done. All should receive the instruction, all should unite in the prayers, all should join in the singing, and, more important still, there should be union and coöperation on the part of all, however varied their conditions and attainments.

So far as the music is concerned, when the trained voices sing, the people should neither listen as outsiders who have no part, nor as an audience to be merely entertained; and when the familiar tunes are sung, the trained voices should not lose interest by feeling that their best powers are not called into action.

There should be no antagonism nor even separation of

interests between choirs and congregations, and yet each should have to sing that which is suited to the needs and attainments of each. But how shall all this be accomplished, and all be made to coöperate harmoniously toward a higher usefulness for the music of the church and a nobler enjoyment of it?

This question, it is the object of these further explanations, and of this book, to answer.

There is not a familiar hymn that has not some Scripture or other words appropriate to it for illustration, introduction, or preparation. There is not a standard tune that may not receive new interest by an appropriate prelude. Let the choir sing such words as illustrate, lead to, and prepare for, the familiar hymn and tune, in music that is suited for that object rather than for vocal display, and then let "all the people" join in the tune as a chorus or climax, and, it is confidently asserted, the following results will be realized:

1st. The musical effect not being at its best without the voices of the congregation to make the tune a climax, and the climax not being reached without the illustration and preparation by the choir, a need is created—of the choir for the people, and of the people for the choir—that forms a basis for union, good will and mutual coöperation.

2d. The congregation, seeing just what the words mean that the choir sing, and why they are sung—watching their progress, and their appropriateness as they prepare for, and lead to, the final song—are much removed from the temptation now so common, to listen to the trained voices for musical entertainment instead of devotional assistance; and the choir, realizing the higher nature of their work, will be equally relieved from the temptation (or perhaps necessity) also common, to sing for the mere entertainment of their listeners.

3d. A new and better interest in the solos, duets, quartets, and anthems of the choir will spring up. Heretofore the more religious the meetings of a church, the less trained choir performances were wanted; the obvious reason being that the latter subserved little, if any, religious use; but the plan of CHOIR AND CONGREGATION will lead surely and safely to a union of worship and musical culture; for the more perfect and impressive the rendering by the choir of,

> "He is despised and rejected of men,"

the more heart-felt will be the response—

> "My faith looks up to thee,
> Thou Lamb of Calvary."

In proportion as

> "Now is the accepted time"

is sung persuasively so will be

> "Hear, O sinner, mercy hails you,
> Now with sweetest voice she calls!"

or as the choir describe the struggle with our spiritual enemies in the words:

> "They be many that fight against me,"

will the congregation be inclined to sing with new earnestness and resolution,

> "My soul, be on thy guard,
> Ten thousand foes arise,"

and so these services will be welcome and helpful in the most religious meetings of the church.

When shall these Scripture selections which precede the hymns and tunes be used, or at what part of divine service shall choir and congregation unite in these tune services? Shall it be only at opening or closing, or shall it be during service when the hymns are usually sung?

Whenever a hymn is appropriate its appropriate Scripture will be in order. A case can hardly be imagined where the two would not properly go together. It will be always, and only, a question of the preparation of the choir—the tune will always be ready. At first the choir may not have time to prepare preludes for all the hymns, but as they become familiar with the book they can accompany every hymn with a Scripture selection, if it is desired.

When this is to be done, it is suggested that the minister announce and read both selection and hymn. To facilitate this, the words of the selection are generally printed by themselves at the top of the hymn page. When the minister announces and reads both selection and hymn it will be understood that both are to be sung; when he announces and reads only the hymn it will be understood that the prelude is to be omitted. The congregation can either rise with the choir and stand during the prelude, or they can remain seated during the prelude and rise only for the hymn. The advantage of the first way is that they are then all ready for the hymn, without the trouble and confusion of rising during the singing. The tune should join the prelude without interlude or delay, except in the special cases hereafter mentioned.

RESPONSIVE SERVICES.

The growing feeling that all should have something to do in the services of the church, has already led extensively to alternate reading, by minister and people, of psalms and other portions of Scripture as a part of divine service.

The value of this exercise can not be questioned. Beside helping to fix the attention on what is read, all know that there is a reflex influence from spoken words upon him who speaks them, that thought alone can not produce.

There are, however, two difficulties in the spoken responses of a congregation, that to many people are hindrances to their usefulness,

The first is the disagreement—almost impossible to avoid—caused by not speaking the words together, and the second is the disorder that cannot be avoided, of voices at all sorts of pitches from low to high, mingling in a confused mass.

The obvious remedy for both these difficulties is chanting, and, however the spoken responses may have served a purpose, when once the measured and harmonious utterance of the chant form has been attained, the "confusion of tongues" inevitable in spoken responses, becomes a serious trouble to the sensitive, thoughtful, and devout. All may be assured that the chant is more easily and successfully acquired by a congregation than any tune, provided the chant is a proper one, and the words to it rightly set. That the musical utterances of responses is more emotional and more calculated to excite devotional feelings than spoken ones, needs no argument. The Responsive Services of the CHOIR AND CONGREGATION are therefore put forth with the strong conviction that the idea on which they are based, is an advanced one in this important and growing department of divine service.

It is believed, also, that the chants here used are proper chants, and that the words to them are so set that congregations will find no difficulty in using them.

The Responsive Service may take the place of one of the hymns, or of one of the Scripture readings; or, if minister and people have been accustomed to read alternately, it may take the place of that exercise. Many of the Responsive Services would come in with great appropriateness just before prayer, for they would tend to prepare the minds of both minister and people for that act. In fact, many of them would commence the prayer, which the minister as the mouth-piece of the people might continue. In another view, the Responsive Service might be the Old Testament Scripture, which might be followed the people being seated—by a New Testament selection or the portion of Scripture containing the text, read by the minister for instruction; the Responsive Service being always more for worship than for instruction. In Responsive Services the connection between minister and choir and congregation should be close. The instant one closes, the other should begin; there should be no hiatus between minister and response, nor between response and minister. The whole exercise should be continuous and cumulative.

ADDITIONAL HYMNS AND SELECTIONS.

Additional hymns and selections are placed separately, because they could not well be classified with the selections and hymns in the body of the book. This does not, however, affect their usefulness wherever they are found appropriate, either in public or social worship.

ABBREVIATIONS.

Where long hymns could be abbreviated it has been done, because the added Scripture selection lengthens the singing service. In many cases, however, it was not easy to see how abbreviations could be made, and such are left to be abbreviated according to the subject with which they are connected, or according to the taste of the minister.

The singing service may often be shortened advantageously by omitting instrumental interludes, for it is often the case that listening to instrumental music between verses breaks their connection in the mind, and causes mere musical considerations to take the place of spiritual ones. It is often the case that the subject of a hymn cannot safely be disturbed from the beginning to the end of it. This refers to devotional hymns and not to descriptive ones, in which interludes are sometimes serviceable.

SELECTION and HYMN, and PRELUDE and TUNE COMBINATIONS.

In addition to the combinations for choir and congregation indicated in this book, others may be made by chorister or minister. First, more combinations may be made on the plan of those already made, viz.: identity of keys and subjects, (with an occasional connection of relative minor and major.) Secondly, combinations may be made where preludes and tunes are in different keys, provided it is understood that the organist will play an interlude between prelude and tune, modulating from one to the other. This plan would open the way to hundreds of new combinations. No interlude should be played between prelude and tune unless this necessity arises. It is suggested that the minister always announce the Selection and Hymn whatever combinations be made.

G. F. R.

NOTE.—Will musical authors and publishers allow the author of this work, as one of the fraternity, frankly to remind them of the outlay of labor, time, and money that they see must have been expended in perfecting this idea and making it generally known? He is confident that all honorable and Christian men will give him a fair field for his experiment, and will not seek, by making use of the ideas and plans that he has originated, to reap for themselves the reward of his labors after the hard work has been done.

NEW CHOIR AND CONGREGATION.

Selection 1.—DOXOLOGY SERVICE.—Let the people praise thee, O God.

This Prelude may also be used with Hymns 1, 2, 3, 4, 5, or 6 when preferred.

G. F. R.

Let the peo - ple praise thee, O God, . . let ALL THE PEO - PLE praise thee; Oh, let the na-tions be

glad and sing for joy, For thou shalt judge the peo-ple right-eous-ly And gov - ern the na - tions,

gov - ern the na - tions, gov - ern the na - tions up - on earth; Let the peo - ple praise thee, O

God, O God, Let ALL THE PEO-PLE praise . . . thee,

God,

Cho'r and Congregation. *

Praise God, from whom all bless-
  ings flow ;
Praise him, all creatures here be-
  low ;
Praise him above, ye heavenly
  host,
Praise Father, Son, and Holy
  Ghost.

* It is intended that this Doxology shall follow the foregoing Prelude. without interlude or delay, to the tune " Old
Hundr:d." It should be given with the voices of " all the people." (For tune, see next page.)

(5)

Selection 2.—OLD HUNDRED SERVICE.—Praise ye the Lord.

Selection 2.

PRAISE YE THE LORD. Kings of the earth and all people; princes and all judges of the earth: both young men and maidens, old men and children.

For the Lord is good, His mercy is everlasting, and His truth endureth to all generations. Let every thing that hath breath praise the Lord.

OLD HUNDRED. L. M.

Choir and Congregation.

W. FRANC.

Praise God, from whom all bless-ings flow; Praise him, all creat-ures here be-low;

Praise him a-bove, ye heaven-ly host; Praise Fa-ther, Son, and Ho-ly Ghost.

1 KETHE.

1 All people that on earth do dwell,
Sing to the Lord with cheerful voice;
Him serve with fear, his praise forth tell,
Come ye before him and rejoice.

2 The Lord, ye know, is God indeed,
Without our aid he did us make;
We are his flock, he doth us feed,
And for his sheep he doth us take.

3 Oh, enter, then, his gates with praise,
Approach with joy his courts unto;
Praise, laud, and bless his name always,
For it is seemly so to do.

4 For why? the Lord our God is good,
His mercy is forever sure;
His truth at all times firmly stood,
And shall from age to age endure.

2 TATE & BRADY.

1 Be thou, O God, exalted high;
And as thy glory fills the sky,
So let it be on earth displayed,
Till thou art here, as there, obeyed.

2 Thy praises, Lord, we will resound
To all the listening nations round:
Thy mercy highest heaven transcends;
Thy truth unto the clouds extends.

3 WATTS.

1 From all that dwell below the skies,
Let the Creator's praise arise:
Let the Redeemer's name be sung,
Thro' ev'ry land by ev'ry tongue.

2 Eternal are thy mercies, Lord,
Eternal truth attends thy word:
Thy praise shall sound from shore to shore,
Till suns shall rise and set no more.

4 TATE & BRADY.

1 With one consent let all the earth
To God their cheerful voices raise;
Glad homage pay, with hallowed mirth,
And sing before him songs of praise.

2 The Lord is God; 'tis he alone
Doth life, and breath, and being give;
We are his work, and not our own,
The sheep that on his pastures live.

3 Enter his gates with songs of joy,
With praises to his courts repair;
And make it your divine employ,
To pay your thanks and honors there.

4 For he is good, supremely good;
His mercy is forever sure;
· His truth, which always firmly stood,
To endless ages shall endure.

5 WATTS.

1 Before Jehovah's awful throne,
Ye nations, bow with sacred joy.
Know that the Lord is God alone;
He can create, and he destroy.

2 His sovereign power, without our aid
Made us of clay, and formed us men;
And when, like wand'ring sheep, we strayed,
He brought us to his fold again.

3 We are his people, we his care—
Our souls, and all our mortal frame:
What lasting honors shall we rear,
Almighty Maker, to thy name?

4 We'll crowd thy gates with thankful songs,
High, as the heaven, our voices raise;
And earth, with all her thousand tongues,
Shall fill thy courts with sounding praise.

6 WATTS.

1 Wide as his vast dominion lies,
Let the Creator's name be known;
Loud as his thunder, shout his praise,
And sound it lofty as his throne.

2 Oh, sing the wonders of that love,
That thrills all heaven with grand accord;
Let all below and all above,
Shout hallelujahs to the Lord.

Selection 3.—ROSEDALE SERVICE (No. 1).—How amiable are thy tabernacles.   *

Selection 3.

How amiable are thy tabernacles, O Lord of hosts! My soul longeth, yea, even fainteth, for the courts of the Lord; my heart and my flesh crieth out for the living God. Blessed are they that dwell in thy house; they will be still praising thee.

ROSEDALE. L. M.

Choir and Congregation.

G. F. ROOT.

Great God! at - tend, while Zi - on sings The joy that from thy pres - ence springs;

To spend one day with thee on earth Ex - ceeds a thou - sand days of mirth.

7 WATTS.

1 Great God! attend, while Zion sings
The joy that from thy presence springs;
To spend one day with thee on earth
Exceeds a thousand days of mirth.

2 God is our sun, he makes our day;
God is our shield, he guards our way
From all the assaults of hell and sin,
From foes without, and foes within.

3 All needful grace will God bestow,
And crown that grace with glory, too:
He gives us all things, and withholds
No real good from upright souls.

4 O God, our King, whose sovereign sway
The glorious hosts of heaven obey,
Display thy grace, exert thy power,
Till all on earth thy name adore!

8 WATTS.

1 How pleasant, how divinely fair,
O Lord of hosts, thy dwellings are!
With long desire my spirit faints,
To meet the assemblies of thy saints.

2 Blest are the souls that find a place
Within the temple of thy grace;
There they behold thy gentler rays,
And seek thy face, and learn thy praise.

3 Blest are the men whose hearts are set,
To find the way to Zion's gate;
God is their strength, and thro' the road
They lean upon their helper, God.

4 Cheerful they walk with growing strength,
Till all shall meet in heaven at length;
Till all before thy face appear,
And join in nobler worship there.

9 STENNETT.

1 Another six days' work is done,
Another Sabbath is begun;
Return, my soul! enjoy thy rest,
Improve the day thy God has blessed.

2 Oh, that our tho'ts and thanks may rise,
As grateful incense to the skies;
And draw from heaven that sweet repose,
Which none, but he that feels it, knows.

3 This heavenly calm, within the breast,
Is the dear pledge of glorious rest,
Which for the church of God remains—
The end of cares, the end of pains.

4 In holy duties, let the day,
In holy pleasures, pass away;
How sweet a Sabbath thus to spend,
In hope of one that ne'er shall end.

10 DODDRIDGE.

1 Thine earthly Sabbaths, Lord, we love,
But there's a nobler rest above;
To that our longing souls aspire,
With cheerful hope and strong desire.

2 No more fatigue, no more distress,
Nor sin nor death shall reach the place;
No groans shall mingle with the songs
That warble from immortal tongues.

3 No rude alarms of raging foes,
No cares to break the long repose,
No midnight shade, no clouded sun,
But sacred, high, eternal noon.

11 WATTS.

1 Come gracious Lord, descend and dwell,
By faith and love, in every breast:
Then shall we know, and taste, and feel
The joys that can not be expressed.

2 Come, fill our hearts with inward strength,
Make our enlarged souls possess,
And learn the height, and breadth,
and length
Of thine eternal love and grace.

3 Now to the God whose powers can do
More than our thoughts and wishes know,
Be everlasting honors done,
By all the church, through Christ his Son.

Selection 4.—STEPHENS SERVICE.—"Awake, ye saints, awake!"

G. F. R.

A-wake, ye saints, a-wake! . . . . . In loft-iest songs of praise

And hail this sa-cred day; Your

. . . Your hom-age pay; The

joy-ful hom-age pay; Come, bless the day that God hath blest, The type of heav'ns e-ter-nal rest, The

type of heaven's e-ter-nal rest. A-wake, ye saints, a-wake! . . . . . A-

type of heaven's e-ter-nal rest. . . . . A-wake, and hail this sa-cred day, . .

wake, ye saints, a-wake! . . . In loft-iest songs of praise Your joy-ful

. . . . A-wake, and hail this sa-cred day; . . . Your joy-ful

hom-age pay, your joy-ful hom-age pay; A-wake, ye saints, a-wake! And hail this sa-cred day.

hom-age pay, your joy-ful hom-age pay; A-wake, ye saints, a-wake! And hail this sa-cred day.

Selection 4.

Awake, ye saints, awake! and hail this sacred day; In loftiest songs of praise your joyful homage pay. Come, bless the day that God hath blest, the type of heaven's eternal rest. Awake, ye saints, awake! and hail this sacred day.

STEPHENS. C. M.

WM. JONES.

With joy we hail the sa - cred day Which God hath called his own;

With joy the sum - mons we o - bey, To wor - ship at his throne.

12 LYTE.

1 With joy we hail the sacred day
  Which God hath called his own;
  With joy the summons we obey
  To worship at his throne.

2 Thy chosen temple, Lord, how fair!
  Where willing votaries throng
  To breathe the humble, fervent prayer,
  And pour the choral song.

3 Spirit of grace! oh, deign to dwell
  Within thy church below;
  Make her in holiness excel,
  With pure devotion glow.

4 Let peace within her walls be found;
  Let all her sons unite,
  To spread with grateful zeal around
  Her clear and shining light.

13 WATTS.

1 Lord, in the morning thou shalt hear
  My voice ascending high;
  To thee will I direct my prayer,
  To thee lift up mine eye.

2 Thou art a God, before whose sight
  The wicked shall not stand;
  Sinners shall ne'er be thy delight,
  Nor dwell at thy right hand.

3 But to thy house will I resort
  To taste thy mercies there;
  I will frequent thy holy court,
  And worship in thy fear.

4 Oh, may thy Spirit guide my feet
  In ways of righteousness!
  Make every path of duty straight,
  And plain before my face.

14 BARBAULD.

1 Again the Lord of life and light
  Awakes the kindling ray,
  Dispels the darkness of the night,
  And pours increasing day.

2 Oh, what a night was that which wrapt
  A guilty world in gloom!
  Oh, what a sun which broke this day
  Triumphant from the tomb!

3 This day be grateful homage paid,
  And loud hosannas sung;
  Let gladness dwell in every heart,
  And praise on every tongue.

4 Ten thousand thousand voices join
  To hail this happy morn,
  Which scatters blessings from its wings
  On nations yet unborn.

15 WATTS.

1 This is the day the Lord hath made;
  He calls the hours his own;
  Let heaven rejoice, let earth be glad,
  And praise surround the throne.

2 To-day he rose, and left the dead,
  And Satan's empire fell;
  To-day the saints his triumph spread,
  And all his wonders tell.

3 Hosanna to the anointed King,
  To David's holy Son;
  Help us, O Lord; descend, and bring
  Salvation from thy throne.

16 WATTS.

1 Once more, my soul, the rising day
  Salutes thy waking eyes;
  Once more, my voice, thy tribute pay
  To him that rules the skies.

2 Night unto night his name repeats,
  The day renews the sound,
  Wide as the heaven on which he sits,
  To turn the seasons round.

3 Great God, let all my hours be thine,
  While I enjoy the light;
  Then shall my sun in smiles decline,
  And bring a pleasant night.

Selection 5.—CARMEN SERVICE.—This is the day the Lord hath made.

This is the day the Lord hath made, We will re-joice and be glad in

We will re-joice, we will re-joice,

it, we will re-joice and be glad in it; O-pen to me the gates of right-cous-ness, I will go,-

I will

I will go in-to them, and I will praise the Lord, I will go in-to them, and I will praise the Lord.

I will

This is the day the Lord hath made, We will re-joice and be glad in

We will re-joice, we will re-joice,

and be glad in it, and be glad, . . . and be

it, we will re-joice, . . . and be glad in it, and be glad, and be

and be glad in it,

glad in it. This is the day the Lord hath made, . the day the Lord . hath made.

it. . . . . . . this is the day that the Lord . . hath made.

Selection 5.

This is the day the Lord hath made, we will rejoice and be glad in it.   Open to me the gates of righteousness, I will go into them, and I will praise the Lord.   This is the day the Lord hath made.

CARMEN. H. M.

Arr. by G. F. R.

Choir and Congregation.

{ Wel-come, de-light-ful morn, Thou day of sa-cred rest ; }
{ I hail thy kind re-turn;—Lord, make these mo-ments blest; } From the low train of

mor-tal toys I soar to reach im-mor-tal joys, I soar . . to reach . im-mor-tal joys.

---

17   HAYWARD.

1 Welcome, delightful morn,
    Thou day of sacred rest ;
I hail thy kind return ;—
Lord make these moments blest :
        From the low train
        Of mortal toys,
        I soar to reach
        Immortal joys.

2 Now may the King descend
    And fill his throne of grace ;
Thy sceptre, Lord, extend,
While saints address thy face ;
        Let sinners feel
        Thy quickening word,
        And learn to know
        And fear the Lord.

3 Descend, celestial dove,
    With all thy quickening powers ;
Disclose a Savior's love,
And bless the sacred hours :
        Then shall my soul
        New life obtain,
        Nor Sabbaths be
        Enjoyed in vain.

---

18   WATTS.

1 Lord of the worlds above,
    How pleasant and how fair
The dwellings of thy love,
    Thine earthly temples are !
        To thine abode
        My heart aspires,
        With warm desires,
        To see my God.

2 Oh, happy souls, that pray,
    Where God appoints to hear !
Oh, happy men that pay
    Their constant service there !
        They praise thee still ;
        And happy they
        That love the way
        To Zion's hill.

3 They go from strength to strength,
    Through this dark vale of tears,
Till each arrives at length,
    Till each in heaven appears :
        Oh, glorious seat,
        When God, our King,
        Shall thither bring
        Our willing feet !

---

19   C. WESLEY.

1 Rejoice ! the Lord is King—
    Your God and King adore ;
Mortals, give thanks and sing,
    And triumph evermore :
        Lift up the heart,
        Lift up the voice :
        Rejoice aloud,
        Ye saints, rejoice.

2 His kingdom cannot fail,
    He rules o'er earth and heaven,
The keys of death and hell
    To Jesus Christ are given ;
        Lift up the heart,
        Lift up the voice :
        Rejoice aloud,
        Ye saints, rejoice.

3 He all his foes shall quell,
    Shall all our sins destroy,
And every bosom swell
    With pure seraphic joy ;
        Lift up the heart,
        Lift up the voice :
        Rejoice aloud,
        Ye saints, rejoice.

Selection 6.—KEBLE SERVICE.—Remember the Sabbath day to keep it holy.

Re-mem-ber the Sab-bath day to keep it ho - ly, to keep it ho - ly, For in

six days the Lord made heav'n and earth, The sea and all that in them is, . . . and rest-ed the

seventh day, Where-fore the Lord bless'd the Sabbath day and hal - lowed it, and hal - lowed it.

KEBLE. C. M.

Words by REV. J. MASON.
Music arr. by GEO. F. ROOT.

Choir and Congregation.

20 1. Blest day of God! most calm, most bright, The first, the best of days, The la - b'rer's
2. My Sav-ior's face made thee to shine; His ris - ing thee did raise, And made thee

rest, the saint's de - light, The day of prayer and praise.
heav'n-ly and di - vine, Be - yond all oth - er days.

3 The first-fruits oft a blessing prove
    To all the sheaves behind;
And they the day of Christ who love,
    A happy week shall find.

4 This day I must with God appear;
    For, Lord, the day is thine;
Help me to spend it in thy fear,
    And thus to make it mine.

Selection 4, 5, or 6.

Choir and Congregation.

SANTON. 7s & 6s.

Words by Bishop WORDSWORTH.
Music arr. by G. F. ROOT.

21. 1. Oh, day of rest and glad-ness, Oh, day of joy and light, Oh, balm of care and sad-ness, Most

beau-ti-ful, most bright, On thee the high and low-ly, Bend-ing be-fore the throne, Sing ho-ly, ho-ly,

ho-ly, To thee, great Three in One.

2 To-day on weary nations
  The heavenly manna falls;
To holy convocations
  The silver trumpet calls,
Where gospel light is glowing
  With pure and radiant beams,
And living water flowing
  With soul-refreshing streams.

3 New graces ever gaining
  From this our day of rest,
We reach the rest remaining
  To spirits of the blest.
To Holy Ghost be praises,
  To Father and to Son;
The Church her voice upraises
  To thee, blest Three in One.

Selection 5 or 6.

Choir and Congregation.

SAVANNAH. 10s.

Words by Rev. WM. MASON.
Music by PLEYEL.

22. 1. A-gain the day re-turns of ho-ly rest, Which, when he made the world, Je-ho-vah blest;
    2. Let us de-vote this con-se-crat-ed day To learn his will, and all we learn o-bey;
    3. Fa-ther in heaven! in whom our hopes con-fide, Whose power de-fends us, and whose pre-cepts guide,

When, like his own, he bade our la-bors cease, And all be pi-e-ty, and all be peace.
So shall he hear, when fer-vent-ly we raise Our sup-pli-ca-tions and our songs of praise.
In life our Guar-dian, and in death our Friend, Glo-ry su-preme be thine till time shall end.

Selection 7.—SPANISH HYMN SERVICE.—I laid me down and slept.   † † †

I laid me down and slept; I awaked, for the Lord sustained me; I cried unto the Lord, I cried with my

voice, And he heard me, he heard me out of his ho-ly hill. O Lord, my God, in thee do I put my trust, O

in thee, in thee, in thee,

Lord my God, in thee do I put my trust, in thee, in thee, do I put my trust.

I a-waked, I a-waked,

laid me down and slept; I a-waked, I a-waked, I a-waked, for the Lord sus-tained me.

SPANISH HYMN. 6s & 5s.

Choir and Congregation.   New Arrangement.

23 { 1. Thro' thy pro-tect-ing care, Kept till the dawn-ing. }
   { Taught to draw near in prayer, Heed we the warn-ing; } Oh, thou great One in Three, Glad-ly our

souls would be Ev - er-more praising thee, God of the morn-ing.

2 God of our sleeping hours!
   Watch o'er us waking,
   All our imperfect powers
   In thine hands taking;
   In us thy work fulfill,
   Be with thy children still,
   Those who obey thy will
   Never forsaking.

Selection 8.—LANESBORO' SERVICE.—Early will I seek thee.

Choir. Impressively.

G. F. R.

Cres.

O God, thou art my God; Ear-ly will I seek thee, ear-ly will I seek thee; my soul thirst-eth for

my

Cres. In a dry and thirsty land,

thee, . . . my flesh . . long-eth for thee . . . . in a dry and thirsty

soul thirst-eth for thee, my flesh

Dim. . . . . pp m Cres. . . . . .

land, where no wa-ter is; O God! thou art my God; Ear-ly will I seek thee, early will I seek thee.

LANESBORO'. C. M.

Choir and Congregation.

Words by Dr. Watts.
Music arr. by Dr. Mason.

24
1. Ear-ly, my God, with - out de - lay, I haste to seek thy face; My thirst-y spir - it
2. Not life it - self, with all its joys, Can my best pas-sions move, Or raise so high my
3. Thus, till my last ex - pir - ing day, I'll bless my God and King; Thus will I lift my

faints a - way, My thirst - y spir - it faints a - way, Without thy cheer-ing grace.
cheer - ful voice, Or raise so high my cheer - ful voice, As thy for - giv-ing love.
hands to pray, Thus will I lift my hands to pray, And tune my lips to sing.

2

GENERAL PRAISE.

Selection 9.—STATE ST. SERVICE.—I was glad when they said unto me.

Solo.   J. C. WOODMAN.

I was glad when they said un - to me, We will go in - to the house of the Lord.

Choir.

Our feet shall stand in thy gates, O Je - ru - sa - lem; Je - ru - sa - lem is built as a cit - y that is at

u - ni - ty in it - self, For thith - er the tribes go up, e - ven the tribes of the Lord, to

tes - ti - fy un - to Is - ra - el, to give thanks un - to the Lord, to give thanks un - to the

name, the name of the Lord. I was glad when they said un - to me, We will go in - to the

house of the Lord, for there is the seat of judg-ment, e - ven the seat of the house of Da - vid.

Selection 9.

I was glad when they said unto me, we will go into the house of the Lord.

Our feet shall stand in thy gates, O Jerusalem. Jerusalem is built as a city that is at unity in itself, for thith-er the tribes go up, even the tribes of the Lord, to tes-tify unto Israel, to give thanks unto the name of the Lord. For there is the seat of judgment, even the seat of the house of David.

STATE ST. S. M.

J. C. WOODMAN.

Choir and Congregation.

1. I love thy king - dom, Lord, The house of thine a - bode,

The church our blest Re - deem - er saved With his own pre - cious blood.

---

25 DWIGHT.

1 I love thy kingdom, Lord—
The house of thine abode,
The church our blest Redeemer saved
With his own precious blood.

2 I love thy church, O God!
Her walls before thee stand,
Dear as the apple of thine eye,
And graven on thy hand.

3 For her my tears shall fall,
For her my prayers ascend ;
To her my cares and toils be given,
Till toils and cares shall end.

4 Beyond my highest joy,
I prize her heavenly ways,
Her sweet communion, solemn vows,
Her hymns of love and praise.

26 STENNETT.

1 How charming is the place
Where my Redeemer, God,
Unvails the beauty of his face,
And sheds his love abroad!

2 Not the fair palaces,
To which the great resort,
Are once to be compared with this,
Where Jesus holds his court.

---

3 Here on the mercy-seat,
With radiant glory crowned,
Our joyful eyes behold him sit
And smile on all around.

4 Give me, O Lord, a place
Within thy blest abode,
Among the children of thy grace,
The servants of my God.

27 BULFINCH.

1 Lord, in this sacred hour
Within thy courts we bend,
And bless thy love, and own thy power,
Our Father and our Friend.

2 But thou art not alone
In courts by mortals trod ;
Nor only is the day thine own
When man draws near to God.

3 Thy temple is the arch
Of yon unmeasured sky;
Thy Sabbath, the stupendous march
Of thine eternity.

4 Lord, may that holier day
Dawn on thy servants' sight ;
And purer worship may we pay
In heaven's unclouded light.

---

28 MONTGOMERY.

1 O thou above all praise,
Above all blessing high,
Who would not fear thy holy name,
And laud, and magnify!

2 Oh, for the living flame
From thine own altar brought,
To touch our lips, our souls inspire,
And wing to heaven our thought!

3 God is our strength and song,
And his salvation ours ;
Then be his love in Christ proclaimed
With all our ransomed powers.

29 JERVIS.

1 With joy we lift our eyes
To those bright realms above,
That glorious temple in the skies,
Where dwells eternal Love.

2 Before thy throne we bow,
O thou almighty King ;
Here we present the solemn vow,
And hymns of praise we sing.

3 While in thy house we kneel,
With trust and holy fear,
Thy mercy and thy truth reveal,
And lend a gracious ear.

Selection 10.—DALSTON SERVICE.—I was glad when they said.

This Prelude may also be used with State St., p. 19, and Hymns 25, 26, 27, 28, and 29.

I was glad when they said un-to me, Let us go in-to the house of the Lord, Our

feet shall stand with-in thy gates, O Je-ru-sa-lem, O Je-ru-sa-lem. Pray for the

peace of Je-ru-sa-lem, They shall pros-per that love thee; Peace be with-in thy walls, and pros-

per-i-ty with-in thy pal-a-ces. Oh, come, oh, come, let us go, let us

go in-to the house of the Lord, let us go, let us go in-to the house of the Lord.

Selection 10.

I was glad when they said unto me, let us go into the house of the Lord. Our feet shall stand within thy gates, O Jerusalem. Pray for the peace of Jerusalem, they shall prosper that love thee. Peace be within thy walls, and prosperity within thy palaces. Oh, come, let us go into the house of the Lord.

DALSTON. S. P. M.

Choir and Congregation.

A. WILLIAMS.

1. How pleased and blest was I, To hear the peo-ple cry, "Come, let us seek our God to-day!"

Yes, with a cheer-ful zeal, We'll haste to Zi-on's hill, And there our vows and hon-ors pay.

---

30 WATTS.

1 How pleased and blest was I,
    To hear the people cry,
"Come, let us seek our God to-day!"
Yes, with a cheerful zeal,
We haste to Zion's hill,
And there our vows and honors pay.

2 Zion—thrice happy place—
    Adorned with wondrous grace;
What walls of strength embrace thee
    In thee our tribes appear   [round!
    To pray, and praise, and hear
The sacred gospel's joyful sound.

3 May peace attend thy gate,
    And joy within thee wait,
To bless the soul of every guest:
    The man who seeks thy peace,
    And wishes thine increase,
A thousand blessings on him rest!

4 My tongue repeats her vows,
    " Peace to this sacred house !"
For here my friends and kindred dwell:
    And since my glorious God
    Makes thee his blest abode,
My soul shall ever love thee well.

31 SWAIN.

1 'Tis heaven begun below
    To hear Christ's praises flow
In Zion, where his name is known :
    What will it be above
    To sing redeeming love,
And cast our crowns before his throne !

2 When we adore him there,
    We shall be void of fear,
Nor faith, nor hope, nor patience need :
    Love will absorb us quite,
    Love, in the midst of light,
On God's eternal love shall feed.

3 Oh, what sweet company
    We then shall hear and see !
What harmony will there abound
    When souls unnumbered sing
    The praise of Zion's King,
Nor one dissenting voice is found !

4 Till that blest period come,
    Zion shall be my home;
And may I never thence remove,
    Till from the church below
    To that on high I go,
And there commune in perfect love.

32 WATTS.

1 The Lord Jehovah reigns,
    And royal state maintains,
His head with awful glories crowned;
    Arrayed in robes of light,
    Begirt with sovereign might,
And rays of majesty around.

2 Upheld by thy commands,
    The world securely stands,
And skies and stars obey thy word;
    Thy throne was fixed on high
    Before the starry sky ;
Eternal is thy kingdom, Lord !

3 Let floods and nations rage,
    And all their powers engage—
Let swelling tides assault the sky—
    The terrors of thy frown
    Shall beat their madness down ;
Thy throne forever stands on high.

4 Thy promises are true ;
    Thy grace is ever new ;
There fixed, thy church shall ne'er
    Thy saints, with holy fear,   [remove;
    Shall in thy courts appear,
And sing thine everlasting love.

Selection 11.—TEMPLE SERVICE.—Blessed are they that dwell.

Bless-ed are they that dwell in thy house, that dwell in thy house, O Lord of hosts! For a

day in thy courts is bet-ter than a thou-sand. I had ra-ther be a door-keep-er in the

house of my God than to dwell in the tents of wick-ed-ness, than to dwell in the tents of wick-ed-ness.

For the Lord God is a sun and shield; the Lord will give grace and glo-ry; no good thing will he with-

hold from them that walk up-right-ly. O Lord of hosts! bless-ed are they that dwell in thy house.

Selection 11.

Blessed are they that dwell in thy house, O Lord of hosts! for a day in thy courts is better than a thousand. I had rather be a door-keeper in the house of my God than to dwell in the tents of wickedness.

For the Lord God is a sun and shield; the Lord will give grace and glory; no good thing will he withhold from them that walk uprightly. O Lord of hosts! blessed are they that dwell in thy house.

TEMPLE. 8s & 7s. Double.

Choir and Congregation.   Arr. by G. F. R.

Far from mor - tal cares re - treat-ing, Sor - did hopes and vain de - sires, Here, our will - ing foot-steps meet-ing, Ev - 'ry heart to heaven as-pires; From the Fount of glo - ry beam-ing, Light ce-les - tial cheers our eyes, Mer - cy from a - bove pro-claim-ing Peace and par - don from the skies.

33   TAYLOR.

1 Far from mortal cares retreating,
    Sordid hopes and vain desires,
  Here, our willing footsteps meeting,
    Every heart to heaven aspires;
  From the Fount of glory beaming,
    Light celestial cheers our eyes,
  Mercy from above proclaiming
    Peace and pardon from the skies.

2 Who may share this great salvation?
    Every pure and humble mind;
  Every kindred, tongue, and nation,
    From the dross of guilt refined:
  Blessings all around bestowing,
    God witholds his care from none;
  Grace and mercy ever flowing
    From the fountain of his throne.

3 Every stain of guilt abhorring,
    Firm and bold in virtue's cause,
  Still thy Providence adoring,
    Faithful subjects to thy laws;
  Lord, with favor still attend us,
    Bless us with thy wondrous love!
  Thou, our Sun, our Shield, defend us;
    All our hope is from above.

34   COWPER.

1 Hear what God, the Lord, hath spo-
    O my people, faint and few, [ken;
  Comfortless, afflicted, broken,
    Fair abodes I build for you;
  Scenes of heartfelt tribulation
    Shall no more perplex your ways;
  You shall name your walls "Salvation"
    And your gates shall all be "Praise."

2 There, like streams that feed the garden,
    Pleasures without end shall flow;
  For the Lord, your faith rewarding,
    All his bounty shall bestow.
  Still in undisturbed possession
    Peace and righteousness shall reign;
  Never shall you feel oppression,
    Hear the voice of war again.

3 Ye, no more your suns descending,
    Waning moons no more shall see,
  But, your griefs forever ending,
    Find eternal noon in me.
  God shall rise, and shining o'er you,
    Change to day the gloom of night;
  He, the Lord, shall be your Glory,
    God, your everlasting Light.

Selection 3.—How amiable are thy tabernacles, O Lord of hosts.

FRANKLAND. C. M.

Words by Dr. WATTS.
Music arr. by G. F. ROOT.

Choir and Congregation.

35
1. My soul, how love - ly is the place To which thy God re - sorts! 'Tis heaven to see his
2. There the great Mon - arch of the skies His sav - ing power dis-plays; And light breaks in up-

smil - ing face, Tho' in his earth - ly courts.
on our eyes, With kind and quick - 'ning rays.

3 With his rich gifts, the heavenly Dove
Descends and fills the place;
While Christ reveals his wondrous love,
And sheds abroad his grace.

4 There, mighty God, thy words declare
The secrets of thy will;
And still we seek thy mercy there,
And sing thy praises still.

36 [Sel. 3. Tune, Frankland.]
COWPER.
1 Far from the world, O Lord, I flee,
From strife and tumult far;
From scenes where Satan wages still
His most successful war.

2 The calm retreat, the silent shade,
With prayer and praise agree;
And seem by thy sweet bounty made
For those who follow thee.

3 There, if thy Spirit touch the soul,
And grace her mean abode;
Oh! with what peace, and joy, and love,
She then communes with God.

4 Author and Guardian of my life!
Sweet Source of light divine,
And—all harmonious names in one—
My Savior!—thou art mine!

5 What thanks I owe thee, and what love—
A boundless, endless store—
Shall echo through the realms above,
When time shall be no more.

37 [Sel. 6, Tune, Keble, p. 14.]
BROWNE.
1 Frequent the day of God returns
To shed its quickening beams;
And yet how slow devotion burns;
How languid are its flames!

2 Accept our faint attempts to love,
Our frailties, Lord, forgive;
We would be like thy saints above,
And praise thee while we live.

3 Increase, O Lord, our faith and hope,
And fit us to ascend
Where the assembly ne'er breaks up,
The Sabbath ne'er shall end;—

4 Where we shall breathe in heavenly air,
With heavenly lustre shine,
Before the throne of God appear,
And feast on love divine.

38 [Sel. 6. Tune, Keble, p. 14.]
BARBAULD.
1 When, as returns this solemn day,
Man comes to meet his God,
What rites, what honors shall he pay?
How spread his praise abroad?

2 From marble domes and gilded spires
Shall clouds of incense rise?
And gems, and gold, and garlands deck
The costly sacrifice?

3 Vain, sinful man! creation's lord
Thy offerings well may spare;
But give thy heart, and thou shalt find
Thy God will hear thy prayer.

39 [Sel. 4. Tune, Stephens, p. 11.]
WATTS.
1 Blest morning! whose young dawning rays
Beheld our rising God;
That saw him triumph o'er the dust,
And leave his dark abode.

2 In the cold prison of a tomb
The great Redeemer lay,
Till the revolving skies had brought
The third, the appointed day.

3 Hell and the grave combined their force
To hold our Lord in vain;
The sleeping conqueror arose,
And burst their feeble chain.

4 To thy great name, almighty Lord,
These sacred hours we pay,
And loud hosannas shall proclaim
The triumph of the day.

5 Salvation and immortal praise
To our victorious King!
Let heaven and earth, and rocks and seas,
With glad hosannas ring.

40 [Tune Keble, p. 14.]
MRS. SAFFERY.
1 God of the sun-light hours, how sad
Would evening shadows be,
Or night, in deeper sable clad,—
If aught were dark to thee!

2 How mournfully that golden gleam
Would touch the thoughtful heart,
If, with its soft, retiring beam,
We saw thy love depart.

3 But, tho' the gathering gloom may hide
Those gentle rays awhile,
Yet they who in thy house abide,
Shall ever share thy smile.

4 Then let creation's volume close,
Though every page be bright;
On thine, still open, we repose
With more intense delight.

AUBER. 7s. 6 lines.

Choir and Congregation.   Music arr. by G. F. ROOT.

1. Hail, thou bright and sa-cred morn, Risen with glad-ness in thy beams! Light, which not of earth is born, From thy dawn in glo-ry streams; Airs of heaven are breathed a-round, And each place is ho-ly ground.

41 [*Sel. 4, 5, or 6. Tune, Auber.*]
                                    ELLIOTT.
1 Hail, thou bright and sacred morn,
   Risen with gladness in thy beams!
Light, which not of earth is born,
   From thy dawn in glory streams:
Airs of heaven are breathed around
And each place is holy ground.

2 Great Creator! who this day
   From thy perfect work didst rest;
By the souls that own thy sway
   Hallowed be its hours and blest;
Cares of earth aside be thrown,
This day given to heaven alone!

3 Savior! who this day didst break
   The dark prison of the tomb;
Bid my slumbering soul awake,
   Shine thro' all its sin and gloom:
Let me, from my bonds set free,
Rise from sin, and live to thee.

4 Blessed Spirit! Comforter!
   Sent this day from Christ on high;
Lord, on me thy gifts confer,
   Cleanse, illumine, sanctify!
All thine influence shed abroad,
Fill me with the peace of God.

42 [*Sel. 6. Tune, Auber*]
                                    WHYTEHEAD.
1 Resting from his work to-day,
   In the tomb the Savior lay;
Still he slept, from head to feet
Shrouded in the winding sheet
Lying in the rock alone,
Hidden by the sealed stone.

2 Late at even there was seen
   Watching long the Magdalene;
Early, ere the break of day,
   Sorrowful she took her way
To the holy garden glade,
Where her buried Lord was laid.

3 So with thee, till life shall end,
   I would solemn vigil spend;
Let me hew thee, Lord, a shrine
   In this rocky heart of mine,
Where in pure embalmed cell
None but thee may ever dwell.

4 Myrrh and spices will I bring,
   True affection's offering;
Close the door from sight and sound
Of the busy world around;
And in patient watch remain
Till my Lord appear again.

43   MONTGOMERY.
1 As the hart, with eager looks,
   Panteth for the water-brooks,
So my soul, athirst for thee,
   Pants the living God to see;
When, oh, when, with filial fear,
Lord, shall I to thee draw near?

2 Why art thou cast down, my soul?
   God, thy God, shall make thee whole;
Why art thou disquieted?
   God shall lift thy fallen head,
And his countenance benign
Be the saving health of thine.

44   HASTINGS.
1 Now, from labor and from care,
   Evening shades have set me free;
In the work of praise and prayer,
   Lord! I would converse with thee;
Oh! behold me from above,
Fill me with a Savior's love.

2 Sin and sorrow, guilt and woe,
   Wither all my earthly joys;
Naught can charm me here below,
   But my Savior's melting voice;
Lord! forgive—thy grace restore,
Make me thine for evermore.

3 For the blessings of this day,
   For the mercies of this hour,
For the gospel's cheering ray,
   For the Spirit's quickening power,—
Grateful notes to thee I raise;
Oh! accept my song of praise.

45   AUBER.
1 On thy church, O Power divine,
   Cause thy glorious face to shine,
Till the nations from afar
Hail her as their guiding star;
Till her sons from zone to zone,
Make thy great salvation known.

2 Then shall God, with lavish hand,
   Scatter blessings o'er the land;
Earth shall yield her rich increase,
Every breeze shall whisper peace,
And the world's remotest bound
With the voice of praise resound.

Selection 12.—HENDON SERVICE. No. 1.—Oh, come, let us worship.

Choir.

Come, oh, come, let us wor-ship, Oh, come, let us wor-ship, and bow down, let us kneel be-fore the

Lord, our Ma-ker, for he is our God, And we are the people of his pas-ture and the sheep of his

and the sheep, . . .

hand; Oh, come, let us wor-ship and bow down, let us kneel be-fore the Lord, be-fore the Lord, our Ma-ker.

HENDON. 7s.

Words by Rev. Wᴹ. Hᴀᴍᴍᴏɴᴅ.
Arr. by Dr. L. Mᴀꜱᴏɴ.

Choir and Congregation.

46 1. Lord, we come be-fore thee now, At thy feet we hum-bly bow; Oh, do not our suit dis-dain!

Shall we seek thee, Lord, in vain? Shall we seek thee, Lord, in vain?

2 Lord, on thee our souls depend,
In compassion now descend;
Fill our hearts with thy rich grace,
‖:Tune our lips to sing thy praise.:‖

3 In thine own appointed way
Now we seek thee; here we stay;
Lord, we know not how to go
‖:Till a blessing thou bestow.:‖

Selection 12.

Oh, come, let us worship and bow down; let us kneel before the Lord, our Maker: for he is our God: and we | are the people of his pasture and the sheep of his hand: oh, come, let us worship and bow down.

TEMPLE. 8s, 7s, & 4s.

Choir and Congregation.

Words by Rev. J. Pierpont.
Music arr. by G. F. Root.

47
1. God Al-might-y and All see-ing! Ho-ly One, in whom we all Live, and move, and have our
2. Of all good thou art the Giv-er; Weak and wand'ring ones are we; Then for-ev-er, yea, for-

be-ing, Hear us when on thee we call; Fa-ther hear us, Fa-ther hear us As be-fore thy throne we fall.
ev-er, In thy presence would we be; Oh, be near us, Oh, be near us, That we wan-der not from thee.

48   Kelly.

1 In thy name, O Lord, assembling,
   We, thy people, now draw near;
   Teach us to rejoice with trembling;
   Speak, and let thy servants hear;
   [:Hear with meekness—:]
   Hear thy word with godly fear.

2 While our days on earth are lengthened,
   May we give them, Lord, to thee;
   Cheered by hope, and daily strengthened,
   May we run, nor weary be,
   [:Till thy glory;:]
   Without cloud in heaven we see.

3 There, in worship purer, sweeter,
   All thy people shall adore;
   Tasting of enjoyment greater
   Than they could conceive before;
   [:Full enjoyment, :]
   Full and pure forevermore.

Selection 12.—Oh, come, let us worship.

FEDERAL ST. L. M.

Choir and Congregation.

Words by Rev. John Wesley.
Music by H. K. Oliver.

49
1. Lo, God is here!—let us a-dore! And own how dreadful is this place! Let all with-in us

feel his power, And, si-lent, bow be-fore his face.

2 Lo, God is here! him day and night
   United choirs of angels sing:
   To him, enthroned above all height,
   Let saints their humble worship bring.

3 Lord God of hosts! oh, may our praise
   Thy courts with grateful incense fill!
   Still may we stand before thy face,
   Still hear and do thy sovereign will.

Selection 13.—GRATITUDE SERVICE.—Thou openest thine hand.

Choir. *mf*   *m*   Cres.   *mp*   G. F. R.

Thou o-pen-est thine hand, and sat-is-fi-est the de-sire of ev-'ry liv-ing

thing, Thou mak-est the out-goings of the morn-ing and ev'n-ing to re-joice.

to re-

. . . . . I will sing of the mer-cies of the Lord, of the mer-cies of the Lord for-ev-er.

joice.

Choir and Congregation.

GRATITUDE. L. M.

Words by Dr. Watts.
Music arr. by Dr. Hastings.

50
1. My God, how end-less is thy love! Thy gifts are ev-'ry eve-ning new;
2. Thou spread'st the cur-tains of the night, Great guar-dian of my sleep-ing hours;
3. I yield my powers to thy com-mand, To thee I con-se-crate my days;

And morn-ing mer-cies from a-bove, Gen-tly dis-till like ear-ly dew.
Thy sove-reign word re-stores the light, And quick-ens all my drow-sy powers.
Per-pet-ual bless-ings from thine hand De-mand per-pet-ual songs of praise.

Selection 14.—ROSEHILL SERVICE.—It is a good thing to give thanks.

It is a good thing to give thanks, to give thanks un - to the Lord, And to sing

It is a good thing to give thanks, to give thanks un - to the Lord, And to sing

prais - es un - to thy name, un - to thy name, O Most High; To show forth thy lov - ing

prais - es un - to thy name, un - to thy name, O Most High; To show forth thy lov - ing

kind - ness in the morn - ing, And thy faith - ful-ness ev - 'ry night, And thy faith - ful-ness

kind - ness in the morn - ing, And thy faith - ful-ness ev - 'ry night, And thy faith - ful-ness

This may be sung by a single voice, or the Sopranos of the choir may be divided, a part singing this.

ev - 'ry night. Up - on an in-stru-ment of ten strings, And up-on the psal-ter-y,

ev - 'ry night.

Rosehill Service.—Continued.

and up-on the psal-ter-y, Up-on the harp with sol-emn sound.

It is a good

Lord,

It is a good thing

thing to give thanks un-to the Lord, It is a good thing, it is a good

Lord,

to give thanks un-to the Lord, and to sing prais-es un-to thy name. Praise the

thing to give thanks un-to the Lord, and to sing prais-es un-to thy name. Praise the

Lord . praise the Lord, . praise the name . of the Lord.

Lord, . praise the Lord, . praise the name of the Lord.

praise the Lord, . praise the Lord,

Selection 14.

It is a good thing to give thanks unto the Lord, and to sing praises unto thy name, O Most High; to show forth thy loving kindness in the morning, and thy faithfulness every night. Upon an instrument of ten strings, and upon the psaltery; upon the harp with solemn sound. It is a good thing to give thanks unto the Lord. Praise ye the Lord.

ROSEHILL. L. M.

Choir and Congregation.

J. E. SWEETSER.

1. Sweet is the work, my God, my King, To praise thy name, give thanks, and sing; To show thy love by morn-ing light, And talk of all thy truth at night.

51
WATTS.

1 Sweet is the work, my God, my King,
To praise thy name, give thanks, and sing;
To show thy love by morning light,
And talk of all thy truth at night.

2 Sweet is the day of sacred rest;
No mortal care shall seize my breast;
Oh, may my heart in tune be found,
Like David's harp of solemn sound!

3 Lord, I shall share a glorious part,
When grace hath well refined my heart,
And fresh supplies of joy are shed,
Like holy oil to cheer my head.

4 Then shall I see, and hear, and know
All I desired or wished below;
And every power find sweet employ,
In that eternal world of joy.

52
WATTS.

1 My God, my King, thy various praise
Shall fill the remnant of my days;
Thy grace employ my humble tongue,
Till death and glory raise the song.

2 The wings of every hour shall bear
Some thankful tribute to thine ear;
And every setting sun shall see
New works of duty done for thee.

3 Let distant times and nations raise
The long succession of thy praise;
And unborn ages make my song
The joy and triumph of their tongue.

4 But who can speak thy wondrous deeds?
Thy greatness all our thoughts exceeds;
Vast and unsearchable thy ways!
Vast and immortal be thy praise!

53
TATE & BRADY.

1 Oh, render thanks to God above,
The fountain of eternal love;
Whose mercy firm, through ages past,
Hath stood, and shall forever last.

2 Who can his mighty deeds express,
Not only vast—but numberless?
What mortal eloquence can raise
His tribute to immortal praise?

3 Extend to me that favor, Lord,
Thou to thy chosen dost afford;
When thou return'st to set them free,
Let thy salvation visit me.

4 Oh, render thanks to God above,
The fountain of eternal love:
His mercy firm, through ages past,
Hath stood, and shall forever last.

54
WATTS.

1 Now to the Lord a noble song!
Awake, my soul! awake, my tongue!
Hosanna to th' eternal name,
And all his boundless love proclaim.

2 See where it shines in Jesus' face,—
The brightest image of his grace!
God, in the person of his Son,
Hath all his mightiest works outdone.

3 Grace!—'tis a sweet, a charming theme:
My thoughts rejoice at Jesus' name:
Ye angels! dwell upon the sound:
Ye heavens! reflect it to the ground.

55
DODDRIDGE.

1 Triumphant Lord, thy goodness reigns
Through all the wide celestial plains;
And its full streams unceasing flow
Down to the abodes of men below.

2 Through nature's work its glories shine;
The cares of providence are thine;
And grace erects our ruined frame
A fairer temple to thy name.

3 Oh, give to every human heart
To taste, and feel how good thou art;
With grateful love and reverent fear,
To know how blest thy children are.

Selection 15.—HILLSDALE SERVICE, No. 1.—Oh, give thanks unto the Lord!

Oh, give thanks un-to the Lord! for his mer-cy en-dur-eth for-ev - er; Glo-ry and hon-or

are in his presence, strength and gladness are in his place. He rul-eth by his power, he rul-eth for-

ev - er; give thanks un-to the Lord, give thanks un-to the Lord; his eyes be-hold the na-tions, his

eyes be-hold the nations; give thanks, give thanks un-to the Lord; Oh, give thanks un-to the

Lord, for his mer-cy en-dur-eth for-ev - er, his mer-cy en-dur-eth for-ev - - - er.

Selection 15.

Oh, give thanks unto the Lord, for his mercy endureth forever. Glory and honor are in his presence, strength and gladness are in his place.

He ruleth by his power; he ruleth forever. His eyes behold the nations. Oh, give thanks unto the Lord, for his mercy endureth forever.

HILLSDALE. L. M.

Geo. F. Root.

Choir and Congregation.

Come, O my soul! in sa-cred lays At-tempt thy great Cre - a - tor's praise:

But, oh, what tongue can speak his fame? What mor - tal verse can reach the theme?

56 BLACKLOCK.

1 Come, O my soul! in sacred lays
Attempt thy great Creator's praise:
But, oh, what tngue can speak his fame?
What mortal verse can reach the theme?

2 Enthroned amid the radiant spheres,
He glory like a garment wears;
To form a robe of light divine,
Ten thousand suns around him shine.

3 In all our Maker's grand designs,
Almighty power with wisdom shines;
His works, thro' all this wondrous frame,
Declare the glory of his name.

4 Raised on devotion's lofty wing,
Do thou, my soul, his glories sing;
And let his praise employ thy tongue,
Till listening worlds shall join the song!

57 WATTS.

1 With all my powers of heart and tongue,
I'll praise my Maker in my song;
Angels shall hear the notes I raise,
Approve the song, and join the praise.

2 To God I cried when troubles rose;
He heard me, and subdued my foes:
He did my rising fears control,
And strength diffused through all my soul.

3 Amid a thousand snares I stand
Upheld and guarded by thy hand;
Thy words my fainting soul revive,
And keep my dying faith alive.

4 I'll sing thy truth and mercy, Lord,
I'll sing the wonders of thy word;
Not all thy works and names I below
So much thy power and glory show.

58 WATTS.

1 Jehovah reigns; his throne is high;
His robes are light and majesty;
His glory shines with beams so bright,
No mortal can sustain the sight.

2 His terrors keep the world in awe;
His justice guards his holy law;
Yet love reveals a smiling face,
And truth and promise seal the grace.

3 Through all his works his wisdom shines,
And baffles Satan's deep designs;
His power is sovereign to fulfill
The noblest counsels of his will.

4 And will this glorious Lord descend
To be my Father and my Friend?
Then let my songs with angels' join;
Heaven is secure, if God be mine.

59 CONDER.

1 The Lord is King! lift up thy voice,
O earth, and all ye heavens, rejoice!
From world to world the joy shall ring,
The Lord omnipotent is King!

2 The Lord is King! who then shall dare
Resist his will, distrust his care?
Holy and true are all his ways:
Let every creature speak his praise.

3 The Lord is King! exalt your strains,
Ye saints, your God, your Father reigns!
One Lord, one empire, all secures;
He reigns,—and life and death are yours.

60 NEEDHAM.

1 Awake, my tongue, thy tribute bring
To him who gave thee power to sing;
Praise him, who is all praise above,
The source of wisdom and of love.

2 Through each bright world above, behold
Ten thousand thousand charms unfold;
Earth, air, and mighty seas combine,
To speak his wisdom all divine.

3 But in redemption, oh, what grace!
Its wonders, oh, what thought can trace
Here wisdom shines forever bright;
Praise him, my soul, with sweet delight.

3

Selection 16.—HAMBURG SERVICE.—Sing unto God, ye kingdoms of the earth.

Sing un - to God, ye kingdoms of the earth; oh, sing prais-es un - to the Lord! Sing un - to God, ye

kingdoms of the earth; ascribe ye strength, ascribe ye strength, ascribe ye strength unto God. His excellency is over

Is - ra - el, and his strength is in the clouds. . . . Sing un - to God, ye king-doms of the earth; the

God of Is - ra - el is he that giv-eth strength, is he that giv - eth strength and power un-

to his peo - ple. Sing un - to God! sing un - to God, ye king-doms of the earth!

un - to God.   Sing all ye

Selection 16.

Sing unto God, ye kingdoms of the earth; oh, sing praises unto the Lord. Ascribe ye strength unto God. His excellency is over Israel, and his strength is in the clouds. The God of Israel is he that giveth strength and power unto his people.

Sing unto God, ye kingdoms of the earth.

HAMBURG. L. M.

Choir and Congregation.   Arr. by Dr. L. Mason.

Kingdoms and thrones to God be - long; Crown him, ye na - tions, in your song;

His wondrous names and pow'rs re - hearse; His hon-ors shall en - rich your verse.

61   WATTS.

1 Kingdoms and thrones to God belong;
  Crown him, ye nations, in your song;
  His wondrous names and pow'rs rehearse;
  His honors shall enrich your verse.

2 He shakes the heavens with loud alarms;
  How terrible is God in arms!
  In Israel are his mercies known;
  Israel his peculiar throne.

3 Proclaim him King, pronounce him blest;
  He's your defense, your joy, your rest;
  When terrors rise, and nations faint.
  God is the strength of every saint.

62   ANON.

1 Unto the Lord, unto the Lord,
  Oh, sing a new and joyful song!
  Declare his glory, tell abroad
  The wonders that to him belong.

2 For he is great, for he is great;
  Above all gods his throne is raised;
  He reigns in majesty and state,
  In strength and beauty is he praised.

3 Give to the Lord, give to the Lord
  The glory due unto his name;
  Enter his courts with sweet accord;
  In songs of joy his grace proclaim.

63   WATTS.

1 Come, let our voices join to raise
  A sacred song of solemn praise:
  God is a sovereign King; rehearse
  His honors in exalted verse.

2 Come, let our souls address the Lord,
  Who framed our natures with his word:
  He is our Shepherd, we the sheep
  His mercy chose, his pastures keep.

3 Come, let us hear his voice to-day;
  The counsels of his love obey;
  Nor let our hardened hearts renew
  The sins and plagues that Israel knew.

4 Seize the kind promise while it waits,
  And march to Zion's heavenly gates:
  Believe, and take the promised rest;
  Obey, and be forever blest.

64   ANCIENT HYMN

1 Thee we adore, eternal Lord!
  We praise thy name with one accord;
  Thy saints, who here thy goodness see,
  Through all the world do worship thee.

2 To thee aloud all angels cry,
  The heavens and all the powers on high:
  Thee, holy, holy, holy King,
  Lord God of hosts, they ever sing.

3 Th' apostles join the glorious throng;
  The prophets swell th' immortal song;
  The martyrs' noble army raise
  Eternal anthems to thy praise.

4 From day to day, O Lord, do we
  Highly exalt and honor thee!
  Thy name we worship and adore,
  World without end, for evermore!

65   WATTS.

1 Give to the Lord, ye sons of fame,
  Give to the Lord renown and power;
  Ascribe due honors to his name,
  And his eternal might adore.

2 The Lord proclaims his power aloud,
  O'er all the ocean and the land;
  His voice divides the watery cloud,
  And lightnings blaze at his command.

3 The Lord sits, Sovereign on the flood;
  The Thunderer reigns forever King;
  But makes his church his blest abode,
  Where we his awful glories sing.

4 In gentler language, there the Lord
  The counsels of his grace imparts:
  Amid the raging storm, his word
  Speaks peace and courage to our hearts.

Selection 17.—GREATOREX SERVICE.—The Lord is good to all.

G. F. R.

The Lord is good to all, and his ten-der mer-cies are o-ver all his works. All thy

works shall praise thee, O Lord, and thy saints shall bless thee. They shall a-bun-dant-ly

ut-ter the mem-o-ry, the mem-'ry of thy great good-ness, of thy great good-ness.

And shall sing of thy right-eous-ness, and shall sing of thy right-eous-ness,

And shall sing of thy right-eous-ness, and shall sing of thy

and shall sing of thy right-eous-ness. The Lord is good to all, the

right-eous-ness, shall

Lord is good to all, and his ten-der mer-cies are o-ver all his works.

Selection 17.

The Lord is good to all, and his tender mercies are over all his works. All thy works shall praise thee, O Lord, and thy saints shall bless thee. They shall abundantly ut- ter the memory of thy great goodness, and shall sing of thy righteousness. The Lord is good to all, and his ten- der mercies are over all his works.

GROSSETE. L. M.

Choir and Congregation.   GREATOREX.

1. Give to our God im - mor - tal praise; Mer - cy and truth are all his ways:

Won - ders of grace to God be - long; Re - peat his mer - cies in your song.

63 WATTS.

1 Give to our God immortal praise;
  Mercy and truth are all his ways:
  Wonders of grace to God belong;
  Repeat his mercies in your song.

2 Give to the Lord of lords renown,
  The King of Kings with glory crown:
  His mercies ever shall endure,
  When lords and kings are known no more.

3 He built the earth, he spread the sky,
  And fixed the starry lights on high:
  Wonders of grace to God belong;
  Repeat his mercies in your song.

4 He fills the sun with morning light,
  He bids the moon direct the night:
  His mercies ever shall endure,
  When suns and moons shall shine no more.

67 WATTS.

1 For thee, O God, our constant praise
  In Zion waits, thy chosen seat;
  Our promised altars there we'll raise,
  And all our zealous vows complete.

2 O thou, who to our humble prayer
  Didst always bend thy listening ear,
  To thee shall all mankind repair,
  And at thy gracious throne appear.

3 Our sins, though numberless, in vain
  To stop thy flowing mercy try:
  For grace shall cleanse the guilty stain,
  And wash away the crimson dye.

4 How blest the man, who, near thee placed,
  Within thy heavenly dwelling lives!
  While we, at humbler distance, taste
  The vast delights thy temple gives.

68 LYTE.

1 My God, what monuments I see
  In all around of thine and thee:
  I view thee in the heavens above;
  More high than these is heavenly love

2 I mark the strong eternal hill,
  Thy faithfulness is stronger still:
  I gaze on ocean deep and broad,
  More deep thy counsels are, O Go'.

3 O give me 'neath thy wings to rest,
  To lean on thy parental breast,
  To feed on thee, the living bread,
  And drink at mercy's fountain-head.

4 The springs of life are all thine own,
  They flow from thy eternal throne:
  Light in thy light alone we see,
  O save us, for we rest on thee.

69 WATTS.

1 Bless, O my soul, the living God;
  Call home thy thoughts that rove abroad.
  Let all the powers within me join
  In work and worship so divine.

2 Bless, O my soul, the God of grace;
  His favors claim thy highest praise:
  Why should the wonders he hath wrought
  Be lost in silence and forgot?

3 Let every land his power confess;
  Let all the earth adore his grace:
  My heart and tongue with rapture join,
  In work and worship so divine.

70 STEELE.

1 Praise ye the Lord—let praise employ,
  In his own courts, your songs of joy;
  The spacious firmament around
  Shall echo back the joyful sound.

2 Recount his works in strains divine,
  His wondrous works—how bright they shine!
  Praise him for all his mighty deeds,
  Whose greatness all your praise exceeds.

3 Let all, whom life and breath inspire,
  Attend, and join the blissful choir;
  But chiefly ye, who know his word,
  Adore, and love, and praise the Lord!

Selection 18.—ROOKINGHAM SERVICE.—Not unto us, O Lord.

Not un-to us, O Lord, not un-to us, but un-to thy name give glo-ry, give glo-ry; Oh, that

men wou'd praise the Lord for his good-ness, Oh, that men would praise the Lord for his good-ness a..d

for his won-der-ful works to the chil-dren of men; Oh, that men would praise the Lord would

Not un-to us, O

praise him for his good-ness; Oh, that men would praise the Lord, would praise him for his goodness, and

Lord, not un-to us; Not un-to us, O Lord, not un-to us, but

for his won-der-ful works un-to the chil-dren of men; Oh, that men, oh, that men would praise the

un-to thy name give glo-ry, give glo-ry.

Lord, praise the Lord. Not un-to us, O Lord, not un-to us, but un-to thy name give glo-ry.

Selection 18.

Not unto us, O Lord, not unto us, but unto thy name give glory; oh, that men would praise the Lord for his goodness and for his wonderful works to the children of men. Not unto us, O Lord, but unto thy name give glory.

ROCKINGHAM. L. M.

Choir and Congregation.

Dr. L. Mason.

1. Give thanks to God; he reigns a-bove; Kind are his tho'ts, his name is love:

His mer-cy a-ges past have known, And a-ges long to come shall own.

71 WATTS.

1 Give thanks to God; he reigns above:
Kind are his thoughts, his name is love:
His mercy ages past have known,
And ages long to come shall own.

2 Let the redeemed of the Lord
The wonders of his grace record;
Israel, the nation whom he chose,
And rescued from their mighty foes.

3 He feeds and clothes us all the way,
He guides our footsteps lest we stray ;
He guards us with a powerful hand,
And brings us to the heavenly land.

4 Oh, let the saints with joy record
The truth and goodness of the Lord!
How great his works! how kind his ways!
Let every tongue pronounce his praise.

72 WATTS.

1 The Lord! how wondrous are his ways!
How firm his truth! how large his grace!
He takes his mercy for his throne,
And thence he makes his glories known.

2 Not half so high his power hath spread
The starry heavens above our head,
As his rich love exceeds our praise,
Exceeds the highest hopes we raise.

3 Not half so far has nature placed
The rising morning from the west,
As his forgiving grace removes
The daily guilt of those he loves.

4 His everlasting love is sure
To all his saints, and shall endure ;
From age to age his truth shall reign,
Nor children's children hope in vain.

73 ANON.

1 Lord God of hosts, by all adored !
Thy name we praise with one accord:
The earth and heavens are full of thee:
Thy light, thy love, thy majesty.

2 Loud hallelujahs to thy name
Angels and seraphim proclaim ;
Eternal praise to thee is given
By all the powers and thrones in heaven.

3 The holy church in every place
Throughout the world exalts thy praise:
Both heaven and earth do worship thee
Thou Father of eternity!

4 From day to day, O Lord, do we
Highly exalt and honor thee;
Thy name we worship and adore,
World without end, forevermore.

74 TATE & BRADY.

1 With glory clad, with strength arrayed,
The Lord that o'er all nature reigns,
The world's foundation strongly laid,
And the vast fabric still sustains.

2 How sure established is thy throne !
Which shall no change or period see;
For thou, O Lord, and thou alone,
Art God from all eternity.

3 The floods, O Lord, lift up their voice,
And toss the troubled waves on high ;
But God above can still their noise,
And make the angry sea comply.

75 WATTS

1 Great is the Lord! What tongue can frame
An honor equal to his name?
How awful are his glorious ways !
The Lord is dreadful in his praise!

2 Vast are thy works, Almighty Lord!
All nature rests upon thy word ;
And clouds, and storms, and fire obey
Thy wise and all-controlling sway.

3 Thy glory, fearless of decline,
Thy glory, Lord, shall ever shine ;
Thy praise shall still our breath employ
Till we shall rise to endless joy.

GENERAL PRAISE.

Selection 19.—HILLSDALE SERVICE, No. 2.—How excellent is thy loving kindness.

Selection 19.

How excellent is thy loving kindness, O God! Therefore the children of men put their trust under the shadow of thy wings. How excellent is thy loving kindness, O God!

HILLSDALE. L. M.

Choir and Congregation. GEO. F. ROOT.

My God, in whom are all the springs Of boundless love and grace un-known,

Hide me beneath thy spreading wings, Till the dark cloud is o-ver-blown.

76 WATTS.

1 My God, in whom are all the springs
Of boundless love, and grace unknown,
Hide me beneath thy spreading wings,
Till the dark cloud is overblown.

2 Up to the heavens I send my cry;
The Lord will my desires perform:
He sends his angels from the sky,
And saves me from the threat'ning storm.

3 High o'er the earth thy mercy reigns,
And reaches to the utmost sky;
His truth to endless years remains,
When lower worlds dissolve and die.

4 Be thou exalted, O my God,
Above the heavens where angels dwell;
Thy power on earth be known abroad,
And land to land thy wonders tell.

77 PALGRAVE.

1 Lord God of morning and of night,
We thank thee for thy gift of light;
As in the dawn the shadows fly,
We seem to find thee now more nigh.

2 Fresh hopes have wakened in the heart,
Fresh force to do our daily part;
Thy thousand sleeps our strength restore,
A thousand-fold to serve thee more.

3 Yet whilst thy will we would pursue,
Oft what we would we can not do;
The sun may stand in zenith skies,
But on the soul thick midnight lies.

4 O Lord of lights, 'tis thou alone
Canst make our darkened hearts thine own;
Though this new day with joy we see,
O dawn of God, we cry for thee.

5 Praise God, our Maker and our Friend;
Praise him through time, till time shall end;
Till psalm and song his name adore
Through Heaven's great day of Evermore.

78 KEN.

1 Awake, my soul, and with the sun
Thy daily stage of duty run;
Shake off dull sloth, and joyful rise
To pay thy morning sacrifice.

2 Glory to thee, who safe hast kept,
And hast refreshed me while I slept;
Grant, Lord, when I from death shall wake,
I may of endless life partake.

3 Lord, I my vows to thee renew:
Scatter my sins as morning dew;
Guard my first springs of thought and will,
And with thyself my spirit fill.

4 Direct, control, suggest, this day,
All I design, or do, or say;
That all my powers, with all their might,
In thy sole glory may unite.

79 WATTS.

1 Awake, our souls! away, our fears!
Let every trembling thought be gone;
Awake, and run the heavenly race,
And put a cheerful courage on!

2 True, 'tis a strait and thorny road,
And mortal spirits tire and faint;
But they forget the mighty God,
Who feeds the strength of every saint—

3 The mighty God, whose matchless power
Is ever new and ever young,
And firm endures, while endless years
Their everlasting circles run,

4 From thee, the overflowing spring,
Our souls shall drink a fresh supply;
While such as trust their native strength
Shall melt away, and droop, and die.

5 Swift as an eagle cuts the air,
We'll mount aloft to thine abode;
On wings of love our souls shall fly,
Nor tire amid the heavenly road!

Selection 20.—CHESTERFIELD SERVICE.—I will lift up mine eyes unto the hills.

G. F. R.

Choir. *m*

I will lift up mine eyes un-to the hills, un-to the hills, from whence doth come my help, from whence doth come my

my help cometh from   the   Lord, from the Lord,

help: my help cometh from   the   Lord,   from   the   Lord   which made the heav'ns and earth.

my help cometh from   the   Lord,

SOLO. Tenor or Soprano.

My . . help com - eth from   the   Lord, from the Lord which made heaven   and

p

earth.   He will not suf - fer thy foot to be mov - ed.   He that

Cres.   Cres.   Dim.

keep - eth thee will   not slum - ber,   He   that keep - eth thee will   not slumber.

Choir. *m*   Cres.   *f*   Dim.

I will lift up mine eyes un-to the hills, unto the hills, from whence doth come my help, doth come my   help.

Selection 20.

I will lift up mine eyes unto the hills from whence cometh my help. My help cometh from the Lord which made heaven and earth.

He will not suffer thy foot to be moved. He that keepeth thee will not slumber.
I will lift up mine eyes unto the hills.

CHESTERFIELD. C. M.

Choir and Congregation.

THOS. HAWEIS.

1. Up to the hills I lift mine eyes, There all my hope is laid;

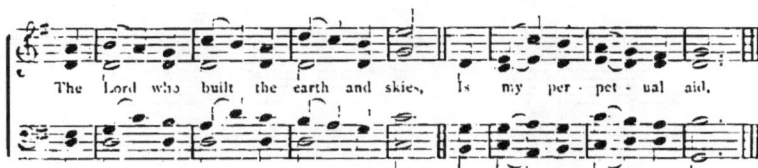

The Lord who built the earth and skies, Is my per-pet-ual aid.

80
WATTS.

1 Up to the hills I lift mine eyes,
  There all my hope is laid;
  The Lord, who built the earth and skies
  Is my perpetual aid.

2 Thy foot unmoved he ever keeps,
  And all thy ways will guard:
  He slumbers not, and never sleeps—
  Thy keeper is the Lord.

3 The Lord, thy keeper, shades thy way,
  Preserves thee in his sight;
  Nor shall the sun smite thee by day,
  Nor shall the moon by night.

4 The Lord preserves thy soul from sin,
  From evils great and sore—
  Thy going out and coming in,
  Now and forevermore.

81
REV. W. J. IRONS.

1 Father of love, our Guide and Friend,
  O lead us gently on,
  Until life's trial-time shall end,
  And heavenly peace be won.

2 We know not what the path may be,
  As yet by us untrod;
  But we can trust our all to thee
  Our Father and our God.

3 If called, like Abraham's child, to climb
  The hill of sacrifice,
  Some angel may be there in time;
  Deliverance shall arise:

4 Or, if some darker lot be good,
  O teach us to endure
  The sorrow, pain, or solitude,
  That make the spirit pure.

82
ANON.

1 Arise, ye people, and adore,
  Exulting strike the chord;
  Let all the earth—from shore to shore,
  Confess th' Almighty Lord.

2 Glad shouts aloud—wide echoing round,
  Th' ascending God proclaim;
  The angelic choir respond the sound,
  And shake creation's frame.

3 They sing of death and hell o'erthrown,
  In that triumphant hour:
  And God exalts his conquering Son
  To his right hand of power.

4 O shout, ye people, and adore,
  Exulting strike the chord;
  Let all the earth—from shore to shore,
  Confess th' Almighty Lord.

83
STEELE.

1 Come, ye that love the Savior's name,
  And joy to make it known;
  The Sovereign of your hearts proclaim,
  And bow before his throne.

2 Behold your King, your Savior, crowned
  With glories all divine;
  And tell the wondering nations round,
  How bright those glories shine.

3 When in his earthly courts we view
  The beauties of our King,
  We long to love as angels do,
  And with their voice to sing.

84
WATTS.

1 Blest are the souls that hear and know
  The gospel's joyful sound:
  Peace shall attend the path they go,
  And light their steps surround.

2 Their joy shall bear their spirits up
  Through their Redeemer's name:
  His righteousness exalts their hope,
  Nor Satan dares condemn.

3 The Lord, our glory and defense,
  Strength and salvation gives:
  Israel, thy King forever reigns,
  Thy God forever lives.

Selection 21.—ST. ANN'S SERVICE.—O Zion, that bringest good tidings.

O Zi - on, that bring - est good tid - ings, get thee up, get thee up in - to the high mountain!

O Je - ru - sa-lem, that bringest good tid-ings, Lift up thy voice, lift up thy voice, lift up thy

voice with strength! Lift it up, be not a-fraid! be not a-fraid! Say un - to the cit - ies of Ju - dah, Be-

hold your God! Be not a - fraid! O Zi - on, that bring - est good tid - ings, O Je - ru - sa-lem, that

bring-est good tid - ings, Lift up thy voice! lift up thy voice! Lift up thy voice with strength!

Selection 21.

O Zion, that bringest good tidings, get thee up into the high mountain. O Jerusalem, that bringest good tidings, lift up thy voice with strength; lift it up, be not afraid. | Say unto the cities of Judah, behold your God. O Jerusalem, that bringest good tidings, lift up thy voice with strength.

ST. ANN'S. C. M.

Dr. Croft.

1. Lift up to God the voice of praise, Whose breath our souls in-spired;

Loud and more loud the an-them raise, With grate-ful ar-dor fired.

85 WARDLAW.

1 Lift up to God the voice of praise,
   Whose breath our souls inspired;
   Loud and more loud the anthem raise,
   With grateful ardor fired.

2 Lift up to God the voice of praise,
   Whose goodness, passing thought,
   Loads every minute, as it flies,
   With benefits unsought.

3 Lift up to God the voice of praise,
   From whom salvation flows,
   Who sent his Son our souls to save
   From everlasting woes.

4 Lift up to God the voice of praise,
   For hope's transporting ray,
   Which lights, through darkest shades of death,
   To realms of endless day.

86 PATRICK.

1 O God! we praise thee, and confess
   That thou the only Lord
   And everlasting Father art,
   By all the earth adored.

2 To thee all angels cry aloud;
   To thee the powers on high,
   Both cherubim and seraphim,
   Continually do cry:—

3 O holy, holy, holy Lord,
   Whom heavenly hosts obey,
   The world is with the glory filled
   Of thy majestic sway!

4 The apostles' glorious company,
   And prophets crowned with light,
   With all the martyrs' noble host,
   Thy constant praise recite.

5 Thy holy church throughout the world,
   O Lord, confesses thee,
   That thou th' eternal Father art,
   Of boundless majesty.

87 WATTS.

1 Praise ye the Lord, immortal choir!
   In heavenly heights above,
   With harp, and voice, and soul of fire,
   Burning with perfect love.

2 Shout to Jehovah, surging main!
   In deep eternal roar;
   Let wave to wave resound the strain,
   And shore reply to shore.

3 And round the wide world let it roll,
   Whilst man shall lead it on;
   Join, every ransomed human soul,
   In glorious unison.

88 WATTS.

1 Begin, my tongue, some heavenly theme,
   And speak some boundless thing:
   The mighty works, or mightier name,
   Of our eternal King.

2 His very word of grace is strong,
   As that which built the skies;
   The voice that rolls the stars along
   Speaks all the promises.

3 Oh, might I hear thy heavenly tongue
   But whisper, "Thou art mine!"
   Those gentle words should raise my song
   To notes almost divine.

89 DODDRIDGE.

1 How rich thy favors, God of grace!
   How various and divine!
   Full as the ocean they are poured,
   And bright as heaven they shine.

2 He to eternal glory calls,
   And leads the wondrous way
   To his own palace, where he reigns
   In uncreated day.

3 The songs of everlasting years
   That mercy shall attend,
   Which leads, through sufferings of an hour,
   To joys that never end.

Selection 22.—ST. MARTIN'S SERVICE.—Great is the Lord, and greatly to be praised.

Great is the Lord, and great-ly to be prais-ed, He is to be fear-ed a-bove all gods,

Great is the Lord, and great-ly to be prais-ed, He is to be fear-ed a-bove all gods,

he is to be fear-ed a-bove all gods. Hon-or and maj-es-ty are be-fore him, strength and

he is to be fear-ed a-bove all gods. Hon-or and maj-es-ty are be-fore him, strength and

beau-ty are in his sanct-u-a-ry; Oh, wor-ship the Lord in the beau-ty of ho-li-ness, Fear ye

beau-ty are in his sanct-u-a-ry; Oh, wor-ship the Lord in the beau-ty of ho-li-ness, Fear be-

fore him, all the earth. Great is the Lord, and great-ly to be prais-ed; Fear ye be-fore him, all the earth.

fore him, all the earth. Great is the Lord, and great-ly to be prais-ed; Fear ye be-fore him, all the earth.

Selection 22.

Great is the Lord, and greatly to be praised. He is to be feared above all gods. Honor and majesty are before him; strength and beauty are in his sanctuary. Oh, worship the Lord in the beauty of holiness; fear before him, all the earth.

ST. MARTINS. C. M.

Choir and Congregation.   WM. TANSUR.

1. O thou, to whom all crea-tures bow With-in this earth-ly frame,

Thro' all the world, how great art thou! How glo-rious is thy name!

---

90   WATTS.

1 O thou, to whom all creatures bow
Within this earthly frame,
Through all the world, how great art thou!
How glorious is thy name!

2 When heaven, thy beauteous work on high,
Employs my wondering sight;
The moon that nightly rules the sky
With stars of feebler light; —

3 Lord, what is man, that thou shouldst deign
To bear him in thy mind!
Or what is race, that thou shouldst prove
To them so wondrous kind!

4 O thou, to whom all creatures bow,
Within this earthly frame,
Through all the world, how great art thou!
How glorious is thy name!

91   H. K. WHITE.

1 The Lord, our God, is full of might,
The winds obey his will:
He speaks,—and, in his heavenly height,
The rolling sun stands still.

2 Rebel, ye waves, and o'er the land
With threatening aspect roar;
The Lord uplifts his awful hand,
And chains you to the shore.

3 Howl, winds of night, your force combine;
Without his high behest,
Ye shall not, in the mountain pine,
Disturb the sparrow's nest.

4 His voice sublime is heard afar,
In distant peals it dies;
He yokes the whirlwind to his car,
And sweeps the howling skies.

5 Ye nations, bend—in reverence bend;
Ye monarchs, wait his nod,
And bid the choral song ascend
To celebrate your God.

92   WATTS.

1 Great God! how infinite art thou!
What worthless worms are we!
Let the whole race of creatures bow,
And pay their praise to thee.

2 Thy throne eternal ages stood,
Ere seas or stars were made;
Thou art the ever-living God,
Were all the nations dead.

3 Eternity, with all its years,
Stands present in thy view;
To thee, there 's nothing old appears
Great God! there 's nothing new.

4 Our lives thro' various scenes are drawn,
And vexed with trifling cares;
While thine eternal thought moves on
Thine undisturbed affairs.

5 Great God! how infinite art thou!
What worthless worms are we!
Let the whole race of creatures bow,
And pay their praise to thee.

93   WATTS.

1 The Lord of glory is my light,
And my salvation, too;
God is my strength,—nor will I fear
What all my foes can do.

2 One privilege my heart desires,—
Oh! grant me an abode,
Among the churches of thy saints,
The temples of my God.

3 When troubles rise, and storms appear,
There may his children hide;
God has a strong pavilion, where
He makes my soul abide.

4 Now shall my head be lifted high,
Above my foes around;
And songs of joy and victory
Within thy temple sound.

Selection 23.—SILVER ST. SERVICE.—The Lord reigneth.

Choir. With dignity.

The Lord reign-eth! He is clothed with maj - es - ty, The Lord is clothed with maj - es - ty, where-

with he hath gird - ed him - self. The world is al - so stab'ished that it can not be moved.

The Lord reign-eth! He is clothed with maj-es-ty, he is clothed with maj-es-ty, A - men, A - men.

Allegro.

Cry out and shout! Cry out and shout! thou in-hab-i-tant of Zi - on, For

Cry out and shout! Cry out and shout! shout!

Cry out and shout! Cry out and shout! shout!

great is the Ho-ly One of Is-rael! Great is the Ho-ly One of Israel! Great, great in the midst of thee.

Cry out and shout! . . Great, great in the midst of thee! Cry out and shout! cry out and shout!

Cry out and shout! oh, cry out and shout!

Selection 23.

The Lord reigneth. He is clothed with majesty; the Lord is clothed with majesty, wherewith he hath girded himself. The world is also stablished that it can not be moved. Cry out and shout, thou inhabitant of Zion, for great is the Holy One of Israel in the midst of thee. Cry out and shout.

SILVER ST. S. M.

Choir and Congregation.

L. SMITH.

1. Come, sound his praise a - broad, And hymns of glo - ry sing:

Je - ho - vah is the sov - 'reign God, The u - ni - ver - sal King.

94
WATTS.

1 Come, sound his praise abroad,
  And hymns of glory sing:
Jehovah is the sovereign God,
  The universal King.

2 He formed the deeps unknown;
  He gave the seas their bound;
The watery worlds are all his own,
  And all the solid ground.

3 Come, worship at his throne,
  Come, bow before the Lord:
We are his work, and not our own,
  He formed us by his word.

4 To-day attend his voice,
  Nor dare provoke his rod;
Come, like the people of his choice,
  And own your gracious God.

95
WATTS.

1 Great is the Lord our God,
  And let his praise be great;
He makes his churches his abode,
  His most delightful seat.

2 These temples of his grace,
  How beautiful they stand!
The honors of our native place,
  And bulwarks of our land.
    4

---

3 In Zion, God is known,
  A refuge in distress:
How bright hath his salvation shone
  Through all her palaces!

4 In every new distress,
  We 'll to his house repair;
We 'll think upon his wondrous grace,
  And seek deliverance there.

96
AUDER.

1 Sweet is the work, O Lord,
  Thy glorious name to sing;
To praise and pray—to hear thy word,
  And grateful offerings bring.

2 Sweet—at the dawning light,
  Thy boundless love to tell;
And when approach the shades of night,
  Still on the theme to dwell.

3 Sweet—on this day of rest,
  To join in heart and voice,
With those who love and serve thee best,
  And in thy name rejoice.

4 To songs of praise and joy
  Be every Sabbath given,
That such may be our blest employ
  Eternally in heaven.

97
DODDRIDGE.

1 Now let our voices join
  To raise a sacred song;
Ye pilgrims! in Jehovah's ways,
  With music pass along.

2 See—flowers of paradise,
  In rich profusion spring;
The sun of glory gilds the path,
  And dear companions sing.

3 See—Salem's golden spires,
  In beauteous prospect, rise;
And brighter crowns than mortals wear,
  Which sparkle through the skies.

4 All honor to his name,
  Who marks the shining way,—
To him who leads the pilgrims on
  To realms of endless day.

98
WATTS.

1 Thy name, Almighty Lord,
  Shall sound through distant lands:
Great is thy grace, and sure thy word;
  Thy truth forever stands.

2 Far be thine honor spread,
  And long thy praise endure,
Till morning light, and evening shade,
  Shall be exchanged no more.

Selection 24.—St. THOMAS SERVICE.—Be joyful in God.

G. F. R.

Be joy-ful in God! be joy-ful in God! oh, let the na-tions be

Be joy-ful in God! be joy-ful in God! oh, let the na-tions be glad, oh, let the na-tions be

glad, let the na-tions be glad, and sing for joy! Let

glad, let the na-tions be glad, and sing for joy! Let all those that put their trust in thee re-joice! Let

all those that put their trust in thee re-joice; let them al-so that love thy name be joy-ful in

all those that put their trust in thee re-joice; let them al-so that love thy name be joy-ful in

thee, let them al-so that love thy name be joy-ful in thee, be joy-ful, be joy-ful in thee!

thee, let them al-so that love thy name be joy-ful in thee, be joy-ful, be joy-ful in thee!

Selection 24.

Be joyful in God! Oh, let the nations be glad, and sing for joy! Let all those that put their trust in thee rejoice; let them also that love thy name be joyful in thee.

ST. THOMAS. S. M.

Choir and Congregation.

WILLIAMS.

1. Come, we who love the Lord, And let our joys be known; Join in a song of sweet accord, And thus surround the throne.

99 WATTS.

1 Come, we who love the Lord,
 And let our joys be known;
 Join in a song of sweet accord,
 And thus surround the throne.

2 Let those refuse to sing
 Who never knew our God;
 But children of the heavenly King
 May speak their joys abroad.

3 The hill of Zion yields
 A thousand sacred sweets
 Before we reach the heavenly fields,
 Or walk the golden streets.

4 Then let our songs abound,
 And every tear be dry;
 We're marching thro' Immanuel's ground
 To fairer worlds on high.

100 MONTGOMERY.

1 Oh, bless the Lord, my soul!
 His grace to thee proclaim
 And all that is within me join
 To bless his holy name.

2 Oh, bless the Lord, my soul!
 His mercies bear in mind:
 Forget not all his benefits:
 The Lord to thee is kind.

3 He pardons all thy sins,
 Prolongs thy feeble breath;
 He healeth thy infirmities,
 And ransoms thee from death.

4 Then bless his holy name,
 Whose grace hath made thee whole!
 Whose loving-kindness crowns thy days;
 Oh, bless the Lord, my soul!

101 [Sel. 5 or 6.] WATTS.

1 Welcome, sweet day of rest,
 That saw the Lord arise!
 Welcome to this reviving breast,
 And these rejoicing eyes!

2 The King himself comes near,
 And feasts his saints to-day;
 Here may we sit, and see him here,
 And love, and praise, and pray.

3 One day, amid the place
 Where my dear Lord hath been,
 Is sweeter than ten thousand days
 Within the tents of sin.

4 My willing soul would stay
 In such a frame as this,
 And sit and sing herself away
 To everlasting bliss.

MONSELL. S. M.

Choir and Congregation.
Andantino.

Words by Rev. J. S. B. MONSELL.
Music written for this work.

102
1. Whene'er we bend, O Lord, Before thy mer-cy-seat, Our souls, a-dor-ing,
2. Where'er thy name is blest, Wher-e'er thy peo-ple meet, 'Tis there we love in

plead thy word, And own thy mer-cy sweet.
thee to rest, And find thy mer-cy sweet.

3 Light thou our earthly way,
 Guide thou our wandering feet,
 That thro' our journey here we may
 Still find thy mercy sweet.

4 Then with the ransomed host
 Eternally repeat,
 To Father, Son, and Holy Ghost,
 Our joy—thy mercy sweet.

Selection 25.—NUREMBERG SERVICE.—Oh, come, let us sing unto the Lord!

Oh, come, let us sing, let us sing un-to the Lord! let us heart-i-ly re-joice in the Rock of our sal-

Oh, come, let us sing, let us sing un-to the Lord! let us heart-i-ly re-joice in the Rock of our sal-

va-tion. Let us come be-fore his presence with thanksgiving, and make a joyful noise un-to him with

va-tion. Let us come be-fore his presence with thanksgiving, and make a joyful noise un-to him with

psalms, and make a joyful noise un-to him with psalms.   For the Lord is a great

psalms, and make a joyful noise un-to him with psalms.   For the Lord is a great

For the Lord is a great God,

God, and a great King a-bove all gods, a great King a-bove all gods. Oh, come, let us sing! Oh, come, let us sing!

God, and a great King a-bove all gods, a great King a-bove all gods. Oh, come, let us sing! Oh, come, let us sing!

Selection 25.

Oh, come, let us sing unto the Lord; let us heartily rejoice in the Rock of our salvation. Let us come before his presence with thanksgiving, and make a joyful noise unto him with psalms. For the Lord is a great God, and a great King above all gods.

Oh, come, let us sing unto the Lord.

NUREMBURG. 7s.

Choir and Congregation. AHLE.

Praise to God, immortal praise, For the love that crowns our days;
Bounteous Source of ev'ry joy, Let thy praise our tongues employ.

---

103 BARBAULD.

1 Praise to God, immortal praise,
For the love that crowns our days;
Bounteous source of every joy,
Let thy praise our tongues employ.

2 For the blessings of the field,
For the stores the gardens yield,
For the joy which harvests bring,
Grateful praises now we sing.

3 All that Spring, with bounteous hand,
Scatters o'er the smiling land;
All that liberal Autumn pours
From her rich o'erflowing stores.

4 Lord, for these our souls shall raise
Grateful vows and solemn praise;
And when every blessing's flown,
Love thee for thyself alone.

104 WRANGHAM.

1 Praise the Lord—his power confess;
Praise him in his holiness;
Praise him as the theme inspires,—
Praise him as his fame requires.

2 Let the trumpet's lofty sound
Spread its loudest notes around;
Let the harp unite, in praise,
With the sacred minstrel's lays.

3 Let the organ join to bless
God, the Lord of righteousness;
Tune your voice to spread the fame
Of the great Jehovah's name.

4 All who dwell beneath his light,
In his praise your hearts unite;
While the stream of song is poured,
Praise and magnify the Lord.

105 TURNER.

1 Lord of hosts, how bright, how fair,
E'en on earth, thy temples are:
Here thy waiting people see
Much of heaven, and much of thee.

2 From thy gracious presence flows
Bliss that softens all our woes:
While thy Spirit's holy fire
Warms our hearts with pure desire.

3 Here we supplicate thy throne;
Here thou mak'st thy glories known;
Here we learn thy righteous ways,
Taste thy love, and sing thy praise.

4 Thus with sacred songs of joy,
We our happy lives employ;
Love, and long to love thee more,
Till from earth to heaven we soar.

106 SANDYS.

1 Thou who art enthroned above,
Thou by whom we live and move!
Oh, how sweet, with joyful tongue,
To resound thy praise in song!

2 From thy works our joys arise,
O thou only good and wise!
Who thy wonders can declare?
How profound thy counsels are!

3 Warm our hearts with sacred fire;
Grateful fervors still inspire;
All our powers, with all their might,
Ever in thy praise unite.

107 LYTE.

1 Praise the Lord, his glories show,
Saints within his courts below,
Angels round his throne above,
All that see and share his love!

2 Praise the Lord, his mercies trace;
Praise his providence and grace—
All that he for man hath done,
All he sends us through his Son.

3 Earth to heaven, and heaven to earth,
Tell his wonders, sing his worth;
Age to age, and shore to shore,
Praise him, praise him, evermore!

Selection 26.—WILMOT SERVICE.—Praise waiteth for thee, O God, in Zion.

Praise waiteth for thee, O God, in Zi - on, and un - to thee shall the vow be performed; Oh, thou that hearest

prayer, un - to thee shall all flesh come; Oh, thou that hear - est prayer, un - to thee shall all flesh come.

Bless - ed is the man whom thou choosest, and causest to approach un - to thee. . . . that he may

dwell, may dwell in thy courts, that he may dwell, may dwell in thy courts. Praise waiteth for thee, O

God, in Zi - on, and un - to thee shall the vow be performed. Praise waiteth for thee, praise waiteth for thee.

Selection 26.

Praise waiteth for thee, O God, in Zion, and unto thee shall the vow be performed. O thou that hearest prayer, unto thee shall all flesh come. Blessed is the man whom thou choosest and causest to approach unto thee, that he may dwell in thy courts. Praise waiteth for thee, O God, in Zion.

WILMOT. 8s & 7s.

Choir and Congregation.   Arr. by DR. MASON.

1 Praise to thee, thou great Cre - a - tor! Praise to thee from ev - ery tongue:

Join, my soul, with ev - ery crea - ture, Join the u - ni - ver - sal song.

---

108 · FAWCETT.

1 Praise to thee, thou great Creator!
  Praise to thee from every tongue:
  Join, my soul, with every creature,
  Join the universal song.

2 Father, Source of all compassion,
  Pure, unbounded grace is thine:
  Hail the God of our salvation!
  Praise him for his love divine.

3 For ten thousand blessings given,
  For the hope of future joy,
  Sound his praise through earth and heaven,
  Sound Jehovah's praise on high.

4 Joyfully on earth adore him,
  Till in heaven our song we raise;
  There, enraptured, fall before him,
  Lost in wonder, love, and praise.

109 · MANT.

1 Praise the Lord! ye heavens, adore him,
  Praise him, angels in the height;
  Sun and moon, rejoice before him;
  Praise him, all ye stars of light!

2 Praise the Lord—for he hath spoken;
  Worlds his mighty voice obeyed;
  Laws which never shall be broken,
  For their guidance he hath made.

3 Praise the Lord—for he is glorious;
  Never shall his promise fail;
  God hath made his saints victorious,
  Sin and death shall not prevail.

4 Praise the God of our salvation,
  Hosts on high his power proclaim;
  Heaven and earth, and all creation,
  Laud and magnify his name.

110 · ROBINSON.

1 Mighty God! while angels bless thee,
  May a mortal lisp thy name?
  Lord of men, as well as angels!
  Thou art every creature's theme:

2 Lord of every land and nation!
  Ancient of eternal days!
  Sounded through the wide creation,
  Be thy just and glorious praise.

3 For the grandeur of thy nature,—
  Grand, beyond a seraph's thought;
  For the wonders of creation,
  Works with skill and kindness wrought;

4 For thy providence, that governs
  Through thine empire's wide domain,
  Wings an angel, guides a sparrow;
  Blessed be thy gentle reign.

111 · ONDERDONK.

1 Blest be thou, O God of Israel,
  Thou, our Father, and our Lord!
  Blest thy majesty forever!
  Ever be thy name adored.

2 Thine, O Lord, are power and greatness,
  Glory, victory, are thine own;
  All is thine in earth and heaven,
  Over all thy boundless throne.

3 Riches come of thee, and honor,
  Power and might to thee belong;
  Thine it is to make us prosper,
  Only thine to make us strong.

4 Lord, to thee, thou God of mercy,
  Hymns of gratitude we raise;
  To thy name, forever glorious,
  Ever we address our praise!

112 · OSLER.

1 Worship, honor, glory, blessing,
  Lord, we offer to thy name;
  Young and old, their thanks expressing,
  Join thy goodness to proclaim :—

2 As the hosts of heaven adore thee,
  We, too, bow before thy throne;
  As the angels serve before thee,
  So on earth thy will be done.

Selection 27.—LENOX SERVICE.—Let every thing that hath breath praise the Lord.

Let ev - 'ry thing that hath breath praise the Lord, ... praise the Lord. Let

praise the Lord, praise the Lord,

ev-'ry thing that hath breath praise the Lord, . . . praise the Lord, praise the Lord. Praise ye him, all his

praise the Lord,

an - gels, praise ye him, all his hosts. Praise ye him, sun and moon; praise him,

an-gels, praise him, all his hosts. Praise ye him, sun and moon; Praise ye him, . .

all ye stars of light. Praise the Lord from the earth, both young men and maid - ens, Old men and

all ye stars of light. Old men and

chil - dren, old men and children, Let ev-'ry-thing that hath breath praise the Lord, praise the Lord, praise the Lord.

Selection 27.

Let every thing that hath breath praise the Lord. Praise ye him, all his angels. Praise ye him, all his hosts. Praise ye him, sun and moon. Praise him, all ye stars of light. | Praise the Lord from the earth, both young men and maidens, old men and children.
Let every thing that hath breath praise the Lord.

LENOX. H. M.

Choir and Congregation. EDSON.

Ye tribes of Ad-am, join With heav'n, and earth, and seas, And of-fer notes di-vine To your Cre-a-tor's praise;

Ye

Ye ho-ly throng Of angels bright, Ye ho-ly throng Of an-gels bright, In worlds of light Begin the song.

holy throng Of angels bright, Ye holy throng Of an-gels bright, In worlds of light

113 WATTS.

1 Ye tribes of Adam, join
    With heaven, and earth, and seas,
And offer notes divine
    To your Creator's praise:
        Ye holy throng
        Of angels bright,
        In worlds of light,
        Begin the song.

2 The shining worlds above
    In glorious order stand;
Or in swift courses move,
    By his supreme command:
        He spake the word,
        And all their frame
        From nothing came,
        To praise the Lord!

3 Let all the nations fear
    The God that rules above;
He brings his people near,
    And makes them taste his love:
        While earth and sky
        Attempt his praise,
        His saints shall raise
        His honors high.

114 DWIGHT.

1 Sing to the Lord most high;
    Let every land adore;
With grateful voice make known
    His goodness and his power:
        With cheerful songs
        Declare his ways,
        And let his praise
        Inspire your tongues.

2 Enter his courts with joy;
    With fear address the Lord;
He formed us with his hand,
    And quickened by his word;
        With wide command
        He spreads his sway,
        O'er every sea
        And every land.

3 His hands provide our food,
    And every blessing give;
We feed upon his care,
    And in his pastures live:
        With cheerful songs
        Declare his ways,
        And let his praise
        Inspire your tongues.

115 STEELE.

1 To your Creator, God,
    Your great Preserver, raise,
Ye creatures of his hand,
    Your highest notes of praise:
        Let every voice
        Proclaim his power,
        His name adore
        And loud rejoice.

2 Let every creature join
    To celebrate his name,
And all their various powers
    Assist th' exalted theme:
        Let nature raise,
        From every tongue,
        A general song
        Of grateful praise.

3 But oh! from human tongues
    Should nobler praises flow;
And every thankful heart
    With warm devotion glow:
        Your voices raise
        Above the rest;
        Ye highly blest!
        Declare his praise.

Selection 28.—LYONS SERVICE.—The Lord is my strength and song.

G. F. R.

Is my strength and song, is my strength and song, And

The Lord is my strength and song, . . .

is be - come my sal - va - tion, and is be - come my sal - va - tion. This gate of the

Lord, in - to which the right-eous shall en - ter. I will praise thee for thou hast

heard me, and art be - come my sal - va - tion; I will praise thee, for thou hast heard me, and art be-

come my sal - va - tion. Is my strength and song, is my strength and song.

The Lord is my strength and song, ...

Selection 28.

The Lord is my strength and song, and is become my salvation. This gate of the Lord, into which the righteous shall enter. I will praise thee, for thou hast heard me, and art become my salvation. The Lord is my strength and song.

LYONS. 10s & 11s.

Choir and Congregation.

HAYDN.

1. Oh, praise ye the Lord; pre-pare your glad voice His praise in the great as - sem - bly to sing; In

their great Cre - a - tor let all men re - joice, And heirs of sal - va-tion be glad in their King.

---

116   TATE & BRADY.

1 Oh, praise ye the Lord; prepare your glad voice
His praise in the great assembly to sing,
In their great Creator let all men rejoice,
And heirs of salvation be glad in their King.

2 Let them his great name devoutly adore;
In loud-swelling strains his praises express,
Who graciously opens his bountiful store,
Their wants to relieve, and his children to bless.

3 With glory adorned, his people shall sing
To God, who defense and plenty supplies;
Their loud acclamations to him, their great King,
Through earth shall be sounded, and reach to the skies.

117   C. WESLEY.

1 Ye servants of God, your Master proclaim,
And publish abroad his wonderful name;
The name all-victorious of Jesus extol;
His kingdom is glorious, he rules over all.

2 God ruleth on high, almighty to save;
And still he is nigh—his presence we have;
The great congregation his triumph shall sing,
Ascribing salvation to Jesus our King.

3 Salvation to God, who sits on the throne,
Let all cry aloud, and honor the Son;
The praises of Jesus the angels proclaim,
Fall down on their faces, and worship the Lamb.

4 Then let us adore, and give him his right,
All glory and power, and wisdom and might;
All honor and blessing, with angels above,
And thanks never ceasing, for infinite love.

118   GRANT.

1 O, worship the King all-glorious above,
And gratefully sing his wonderful love—
Our Shield and Defender, the Ancient of Days,
Pavilioned in splendor, and girded with praise.

2 O tell of his might, and sing of his grace,
Whose robe is the light, whose canopy, space;
His chariots of wrath the deep thunder-clouds form,
And dark is his path on the wings of the storm.

3 Thy bountiful care what tongue can recite?
It breathes in the air, it shines in the light,
It streams from the hills, it descends to the plain,
And sweetly distills in the dew and the rain.

4 Frail children of dust, and feeble as frail,
In thee do we trust, nor find thee to fail;
Thy mercies how tender! how firm to the end!
Our Maker, Defender, Redeemer, and Friend!

5 Father Almighty, how faithful thy love!
While angels delight to hymn thee above,
The humbler creation, though feeble their lays,
With true adoration shall lisp to thy praise.

Selection 20.—**ITALIAN HYMN SERVICE.**—Let my mouth be filled with thy praise. † † †

Let my mouth be fill - ed with thy praise, O Lord, and with thy hon - or all the day; let my mouth . .

Let my

let my mouth be filled, let my mouth be fill - ed

mouth be fill-ed with thy praise, O Lord, let my mouth be fill-ed with thy praise, O Lord,

with thy praise, and with thy hon - or all the day. My God, be not far from me, Oh, my God, make haste for my

help. Un-to thee will I sing with the harp, Oh, thou ho - ly One of Is - ra - el, Un-to

with the harp,

thee will I sing, un - to thee will I sing, Oh, thou ho - ly One, thou ho - ly One of Is - ra -

el. Let my mouth, let my mouth be fill - ed with thy praise.

Let my mouth be fill-ed with thy praise, O Lord,

Selection 29.

Let my mouth be filled with thy praise, O Lord, and with thy honor all the day. My God, be not far from me; oh, my God, make haste for my help.

Unto thee will I sing with the harp, oh, thou holy One of Israel. Let my mouth be filled with thy praise, O Lord.

ITALIAN HYMN. 6s & 4s.

GIARDINI.

Choir and Congregation.

1. Come, thou al-might-y King, Help us thy name to sing, Help us to praise: Fa-ther! all glo-ri-ous, O'er all vic-to-ri-ous, Come, and reign o-ver us, An-cient of Days!

| 119 | MADAN. | 120 | ALLEN. | 121 | BODEN. |

119

1 Come, thou Almighty King,
Help us thy name to sing,
Help us to praise:
Father! all glorious,
O'er all victorious,
Come, and reign over us,
Ancient of Days!

2 Come, thou incarnate Word,
Gird on thy mighty sword;
Our prayer attend;
Come, and thy people bless,
And give thy word success:
Spirit of holiness!
On us descend.

3 Come, holy Comforter!
Thy sacred witness bear,
In this glad hour:
Thou, who almighty art,
Now rule in every heart,
And ne'er from us depart,
Spirit of power!

120

1 Glory to God on high!
Let heaven and earth reply,
"Praise ye his name!"
His love and grace adore,
Who all our sorrows bore;
Sing loud for evermore,
"Worthy the Lamb!"

2 While they around the throne
Cheerfully join in one,
Praising his name,—
Ye who have felt his blood
Sealing your peace with God,
Sound his dear name abroad.
"Worthy the Lamb!"

3 Join, all ye ransomed race,
Our Lord and God to bless,
Praise ye his name!
In him we will rejoice,
And make a joyful noise,
Shouting with heart and voice,
"Worthy the Lamb!"

121

1 Come, all ye saints of God,
Wide through the earth abroad
Spread Jesus' fame;
Tell what his love hath done;
Trust in his name alone;
Shout to his lofty throne,
"Worthy the Lamb!"

2 Hence, gloomy doubts and fears!
Dry up your mournful tears;
Swell the glad theme:
To Christ, our gracious King,
Strike each melodious string;
Join heart and voice to sing,
"Worthy the Lamb!"

3 Hark! how the choirs above,
Filled with the Savior's love,
Dwell on his name!
There, too, may we be found,
With light and glory crowned,
While all the heavens resound,
"Worthy the Lamb!"

Selection 19.

Choir and Congregation.

WILLIAMS. C. M. Double.

Words by HELEN M. WILLIAMS.
Music by GEO. F. ROOT.

122 1 { While thee I seek, protecting Power! Be my vain wishes stilled; }
{ And may this con-se-cra-ted hour With better hopes be filled! } Thy love the power of thought bestowed; To

2 { In each e-vent of life, how clear Thy rul-ing hand I see! }
{ Each blessing to my soul more dear Because conferred by thee. } In ev-'ry joy that crowns my days, In

3 { When gladness wings my favored hour, Thy love my tho'ts shall fill; }
{ Resigned, when storms of sorrow lower, My soul shall meet thy will. } My lift-ed eye, with-out a tear, The

thee my tho'ts would soar: Thy mer-cy o'er my life has flowed; That mer-cy I a-dore.

ev-'ry pain I bear, My heart shall find de-light in praise, Or seek re-lief in prayer.

gath-'ring storm shall see; My stead-fast heart shall know no fear; That heart will rest on thee.

---

123 [Sel. 16. Tune, Williams.]
MONTGOMERY.

1 God, in the high and holy place,
Looks down upon the spheres;
Yet in his providence and grace,
To every eye appears.
He bows the heavens; the mountains stand
A highway for our God;
He walks amid the desert land;
'Tis Eden where he trod.

2 The forests in his strength rejoice;
Hark! on the evening breeze,
As once of old, Jehovah's voice
Is heard among the trees.
In every stream his bounty flows,
Diffusing joy and wealth;
In every breeze his Spirit blows,—
The breath of life and health.

3 His blessings fall in plenteous showers
Upon the lap of earth,
That teems with foliage, fruits, and flowers,
And rings with infant mirth.
If God hath made this world so fair,
Where sin and death abound;
How beautiful, beyond compare,
Will Paradise be found!

---

124 [Sel. 13. Tune, Williams.]
HEGINBOTHAM.

1 Father of mercies! God of love!
My Father and my God!
I'll sing the honors of thy name,
And spread thy praise abroad.
In every period of my life
Thy thoughts of love appear;
Thy mercies gild each transient scene,
And crown each passing year.

2 In all thy mercies, may my soul
A Father's bounty see;
Nor let the gifts thy grace bestows
Estrange my heart from thee.
Teach me, in times of deep distress,
To own thy hand, O God!
And in submissive silence learn
The lessons of thy rod.

3 Through every period of my life,
Each bright, each clouded scene,
Give me a meek and humble mind,
Still equal and serene.
Then may I close my eyes in death,
Redeemed from anxious fear;
For death itself, my God, is life,
If thou art with me there.

---

125 [Sel. 16. Tune, Williams.]
WATTS.

1 With songs and honors sounding loud,
Address the Lord on high;
Over the heavens he spreads his cloud,
And waters vail the sky.
He sends his showers of blessings down,
To cheer the plains below;
He makes the grass the mountains crown,
And corn in valleys grow.

2 His steady counsels change the face
Of the declining year;
He bids the sun cut short his race,
And wintry days appear.
His hoary frost, his fleecy snow,
Descend and clothe the ground;
The liquid streams forbear to flow,
In icy fetters bound.

3 He sends his word and melts the snow,
The fields no longer mourn;
He calls the warmer gales to blow,
And bids the Spring return.
The changing wind, the flying cloud,
Obey his mighty word:
With songs and honors sounding loud,
Praise ye the sovereign Lord,

Selection 13, 16, or 19.

Choir and Congregation.

MILTON. 7s. Double.

Words by JOHN MILTON.
New arr. by G. F. ROOT.

126
1. Let us with a joy-ful mind Praise the Lord, for he is kind, For his mer-cies shall en-dure,
2. Did the sol-id earth or-dain How to rise a-bove the main; Who, by his com-mand-ing might,

Ev-er faith-ful, ev-er sure. Let us sound his name a-broad, For of gods he is the God
Filled the new-made world with light: Caused the golden tress-ed sun All the day his course to run;

Who by wis-dom did cre-ate Heav'n's expanse and all its state;—
And the moon to shine by night, 'Mid her spangled sis-ters bright.

3 All his creatures God doth feed,
His full hand supplies their need;
Let us, therefore, warble forth
His high majesty and worth.
He his mansion hath on high,
'Bove the reach of mortal eye;
And his mercies shall endure,
Ever faithful, ever sure.

---

127   [Sel. 16. Tune, Milton.]
MONTGOMERY.

1 Holy, holy, holy Lord
God of Hosts! when heaven and earth,
Out of darkness, at thy word
Issued into glorious birth,
All thy works before thee stood,
And thine eye beheld them good,
While they sung with sweet accord,
Holy, holy, holy Lord!

2 Holy, holy, holy! thee,
One Jehovah evermore,
Father, Son, and Spirit! we,
Dust and ashes, would adore:
Lightly by the world esteemed,
From that world by thee redeemed,
Sing we here with glad accord,
Holy, holy, holy Lord!

3 Holy, holy, holy! all
Heaven's triumphant choir shall sing,
While the ransomed nations fall
At the footstool of their King:
Then shall saints and seraphim,
Harps and voices, swell one hymn,
Blending in sublime accord,
Holy, holy, holy Lord!

128   [Sel. 16. Tune, Milton.]
MONTGOMERY.

1 Songs of praise the angels sang,
Heaven with hallelujahs rang,
When Jehovah's work begun,
When he spake, and it was done.
Songs of praise awoke the morn,
When the Prince of Peace was born;
Songs of praise arose, when he,
Captive led captivity.

2 Heaven and earth must pass away—
Songs of praise shall crown that day;
God will make new heavens and earth—
Songs of praise shall hail their birth.
And shall man alone be dumb,
Till that glorious kingdom come?
No; the Church delights to raise
Psalms and hymns and songs of praise.

3 Saints below, with heart and voice,
Still in songs of praise rejoice;
Learning here, by faith and love,
Songs of praise to sing above.
Borne upon their latest breath
Songs of praise shall conquer death;
Then, amid eternal joy,
Songs of praise their powers employ.

129   [Sel. 3. Tune, Milton.]
C. WESLEY.

1 Light of life, seraphic fire,
Love divine, thyself impart;
Every fainting soul inspire;
Enter every drooping heart;
Every mournful sinner cheer,
Scatter all our guilty gloom;
Father! in thy grace appear,
To thy human temples come.

2 Come, in this accepted hour,
Bring thy heavenly kingdom in;
Fill us with thy glorious power,
Set us free from all our sin:
Nothing more can we require,
We will covet nothing less;
Be thou all our heart's desire,
All our joy, and all our peace.

130   [Sel. 3. Tune, Milton.]
EDMESTON.

1 Heavenly Spirit! may each heart
Through these sacred hours be thine;
May we from the world depart,
Breathing after things divine.
Lead us forth with joy and peace,
To thy temple, in thy ways;
And when this sweet day shall cease,
May its sun go down with praise.

Selection 94.—The Lord is my Shepherd.

ADDISON. L. M. 6 lines, or Double.

Choir and Congregation.

For L. M. Double
repeat from here.

Words by J. ADDISON.
Music arr. for this work.

131
1. The Lord my pasture shall prepare, And feed me with a shepherd's care; His pres-ence shall my wants supply,
2. When in the sul - try glebe I faint, Or on the thirst-y mountain pant; To fer - tile vales, and dew - y meads,
3. Tho' in the paths of death I tread, With gloomy hor-rors o-ver-spread, My stead-fast heart shall fear no ill,

And guard me with a watchful eye; My noonday walks he shall attend, And all my midnight hours de-fend.
My wea - ry, wand'ring steps he leads; Where peaceful riv - ers, soft and slow, A - mid the ver-dant landscape flow.
For thou, O Lord, art with me still; Thy friend-ly rod shall give me aid, And guide me thro' the dreadful shade.

---

132 [L. M. 6 lines]
MOORE.

1 Thou art, O God, the life and light
Of all this wondrous world we see;
Its glow by day, its smile by night,
Are but reflections caught from thee;
Where'er we turn, thy glories shine,
And all things fair and bright are thine.

2 When day, with farewell beam, delays
Among the opening clouds of even,
And we can almost think we gaze
Through opening vistas into heaven,—
Those hues that mark the sun's decline,
So soft, so radiant, Lord, are thine.

3 When night, with wings of starry gloom,
O'ershadows all the earth and skies,
Like some dark, beauteous bird, whose plume
Is sparkling with unnumbered eyes,
That sacred gloom, those fires divine,
So grand, so countless, Lord, are thine.

4 When youthful Spring around us breathes,
Thy Spirit warms her fragrant sigh;
And every flower that summer wreathes,
Is born beneath thy kindling eye;
Where'er we turn, thy glories shine,
And all things fair and bright are thine.

133 [L. M. Double]
ADDISON.

1 The spacious firmament on high,
With all the blue ethereal sky,
And spangled heavens, a shining frame,
Their great Original proclaim:
Th' unwearied sun, from day to day,
Does his Creator's power display;
And publishes to every land
The work of an almighty hand.

2 Soon as the evening shades prevail,
The moon takes up the wondrous tale,
And nightly, to the listening earth,
Repeats the story of her birth;
While all the stars that round her burn,
And all the planets in their turn,
Confirm the tidings as they roll,
And spread the truth from pole to pole.

3 What though in solemn silence, all
Move round the dark terrestrial ball,—
What though no real voice nor sound
Amid their radiant orbs be found,—
In reason's ear they all rejoice,
And utter forth a glorious voice,
Forever singing as they shine,—
"The hand that made us is divine."

134 [L. M. Double.]
DR. HOLMES.

1 Lord of all being; throned afar,
Thy glory flames from sun and star;
Centre and soul of every sphere,
Yet to each loving heart how near!
Sun of our life, thy quickening ray
Sheds on our path the glow of day;
Star of our hope, thy softened light
Cheers the long watches of the night.

2 Lord of all being; throned afar,
Thy glory flames from sun and star;
Centre and soul of every sphere,
Yet to each loving heart how near!
Our midnight is thy smile withdrawn;
Our noontide is thy gracious dawn;
Our rainbow arch thy mercy's sign;
All, save the clouds of sin, are thine!

3 Lord of all life, below, above,
Whose light is truth, whose warmth is love,
Before thy ever-blazing throne
We ask no lustre of our own.
Grant us thy truth to make us free,
And kindling hearts that burn for thee,
Till all thy living altars claim
One holy light, one heavenly flame!

Selection 30.—PALESTRINA SERVICE.—The Lord is my Rock.

G. F. R.

The Lord is my Rock, and my Fort-ress, and my De-liv-'rer, my God, my Strength, in whom I will trust; For who is God save the Lord? or who is a Rock save our God? For who is God save the Lord? or who is a Rock save our God? He de-liv-ered me from my strong en-e-my, from my strong en-e-my, He brought me forth al-so in-to a large place; Oh, who is God save the Lord, and who is a Rock save our God?

PALESTRINA. C. M.

Choir and Congregation.

PALESTRINA.

135 1. No change of time shall ev-er shock My trust, O Lord, in thee; For thou hast al-ways been my Rock, A sure de-fense to me.

2 Thou my deliv'rer art, O God ;
My trust is in thy pow'r:
Thou art my Shield from foes abroad,
My Safeguard and my Tower.

3 Then let Jehovah be adored.
On whom our hopes depend ;
For who, except the mighty Lord,
His people can defend ?

5

Selection 31.—ANGELS' STORY SERVICE.—And there were in the same country.

Choir. Recitative.   G. F. R.

And there were in the same country } shep-herds a-bid-ing in the field, keep-ing watch o-ver their flocks by

And lo!   and his glo-ry shone a-
night. And lo! the an-gel of the Lord came up-on them, and the glo-ry of the Lord shone round a-

bout them! and they were sore a-fraid.   And the angel said un-to them, Fear not, Fear not; for be-

hold, I bring you good tid-ings, good tid-ings of great joy, which shall be to all peo-ple. For

un-to you is born this day in the cit-y of Da-vid a Sav-ior, a Sav-ior which is

Christ the Lord; a Sav-ior, a Sav-ior which is Christ the Lord.

Selection 31.

And there were in the same country shepherds abiding in the field, keeping watch over their flocks by night. And lo! the angel of the Lord came upon them, and the glory of the Lord shone round about them, and they were sore afraid. And the angel said unto them: Fear not, for behold I bring you good tidings of great joy, which shall be to all people. For unto you is born this day in the city of David a Savior which is Christ the Lord.

(Let the children join.)
Choir and Congregation.

ANGELS' STORY. 7s & 6s.

Words by MRS. E. H. MILLER.
Music by GEO. F. ROOT.

Fine.

136 1. I love to hear the sto-ry Which an-gel voic-es tell, How once the King of glo-ry
D. C. The Lord came down to save me, Be-cause he loved me so.
2. I'm glad my bless-ed Sav-ior Was once a child like me, To show how pure and ho-ly
D. C. He nev-er will for-get me, Be-cause he loves me so.
3. To sing his love and mer-cy My sweet-est songs I'll raise; And tho' I can not see him,
D. C. To sing a-mong his an-gels, Be-cause he loves me so.

D. C.

Came down on earth to dwell; I am both weak and sin-ful, But this I sure-ly know,
His lit-tle ones might be; And if I try to fol-low His foot-steps here be-low,
I know he hears my praise; For he has kind-ly prom-ised That I shall sure-ly go

When this piece is connected with the foregoing prelude, an interlude modulating to this key should be played.

THERE'S A SONG IN THE AIR.

Words by J. G. HOLLAND.
Music by GEO. F. ROOT.

Choir and Congregation.

137 1. There's a song in the air, There's a star in the sky, There's a mother's deep prayer, And a baby's low cry;
2. There's a tu-mult of joy O'er the won-der-ful birth, For the Virgin's sweet boy Is the Lord of the earth;
3. In the light of that star Lie the a-ges impearled, And the song from a-far Has swept o-ver the world.
4. We re-joice in the light, And we ech-o the song That comes down thro' the night From the heavenly throng.

A little faster.

And the star rains its fire while the beau-ti-ful sing, For the man-ger of Beth-le-hem cra-dles a King.
Ay! the star rains its fire while the beau-ti-ful sing, For the man-ger of Beth-le-hem cra-dles a King.
Ev-'ry hearth is aflame and the beau-ti-ful sing In the homes of the nations, that Je-sus is King.
Ay! we shout to the love-ly e-van-gel they bring, And we greet in his cra-dle our Sav-ior and King.

Selection 32.—MOZART SERVICE.—Glory to God in the highest.

G. F. R.

Selection 32.

Glory to God in the highest! Peace on earth, good-will toward men.

MOZART. 7s.

Words by Rev. C. WESLEY.
MOZART.

Choir and Congregation.

138
1. Hark! the her - ald an - gels sing, "Glo-ry to the new-born King! Peace on earth,and mer - cy mild;
2. Joy ful, all ye na - tions, rise, Join the tri - umph of the skies; With th' angel - ic hosts pro-claim,

God and sin - ners rec - on-ciled, God and sin - ners rec - on-ciled."
Christ is born in Beth-le - hem, Christ is born in Beth-le - hem.

3 Hail, the heaven-born Prince of Peace!
Hail, the Sun of Righteousness!
Light and life to all he brings,
:Risen with healing on his wings:!

4 Let us then with angels sing,
"Glory to the new-born King!
Peace on earth, and mercy mild;
:God and sinners reconciled!":

Selection 32.

XAVIER. 8s & 7s. Double.

Words by Rev. JOHN CAWOOD.
Music arr. for this work.

Choir and Congregation.

139
1. Hark! what mean those ho - ly voic - es, Sweet - ly sound - ing thro' the skies? Lo! th' angel - ic
2. "Peace on earth, good - will from heav-en," Reach - ing far as man is found; Souls redeemed, and

host re - joic - es; Heav'n - ly hal - le - lu - jahs rise! Hear them tell the won-drous sto - ry,
sins for - giv - en! Loud our gold - en harps shall sound!"Christ is born, the great a - noint - ed;

Hear them chant in hymns of joy: "Glo-ry in the high-est, glo - ry! Glo - ry be to God most high!
Heaven and earth his prais - es sing! Oh, re-ceive whom God ap-point - ed, For your Prophet, Priest,and King!"

Selection 33.—FOLSOM SERVICE.—When marshall'd on the nightly plain.

G. F. R.

When marshall'd on the night-ly plain, The glitt'ring host be-stud the sky, One star a-lone of all the
train Can fix the sin-ner's wand'ring eye; Hark! hark! to God the cho-rus breaks From ev-ery
host, from ev-ery gem, But one a-lone, the Sav-ior speaks, It is the star of Beth-le-
hem, it is the star of Beth-le-hem. But one a-lone, the Sav-ior speaks, but one a-lone, the
star, the star of Beth-le-hem, the star of Beth-le-hem, the star of Beth-le-hem.

But one,   but one,   the
star,

Selection 33.

When marshalled on the nightly plain, The glittering host bestud the sky, One star alone of all the train Can fix the sinner's wandering eye :—

Hark! hark! to God the chorus breaks From every host, from every gem, But one alone the Savior speaks, It is the star of Bethlehem.

FOLSOM. 11s & 10s.

HEBER.
Arr. by Dr. L. Mason.

Choir and Congregation.

140 1. Bright-est and best of the sons of the morn-ing! Dawn on our darkness, and lend us thine aid;

Star of the East, the ho - ri - zon a - dorn-ing, Guide where our in - fant Re - deem-er is laid

(*For 1st verse see tune.*)

2 Cold on his cradle the dew-drops are shining;
 Low lies his head with the beasts of the stall:
Angels adore him, in slumber reclining,
 Maker, and Monarch, and Savior of all!

3 Say, shall we yield him, in costly devotion,
 Odors of Edom, and offerings divine ?
Gems of the mountain, and pearls of the ocean,
 Myrrh from the forest, or gold from the mine ?

4 Vainly we offer each ample oblation,
 Vainly with gold would his favors secure ;
Richer, by far, is the heart's adoration ;
 Dearer to God are the prayers of the poor.

5 Brightest and best of the sons of the morning !
 Dawn on our darkness, and lend us thine aid;
Star of the East, the horizon adorning,
 Guide where our infant Redeemer is laid.

ZERAH. C. M.

Words by Michael Bruce.
Music by Dr. L. Mason.

Choir and Congregation.

141 1. To us a child of hope is born, To us a Son is given; Him shall the tribes of earth o - bey,
    2. His name shall be the Prince of Peace, For ev - er-more a - dored; The Won-der-ful, the Counsel - or,
    3. His pow'r, increasing, still shall spread ; His reign no end shall know : Jus - tice shall guard his throne above,

Him all the hosts of heaven; Him shall the tribes of earth o - bey, Him all the hosts of heaven.
The great and mighty Lord! The Won-der - ful, the Counsel - or, The great and might-y Lord!
And peace abound be - low ; Jus-tice shall guard his throne a - bove, And peace a - bound be - low.

Selection 33.

Choir and Congregation.

WHILE SHEPHERDS WATCHED.

Words by Nahum Tate.
Old melody, arr. for this work.

Fine.

142

1 { While shepherds watched their flocks by night, All seat - ed on the ground, }
   { The an - gel of the Lord came down, And glo - ry shone a - round. }   "Fear not," said he, for mighty dread

D. C. "Glad tid - ings of great joy I bring To you and all man-kind.

D. C.

Had seized their troubled mind,

2 "To you, in David's town, this day,
Is born of David's line,
The Savior, who is Christ, the Lord,
And this shall be the sign : —
The heavenly babe you there shall find
To human view displayed,
All meanly wrapped in swathing bands,
And in a manger laid."

3 Thus spake the seraph, and forthwith
Appeared a shining throng
Of angels, praising God, who thus
Addressed their joyful song : —
"All glory be to God on high,
And to the earth be peace;
Good-will henceforth from heaven to men
Begin, and never cease ! "

Selection 33.

Choir and Congregation.

SEARS. C. M. Double.

Words by Rev. E. H. Sears.
Music arr. by Geo. F. Root.

143

1. It came up - on the mid-night clear, That glo - rious song of old, From an - gels bend - ing
2. Still thro' the clo - ven skies they come, With peace - ful wings un-furled ; And still ce - les - tial
3. Oh, ye, be-neath life's crush-ing load, Whose forms are bend - ing low, Who toil a - long the

near the earth To touch their harps of gold ; "Peace to the earth, good-will to man, From heav'n's all-gracious King !"
mu - sic floats O'er all the wea - ry world ; A - bove its sad and low-ly plains They bend on heav'nly wing,
climbing way, With pain-ful steps and slow ; — Look up ! for glad and golden hours Come swift-ly on the wing ;

REFRAIN.

The earth in sol - emn still - ness lay, To hear the an - gels sing, To hear the an - gels sing,
And ev - er o'er the Ba - bel sounds, The bless - ed an - gels sing, The bless - ed an - gels sing,
Oh, rest be - side the wea - ry road, And hear the an - gels sing ! And hear the an - gels sing,

SEARS. Concluded.

To hear the an-gels sing, The earth in sol-emn still-ness lay To hear the an-gels sing.
The bless-ed an-gels sing, And ev-er o'er its Ba-bel sounds, The bless-ed an-gels sing.
And hear the an-gels sing, Oh, rest be-side the wea-ry road, And hear the an-gels sing.

Selection 32.

Choir and Congregation.

BOND. C. M.

Words by Rev. E. H. SEARS.
Music by G. F. ROOT.

144 1. Calm on the list-'ning ear of night, Come heav'n's me-lo-dious strains, Where wild Ju - de - a
2. Ce - les - tial choirs, from courts a - bove, Shed sa - cred glo - ries there, And an - gels, with their

stretch - es far Her sil - ver - man - tled plains.
spark - ling lyres, Make mu - sic on the air.

3 The answering hills of Palestine
Send back the glad reply,
And greet, from all their holy heights,
The day-spring from on high.

4 "Glory to God!" the sounding skies
Loud with their anthems ring—
"Peace to the earth, good-will to men,
From heaven's eternal King!"

Selection 32.

Choir and Congregation.

SILENT NIGHT! HOLY NIGHT!

Old German Christmas Song.
Arranged for this work.

145 1. Si - lent night! Ho - ly night! All is calm, All is bright: Round yon vir - gin moth - er and child,
2. Si - lent night! Ho - ly night! Shepherds quake At the sight; Glo - ries stream from heav - en a - far,
3. Si - lent night! Ho - ly night! Son of God, Love's pure light Radiant beams from thy ho - ly face,

Ho - ly In - fant, so ten - der and mild, Falls a heav-en-ly peace, Falls a heav - en - ly peace.
Heav'n-ly hosts, sing al - le - lu - ia! Christ the Sav-ior is born, Christ the Sav - ior is born.
With the dawn of re - deem - ing grace, Jesus, Lord, at thy birth, Je - sus, Lord, at thy birth.

Selection 34.—ANTIOCH SERVICE.—The people that walked in darkness.

The people that walked in darkness have seen a great light; They that dwell in the land of the shad-ow of death, Up-on them hath the light shin-ed; For un-to us a Child is born, un-to us a Son is giv-en, And the government shall be up-on his shoul-der, And his name shall be call-ed Won-der-ful! Coun-sel-lor! The might-y God! The ev-er-last-ing Fa-ther! The Prince of Peace!

Here let Choir and Congregation sing 1st verse of hymn.

Hal-le-lu-jah, Hal-le-lu-jah, The kingdoms of this world are be-come the King-dom of our

Here let Choir and Congregation sing 2d, 3d, and 4th verses.

Lord and of his Christ, and of his Christ, and he shall reign for-ev-er and ev-er.

Selection 34.

The people that walked in darkness have seen a great light; they that dwell in the land of the shadow of death, upon them hath the light shined.

For unto us a child is born, unto us a Son is given;

and the government shall be upon his shoulder: and his name shall be called Wonderful, Counsellor, the mighty God, the everlasting Father, the Prince of Peace.

ANTIOCH. C. M.

WATTS.
From HANDEL, by DR. L. MASON.

Choir and Congregation.

146 Joy to the world, the Lord is come! Let earth re-ceive her King; Let ev-'ry heart pre-pare him room, And heav'n and nature sing, And heav'n and nature sing, And heav'n, and heav'n and nature sing.

And heav'n and nature sing, And heav'n and nature sing,

(For 1st verse see tune.)

Hallelujah! the kingdoms of this world are become the kingdom of our Lord and of his Christ, and he shall reign forever and ever.

2 Joy to the world, the Savior reigns; Let men their songs employ; While fields and floods, rocks, hills and plains, Repeat the sounding joy.

3 No more let sin and sorrow grow, Nor thorns infest the ground; He comes to make his blessings flow Far as the curse is found.

4 He rules the world with truth and grace, And makes the nations prove The glories of his righteousness, And wonders of his love.

147

HERR.

1 Angels rejoiced and sweetly sung At our Redeemer's birth; Mortals, awake! let every tongue Proclaim his matchless worth.

2 Good-will to men; ye fallen race! Arise, and shout for joy; He comes, with rich abounding grace, To save, and not destroy.

Selection 34. (Without interlude.)

ST. ANN'S. C. M.

Words by DR. DODDRIDGE.
Music by DR. CROFT.

Choir and Congregation.

148 1. Hark, the glad sound! the Sav-ior comes, The Sav-ior prom-ised long; Let ev-'ry heart pre-pare a throne, And ev-'ry voice a song.

2. He comes, the pris-'ner to re-lease, In Sa-tan's bond-age held; The gates of brass be-fore him burst, The i-ron fet-ters yield.

3 He comes, from thickest films of vice To clear the mental ray, And, on the eyes long closed in night, To pour celestial day.

4 Our glad hosannas, Prince of Peace, Thy welcome shall proclaim, And heaven's eternal arches ring With thy beloved name.

GETHSEMANE.

Selection 35.—WINDHAM SERVICE, No. 2.—My soul is exceedingly sorrowful.

Choir.

My soul is ex-ceed-ing-ly sor-row-ful, e-ven un-to death. O, my Fa-ther!

O, my Fa-ther! if it be pos-si-ble, let this cup pass from me, let this cup pass

from me. But not my will, not my will, not my will, but thine be done.

WINDHAM. L. M.

Words by REV. W. B. TAPPAN.
Music by DANIEL READ.

Choir and Congregation.

149
1. 'Tis midnight; and on Ol-ive's brow The star is dimmed that late-ly shone: 'Tis midnight; in the
2. 'Tis midnight; and from all removed, The Sav-ior wres-tles lone with fears; Ev'n that dis-ci-ple

gar-den, now, The suf-f'ring Sav-ior prays a-lone.
whom he loved Heeds not his Mas-ter's grief and tears.

3 'Tis midnight; and for others' guilt
   The Man of Sorrows weeps in blood;
   Yet he that hath in anguish knelt
   Is not forsaken by his God.

4 'Tis midnight; and from ether-plains
   Is borne the song that angels know;
   Unheard by mortals are the strains
   That sweetly soothe the Savior's woe.

Selection 35.

My soul is exceedingly sorrowful, even unto death. O, | But not my will but thine be done.
my Father, if it be possible, let this cup pass from me. |

GETHSEMANE. 7s. 6 lines.

Choir and Congregation.   Arranged for this work.

1. Go to dark Geth-sem-a - ne, Ye that feel the tempter's power; Your Re-deem-er's con - flict see,

Watch with him one bit-ter hour; Turn not from his griefs a - way, Learn of Je-sus Christ to pray.

(For 1st verse see tune.)

150
MONTGOMERY.

2 Follow to the judgment-hall;
  View the Lord of life arraigned;
Oh, the wormwood and the gall!
  Oh, the pangs his soul sustained!
Shun not suffering, shame, or loss;
Learn of him to bear the cross.

3 Calvary's mournful mountain climb;
  There, adoring at his feet,
Mark that miracle of time,
  God's own sacrifice complete:
"It is finished," hear him cry ;—
Learn of Jesus Christ to die.

4 Early hasten to the tomb,
  Where they laid his breathless clay;
All is solitude and gloom,
  Who hath taken him away?
Christ is risen ;—he meets our eyes;
Savior, teach us so to rise!

151 [L. M. Tune, Windham.]
WATTS.

1 He dies!—the friend of sinners dies ;
  Lo! Salem's daughters weep around ;
A solemn darkness vails the skies ;
  A sudden trembling shakes the ground.

2 Here's love and grief beyond degree :
  The Lord of glory dies for men ;
But lo! what sudden joys we see,
  Jesus, the dead, revives again.

3 Break off your tears, ye saints, and tell
  How high our great Deliverer reigns;
Sing how he spoiled the hosts of hell,
  And led the tyrant Death in chains.

4 Say—live forever, glorious King,
  Born to redeem, and strong to save!
Where now, O death, where is thy sting?
  And where thy victory, boasting grave?

152 [L. M. Tune, Windham.]
BONAR.

1 Jesus, whom angel hosts adore,
  Became a man of griefs for me ;
In love, though rich, becoming poor,
  That I through him enriched might be.

2 Though Lord of all, above, below,
  He went to Olivet for me :
There drank my cup of wrath and woe,
  When bleeding in Gethsemane.

3 Jesus, whose dwelling is the skies,
  Went down into the grave for me ;
There overcame my enemies,
  There won the glorious victory.

4 'T is finished all : the vail is rent,
  The welcome sure, the access free :—
Now then, we leave our banishment,
  O Father, to return to thee!

153 [L. M. Tune, Windham.]
STENNETT.

1 "'T is finished !"—so the Savior cried,
  And meekly bowed his head and died:
"'T is finished !"—yes, the race is run,
  The battle fought, the victory won.

2 'T is finished !—all that heaven foretold
  By prophets in the days of old;
And truths are opened to our view
  That kings and prophets never knew.

3 'T is finished !—Son of God, thy power
  Hath triumphed in this awful hour ;
And yet our eyes with sorrow see
  That life to us was death to thee.

4 'T is finished !—let the joyful sound
  Be heard through all the nations round ;
'T is finished !—let the triumph rise,
  And swell the chorus of the skies.

Selection 36.—STOW SERVICE.—Come, every pious heart.   G. F. R.

Come, ev'ry pi - ous heart, That loves the Sav - ior's name, Your no - blest pow'rs ex - ert, To

cel - e - brate his fame. He left his star - ry crown, And laid his robes a - side; On

wings of love came down, On wings of love came down, And wept, and bled, and died.

From the dark grave he rose, The man - sion of the dead, And thence his might - y foes, In

glo - rious tri - umph led, And thence his might - y foes In glo - rious tri - umph led.

Selection 36.

Come every pious heart, That loves the Savior's name,
Your noblest powers exert To celebrate his fame, He left
his starry crown, And laid his robes aside;

On wings of love came down, And wept, and bled, and
died. From the dark grave he rose, The mansion of the
dead, And thence his mighty foes In glorious triumph led.

STOW. H. M.

Words by Dr DODDRIDGE.
Music by Dr. L. MASON.

Choir and Congregation.

154

1. Yes, the Re-deem-er rose; The Sav-ior left the dead; And o'er our hell-ish foes High
2. All hail! tri-umph-ant Lord, Who sav'st us with thy blood! Wide be thy name a-dored, Thou

raised his conq'ring head; In wild dis-may, The guards a-round Fa'l to the ground, And sink a-way.
ris-ing, reign-ing God! With thee we rise, With thee we reign, And em-pires gain Be-yond the skies.

Selection 36.

BLOW YE THE TRUMPET. H. M.

Words by Rev. C. WESLEY.
Music by G. F. ROOT

Choir and Congregation.

155

1. Blow ye the trum-pet, blow! The glad-ly sol-emn sound: Let all the na-tions know, To
2. Ye slaves of sin and hell! Your lib-er-ty re-ceive, And safe in Je-sus dwell, And
3. The gos-pel trum-pet hear, The news of pard'ning grace: Ye hap-py souls, draw near: Be-

The year of ju - - - bi-lee is

CHORUS.

earth's re-mot-est bound;
blest in Je-sus live. The year of ju-bi-lee is come, The year of ju-bi-
hold your Sav-ior's face:

come; Re-turn, ye ran - - somed sin - ners, home.

lee is come; Re-turn, ye ran-somed sin-ners, home, ye ran-somed sin-ners, home.

Selection 37.—ADDISON SERVICE.—Lift up your heads, O ye gates.

Arr. for this work.

Lift up your heads, O ye gates, and be ye lift-ed up, ye ev-er-last-ing doors, and the

King of glo-ry shall come in, the King of glo-ry shall come in. Who is this King of glo-ry?

Who is this King of glo-ry? The Lord, strong and mighty, the Lord, strong and mighty, the Lord mighty in

bat-tle. Lift up your heads, O ye gates, e-ven lift them up, ye ev-er-last-ing doors, and the

King of glo-ry shall come in, the King of glo-ry shall come in. Who is this King of glo-ry?

Who is this King of glo-ry? The Lord of hosts, the Lord of hosts, He is the King of glo-ry.

Selection 37.

Lift up your heads, O ye gates, and be ye lifted up, ye everlasting doors, and the King of glory shall come in. Who is this King of glory? The Lord, strong and mighty, the Lord mighty in battle.

Lift up your heads, O ye gates, even lift them up, ye everlasting doors, and the King of glory shall come in. Who is this King of glory? The Lord, strong and mighty, he is the King of glory.

Choir and Congregation.

ADDISON. L. M. Double.

Words by C. WESLEY.
Arr. for this work.

156 1. Our Lord is ris - en from the dead, Is ris-en to the realms on high ;)
The pow'rs of hell are captive led, Dragg'd to the portals of the sky. } There his tri-umph-al chariot waits,

And an-gels chant the solemn lay :—"Lift up your heads, ye heav'nly gates ! Ye ev-er - lasting doors ! give way."

1 Our Lord is risen from the dead,
Is risen to the realms on high ;
The powers of hell are captive led,
Dragged to the portals of the sky.
There his triumphal chariot waits,
And angels chant the solemn lay :—
"Lift up your heads, ye heavenly gates!
Ye everlasting doors ! give way."

2 Loose all your bars of massy light,
And wide unfold th'ethereal scene ;
He claims those mansions as his right ;
Receive the King of glory in.
Who is the King of glory—who ?
The Lord who all our foes o'ercame ;
Who sin, and death, and hell o'erthrew ;
And Jesus is the conqueror's name.

3 Lo! his triumphal chariot waits,
And angels chant the solemn lay :—
"Lift up your heads, ye heavenly gates!
Ye everlasting doors ! give way."
Who is the King of glory—who ?
The Lord of boundless pow'r possessed ;
The King of saints and angels, too,
God over all, forever blessed.

Selection 37.

Choir and Congregation.

MOZART. 7s.

Words by C. WESLEY.
Music by MOZART.

157 1. Christ the Lord is ris'n to-day, Sons of men, and an - gels say : Raise your joys and triumphs high !
2. Vain the stone, the watch, the seal, Christ hath burst the gates of hell ; Death in vain for - bids his rise ;

Sing, ye heav'ns, and earth re-ply ! Sing, ye heav'ns, and earth re - ply !
Christ hath o - pened Par - a - dise, Christ hath o - pened Par - a - dise.

3 Lives again our glorious King ;
"Where, O Death, is now thy sting ?"
Once he died our souls to save ;
"Where's thy vict'ry, boasting Grave?"

4 Soar we now where Christ has led,
Following our exalted Head ;
Made like him, like him we rise,
Ours the cross, the grave, the skies!

6

Selection 38.—LOVING KINDNESS SERVICE.—Hark! hark! the notes of joy.

G. F. R.

Hark! hark! the notes of joy Roll o'er the heav'n-ly plains, And ser-aphs find em-

ploy For their sub-lim-est strains; Hark! hark! the sounds draw nigh, The heav'n-ly King de-

scends, And from his throne on high, To earth his glo-ry bends. Strike, strike the harp a-

gain, To great Im-man-uel's name; A-rise, ye sons of men! And all his grace pro-

claim, An-gels and men! wake ev-'ry string! 'Tis God the Sav-ior's praise we sing!

Selection 38.

Hark! hark! the notes of joy Roll o'er the heavenly plains, And seraphs find employ For their divinest strains. Hark! hark! the sounds draw nigh, The heavenly King descends, And from his throne on high To earth his glory bends. Strike, strike the harps again, To great Immanuel's name. Arise, ye sons of men! And all his grace proclaim. Angels and men, wake every string! 'Tis God the Savior's praise we sing!

LOVING-KINDNESS. L. M.

Choir and Congregation.   Old American Melody.

A-wake, my soul, to joyful lays, And sing thy great Redeemer's praise; He just-ly claims a song from me:

CHORUS.

His lov-ing-kindness, oh, how free! Lov-ing-kindness, loving-kindness, His lov-ing-kind-ness, oh, how free!

158   MEDLEY.

1 Awake, my soul, to joyful lays,
And sing the great Redeemer's praise;
He justly claims a song from me:
His loving-kindness, oh, how free!

2 He saw me ruined in the fall,
Yet loved me, notwithstanding all;
He saved me from my lost estate:
His loving-kindness, oh, how great!

3 Tho' numerous hosts of mighty foes,
Tho' earth and hell my way oppose,
He safely leads my soul along:
His loving-kindness, oh, how strong!

4 When trouble, like a gloomy cloud,
Has gathered thick and thundered loud,
He near my soul has always stood:
His loving-kindness, oh, how good!

5 Soon shall I pass the gloomy vale;
Soon all my mortal powers must fail:
Oh, may my last expiring breath
His loving-kindness sing in death!

6 Then let me mount and soar away
To the bright world of endless day;
And sing, with rapture and surprise,
His loving-kindness in the skies!

Selection 38.

GOLDEN GATE. L. M. 6 lines.

Choir and Congregation.   Words by REV. GEO. WEISSEL.
Music by GEO. F. ROOT.

159
1. Lift up your heads, ye might-y gates, Be-hold the King of glo-ry waits; The King of kings is drawing
2. Fling wide the portals of your heart, Make it a tem-ple set a - part From earthly use for heav'n's em-
3. Redeemer, come, I o - pen wide My heart to thee; here, Lord, abide: Let me thy in - ner presence

CHORUS.

near, The Sav-ior of the world is here. O happy hearts and happy homes, To whom this King of triumph comes!
ploy, Adorned with prayer and love and joy. O happy hearts and happy homes, To whom this King of triumph comes!
feel, Thy grace and love in me re-veal. So come, my Sovereign, enter in; Let new and nobler life be-gin.

Selection 39.—PARK ST. SERVICE.—And the number of them.

Selection 39.

And the number of them was ten thousand times ten thousand and thousands of thousands, saying with a loud voice, Worthy is the Lamb that was slain, to receive power, and riches, and wisdom, and strength, and honor, and glory, and blessing. And every creature which is in heaven, and on the earth, heard I saying, Blessing, and honor, and glory, and power be unto him that sitteth upon the throne, and unto the Lamb forever and ever. And all the angels fell before the throne on their faces, and worshiped God, saying, Amen: Blessing, and glory, and wisdom, and thanksgiving, and honor, and power, and might, be unto our God forever and ever. Amen.

PARK ST. L. M.

VENUA.

Choir and Congregation.

1. Hark! how the cho-ral song of heav'n Swells full of peace and joy a - bove; Hark! how they strike their gold-en harps, And raise the tune-ful notes of love, And raise the tune-ful notes of love.

160   ANON.

1 Hark! how the choral song of heaven
   Swells full of peace and joy above;
   Hark! how they strike their golden harps,
   And raise the tuneful notes of love.

2 No anxious care nor thrilling grief,
   No deep despair, nor gloomy woe
   They feel, when high their lofty strains
   In noblest, sweetest concord flow.

3 When shall we join the heavenly host,
   Who sing Immanuel's praise on high,
   And leave behind our doubts and fears,
   To swell the chorus of the sky?

4 Oh, come, thou rapture-bringing morn!
   And usher in the joyful day;
   We long to see thy rising sun
   Drive all these clouds of grief away.

161   MONTGOMERY.

1 Come, let us sing the song of songs—
   The saints in heaven began the strain—
   The homage which to Christ belongs:
   "Worthy the Lamb, for he was slain!"

2 Slain to redeem us by his blood,
   To cleanse from every sinful stain,
   And make us kings and priests to God—
   "Worthy the Lamb, for he was slain!"

3 To him who suffered on the tree,
   Our souls, at his soul's price, to gain,
   Blessing, and praise, and glory be:
   "Worthy the Lamb, for he was slain!"

4 To him, enthroned by filial right,
   All power in heaven and earth proclaim,
   Honor, and majesty, and might:
   "Worthy the Lamb, for he was slain!"

162   WATTS.

1 Now to the Lord, who makes us know
   The wonders of his dying love,
   Be humble honors paid below,
   And strains of nobler praise above:

2 To Jesus, our atoning Priest,
   To Jesus, our eternal King,
   Be everlasting power confessed!
   Let every tongue his glory sing.

3 Behold! on flying clouds he comes,
   And every eye shall see him move:
   Tho' with our sins we pierced him once,
   He now displays his pardoning love.

4 The unbelieving world shall wail,
   While we rejoice to see the day;
   Come, Lord! nor let thy promise fail,
   Nor let thy chariot long delay.

163   WATTS.

1 Now be my heart inspired to sing
   The glories of my Savior King,—
   Jesus the Lord; how heavenly fair
   His form! how bright his beauties are!

2 O'er all the sons of human race,
   He shines with a superior grace;
   Love from his lips divinely flows,
   And blessings all his state compose.

3 Thy throne, O God, forever stands;
   Grace is the sceptre in thy hands;
   Thy laws and works are just and right;
   Justice and grace are thy delight.

164   SHRUBSOLE.

1 Arm of the Lord, awake, awake;
   Put on thy strength, the nations shake;
   Now let the world, adoring, see
   Triumphs of mercy wrought by thee.

2 Say to the heathen, from thy throne,
   "I am Jehovah, God alone:"
   Thy voice their idols shall confound,
   And cast their altars to the ground.

3 Almighty God, thy grace proclaim
   Through every clime, of every name;
   Let adverse powers before thee fall,
   And crown the Savior Lord of all!

PRAISE TO THE RISEN LORD.

Selection 40.—DENFIELD SERVICE.—Worthy is the Lamb that was slain.

G. F. R.

Wor - thy is the Lamb, is the Lamb that was slain, to receive pow -er, and rich - es, and wis-dom, and

Wor - thy is the Lamb, is the Lamb that was slain, to receive pow -er, and rich - es, and wis-dom, and

strength, and hon - or, and glo - ry, and bless -ing; strength, and hon - or, and glo - ry, and bless - ing.

strength, and hon - or, and glo - ry, and bless -ing; strength, and hon - or, and glo - ry, and bless - ing.

Bless-ing, hon - or, glo - ry, pow - er, be un - to him, be

Bless - ing, and hon - or, and glo - ry, and pow - er, be un - to him, be

Bless-ing, hon - or, glo - ry, pow - er,

un - to him that sit-teth up-on the throne, and un - to the Lamb for - ev - er and ev - er.

Selection 40.

Worthy is the Lamb that was slain, to receive power, and riches, and wisdom, and strength, and honor, and glory, and blessing.

Blessing, and honor, and glory, and power be unto him that sitteth upon the throne, and unto the Lamb forever.

DENFIELD. C. M.

Choir and Congregation.

Dr. L. MASON.

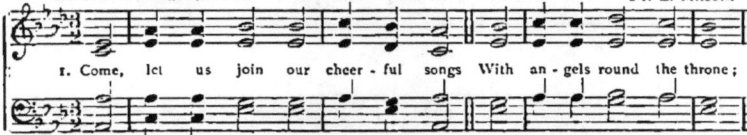

1. Come, let us join our cheer-ful songs With an-gels round the throne;

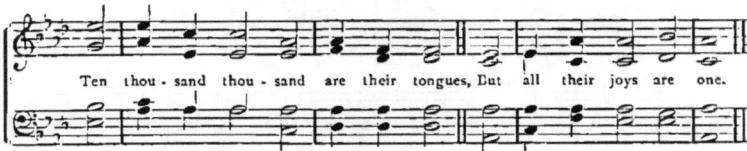

Ten thou-sand thou-sand are their tongues, But all their joys are one.

165
WATTS.

1 Come, let us join our cheerful songs
With angels round the throne;
Ten thousand thousand are their tongues,
But all their joys are one.

2 "Worthy the Lamb that died," they cry,
"To be exalted thus!"
"Worthy the Lamb!" our lips reply,
"For he was slain for us."

3 Jesus is worthy to receive
Honor and power divine;
And blessings, more than we can give,
Be, Lord, forever thine!

4 Let all that dwell above the sky,
And air, and earth, and seas,
Conspire to lift thy glories high,
And speak thine endless praise.

5 The whole creation join in one,
To bless the sacred name
Of him who sits upon the throne,
And to adore the Lamb!

166
PIRIE.

1 Come, let us join our songs of praise,
To our ascended Priest;
He entered heaven with all our names
Engraven on his breast.

2 Clothed with our nature still, he knows
The weakness of our frame,
And how to shield us from the foes
Whom he himself o'ercame.

3 Nor time, nor distance, e'er shall quench
The fervor of his love;
For us he died in kindness here,
For us he lives above.

4 Oh! may we ne'er forget his grace,
Nor blush to bear his name;
Still may our hearts hold fast his faith—
Our lips his praise proclaim.

167
MONTGOMERY.

1 Sing we the song of those who stand
Around the eternal throne,
Of every kindred, clime, and land,
A multitude unknown.

2 Life's poor distinctions vanish here;
To-day the young, the old,
Our Savior and his flock appear
One Shepherd and one fold.

3 Toil, trial, suffering still await
On earth the pilgrims' throng;
Yet learn we in our low estate
The Church Triumphant's song.

4 "Worthy the Lamb for sinners slain,"—
Cry the redeemed above,
"Blessing and honor to obtain,
And everlasting love!"

5 "Worthy the Lamb," on earth we sing,
"Who died our souls to save!
Henceforth, O Death! where is thy sting?
Thy victory, O Grave!"

168
WATTS.

1 Oh! for a shout of sacred joy
To God, the sovereign King;
Let all the lands their tongues employ,
And hymns of triumph sing.

2 Jesus, our God, ascends on high;
His heavenly guards around
Attend him rising through the sky,
With trumpets' joyful sound!

3 While angels shout and praise their King,
Let mortals learn their strains;
Let all the earth his honor sing;
O'er all the earth he reigns.

4 Rehearse his praise, with awe profound;
Let knowledge lead the song;
Nor mock him with a solemn sound
Upon a thoughtless tongue.

Selection 41.—GEER SERVICE.—And they shall call his name Emmanuel.

And they shall call his name EM-MAN - U - EL, Em-man-u-el, And they shall call his name EM-

MAN-U-EL, Em-man-u-el, And they shall call his name Em-man-u-el, Em-man-u-el, God with us!

That at the name of Je - sus ev - ery knee should bow, and ev - ery tongue con-

fess that Je - sus Christ is Lord, To the

To the glo - ry of God the Fa - ther,

glo - ry of God the Fa - ther, To the glo-ry of God the Fa - ther. A - men, A - men.

Selection 41.

And they shall call his name EMMANUEL, GOD WITH US. | tongue confess that Jesus Christ is Lord, to the glory of
That at the name of Jesus every knee should bow and every | God the Father. Amen.

GEER. C. M.

1. To our Re-deem-er's glo-rious name, A-wake the sa-cred song!

Oh! may his love—im-mor-tal flame—Tune ev-ery heart and tongue!

---

169 STEELE.

1 To our Redeemer's glorious name,
   Awake the sacred song!
   Oh! may his love—immortal flame—
   Tune every heart and tongue!

2 His love, what mortal thought can reach?
   What mortal tongue display?
   Imagination's utmost stretch,
   In wonder, dies away.

3 Dear Lord! while we adoring pay
   Our humble thanks to thee,
   May every heart with rapture say,—
   "The Savior died for me!"

170 STEELE.

1 Come, thou desire of all thy saints!
   Our humble strains attend,
   While with our praises and complaints,
   Low at thy feet we bend.

2 How should our songs, like those above,
   With warm devotion rise!
   How should our souls on wings of love,
   Mount upward to the skies!

3 Come, Lord! thy love alone can raise
   In us the heavenly flame;
   Then shall our lips resound thy praise,
   Our hearts adore thy name.

171 BERNARD.

1 Jesus, the very thought of thee,
   With sweetness fills my breast:
   But sweeter far thy face to see,
   And in thy presence rest.

2 Nor voice can sing, nor heart can frame,
   Nor can the memory find
   A sweeter sound than thy blest name,
   O Savior of mankind!

3 O Hope of every contrite heart!
   O Joy of all the meek!
   To those who fall, how kind thou art!
   How good to those who seek!

4 Jesus, our only joy be thou,
   As thou our prize wilt be;
   Jesus, be thou our glory now,
   And through eternity.

172 KELLY.

1 The head that once was crowned with thorns,
   Is crowned with glory now;
   A royal diadem adorns
   The mighty Victor's brow.

2 The highest place that heaven affords,
   Is his by sovereign right;
   The King of kings, and Lord of lords,
   He reigns in glory bright;—

3 The joy of all who dwell above,
   The joy of all below,
   To whom he manifests his love,
   And grants his name to know.

4 To them the cross with all its shame,
   With all its grace is given;
   Their name—an everlasting name
   Their joy—the joy of heaven.

173 STEELE.

1 The Savior! oh, what endless charms
   Dwell in the blissful sound!
   Its influence every fear disarms,
   And spreads sweet comfort round.

2 The almighty Former of the skies
   Stooped to our vile abode;
   While angels viewed with wondering eyes
   And hailed the incarnate God.

3 Oh! the rich depths of love divine!
   Of bliss a boundless store!
   Dear Savior, let me call thee mine;
   I can not wish for more.

4 On thee alone my hope relies
   Beneath thy cross I fall;
   My Lord, my Life, my Sacrifice,
   My Savior, and my All!

Selection 42.—CORONATION SERVICE.—All power is given unto me.   G. F. R.

Choir. With dignity and reverence.

All pow'r is giv-en un-to me in heav'n and in earth, The king-doms of this world are be-come the

All pow'r is giv-en un-to me in heav'n and in earth, The king-doms of this world are be-come the

King-dom of our Lord, the King-dom of our Lord, and of his Christ, And he shall reign . . for-

King-dom of our Lord, the King-dom of our Lord, and of his Christ, And he shall reign . .

for-

ev - er, and ev - er, and ev - er, he shall reign for-ev - er, and ev - er, and ev - er,

he shall reign

ev - er, and ev - er, and ev - er, for - ev - er, and ev - er, and ev - er,

King of kings and Lord of lords, KING OF KINGS AND LORD OF LORDS, FOR-EV-ER AND EV - ER - MORE.

King of kings and Lord of lords, KING OF KINGS AND LORD OF LORDS, FOR-EV-ER AND EV - ER - MORE.

Selection 42.

All power is given unto me in heaven and in earth.
The kingdoms of this world are become the Kingdom
of our Lord, the Kingdom of our Lord and of his Christ,

and he shall reign forever and ever. KING OF KINGS
AND LORD OF LORDS FOREVER AND EVERMORE.

CORONATION. C. M.

Choir and Congregation.

O. HOLDEN.

1. All hail the pow'r of Je - sus' name! Let an - gels pros-trate fall; Bring forth the roy - al di - a - dem,

And crown him Lord of all; Bring forth the roy - al di - a - dem, And crown him Lord of all.

174

PERRONETT.

1 All hail the power of Jesus' name!
Let angels prostrate fall;
Bring forth the royal diadem,
And crown him Lord of all.

2 Crown him, ye martyrs of our God,
Who from his altar call;
Extol the stem of Jesse's rod,
And crown him Lord of all.

3 Ye chosen seed of Israel's race,
Ye ransomed from the fall;
Hail him, who saves you by his grace,
And crown him Lord of all.

4 Sinners, whose love can ne'er forget
The wormwood and the gall,
Go, spread your trophies at his feet,
And crown him Lord of all.

5 Let every kindred, every tribe,
On this terrestrial ball,
To him all majesty ascribe,
And crown him Lord of all.

6 Oh! that with yonder sacred throng,
We at his feet may fall;
We 'll join the everlasting song,
And crown him Lord of all.

Selection 42.

CALDERWOOD. 7s, 6 lines.

Choir and Congregation.

Words by Rev. C. WESLEY.
Music arr. by G. F. R.

175
1. Christ, whose glo-ry fills the skies, Christ, the true, the on - ly light, Sun of Righteousness, a - rise,
2. Dark and cheer-less is the morn, If thy light is hid from me; Joy - less is the day's re-turn,
3. Vis - it, then, this soul of mine; Pierce the gloom of sin and grief; Fill me, ra-diant Sun di-vine!

Tri-umph o'er the shades of night; Day-spring from on high, be near, Day-star, in my heart ap-pear.
Till thy mer - cy's beams I see; Till they in - ward light im - part, Warmth and glad-ness to my heart.
Scat - ter all my un - be - lief; More and more thy-self dis - play, Shin-ing to the per-fect day.

Selection 43.—ORTONVILLE SERVICE.—Rejoice greatly, O Daughter of Zion.

G. F. R.

Re-joice greatly, O daughter of Zi-on, Shout, O daughter of Je-ru-salem! Be-hold, thy King

com-eth, he com-eth un-to thee; How great is his good-ness, how great is his beau-ty! He is

al-to-geth-er love-ly, al-to-geth-er, al-to-geth-er love-ly. Thus saith the Lord your Re-

deem-er, The Ho-ly One of Is-ra-el,.. I, e-ven I, am the Lord, Look un-to

me, and be ye saved, look un-to me, and be ye saved, all the ends of the earth.

How great is his goodness! how great is his beau-ty! He is al-to-geth-er love-ly.

Selection 43.

Rejoice greatly, O daughter of Zion, shout, O daughter of Jerusalem ; behold thy King cometh, he cometh unto thee. How great is his goodness! how great is his beauty! He is altogether lovely.

Thus saith the Lord your Redeemer, the Holy One of Israel: I, even I, am the Lord, look unto me, and be ye saved, all the ends of the earth. How great is his goodness! how great is his beauty! He is altogether lovely.

ORTONVILLE. C. M.

Dr. T. Hastings.

1. Ma-jes-tic sweetness sits enthroned Up-on the Sav-ior's brow ; His head with radiant glo-ries crowned, His lips with grace o'er-flow, His lips with grace o'er-flow.

176 STENNETT.

1 Majestic sweetness sits enthroned
   Upon the Savior's brow ;
His head with radiant glories crowned,
His lips with grace o'erflow.

2 No mortal can with him compare,
   Among the sons of men ;
Fairer is he than all the fair
That fill the heavenly train.

3 To him I owe my life and breath,
   And all the joys I have ;
He makes me triumph over death,
He saves me from the grave.

Since from his bounty I receive
   Such proofs of love divine,
Had I a thousand hearts to give,
Lord! they should all be thine.

177 WESLEY.

1 Oh! for a thousand tongues to sing
   My dear Redeemer's praise!
The glories of my God and King,
The triumphs of his grace!

2 My gracious Master and my God !
   Assist me to proclaim,
To spread, through all the earth abroad,
The honors of thy name.

3 Jesus—the name that calms my fears,
   That bids my sorrows cease ;
'Tis music to my ravished ears;
'Tis life, and health, and peace.

4 He breaks the power of reigning sin.
   He sets the prisoner free ;
His blood can make the foulest clean ;
His blood availed for me.

178 WATTS.

1 Behold the glories of the Lamb,
   Amid the eternal throne;
Prepare new honors for his name,
And songs before unknown.

2 Let elders worship at his feet,
   The church adore around,
With vials full of odors sweet,
And harps of sweeter sound.

3 Now to the Lamb that once was slain,
   Be endless blessings paid !
Salvation, glory, joy remain
   Forever on thy head !

4 Thou hast redeemed our souls with blood,
   Hast set the prisoners free,
Hast made us kings and priests to God,
And we shall reign with thee.

179 ENFIELD.

1 Behold, where, in a mortal form,
   Appears each grace divine !
The virtues, all in Jesus met,
With mildest radiance shine.

2 To spread the rays of heavenly light,
   To give the mourner joy,
To preach glad tidings to the poor,
Was his divine employ.

3 Be Christ our pattern, and our guide
   His image may we bear ;
Oh ! may we tread his holy steps,-
His joy and glory share.

180 WATTS.

1 Hosanna to the Prince of light,
   That clothed himself in clay ;
Entered the iron gates of death,
And tore the bars away.

2 Raise your devotion, mortal tongues,
   To reach his blest abode ;
Sweet be the accents of your songs
To our incarnate God.

3 Bright angels ! strike your loudest strings,
   Your sweetest voices raise ;
Let heaven, and all created things,
Sound our Immanuel's praise.

Selection 44.—HARWELL SERVICE.—Hallelujah! for the Lord God Omnipotent reigneth!

Choir. Begin with distant effect. *mf*   *m*   G. F. R.

Hal - le - lu - jah! Hal - le - lu - jah! For the Lord God Om-ni-po-tent reigneth! Hal-le - lu - jah! Hal - le - lu - jah!

For the Lord reigneth! The kingdoms of this world are become the Kingdom of our Lord, The Kingdom of our

Lord and of his Christ, Halle-lu-jah! Hal - le - lu - jah! Hal - le - lu - jah! And he shall reign for-ev - er,

Hal - le - lu - jah! Hal - le - lu - jah! For-ev - er and ev - er! Hal - le - lu - jah! Hal - le - lu - jah!
King of kings . . . . . and

Hal - le - lu - jah! Hal - le - lu - jah! Hal - le - lu - jah! Hal-le - lu - jah! for-ev - er and ev - er!
Lord of lords, He shall reign for - ev - er and ev - er!

Hal - le - lu - jah! Hal - le - lu - jah! Hal - le - lu - jah! Hal-le-lu-jah! for-ev - er and ev - er!

Selection 44.

Hallelujah, for the Lord God omnipotent reigneth. The kingdoms of this world are become the Kingdom of our Lord and of his Christ; and he shall reign forever, King of kings and Lord of lords.

HARWELL. 8s & 7s. 6 lines.

Dr. L. Mason.

Choir and Congregation.

1. Hark! ten thousand harps and voic - es Sound the notes of praise a - bove; Je - sus reigns, and heav'n re-

joic - es: Je - sus reigns, the God of love: See, he sits on yon - der throne; Je - sus
See, he sits

Je - sus rules the world a - lone: Hal - le - lu - jah! Hal - le - lu - jah! Hal - le - lu - jah! A - men!
rules

(For 1st verse see tune.)

181 KELLY.

2 King of glory! reign forever—
Thine an everlasting crown;
Nothing from thy love shall sever
Those whom thou hast made thine own;
Happy objects of thy grace,
Destined to behold thy face.
Hallelujah! hallelujah!
Hallelujah! Amen!

3 Savior! hasten thine appearing;
Bring, oh, bring the glorious day,
When the awful summons hearing,
Heaven and earth shall pass away;
Then, with golden harps we'll sing,
"Glory, glory to our King!"
Hallelujah! hallelujah!
Hallelujah! Amen!

182 BAKEWELL.

1 Hail, thou once despised Jesus!
Crowned in mockery a king!
Thou didst suffer to release us;
Thou didst free salvation bring.
Hail, thou agonizing Savior,
Bearer of our sin and shame!
By thy merits we find favor;
Life is given through thy name.

2 Worship, honor, power and blessing
Thou art worthy to receive;
Loudest praises, without ceasing,
Meet it is for us to give.
Help, ye bright angelic spirits;
Bring your sweetest, noblest lays;
Help to sing our Savior's merits;
Help to chant Immanuel's praise.

183 GOODE.

1 Crown his head with endless blessing,
Who, in God the Father's name,
With compassions never ceasing,
Comes salvation to proclaim.
Hail, ye saints, who know his favor!
Who within his gates are found;
Hail, ye saints, the exalted Savior!
Let his courts with praise resound.

2 Lo, Jehovah, we adore thee;
Thee our Savior! thee our God!
From his throne his beams of glory
Shine through all the world abroad.
In his word his light arises,
Brightest beams of truth and grace;
Bind, oh, bind your sacrifices,
In his courts your offerings place.

Selection 45.—ARIEL SERVICE.—And I heard the voice of many angels.   G. F. R.

Selection 45.

And I heard the voice of many angels saying, Worthy is the Lamb that was slain, to receive power, and riches, and wisdom, and strength, and glory, and honor, and blessing. | Blessing, and honor, and power be unto him that sitteth upon the throne, and unto the Lamb forever and ever.

ARIEL. C. P. M.

Dr. L. MASON.

Choir and Congregation.

1. Oh, could I speak the match-less worth, Oh, could I sound the glo-ries forth, Which in my Sav - ior shine!

I'd soar, and touch the heav'n - ly strings, } In notes al-most di-vine, In notes al-most di - vine.
And vie with Ga - briel while he sings }

184 MEDLEY.

1 Oh, could I speak the matchless worth,
Oh, could I sound the glories forth,
Which in my Savior shine!
I'd soar, and touch the heavenly strings,
And vie with Gabriel while he sings
In notes almost divine.

2 I'd sing the precious blood he spilt,
My ransom from the dreadful guilt,
Of sin and wrath divine!
I'd sing his glorious righteousness,
In which all-perfect heavenly dress
My soul shall ever shine.

3 I'd sing the characters he bears,
And all the forms of love he wears,
Exalted on his throne:
In loftiest songs of sweetest praise,
I would to everlasting days
Make all his glories known.

185 C. WESLEY.

1 O Love divine, how sweet thou art!
When shall I find my willing heart
All taken up by thee?
I thirst, and faint, and die to prove
The greatness of redeeming love,
The love of Christ to me.

7

2 Stronger his love than death or hell;
Its riches are unsearchable;
The first-born sons of light
In vain desire its depths to see;
They can not reach the mystery,
The length, and breadth, and height.

3 God only knows the love of God;
O that it now were shed abroad
In this poor, stony heart!
For love I sigh, for love I pine:
This only portion, Lord, be mine,
Be mine this better part.

186 ALTENBURG.

1 Fear not, O little flock, the foe
Who madly seeks your overthrow;
Dread not his rage and power;
What tho' your courage sometimes faints,
His seeming triumph o'er God's saints
Lasts but a little hour.

2 Amen, Lord Jesus, grant our prayer!
Great Captain, now thine arm make bare,
Fight for us once again!
So shall thy saints and martyrs raise
A mighty chorus to thy praise,
World without end: Amen!

187 ANON.

1 Come join, ye saints, with heart and voice,
Alone in Jesus to rejoice,
And worship at his feet;
Come, take his praises on your tongues,
And raise to him your thankful songs,
" In him ye are complete!"

2 In him, who all our praise excels,
The fullness of the Godhead dwells,
And all perfections meet:
The head of all celestial powers,
Divinely theirs, divinely ours;
" In him ye are complete!"

3 Still onward urge your heavenly way,
Dependent on him day by day,
His presence still entreat;
His precious name forever bless,
Your glory, strength and righteousness,
" In him ye are complete!"

4 Nor fear to pass the vale of death;
In his dear arms resign your breath,
He'll make the passage sweet;
The gloom and fears of death shall flee,
And your departing souls shall see
" In him ye are complete!"

Selection 46.—DUKE ST. SERVICE.—And he led them out as far as to Bethany.

G. F. R.

Solo.

And he led them out as far as to Beth-a-ny, and he lift-ed up his hands and blessed them.

Choir. p   *m*   *Cres.*   *f*

And it came to pass, as he bless-ed them, he was part-ed from them, and car-ried up in-to heaven.

DUKE ST. L. M.

Choir and Congregation.   HATTON.

188
1. Lord, when thou did-st as - cend on high, Ten thousand an - gels filled the sky;
2. Raised to his Fa - ther's glo - rious throne, He sent his Ho - ly Spir - it down;

Those heav'nly guards a - round thee wait, Like chariots that at - tend thy state.
With gifts and grace for reb - el men, That he might dwell on earth a - gain.

Choir (between 1st & 2d verses.)   *p*   *Cres.*   *f*   *m*   *Cres.*

{ And when the day of Pen - te - cost was ful - ly come, }
{ They were all . . . with one ac - cord in one place, } And sud - den - ly there came a sound from

ff   *m*   *Cres.*   *(End with tune. 2d verse.)* *Dim.*

heaven, as of a rush-ing mighty wind, and it filled all the house where they were sit - ting.

Selection 47.—WARD SERVICE.—And he showed me a pure river.

And he showed me a pure riv-er of wa-ter of life, Clear as crys-tal,

clear as crys-tal, pro-ceeding out of the throne of God, of God and of the Lamb.

Clear as crys-tal, clear as crys-tal proceeding out of the throne of God, of God and of the Lamb.

WARD. L. M.

Words by Dr. WATTS.
Music arr. by Dr. L. MASON.

Choir and Congregation.

189
1. There is a stream, whose gen-tle flow Sup-plies the cit-y of our God;
2. That sacred stream, thine ho-ly word, Our grief al-lays, our fear con-trols;

Life, love, and joy still glid-ing through, And wa-t'ring our di-vine a-bode.
Sweet peace thy prom-is-es af-ford, And give new strength to faint-ing souls.

Selection 48.—UXBRIDGE SERVICE.—The word of the Lord is right.

The word of the Lord is right, and all his works are done in truth. His mer-ci-ful kindness is

The word of the Lord is right, and all his works are done in truth.

great to - ward us. And the truth of the Lord en - dur - eth for - ev - er.

The heav'ns de - clare the glo - ry of God, and the fir - ma - ment shew - eth his han - di-work.

Day un - to day ut - ter - eth speech, and night un - to night sheweth knowledge ; there is no speech nor

language, there is no speech nor language, no speech nor language, where their voice is not heard.

Selection 48.

The word of the Lord is right, and all his works are done in truth.

His merciful kindness is great toward us. And the truth of the Lord endureth forever.

The heavens declare the glory of God, and the firmament sheweth his handiwork. Day unto day uttereth speech, and night unto night sheweth knowledge ; there is no speech nor language, where their voice is not heard.

UXBRIDGE. L. M.

Choir and Congregation.

Dr. L. MASON.

1. The heav'ns de - clare thy glo - ry, Lord! In ev - 'ry star thy wis - dom shines;

But when our eyes be - hold thy word, We read thy name in fair - er lines.

190
WATTS.

1 The heavens declare thy glory, Lord !
In every star thy wisdom shines;
But when our eyes behold thy word,
We read thy name in fairer lines.

2 The rolling sun, the changing light,
And nights and days thy power confess,
But the blest volume thou hast writ,
Reveals thy justice and thy grace.

3 Sun, moon, and stars, convey thy praise
Round the whole earth, and never stand :
So, when thy truth began its race,
It touched and glanced on every land.

4 Nor shall thy spreading gospel rest,
Till through the world thy truth has run ;
Till Christ has all the nations blessed
That see the light, or feel the sun.

191
GRANT.

1 The starry firmament on high,
And all the glories of the sky,
Yet shine not to thy praise, O Lord,
So brightly as thy written word.

2 The hopes that holy word supplies,
Its truths divine and precepts wise,
In each a heavenly beam I see,
And every beam conducts to thee.

3 Almighty Lord, the sun shall fail,
The moon forget her nightly tale,
And deepest silence hush on high
The radiant chorus of the sky ;—

4 But fixed for everlasting years,
Unmoved, amid the wreck of spheres,
Thy word shall shine in cloudless day,
When heaven and earth have passed away.

192
BOWRING.

1 Upon the Gospel's sacred page
The gathered beams of ages shine ;
And, as it hastens, every age
But makes its brightness more divine.

2 On mightier wing, in loftier flight,
From year to year does knowledge soar ;
And, as it soars, the Gospel light
Becomes effulgent more and more.

3 More glorious still, as centuries roll,
New regions blest, new powers unfurled,
Expanding with the expanding soul,
Its radiance shall o'erflow the world,—

4 Flow to restore, but not destroy ;
As when the cloudless lamp of day
Pours out its floods of light and joy,
And sweeps the lingering mist away.

193
BEDDOME.

1 God, in the gospel of his Son,
Makes his eternal counsels known,
Where love in all its glory shines,
And truth is drawn in fairest lines.

2 Here, sinners of an humble frame
May taste his grace, and learn his name ;
May read, in characters of blood,
The wisdom, power, and grace of God.

3 Here, faith reveals, to mortal eyes,
A brighter world beyond the skies ;
Here, shines the light which guides our way
From earth to realms of endless day.

4 Oh ! grant us grace, almighty Lord !
To read and mark thy holy word,
Its truths with meekness to receive,
And by its holy precepts live.

194
WATTS.

1 Great Sun of Righteousness, arise !
Oh, bless the world with heavenly light!
Thy gospel makes the simple wise :
Thy laws are pure, thy judgments right.

2 Thy noblest wonders here we view,
In souls renewed and sins forgiven :—
Lord, cleanse my sins, my soul renew,
And make thy word my guide to heaven.

Selection 49.—MANOAH SERVICE.—Thy testimonies are wonderful.

Thy tes - ti - mo nies are won-der-ful, are won - der - ful, there - fore doth my soul keep them. The

Thy tes - ti - mo-nies are won-der-ful, are won - der - ful, there - fore doth my soul keep them. The

en - trance of thy word giv - eth light,

en - trance of thy word giv - eth light, it giv - eth un - der-stand-ing to the sim - ple.

Oh, how love I thy law, it is my med - i - ta - tion all the day. how love . . I thy law, . .

Oh, how love I thy law, it is my med - i - ta - tion all the day, how love I thy law, oh, how I

law, . .

how love I thy law. Thy tes - ti - mo-nies are won-der-ful, thy tes - ti - mo-nies are won - der - ful.

how love I

love . . thy law. Thy tes - ti - mo-nies are won-der-ful, thy tes - ti - mo-nies are won - der ful.

how love I

Selection 49.

Thy testimonies are wonderful, therefore doth my soul keep them. The entrance of thy word giveth light, it giveth understanding to the simple. Oh, how love I thy law! it is my meditation all the day. (*After 1st verse.*)

Thy word is a lamp to my feet and a light to my path. (*After 3d verse.*) And the Word was God. All things were made by him, and without him was not any thing made that was made. In him was life, and the life was the light of men.

MANOAH. C. M.

Words by WM. COWPER.
Music arr. by H. W. GREATOREX.

Choir and Congregation.

195
1. A glo - ry gilds the sa - cred page; Ma - jes - tic like the sun, It gives a
2. The Pow'r that gave it still sup - plies The gra - cious light and heat; Its truth up-

light to ev - 'ry age, It gives, but bor - rows none.
on the na - tions rise; They rise, and nev - er set.

3 Let everlasting thanks be thine,
  For such a bright display,
  As makes a world of darkness shine
  With beams of heavenly day.

4 My soul rejoices to pursue
  The steps of him I love,
  Till glory breaks upon my view,
  In brighter worlds above.

Between 1st and 2d verses.
Choir. m   Cres.   *From here to 2d and 3d verses.* Dim.

Thy word is a lamp to my feet, and a light un - to my path.

Between 3d and 4th verses.
With dignity.   Cres.

And the Word was God. All things were made by him, and with-out him was not

Dim.   Cres.   mf   Cres. (*End with tune, 4th verse.*)

an - y - thing made that was made. In him was life, and the life was the light of men.

Selection 50.—BALERMA SERVICE.—Lord, what love have I unto thy law.

Solo. Tone clear toward joyfulness.   **Duet.** **Cres.** · · · · J. C. WOODMAN.

Lord, what love have I un - to thy law, Lord, what love have I un - to thy law;

all the day long is my stud - y in it. Lord, what love have I un - to thy law, all the day

long is my stud - y in it. Oh, how sweet are thy

words un - to my throat . . . yea . . . sweet - er than hon - ey un - to my mouth!

Thro' thy com - mand - ments I get un - der - stand - ing : therefore I hate all e - vil ways.

Lord, what love have I un - to thy law, all the day long is my stud - y in it.

Selection 50.

Lord, what love have I unto thy law, all the day long is my study in it.

Oh, how sweet are thy words unto my throat, yea, sweeter than honey unto my mouth!

Through thy commandments I get understanding: therefore I hate all evil ways.

Lord, what love have I unto thy law, all the day long is my study in it.

BALERMA. C. M.

Choir and Congregation.   Arr. by Dr. L. Mason.

Oh, hap - py is the man who hears In - struc - tion's warn - ing voice;

And who ce - les - tial wis - dom makes His ear - ly, on - ly choice.

196   Logan.

1 Oh, happy is the man who hears
    Instruction's warning voice;
    And who celestial wisdom makes
    His early, only choice.

2 For she hath treasures greater far
    Than east and west unfold;
    And her rewards more precious are
    Than all their stores of gold.

3 She guides the young with innocence
    In pleasure's paths to tread;
    A crown of glory she bestows
    Upon the hoary head.

4 According as her labors rise,
    So her rewards increase;
    Her ways are ways of pleasantness,
    And all her paths are peace.

197   Fawcett.

1 How precious is the book divine,
    By inspiration given;
    Bright as a lamp its doctrines shine,
    To guide our souls to heaven.

2 O'er all the strait and narrow way
    Its radiant beams are cast;
    A light whose never weary ray
    Grows brightest at the last.

3 It sweetly cheers our drooping hearts
    In this dark vale of tears;
    Life, light, and joy it still imparts,
    And quells our rising fears.

4 This lamp, through all the tedious night
    Of life, shall guide our way,
    Till we behold the clearer light
    Of an eternal day.

198   Watts.

1 Lord, I have made thy word my choice,
    My lasting heritage;
    There shall my noblest powers rejoice,
    My warmest thoughts engage.

2 I 'll read the hist'ries of thy love,
    And keep thy laws in sight;
    While through the promises I rove,
    With ever fresh delight.

3 'T is a broad land, of wealth unknown,
    Where springs of life arise,
    Seeds of immortal bliss are sown,
    And hidden glory lies.

4 The best relief that mourners have;
    It makes our sorrows blest;
    Our fairest hope beyond the grave,
    And our eternal rest.

199   Watts.

1 Laden with guilt, and full of fears,
    I fly to thee, my Lord,
    And not a glimpse of hope appears,
    But in thy written word.

2 The volume of my Father's grace
    Does all my grief assuage;
    Here I behold my Savior's face
    Almost in every page.

3 Here consecrated water flows,
    To quench my thirst of sin;
    Here the fair tree of knowledge grows,
    Nor danger dwells therein.

4 This is the field where hidden lies
    The pearl of price unknown;
    That merchant is divinely wise,
    Who makes the pearl his own.

5 This is the judge that ends the strife,
    Where wit and reason fail,
    My guide to everlasting life,
    Through all this gloomy vale.

6 O may thy counsels, mighty God,
    My roving feet command;
    Nor I forsake the happy road,
    That leads to thy right hand.

Selection 51.—GUIDE SERVICE.—Blessed art thou, O Lord; teach me thy statutes.

G. F. R.

Bless - ed art thou, O Lord, teach me thy stat - utes; Give me un -der-stand-ing, and I shall keep thy

law,   Yea, I shall ob-serve it   with my whole heart,   yea, I shall ob-serve it   with my whole heart.

Make me to go   in the path of thy commandments, for there - in   do I   de - light.

Make me to   go   in the path of thy com-mand-ments, for there-in do I de-light, there-in do I de-light.

Selection 51.

Blessed art thou, O Lord; teach me thy statutes; give me understanding, and I shall keep thy law, yea, I shall observe it with my whole heart. Make me to go in the path of thy commandments, for therein do I delight. Blessed art thou, O Lord; teach me thy statutes; give me understanding, and I shall keep thy law.

Selection 50 may be used here if preferred.

GUIDE. C. M.

Choir and Congregation.

Dr. H. Webster Jones.

1. Oh, that the Lord would guide my ways, To keep his stat - utes still;

Oh, that my God would grant me grace, To know and do his will.

200

WATTS.

1 Oh that the Lord would guide my ways
　To keep his statutes still!
Oh that my God would grant me grace
　To know and do his will!

2 Oh, send thy Spirit down, to write
　Thy law upon my heart;
Nor let my tongue indulge deceit,
　Nor act the liar's part.

3 Order my footsteps by thy word,
　And make my heart sincere;
Let sin have no dominion, Lord,
　But keep my conscience clear.

4 Make me to walk in thy commands—
　'T is a delightful road;
Nor let my head, nor heart, nor hands
　Offend against my God.

201

STEELE.

1 Father of mercies, in thy word
　What endless glory shines!
Forever be thy name adored,
　For these celestial lines.

2 Here may the wretched sons of want
　Exhaustless riches find;
Riches above what earth can grant,
　And lasting as the mind.

3 Here the Redeemer's welcome voice
　Spreads heavenly peace around,
And life and everlasting joys
　Attend the blissful sound.

4 Oh, may these heavenly pages be
　My ever dear delight;
And still new beauties may I see,
　And still increasing light.

5 Divine Instructor, gracious Lord,
　Be thou forever near;
Teach me to love thy sacred word,
　And view my Savior there.

202

STEELE.

1 Thou lovely Source of true delight,
　Whom I unseen adore!
Unvail thy beauties to my sight,
　That I may love thee more.

2 Thy glory o'er creation shines;
　But in thy sacred word,
I read in fairer, brighter lines,
　My bleeding, dying Lord.

3 'T is here, whene'er my comforts droop,
　And sins and sorrows rise,
Thy love with cheerful beams of hope,
　My fainting heart supplies.

4 Jesus, my Lord, my Life, my Light,
　Oh! come with blissful ray;
Break radiant thro' the shades of night,
　And chase my fears away.

5 Then shall my soul with rapture trace
　The wonders of thy love;
But the full glories of thy face
　Are only known above.

203

WATTS.

1 Oh, how I love thy holy law!
　'T is daily my delight;
And thence my meditations draw
　Divine advice by night.

2 My waking eyes prevent the day
　To meditate thy word;
My soul with longing melts away
　To hear thy gospel, Lord.

3 How doth thy word my heart engage?
　How well employ my tongue!
And in my tiresome pilgrimage
　Yields me a heavenly song.

4 When nature sinks, and spirits droop,
　Thy promises of grace
Are pillars to support my hope,
　And there I write thy praise.

Selection 52.—NASHVILLE SERVICE.—The law of the Lord is perfect.

The Law of the Lord is per-fect, con-vert-ing the soul. The witness of the Lord is

sure, mak-ing wise the sim-ple. The stat-utes of the Lord are right, re--joic-ing the heart.

The commandment of the Lord is pure, en--light-'ning the eyes. The fear of the Lord is

clean, en--dur-ing for-ev-er. The judgments of the Lord are true, and righteous al-to-geth-er.

More to be desired are they than gold, yea, than much fine gold. Sweeter al-so than hon-ey, and the honey-comb.

More-o-ver by them is thy ser-vant warn-ed, and in keep-ing of them there is great re-ward.

Selection 52.—The Law of the Lord is perfect. (*Read from page* 108.)

NASHVILLE. L. P. M.

Choir and Congregation.

Words by DR. WATTS.
Music arr. by DR. L. MASON.

204
1. I love the volume of thy word; What light and joy those leaves afford To souls benighted and dis - tressed:
2. Thy threat'nings wake my slumb'ring eyes, And warn me where my danger lies; But 'tis thy blessed gospel, Lord,
3. Who knows the errors of his thoughts? My God, forgive my secret faults, And from presumptious sins restrain;

Thy precepts guide my doubtful way, Thy fear forbids my feet to stray, Thy promise leads my heart to rest.
That makes my guilty conscience clean, Converts my soul, subdues my sin, And gives a free, but large re-ward.
Ac-cept my poor attempts of praise, That I have read thy book of grace, And book of na - ture, not in vain.

Selection 52.

EWING. 7s & 6s.

Choir and Congregation.

Words by REV. W. W. HOW.
Music by ALEX. EWING.

205
1. O Word of God in - car - nate, O Wis - dom from on high, O Truth unchanged, un-chang - ing,
2. The Church from thee, her Mas - ter, Re-ceived the gift di - vine; And still that light she lift - eth
3. It float - eth like a ban - ner Be - fore God's host un - furled; It shin - eth like a bea - con

O Light of our dark sky; We praise thee for the ra - diance That from the hal-lowed page,
O'er all the earth to shine. It is the gold - en cas - ket Where gems of truth are stored;
A - bove the dark-ling world; It is the chart and com - pass, That o'er life's surg-ing sea,

A lan - tern to our foot-steps, Shines on from age to age.
It is the heaven-drawn pic-ture Of thee, the liv - ing Word.
Mid mists, and rocks, and quicksands, Still guide, O Christ, to thee.

4 O make thy Church, dear Savior,
A lamp of burnished gold,
To bear before the nations
Thy true light, as of old.
O teach thy wandering pilgrims
By this their path to trace,
Till, clouds and darkness ended,
They see thee face to face.

Selection 53.—CAMBRIDGE SERVICE.—The Lord hath made bare his holy arm.

The Lord hath made bare his ho - ly arm in the eyes of all the na-tions,

And all the ends of the earth shall see, shall see the sal - va - tion of our God.

the sal - va - - - tion

Solo. Tenor or Soprano.

The Lord hath made bare his ho - ly arm in the eyes of all the na - - -

tions, And all the ends of the earth shall see the sal - va - tion of our God.

Selection 53.

The Lord hath made bare his holy arm in the eyes of all the nations. | And all the ends of the earth shall see the salvation of our God. (*Repeated.*)

CAMBRIDGE. C. M.

Choir and Congregation.

Dr. Randall.

206

1. Sing to the Lord a new made song, Who won-drous deeds hath done; With his right hand and
2. Let all the peo-ple of the earth Their cheer-ful voic-es raise; Let all, with u-ni-

ho-ly arm, The conquest he hath won, The con-quest he hath won, The con-quest he hath won.
ver-sal joy, Resound their Maker's praise, Re-sound their Mak-er's praise, Re-sound their Mak-er's praise.

Selection 53.

Choir and Congregation.

CLARION. 7s. Double.

Words by Rev. J. F. Bahnmaier.
Music by Geo. F. Root.

207

1. Spread, O spread, thou might-y word, Spread the king-dom of the Lord, Where-so-
2. Tell them of the Spir-it given Now, to guide us up to heaven, Strong and

e'er his breath has given Life to be-ings meant for heaven. Tell them how the Fa-ther's will
ho-ly, just and true, Working both to will and do. Word of life, most pure and strong,

Made the world, and keeps it still; How he sent his Son to save All who help and comfort crave.
Lo, for thee the na-tions long: Spread, till from its drear-y night All the world a-wakes to light.

Selection 54.—GLASGOW SERVICE.—Ho! every one that thirsteth.

G. F. R.

Ho! ev-ery one that thirsteth, come ye to the wa-ters, and he that hath no mon-ey, come ye, buy and

eat;   yea, come buy wine and milk without money and without price, without mon-ey and with-out price.

Wherefore do ye spend money for that which is not bread, and your la-bor for that which sa-tis-fi-eth not, which

sat-is-fi-eth not. Hear-ken di-li-gent-ly un-to me, and eat ye that which is

good. In-cline your ear, and come un-to me. Hear, and your soul shall live, your soul shall live.

Selection 54.

Ho! every one that thirsteth, come ye to the waters, and he that hath no money, come ye, buy and eat; yea, come buy wine and milk without money and without price. Wherefore do ye spend money for that which is not bread, and your labor for that which satisfieth not. Hearken diligently unto me, and eat ye that which is good. Incline your ear, and come unto me. Hear, and your soul shall live.

GLASGOW. C. M.

Choir and Congregation.

GEO. F. ROOT.

1. Let ev - ery mor - tal ear at - tend, And ev - ery heart re - joice;

The trum - pet of the gos - pel sounds, With an in - vit - ing voice.

208 WATTS.

1 Let every mortal ear attend,
   And every heart rejoice;
   The trumpet of the gospel sounds,
   With an inviting voice.

2 Ho! ye that pant for living streams,
   And pine away and die—
   Here may you quench your raging thirst
   With springs that never dry.

3 Rivers of love and mercy here
   In a rich ocean join;
   Salvation in abundance flows,
   Like floods of milk and wine.

4 The happy gates of gospel grace
   Stand open night and day;—
   Lord—we are come to seek supplies,
   And drive our wants away.

209 STEELE.

1 The Savior calls! let every ear
   Attend the heavenly sound:
   Ye doubting souls, dismiss your fear;
   Hope smiles reviving round.

2 For every thirsty, longing heart
   Here streams of bounty flow;
   And life, and health, and bliss impart
   To banish mortal woe.
S

3 Here springs of sacred pleasure rise
   To ease your every pain—
   Immortal fountain! full supplies!—
   Nor shall you thirst in vain.

4 Dear Savior, draw reluctant hearts!
   To thee let sinners fly,
   And take the bliss thy love imparts,
   And drink and never die.

210 COLLYER.

1 Return, O wanderer, now return,
   And seek thy Father's face!
   Those new desires, which in thee burn,
   Were kindled by his grace,

2 Return, O wanderer, now return!
   He hears thy humble sigh;
   He sees thy softened spirit mourn,
   When no one else is nigh.

3 Return, O wanderer, now return!
   Thy Savior bids thee live:
   Go to his bleeding feet, and learn
   How freely he'll forgive.

4 Return, O wanderer, now return,
   And wipe the falling tear!
   Thy Father calls—no longer mourn:
   His love invites thee near.

211 STEELE.

1 Ye wretched, hungry, starving poor,
   Behold a royal feast!
   Where mercy spreads her bounteous store
   For every humble guest.

2 See, Jesus stands with open arms;
   He calls, he bids you come;
   Guilt holds you back, and fear alarms;
   But see, there yet is room.

3 Oh, come, and with his children taste
   The blessings of his love;
   While hope attends the sweet repast
   Of nobler joys above.

212 HASTINGS.

1 Return, O wanderer, to thy home,
   Thy Father calls for thee:
   No longer now an exile roam
   In guilt and misery.

2 Return, O wanderer, to thy home;
   Thy Savior calls for thee:
   "The Spirit and the Bride say, Come;"
   Oh, now for refuge flee!

3 Return, O wanderer, to thy home,
   'T is madness to delay:
   There are no pardons in the tomb;
   And brief is mercy's day!

Selection 55.—BERA SERVICE.—Lay not up for yourselves treasures upon earth.

Lay not up for yourselves treas-ures up - on earth, where moth and rust doth cor-rupt, and where thieves

break thro' and steal; But lay up for yourselves treasures in heav'n, where neith-er moth nor rust doth corrupt,

and where thieves do not break thro' nor steal. For where your treas-ure is, there will your heart be al - so.

BERA. L. M.

Words by Dr. DODDRIDGE.
Music by J. E. GOULD.

Choir and Congregation.

213
1. Why will ye waste on tri - fling cares The life which God's com - pas - sion spares? While, in the
2. Shall God in - vite you from a - bove? Shall Je - sus urge his dy - ing love? Shall troubled

va - rious range of thought, The one thing need-ful is for-got?
con - science give you pain? And all these pleas u - nite in vain?

3 Not so your eyes will always view
   Those objects which you now pursue :
   Not so will heaven and hell appear,
   When death's decisive hour is near.

4 Almighty God! thy grace impart;
   Fix deep conviction on each heart;
   Nor let us waste on trifling cares
   That life which thy compassion spares.

Selection 56.—HEROLD SERVICE.—Why stand ye here all the day idle?

G. F. R.

Choir. *mf*

Why stand ye here all the day i - dle? Go ye al - so in - to the vineyard, go ye al - so in - to the vineyard, and

p   Cres.   *p*   *m*   *mf*

what-so - ev - er is right I will give you. Why stand ye here? why stand ye here? Go ye al - so in-

m   *p*   Cres.

to the vineyard, go ye al - so in - to the vineyard, and what-so - ev - er is right I will give you.

HEROLD. P. M.

Choir and Congregation.

Words by Rev. B. R. Hanby.
Music from HEROLD.

214.
1. Work in the vine - yard, Je - sus hath call'd thee, Call'd thee from dark - ness in - to the light;
2. Faith - ful thy God hath prom - ised sal - va - tion, Faith - ful thy load of sor - row he 'll bear;
3. Youth in its ar - dor, man - hood in glo - ry, Child - hood whose life - path is yet un - trod,

Break - ing the chain that so long hath en-thrall'd thee, Work while the day lasts, and work with thy might.
Lead - ing the con - trite thro' ev - 'ry temp-ta - tion, Up to the man-sion he goes to pre - pare.
Old age with locks sil - ver'd o - ver, and hoar - y, All have a work in the vine-yard of God.

Selection 57.—WINDHAM SERVICE, No. 1.—Enter ye in at the strait gate.

Selection 57.

Enter ye in at the strait gate: for wide is the gate, and broad is the way, that leadeth to destruction, and many there be that go in thereat; because strait is the gate, and narrow is the way, which leadeth unto life, and few there be that find it.

WINDHAM. L. M.

Choir and Congregation. DANIEL READ.

1. Broad is the road that leads to death, And thou-sands walk to-geth-er there;

But wis-dom shows a nar-row path, With here and there a trav-el-er.

215 WATTS.

1 Broad is the road that leads to death,
   And thousands walk together there;
   But wisdom shows a narrow path,
   With here and there a traveler.

2 "Deny thyself and take thy cross,"—
   Is the Redeemer's great command:
   Nature must count her gold but dross,
   If she would gain this heavenly land.

3 The fearful soul that tires and faints,
   And walks the ways of God no more,
   Is but esteemed almost a saint,
   And makes his own destruction sure.

4 Lord! let not all my hopes be vain:
   Create my heart entirely new:
   Which hypocrites could ne'er attain,
   Which false apostates never knew.

216 COLLYER.

1 Haste, traveler, haste! the night comes on,
   And many a shining hour is gone;
   The storm is gathering in the west,
   And thou far off from home and rest.

2 The rising tempest sweeps the sky;
   The rains descend, the winds are high;
   The waters swell, and death and fear
   Beset thy path, nor refuge near.

3 Oh, yet a shelter you may gain,
   A covert from the wind and rain;
   A hiding-place, a rest, a home,
   A refuge from the wrath to come!

4 Then linger not in all the plain;
   Flee for thy life; the mountain gain;
   Look not behind; make no delay;
   Oh, speed thee, speed thee on thy way!

217 WATTS.

1 Show pity, Lord! O Lord, forgive;
   Let a repenting rebel live;
   Are not thy mercies large and free?
   May not a sinner trust in thee?

2 Oh, wash my soul from every sin,
   And make my guilty conscience clean!
   Here on my heart the burden lies,
   And past offences pain mine eyes.

3 My lips with shame my sins confess,
   Against thy law, against thy grace:
   Lord, should thy judgment grow severe,
   I am condemned, but thou art clear.

4 Yet save a trembling sinner, Lord!
   Whose hope, still hovering round thy word,
   Would light on some sweet promise there,
   Some sure support against despair.

218 WATTS.

1 What shall the dying sinner do,
   That seeks relief for all his woe?
   Where shall the guilty conscience find
   Ease for the torment of the mind?

2 In vain we search, in vain we try,
   Till Jesus brings his gospel nigh!
   'T is there the power and glory dwell,
   That save rebellious souls from hell.

3 This is the pillar of our hope,
   That bears our fainting spirits up;
   We read the grace, we trust the word,
   And find salvation in the Lord.

219 STEELE.

1 Come, weary souls, with sins distressed,
   Come, and accept the promised rest;
   The Savior's gracious call obey,
   And cast your gloomy fears away.

2 Oppressed with guilt,—a painful load,—
   Oh, come and bow before your God!
   Divine compassion, mighty love
   Will all that painful load remove.

3 Here mercy's boundless ocean flows,
   To cleanse your guilt and heal your woes;
   Pardon, and life, and endless peace—
   How rich the gift, how free the grace!

Selection 58.—GRIGG SERVICE.—Behold, I stand at the door and knock.

Be-hold, I stand at the door and knock; If a-ny man hear my voice, and o-pen the door, and

o-pen the door, I will come in to him, and will sup with him, and he with me, and he with me. Be-

hold, ... Be-hold, ...

I stand at the door and knock, I stand at the door and knock, I stand at the door and knock.

GRIGG. L. M.

Words by Rev. Dr. GRIGG.
Music arr. for this work.

Choir and Congregation.

220

1. Be-hold a stran-ger at the door: He gen-tly knocks, has knock'd before; Has wait-ed long, is
2. Oh, love-ly at-ti-tude! he stands With melt-ing heart and o-pen hands: Oh, matchless kind-ness!

wait-ing still: You treat no oth-er friend so ill.
and he shows This matchless kind-ness to his foes!

3 Rise, touched with gratitude divine,
Turn out his enemy and thine;
Turn out thy soul-enslaving sin,
And let the heavenly Stranger in.

4 Oh, welcome him, the Prince of Peace!
Now may his gentle reign increase!
Throw wide the door, each willing mind,
And be his empire all mankind.

Selection 55.—Lay not up for yourselves treasures upon earth : or Sel. 59.—Behold, now is the accepted time.

BERA. L. M.

Choir and Congregation.   J. E. GOULD.

1. God call-ing yet! shall I not hear? Earth's pleasures shall I still hold dear?

Shall life's swift pass-ing years all fly, And still my soul in slum - bers lie?

221   TERSTEEGEN.

1 God calling yet! shall I not hear?
   Earth's pleasures shall I still hold dear?
   Shall life's swift passing years all fly,
   And still my soul in slumbers lie?

2 God calling yet! shall I not rise?
   Can I his loving voice despise,
   And basely his kind care repay?
   He calls me still; can I delay?

3 God calling yet! and shall he knock,
   And I my heart the closer lock?
   He still is waiting to receive,
   And shall I dare his Spirit grieve?

4 God calling yet! I can not stay;
   My heart I yield without delay :
   Vain world, farewell, from thee I part;
   The voice of God hath reached my heart.

223   [Sel. 55 or 59.   Tune, Bera]
                   DWIGHT.

1 While life prolongs its precious light,
   Mercy is found, and peace is given;
   But soon, ah! soon, approaching night
   Shall blot out every hope of heaven.

2 While God invites, how blest the day!
   How sweet the gospel's charming sound!
   Come, sinners, haste, oh, haste away,
   While yet a pardoning God is found.

3 Soon, borne on time's most rapid wing,
   Shall death command you to the grave,
   Before his bar your spirits bring,
   And none be found to hear or save.

4 In that lone land of deep despair
   No Sabbath's heavenly light shall rise :
   No God regard your bitter prayer,
   Nor Savior call you to the skies.

5 Now God invites—how blest the day!
   How sweet the gospel's charming sound!
   Come, sinners, haste, oh, haste away,
   While yet a pardoning God is found.

(These hymns may both be sung to Grigg, with Sel. 58, if preferred.)

222   [Tune, Glasgow, p. 111.]
                   WATTS.

1 How sad our state by nature is!
   Our sin—how deep it stains!
   And Satan holds our captive minds
   Fast in his slavish chains.

2 But there's a voice of sovereign grace,
   Sounds from the sacred word :
   " Ho! ye despairing sinners, come,
   And trust a pardoning Lord."

3 My soul obeys the almighty call,
   And runs to this relief;
   I would believe thy promise, Lord :
   Oh, help my unbelief!

4 A guilty, weak, and helpless worm,
   On thy kind arms I fall :
   Be thou my Strength and Righteousness
   My Savior and my All.

224   [Tune, Glasgow, p. 111.]
                   STEELE.

1 How helpless guilty nature lies,
   Unconscious of its load!
   The heart, unchanged, can never rise
   To happiness and God.

2 Can aught, beneath a power divine,
   The stubborn will subdue?
   'T is thine, almighty Spirit! thine,
   To form the heart anew.

3 'T is thine, the passions to recall,
   And upward bid them rise;
   To make the scales of error fall,
   From reason's darkened eyes;—

4 To chase the shades of death away,
   And bid the sinner live;
   A beam of heaven, a vital ray,
   'T is thine alone to give.

225   [Tune, Glasgow, p. 111]
                   WATTS.

1 Plunged in a gulf of dark despair,
   We wretched sinners lay,
   Without one cheerful beam of hope,
   Or spark of glimmering day.

2 With pitying eyes the Prince of grace
   Beheld our helpless grief;
   He saw, and—oh, amazing love!—
   He ran to our relief.

3 Down from the shining seats above,
   With joyful haste he fled,
   Entered the grave in mortal flesh,
   And dwelt among the dead.

4 Oh! for this love let rocks and hills
   Their lasting silence break;
   And all harmonious human tongues
   The Savior's praises speak.

Selection 59.—VESPER HYMN SERVICE.—Behold! now is the accepted time.

Be-hold! be-hold! now is th'ac-cept-ed time; Be-hold! now is the day of sal - va - tion. To-

day, if ye will hear his voice, hard - en not your heart, hard - en not your heart.

Come, while it is called to - day, come, while it is called to - day; Now is th'accept - ed

time, now is the d y of sal - va - tion. Ask, and it shall be giv - en you; seek, and ye shall

the ac-cept-ed t'me, and the day of sal - va - tion.

find; knock, and it sha'l be o-pened, shall be o - pened un - to you. Now is th'ac-cept - ed

time, now is the day cf sal - va - tion, the day of sal - va - tion.

the ac - cept - ed time, now is t..e

Selection 59.

Behold! now is the accepted time, now is the day of salvation. To-day, if ye will hear his voice, harden not your
heart. Come, while it is called to-day. Ask, and ye

shall receive; seek, and ye shall find; knock, and it shall
be opened unto you. Behold! now is the accepted time,
now is the day of salvation.

VESPER HYMN. 8s & 7s. 6 lines.

Choir and Congregation. New arrangement.

1. Hear, O sinner! mercy hails you, Now with sweetest voice she calls; Bids you haste to seek the Savior,

Ere the hand of jus-tice falls; Hear, O sinner! hear, O sinner! 'Tis the voice of mer-cy calls.

226 REED.

1 Hear, O sinner! mercy hails you,
　Now with sweetest voice she calls;
Bids you haste to seek the Savior,
　Ere the hand of justice falls;
　Hear, O sinner!
　'Tis the voice of mercy calls.

2 Haste, O sinner, to the Savior!
　Seek his mercy while you may;
Soon the day of grace is over;
　Soon your life will pass away:
　Haste, O sinner!
　You must perish if you stay.

227 MASON.

1 Welcome, welcome, dear Redeemer—
　Welcome to this heart of mine;
Lord, I make a full surrender,
　Every power and thought be thine,
　Thine entirely,
　Through eternal ages thine.

2 Known to all to be thy mansion,
　Earth and hell will disappear;
Or in vain attempt possession,
　When they find the Lord is near;
　Shout, O Zion!
　Shout, ye saints! the Lord is here.

228 HART.

1 Come, ye sinners, poor and wretched,
　Weak and wounded, sick and sore,
Jesus ready stands to save you,
　Full of pity, love and power,
　He is able,
　He is willing, doubt no more.

2 Ho, ye needy; come, and welcome;
　God's free bounty glorify!
True belief and true repentance,
　Every grace that brings us nigh,
　Without money,
　Come to Jesus Christ, and buy.

3 Let not conscience make you linger,
　Nor of fitness fondly dream;
All the fitness he requireth
　Is to feel your need of him;
　This he gives you:
　'Tis the Spirit's rising beam.

229 MONTGOMERY.

1 Come to Calvary's holy mountain,
　Sinners, ruined by the fall!
Here a pure and healing fountain
　Flows to you, to me, to all,—
　In a full, perpetual tide,
　Opened when our Savior died.

2 Come, in sorrow and contrition,
　Wounded, impotent, and blind!
Here the guilty, free remission,
　Here the troubled, peace may find;
　Health this fountain will restore,
　He that drinks shall thirst no more—

3 He that drinks shall live forever;
　'Tis a soul-renewing flood;
God is faithful; God will never
　Break his covenant in blood,
　Signed when our Redeemer died,
　Sealed when he was glorified.

230 SWAIN.

1 Come, ye souls by sin afflicted,
　Bowed with fruitless sorrow down,
By the perfect law convicted,
　Through the cross behold the crown;
　Look to Jesus;
　Mercy flows through him alone.

2 Take his easy yoke, and wear it;
　Love will make obedience sweet;
Christ will give you strength to bear it,
　While his wisdom guides your feet
　Safe to glory,
　Where his ransomed captives meet.

Selection 60.—HASTINGS SERVICE.—Cast away your transgressions.

Choir.

Cast a-way from you all your trans-gres-sions, where-by ye have trans-gress-ed, and

make you a new heart and a new spir-it, For why will ye die, O house of Is-ra-el?

For I have no pleas-ure in the death of him that die-eth, saith the Lord God, saith the

Lord God; where-fore turn your-selves and live ye, turn your-selves and live ye.

HASTINGS. 6s & 4s.

Choir and Congregation.

FINE. D. C.

1. { Child of sin and sor-row! Fill'd with dis-may, }
   { Wait not for to-mor-row, Yield thee to-day: } Heav'n bids thee come, While yet there's room.
D. C. Child of sin and sor-row, Hear and o-bey.

231 HASTINGS.

1 Child of sin and sorrow!
   Filled with dismay,
  Wait not for to-morrow,
   Yield thee to-day:
    Heaven bids thee come,
    While yet there 's room.
  Child of sin and sorrow!
   Hear and obey.

2 Child of sin and sorrow,
   Why wilt thou die?
  Come while thou canst borrow
   Help from on high :
    Grieve not that love
    Which, from above,
  Child of sin and sorrow,
   Would bring thee nigh.

3 Child of sin and sorrow,
   Thy moments glide,
  Like the flitting arrow,
   O'er the rushing tide;
    Ere time is o'er
    Heaven's grace implore;
  Child of sin and sorrow,
   In Christ confide.

Selection 60.—Cast away from you all your transgressions.

EXPOSTULATION. 11s.

Choir and Congregation.   J. HOPKINS.

1. Oh, turn ye, oh, turn ye, for why will ye die, When God, in great mer-cy is com-ing so nigh?

Now Je-sus in-vites you, the Spir-it says Come, And an-gels are wait-ing to wel-come you home.

232   HOPKINS.

1 Oh, turn ye, oh, turn ye, for why will ye die,
  When God, in great mercy, is coming so nigh?
  Now Jesus invites you, the Spirit says, Come,
  And angels are waiting to welcome you home.

2 And now Christ is ready your souls to receive,
  Oh! how can you question, if you will believe?
  If sin is your burden, why will you not come?
  'T is you he bids welcome; he bids you come home.

233   [Sel. 60, Tune, Expostulation.]
                          KNOX.

1 Acquaint thyself quickly, O sinner, with God,
  And joy, like the sunshine, shall beam on thy road;
  And peace, like the dew-drop, shall fall on thy head,
  And sleep, like an angel, shall visit thy bed.

2 Acquaint thyself quickly, O sinner, with God,
  And he shall be with thee when fears are abroad;
  Thy Safeguard in danger that threatens thy path;
  Thy Joy in the valley and shadow of death.

234   [Sel. 60, Tune, Expostulation.]
                          HASTINGS.

1 Delay not, delay not, O sinner, draw near,
  The waters of life are now flowing for thee;
  No price is demanded, the Savior is here;
  Redemption is purchased, salvation is free.

2 Delay not, delay not, O sinner, to come,
  For Mercy still lingers and calls thee to-day:
  Her voice is not heard in the vale of the tomb;
  Her message unheeded will soon pass away.

3 Delay not, delay not, the Spirit of grace,
  Long grieved and resisted, may take his sad flight,
  And leave thee in darkness to finish thy race,
  To sink in the gloom of eternity's night.

4 Delay not, delay not, the hour is at hand,
  The earth shall dissolve, and the heavens shall fade,
  The dead, small and great, in the judgment shall stand;
  What power then, O sinner, will lend thee its aid!

Selection 59.—Behold, now is the accepted time.

TO-DAY. 6s & 4s.   Words by Dr. HASTINGS.
                                     Music by Dr. L. MASON.

Choir and Congregation.

235
1. To-day the Sav-ior calls! Ye wan-d'rers, come; Oh, ye be-night-ed souls, Why long-er roam?
2. To-day the Sav-ior calls; Oh, hear him now; With-in these sa-cred walls To Je-sus bow.
3. To-day the Sav-ior calls; For ref-uge fly; The storm of jus-tice falls, And death is nigh.
4. The Spir-it calls to-day: Yield to his pow'r; Oh, grieve him not a-way: 'T is mer-cy's hour.

Selection 61.—HORTON SERVICE.—Have mercy upon me, O God.

Choir. Somber.   G. F. R.

Have mer - cy   up - on me, O God,   ac - cord - ing to thy lov - ing - kind - ness: ac-

- cord - ing to the mul - ti - tude   of thy ten - der mer - cies   blot   out   my trans-
blot

- gres - sions. Have mer - cy, have mer - cy, have mer - cy   up - on me   ac - cord - ing   to   thy

lov - ing - kind - ness. Wash me thor - ough - ly from my in - i - qui - ty, and cleanse me from   my

sin, For I ac - knowl - edge my trans - gres - sions: and my sin is ev - er be - fore   me.

Selection 61.

Have mercy upon me, O God, according to thy loving-kindness; according to the multitude of thy tender mercies blot out my transgressions. Wash me thoroughly from my iniquity, and cleanse me from my sin, for I acknowledge my transgressions: and my sin is ever before me. Have mercy upon me, O God.

HORTON. 7s.

Choir and Congregation.   Arr. by Dr. MASON.

1. Come, said Jesus' sacred voice, Come, and make my paths your choice; I will guide you to your home; Wea - ry pil - grim, hith - er come.

---

236   BARBAULD.

1 Come, said Jesus' sacred voice,
  Come, and make my paths your choice;
  I will guide you to your home;
  Weary, till mercy speaks within.

2 Thou who, homeless and forlorn,
  Long hast borne the proud world's scorn;
  Long hast roamed the barren waste,
  Weary wanderer, hither haste.

3 Hither come, for here is found
  Balm that flows for every wound!
  Peace, that ever shall endure,
  Rest eternal, sacred, sure.

237   CRABBE.

1 Pilgrim, burdened with thy sin,
  Come the way to Zion's gate;
  There, till mercy speaks within,
  Knock, and weep, and watch, and wait:

2 Knock—he knows the sinner's cry;
  Weep—he loves the mourner's tears;
  Watch, for saving grace is nigh;
  Wait, till heavenly grace appears.

3 Hark! it is the Savior's voice,
  "Welcome, pilgrim, to thy rest!"
  Now within the gate rejoice,
  Safe, and owned, and bought, and blest.

238   SCOTT.

1 Haste, O sinner! now be wise,
  Stay not for the morrow's sun:
  Wisdom if you still despise,
  Harder is it to be won.

2 Haste, and mercy now implore;
  Stay not for the morrow's sun,
  Lest thy season should be o'er
  Ere the morrow is begun.

3 Haste, O sinner! now return;
  Stay not for the morrow's sun,
  Lest thy lamp should cease to burn
  Ere salvation's work is done.

4 Lord! do thou the sinner turn—
  Turn him from his fearful state
  Let him not thy counsel spurn,
  Nor lament his choice too late!

239   NEVIN.

1 "Come up hither! come away;"
  Thus the ransomed spirits sing;
  Here is cloudless, endless day;
  Here is everlasting spring.

2 Come up hither; come and dwell
  With the living hosts above;
  Come, and let your bosoms swell
  With their burning songs of love.

3 Come up hither; come and share
  In the sacred joys that rise,
  Like an ocean, everywhere
  Through the myriads of the skies.

4 Come up hither; come and shine
  In the robes of spotless white;
  Palms, and harps, and crowns are thine;
  Hither, hither wing your flight.

5 Come up hither; hither speed;
  Rest is found in heaven alone;
  Here is all the wealth you need;
  Come and make this wealth your own.

240   CLARKE.

1 Brother, hast thou wandered far
  From thy Father's happy home,
  With thyself and God at war?
  Turn thee, brother; homeward come.

2 Hast thou wasted all the powers
  God for noble uses gave?
  Squandered life's most golden hours
  Turn thee, brother; God can save

3 He can heal thy bitterest wound,
  He thy faintest prayer can hear;
  Seek him, for he may be found;
  Call upon him; he is near.

Come un-to me, all ye that la-bor, All ye that la-bor and are heavy la-den. Take my yoke upon you, and

learn of me, For I am meek and lowly of heart, and ye shall find rest un-to your souls. Come un-to me

Come un-to me, and I will give you rest, and I will give you rest. Come un-to me, Come un-to me.

Choir and Congregation.

DENNIS. S. M.

Words by Dr. DODDRIDGE.
Music arr. by Dr. MASON.

241
1. How gen-tle God's commands! How kind his pre-cepts are! Come, cast your bur-dens
2. Be-neath his watch-ful eye His saints se-cure-ly dwell; That hand which bears cre-

on the Lord, And trust his con-stant care.
a-tion up Shall guard his chil-dren well.

3 Why should this anxious load
  Press down your weary mind?
  Haste to your heavenly Father's throne,
  And peace and safety find.

4 His goodness stands approved,
  Unchanged from day to day;
  I'll drop my burden at his feet,
  And bear a song away.

Selection 62.—Come unto me.

ELLIOTT. L. M.

Words by C. ELLIOTT.
Music arr. by G. F. ROOT.

Choir and Congregation.

242
1. Just as I am, with-out one plea, But that thy blood was shed for me, And that thou
2. Just as I am, though tossed a-bout With many a con-flict, many a doubt, Fightings wih-

bid'st me come to thee, O Lamb of God, I come! I come!
in, and fears with-out, O Lamb of God, I come! I come!

3 Just as I am—poor, wretched, blind;
Sight, riches, healing of the mind,
Yea, all I need, in thee to find,
O Lamb of God, I come! I come!

4 Just as I am—thou wilt receive,
Wilt welcome, pardon, cleanse, relieve,
Because thy promise I believe,
O Lamb of God, I come! I come!

243 [Sel. 62. Tune, Elliott.]
MEDLEY.

1 Jesus, engrave it on my heart,
That thou the one thing needful art
I could from all things parted be,
But never, never, Lord, from thee.

2 Needful thy presence, dearest Lord,
True peace and comfort to afford:
Needful thy promise, to impart
Fresh life and vigor to my heart.

3 Needful art thou, my guide, my stay,
Through all life's dark and dreary way;
Nor less in death thou'lt needful be,
To bring my spirit home to thee.

4 Then needful still, my God, my King,
Thy name eternally I'll sing!
Glory and praise be ever his,—
The one thing needful Jesus is!

244 [Sel. 62. Tune, Elliott.]
C. WESLEY.

1 Oh! that my load of sin were gone!
Oh! that I could at last submit
At Jesus' feet to lay it down—
To lay my soul at Jesus' feet!

2 Rest for my soul I long to find:
Savior of all, if mine thou art,
Give me thy meek and lowly mind,
And stamp thine image on my heart.

3 Break off the yoke of inbred sin,
And fully set my spirit free;
I can not rest, till pure within—
Till I am wholly lost in thee.

245 [Sel. 62. Tune, Elliott.]
WATTS.

1 "Come hither, all ye weary souls;
Ye heavy-laden sinners, come!
I'll give you rest from all your toils,
And raise you to my heavenly home.

2 "They shall find rest who learn of me:
I'm of a meek and lowly mind;
But passion rages like the sea,
And pride is restless as the wind.

3 "Blest is the man whose shoulders take
My yoke, and bear it with delight:
My yoke is easy to his neck,
My grace shall make the burden light."

4 Jesus, we come at thy command;
With faith, and hope, and humble zeal;
Resign our spirits to thy hand,
To mould and guide us at thy will.

246 [Sel. 62. Tune, Elliott.]
WATTS.

1 A broken heart, my God, my King,
Is all the sacrifice I bring:
The God of grace will ne'er despise
A broken heart for sacrifice.

2 My soul lies humbled in the dust,
And owns thy dreadful sentence just:
Look down, O Lord, with pitying eye,
And save the soul condemned to die.

3 Then will I teach the world thy ways;
Sinners shall learn thy sovereign grace:
I'll lead them to my Savior's blood,
And they shall praise a pardoning God.

247 [Sel. 62. Tune, Elliott.]
C. ELLIOTT.

1 With tearful eyes I look around;
Life seems a dark and stormy sea;
Yet, 'mid the gloom, I hear a sound,
A heavenly whisper, "Come to me;"

2 It tells me of a place of rest;
It tells me where my soul may flee:
Oh, to the weary, faint, oppressed,
How sweet the bidding, "Come to me!"

3 "Come, for all else must fail and die!
Earth is no resting-place for thee;
To heaven direct thy weeping eye,
I am thy portion; Come to me."

4 O voice of mercy! voice of love!
In conflict, grief, and agony,
Support me, cheer me from above!
And gently whisper, "Come to me."

248 [Sel. 62. Tune, Elliott.]
WATTS.

1 My God, permit me not to be
A stranger to myself and thee;
Amid a thousand thoughts I rove,
Forgetful of my highest love.

2 Why should my passions mix with earth,
And thus debase my heavenly birth?
Why should I cleave to things below,
And let my God, my Savior, go?

3 Be earth, with all her scenes withdrawn,
Let noise and vanity be gone:
In secret silence of the mind
My heaven, and there my God, I find.

Selection 63.—CHRISTMAS SERVICE.—Let us lay aside ev'ry weight.

Let us lay a-side ev-'ry weight, and the sin that doth so ea-si-ly be-set us, and let us run with

pa-tience the race that is be-fore us, Look-ing un-to Je-sus, look-ing un-to Je-sus, the

Au-thor of faith, the Au-thor and Fin-ish-er of faith, the Au-thor and Fin-ish-er of faith.

Solo or Semi-Chorus.

Bless-ed is the man that en-dur-eth tempt-a-tion, He shall re-

ceive the crown of life, He shall re-ceive the crown of life.

Selection 63.

Let us lay aside every weight, and the sin that doth so easily beset us, and let us run with patience the race that is before us, looking unto Jesus, the Au- thor and Finisher of faith. Blessed is the man that endureth temptation, he shall receive the crown of life.

CHRISTMAS. C. M.

HANDEL.

Choir and Congregation.

1. A - wake, my soul! stretch ev - 'ry nerve, And press with vig - or on; A heav'nly race de-mands thy zeal, And an im - mor - tal crown, And an im - mor - tal crown.

249 DODDRIDGE

1 Awake, my soul, stretch every nerve,
And press with vigor on ;
A heavenly race demands thy zeal,
And an immortal crown.

2 A cloud of witnesses around
Hold thee in full survey ;
Forget the steps already trod,
And onward urge thy way.

3 'T is God's all-animating voice,
That calls thee from on high ;
'T is his own hand presents the prize
To thine aspiring eye.

4 Blest Savior, introduced by thee,
Have I my race begun ;
And, crowned with victory, at thy feet
I 'll lay my honors down.

250 NEEDHAM.

1 Rise, O my soul, pursue the path
By ancient worthies trod ;
Aspiring, view those holy men
Who lived and walked with God.

2 Though dead, they speak in reason's ear,
And in example live ;
Their faith, and hope, and mighty deeds
Still fresh instruction give.

9

3 'Twas through the Lamb's most precious blood
They conquered every foe ;
And to his power and matchless grace
Their crowns of life they owe.

4 Lord, may I ever keep in view
The patterns thou hast given,
And ne'er forsake the blessed road
That led them safe to heaven.

251 WESLEY.

1 Eternal Sun of righteousness,
Display thy beams divine,
And cause the glory of thy face,
Upon my heart to shine.

2 Light, in thy light, oh, may I see,
Thy grace and mercy prove,
Revived, and cheered, and blest by thee,
The God of pardoning love.

3 Lift up thy countenance serene,
And let thy happy child
Behold, without a cloud between,
The Father reconciled.

4 On me thy promised peace bestow,
The peace by Jesus given ;—
The joys of holiness below,
And then the joys of heaven.

252 STEELE.

1 Oh! could our thoughts and wishes fly,
Above these gloomy shades,
To those bright worlds, beyond the sky,
Which sorrow ne'er invades !—

2 There joys, unseen by mortal eyes,
Or reason's feeble ray,
In ever-blooming prospects rise,
Unconscious of decay.

3 Lord! send a beam of light divine,
To guide our upward aim ;
With one reviving touch of thine,
Our languid hearts inflame.

4 Oh ! then, on faith's sublimest wing,
Our ardent hope shall rise
To those bright scenes, where pleasures spring
Immortal in the skies.

253 BEDDOME.

1 Ye trembling souls, dismiss your fears ;
Be mercy all your theme ;
Mercy, which like a river flows
In one continued stream.

2 Fear not the powers of earth and hell :
God will these powers restrain ;
His mighty arm their rage repel,
And make their efforts vain.

Selection 64.—LITCHFIELD SERVICE.—They that wait upon the Lord.

G. F. R.

Solo. m   **Cres.**   f

They that wait up-on the Lord shall re-new, shall re-new their strength . . . They shall

Cres.   f   m   **Cres.**   f   m   **Dim.**

mount up with wings, they shall mount up as ea-gles; They shall run, and not be wea-ry, they sha'l

m   **Dim.**   m

walk, and not faint, they shall run, and not be wea-ry, they shall walk, and not faint.

Choir. m   **Cres.**   f   **Dim.**   **Cres.**   **Dim.**   **Cres.**

They that wait up-on the Lord shall re-new, shall re-new their strength . . . They shall mount up with

They shall mount,

f   m   **Cres.**   f   m   p

wings, they shall mount up as ea-gles, They shall run, and not be wea-ry, They shall walk, and not faint.

Selection 64.

They that wait upon the Lord shall renew their strength, | eagles; they shall run, and not be weary; they shall walk,
they shall mount up with wings, they shall mount up as | and not faint. (*Repeated.*)

LITCHFIELD. C. M.

Choir and Congregation.

Dr. L. Mason.

1. Ye hearts, with youth - ful vig - or warm, In smil - ing crowds draw near;

And turn from ev - 'ry mor - tal charm, A Sav - ior's voice to hear.

254
DODDRIDGE.

1 Ye hearts, with youthful vigor warm,
   In smiling crowds draw near,
   And turn from every mortal charm
   A Savior's voice to hear.

2 "The soul that longs to see my face,
   Is sure my love to gain;
   And those that early seek my grace,
   Shall never seek in vain."

3 What object, Lord, my soul should move,
   If once compared with thee?
   What beauty should command my love,
   Like what in Christ I see?

4 Away, ye false, delusive toys,
   Vain tempters of the mind!
   'T is here I fix my lasting choice,
   For here true bliss I find.

255
STEELE.

1 O thou, whose tender mercy hears
   Contrition's humble sigh;
   Whose hand indulgent wipes the tears
   From sorrow's weeping eye;—

   See, Lord, before thy throne of grace,
   A wretched wanderer mourn:
   Hast thou not bid me seek thy face?
   Hast thou not said—"Return?"

3 And shall my guilty fears prevail
   To drive me from thy feet?
   Oh, let not this dear refuge fail,
   This only safe retreat!

4 Oh, shine on this benighted heart,
   With beams of mercy shine!
   And let thy healing voice impart
   The sense of joy divine.

256
NEWTON.

1 Approach, my soul! the mercy-seat,
   Where Jesus answers prayer;
   There humbly fall before his feet,
   For none can perish there.

2 Thy promise is my only plea,
   With this I venture nigh:
   Thou callest burdened souls to thee,
   And such, O Lord! am I.

3 Bowed down beneath a load of sin,
   By Satan sorely pressed;
   By wars without, and fears within,
   I come to thee for rest.

4 Oh! wondrous Love—to bleed and die,
   To bear the cross and shame,
   That guilty sinners, such as I,
   Might plead thy gracious name!

257
WESLEY.

1 Oh, for a lowly, contrite heart,
   Believing, true, and clean!
   Which neither life nor death can part
   From him that dwells within.

2 A heart in every thought renewed,
   And filled with love divine;
   Perfect, and right, and pure, and good;
   An image, Lord! of thine.

3 Thy nature, gracious Lord! impart;
   Come quickly from above;
   Write thy new name upon my heart,—
   Thy new, best name of Love.

258
BOURNE.

1 Welcome, O Savior! to my heart;
   Possess thine humble throne;
   Bid every rival hence depart,
   And claim me for thine own.

2 The world and Satan I forsake—
   To thee, I all resign;
   My longing heart, O Jesus! take,
   And fill with love divine.

3 Oh! may I never turn aside,
   Nor from thy bosom flee;
   Let nothing here my heart divide—
   I give it all to thee.

Selection 65.—BEMERTON SERVICE, No. 1.—Create in me a clean heart, O God.

Cre-ate   in me a clean heart,   O God, and re - new a right spir - it with - in   me;

Wash   me thoroughly from   mine   in - i - qui-ty and cleanse   me   from   my sin,   For I ac-

knowl-edge my trans-gres - sions: for my sin   is ev - er be - fore   me, is ev - er be-fore me.

BEMERTON. C. M.

Words by Rev. J. D. Carlyle.
Music by H. W. Greatorex.

Choir and Congregation.

259 1. Lord! when we bend be - fore thy throne, And our con - fes - sions pour,   Oh, may we
      2. Our con - trite spir - its pity - ing see: True pen - i - tence im - part;   And let a

feel the sins   we   own, And hate what we   de - plore.
heal - ing ray   from   thee Beam hope on ev - 'ry heart.

3 When we disclose our wants in prayer,
   May we our wills resign;
Nor let a thought our bosom share,
   Which is not wholly thine.

4 Let faith each meek petition fill,
   And waft it to the skies;
And teach our heart 't is goodness still
   That grants it or denies.

Selection 66.—HARVILLE SERVICE.--Blessed are they that mourn,

G. F. R.

Bless-ed are they that mourn, are they that mourn, for they shall be com-fort-ed, be com - fort - ed.

Like as a fa - ther pit - i - eth his chil - dren, so the Lord pit-ieth them that fear him.

Bless-ed are they that mourn, are they that mourn, for they shall be com-fort-ed, be com - fort - ed.

HARVILLE. C. M.

Words by THOS. MOORE.
Music by JAMES FLINT.

Choir and Congregation.

260

1. Oh, thou who driest the mourn-er's tear! How dark this world would be If, when de-
2. When joy no long - er soothes or cheers, And ev'n the hope that threw A mo - ment's

ceived and wound-ed here, We could not fly to thee!
spar - kle o'er our tears Is dimmed and van-ished too;—

3 Oh, who would bear life's stormy doom,
  Did not thy wing of love
Come, brightly wafting thro' the gloom,
  Our peace-branch from above?

4 Then sorrow touched by thee grows bright,
  With more than rapture's ray;
As darkness shows us worlds of light
  We never saw by day.

Selection 67.— DEDHAM SERVICE.—Tho' your sins be as scarlet.

Hear ye! hear ye the word of the Lord: Tho' your sins be as scar - let, they shall

be as white as snow, tho' they be red like crim - son, they shall be as wool, Tho' your

sins be as scar - let, they shall be as white as snow, tho' they be red like crim - son,

they shall be as wool, tho' they be red like crim - son, they shall be as wool; Tho' your

sins be as scar - let, they shall be as white as snow, they shall be as white as snow.

Selection 67.

Hear ye the word of the Lord: as snow; though they be red like crimson, they shall
Though your sins be as scarlet, they shall be as white be as wool.

DEDHAM. C. M.

Choir and Congregation.　　　　　　　　　　　　WM. GARDINER.

Sweet was the time when first I felt The Sav - ior's pard - 'ning blood

Ap - plied to cleanse my soul from guilt, And bring me home to God.

261　　　　NEWTON.

1 Sweet was the time when first I felt
　The Savior's pardoning.blood
　Applied to cleanse my soul from guilt,
　And bring me home to God.

2 Soon as the morn the light revealed,
　His praises tuned my tongue;
　And, when the evening shade prevailed,
　His love was all my song.

3 In prayer, my soul drew near the Lord,
　And saw his glory shine;
　And when I read his holy word,
　I called each promise mine.

4 Now, when the evening shade prevails,
　My soul in darkness mourns:
　And, when the morn the light reveals,
　No light to me returns.

5 Rise, Savior! help me to prevail,
　And make my soul thy care;
　I know thy mercy can not fail,
　Let me that mercy share.

262　　　　C. WESLEY.

1 Oh! for that tenderness of heart,
　That bows before the Lord;
　That owns how just and good thou art,
　And trembles at thy word.

2 Oh! for those humble, contrite tears,
　Which from repentance flow;
　That sense of guilt, which, trembling, fears
　The long-suspended blow!

3 Savior! to me, in pity give,
　For sin, the deep distress;
　The pledge thou wilt, at last, receive,
　And bid me die in peace.

4 Oh! fill my soul with faith and love,
　And strength to do thy will;
　Raise my desires and hopes above,—
　Thyself to me reveal.

263　　　　STEELE.

1 Alas! what hourly dangers rise!
　What snares beset my way!
　To heaven, oh, let me lift mine eyes,
　And hourly watch and pray.

2 How oft my mournful thoughts complain,
　And melt in flowing tears!
　My weak resistance, ah, how vain!
　How strong my foes and fears!

3 O gracious God! in whom I live,
　My feeble efforts aid;
　Help me to watch, and pray, and strive,
　Though trembling and afraid.

4 Increase my faith, increase my hope,
　When foes and fears prevail;
　And bear my fainting spirit up,
　Or soon my strength will fail.

5 Oh, keep me in thy heavenly way,
　And bid the tempter flee!
　And let me never, never stray
　From happiness and thee.

264　　　　CLEAVELAND.

1 Oh! could I find, from day to day,
　A nearness to my God,
　Then would my hours glide sweet away
　While leaning on his word.

2 Lord, I desire with thee to live
　Anew from day to day,
　In joys the world can never give,
　Nor ever take away.

3 Blest Jesus, come and rule my heart,
　And make me wholly thine,
　Then I may never more depart,
　Nor grieve thy love divine.

4 Thus, till my last, expiring breath,
　Thy goodness I'll adore;
　And when my frame dissolves in death,
　My soul shall love thee more.

Selection 68.—SEYMOUR SERVICE.—Against thee only have I sinned.

Recitative.

Against thee, thee on - ly, have I sinned, and done this e - vil in thy sight; For I ac-

knowledge my transgressions, and my sin is ev-er be - fore me. Cast me not a - way from thy presence, and

(Go to 2d verse of Hymn.)   *Interlude between 2d and 3d verses.*

take not thy Ho - ly Spir - it from me. Have mer - cy up-on me, up - on me, O God, ac - cor-ding to thy

(End with tune, 3d verse.)

lov - ing kind - ness; ac - cording to the mul - ti-tude of thy ten - der mercies blot out my trans-gres-sions.

Selection 68.

Against thee, thee only have I sinned, and done this evil in thy sight ;　For I acknowledge my transgressions, and my sin is ever before me.

SEYMOUR. 7s.

Choir and Congregation.　　　　　　　　　　　　　　From WEBER.

God of mercy ! God of grace ! Hear our sad repentant song ; Sorrow dwells on ev'ry face, Pen - itence on every tongue.

265　　　J. TAYLOR.

1 God of mercy ! God of grace !
  Hear our sad, repentant song ;
  Sorrow dwells on every face,
  Penitence on every tongue.

Choir.

Cast me not away from thy presence ; and take not thy Holy Spirit from me.

Choir and Congregation.

2 Every sin and secret fault,
  Filled with grief and shame we own ;
  Humbled at thy feet we lie,
  Seeking pardon from thy throne.

Choir.

Have mercy upon me, O God, according to thy loving kindness : according to the multitude of thy tender mercies blot out my transgressions.

Choir and Congregation.

3 God of mercy ! God of grace !
  Hear our sad repentant songs ;
  Oh, restore thy suppliant race,
  Thou to whom all praise belongs.

(Use only prelude, without interludes, with the f llowing hymns.)

266　　　C. WESLEY.

1 When, my Savior, shall I be
  Perfectly resigned to thee ?
  Poor and vile in mine own eyes,
  Only in thy wisdom wise ?

2 Only thee content to know,
  Ignored of all below ?
  Only guided by thy light,
  Only mighty in thy might ?

3 Fully in my life express
  All the heights of holiness ?
  Sweetly let my spirit prove
  All the depths of humble love.

267　　　TOPLADY.

1 Source and Giver of repose,
  From thee all my comfort flows :
  Peace and happiness are thine ;
  Mine they are, if thou art mine.

2 Thee to praise and thee to know
  Constitute my bliss below ;
  Thee to see and thee to love
  Constitute my bliss above.

3 Lord ! it is not life to live,
  If thy presence thou deny :
  Lord ! if thou thy presence give,
  'T is no longer death to die.

268　　　ANON.

1 Prince of Peace, control my will ;
  Bid this struggling heart be still ;
  Bid my fears and doubtings cease ;
  Hush my spirit into peace.

2 May thy will, not mine, be done ;
  May thy will and mine be one ;
  Chase these doubtings from my heart ;
  Now thy perfect peace impart.

3 Savior ! at thy feet I fall ;
  Thou my life, my God, my all !
  Let thy happy servant be
  One forevermore with thee !

269　　　MONTGOMERY.

1 Hasten, Lord ! to my release,
  Haste to help me, O my God !
  Foes, like armed bands, increase :
  Turn them back the way they trod.

2 Dark temptations round me press,
  Evil thoughts my soul assail ;
  Doubts and fears, in my distress,
  Rise, till flesh and spirit fail.

3 Those that seek thee shall rejoice ;
  I am bound with misery ;
  Yet I make thy law my choice ;
  Turn, my God ! and look on me.

4 Thou mine only Helper art,
  My Redeemer from the grave ;
  Strength of my desiring heart !
  Do not tarry, haste to save.

270　[7s. d. Sel. 6s. Tune, Martyn, p. 159.]

Come unto me all ye that labor and are heavy laden.
　　　　　　　　　　　　　C. WESLEY.

1 Sinners, turn, why will ye die ?
  God, your Maker, asks you—Why ?
  God, who did your being give,
  Made you with himself to live ;
  He the fatal cause demands,
  Asks the work of his own hands,—
  Why, ye thankless creatures, why
  Will ye cross his love, and die ?

2 Sinners, turn, why will ye die ?
  God, your Savior, asks you—Why ?
  He who did your souls retrieve,
  Died himself, that ye might live :
  Will ye let him die in vain ?
  Crucify your Lord again ?
  Why, ye ransomed sinners, why
  Will ye slight his grace, and die ?

3 Sinners, turn, why will ye die ?
  God, the Spirit, asks you—Why ?
  He, who all your lives hath strove,
  Urged you to embrace his love :
  Will ye not his grace receive ?
  Will ye still refuse to live ?
  O ye dying sinners ! why,
  Why will ye forever die ?

Selection 69.—BEMERTON SERVICE, No. 2.—O Lord, thou hast searched me.

O Lord, thou hast searched me, and known me. Thou com-pass-est my path and my

ly - ing down, and art ac-quaint-ed with all my ways; For there is not a word in my tongue,but

lo, O Lord, thou know-est it al - to-geth - er. Whith-er shall I go from thy Spir - it? or

whith-er shall I flee from thy presence? If I as-cend up in - to heav'n, thou art there,thou art there; if I

make my bed in hell, be-hold, thou art there. If I take the wings of the morn-ing, and dwell, dwell in the

ut-ter-most part of the sea; e-ven there shall thy hand lead me, and thy right. hand shall hold me.

Selection 69.

O Lord, thou hast searched me, and known me. Thou compassest my path and my lying down, and art acquainted with all my ways. For there is not a word in my tongue, but, lo, O Lord, thou knowest it altogether. Whither shall I go from thy spirit? or whither shall I flee from thy presence? If I ascend up into heaven, thou art there; if I make my bed in hell, behold, thou art there. If I take the wings of the morning, and dwell in the uttermost part of the sea, even there shall thy hand lead me, and thy right hand shall hold me.

BEMERTON. C. M.

GREATOREX.

Choir and Congregation.

1. In all my vast con-cerns with thee, In vain my soul would try

To shun thy pres-ence, Lord, or flee The no-tice of thine eye.

271
WATTS.

1 In all my vast concerns with thee,
In vain my soul would try
To shun thy presence, Lord, or flee
The notice of thine eye.

2 Thine all-surrounding sight surveys
My rising and my rest,
My public walks, my private ways,
And secrets of my breast.

3 Oh, wondrous knowledge, deep and high!
Where can a creature hide?
Within thy circling arms I lie,
Enclosed on every side.

4 So let thy grace surround me still,
And like a bulwark prove,
To guard my soul from every ill,
Secured by sovereign love.

272
FAWCETT.

1 Thy way, O Lord, is in the sea;
Thy paths I can not trace,
Nor comprehend the mystery
Of thine unbounded grace.

2 As through a glass, I dimly see
The wonders of thy love,
How little do I know of thee,
Or of the joys above!

3 'Tis but in part I know thy will;
I bless thee for the sight:
When will thy love the rest reveal,
In glory's clearer light?

4 With rapture shall I then survey
Thy providence and grace;
And spend an everlasting day
In wonder, love, and praise.

273
DODDRIDGE.

1 Great Ruler of all nature's frame!
We own thy power divine;
We hear thy breath in every storm,
For all the winds are thine.

2 Wide as they sweep their sounding way,
They work thy sovereign will;
And, awed by thy majestic voice,
Confusion shall be still.

3 Thy mercy tempers every blast,
To them that seek thy face,
And mingles with the tempest's roar
The whispers of thy grace.

4 Those gentle whispers let me hear,
Till all the tumult cease;
And gales of Paradise shall lull
My weary soul to peace.

274
COWPER.

1 God moves in a mysterious way
His wonders to perform;
He plants his footsteps in the sea;
And rides upon the storm.

2 Judge not the Lord by feeble sense,
But trust him for his grace;
Behind a frowning providence
He hides a smiling face.

3 His purposes will ripen fast,
Unfolding every hour;
The bud may have a bitter taste,
But sweet will be the flower.

275
THOMSON.

1 Jehovah God! thy gracious power
On every hand we see;
Oh, may the blessings of each hour
Lead all our thoughts to thee.

2 Thy power is in the ocean deeps
And reaches to the skies;
Thine eye of mercy never sleeps
Thy goodness never dies.

3 In all the varying scenes of time,
On thee our hopes depend;
In every age, in every clime,
Our Father and our Friend.

Selection 70.—NAOMI SERVICE.—Blessed is the man whom thou chastenest.

Bless - ed is the man whom thou chas - ten - est, O Lord, that thou may'st give him

rest, that thou may'st give him rest, rest from the days of ad - ver - - si - ty.

Bless - ed is the man whom thou chas - ten - est, O Lord, that thou may'st give him rest, that

thou may'st give him rest, rest from the days of ad - ver - si - ty, that thou may'st give him rest.

Bless - ed is the man whom thou chas - ten - est, O Lord, that thou may'st give him rest, that

thou may'st give him rest, rest from the days of ad - ver - si - ty, that thou may'st give him rest.

Selection 70.

Blessed is the man whom thou chastenest, O Lord, that thou mayest give him rest from the days of adversity.

NAOMI. C. M.

Choir and Congregation.

Dr. L. Mason.

Fa-ther! what-e'er of earth-ly bliss Thy sov-'reign will de-nies,

Ac-cept-ed at thy throne of grace, Let this pe-ti-tion rise:—

276 STEELE.

1 Father! whate'er of earthly bliss
Thy sovereign will denies,
Accepted at thy throne of grace,
Let this petition rise :—

2 "Give me a calm, a thankful heart,
From every murmur free;
The blessings of thy grace impart,
And make me live to thee.

3 "Let the sweet hope that thou art mine
My life and death attend ;
Thy presence through my journey shine,
And crown my journey's end."

277 BONAR.

1 Calm me, my God, and keep me calm ;
Let thine outstretched wing
Be like the shade of Elim's palm,
Beside her desert spring.

2 Yes, keep me calm, though loud and rude
The sounds my ear that greet,—
Calm in the closet's solitude,
Calm in the bustling street,—

3 Calm in the hour of buoyant health,
Calm in the hour of pain,
Calm in my poverty or wealth,
Calm in my loss or gain,—

4 Calm in the sufferance of wrong,
Like him who bore my shame,
Calm 'mid the threatening, taunting throng,
Who hate thy holy name.

5 Calm me, my God, and keep me calm,
Soft resting on thy breast ;
Soothe me with holy hymn and praise,
And bid my spirit rest.

278 DARTON.

1 Walk in the light! so shalt thou know
That fellowship of love,
His Spirit only can bestow,
Who reigns in light above.

2 Walk in the light! and thou shalt find
Thy heart made truly his,
Who dwells in cloudless light enshrined,
In whom no darkness is.

3 Walk in the light! and ev'n the tomb
No fearful shade shall wear ;
Glory shall chase away its gloom,
For Christ hath conquered there.

4 Walk in the light! and thou shalt see
Thy path, though thorny, bright,
For God by grace shall dwell in thee,
And God himself is light.

279 WREFORD.

1 Lord, I believe, thy power I own ;
Thy word I would obey:
I wander comfortless and lone,
When from thy truth I stray.

2 Lord, I believe ; but gloomy fears
Sometimes bedim my sight ;
I look to thee with prayers and tears,
And cry for strength and light.

3 Lord, I believe; but oft, I know,
My faith is cold and weak:
My weakness strengthen, and bestow
The confidence I seek.

4 Yes! I believe; and only thou
Canst give my soul relief:
Lord to thy truth my spirit bow;
"Help thou mine unbelief!"

280 WATTS.

1 O God of mercy! hear my call,
My load of guilt remove;
Break down this separating wall,
That bars me from thy love.

2 Give me the presence of thy grace ;
Then my rejoicing tongue
Shall speak aloud thy righteousness,
And make thy praise my song.

Selection 71.—ERDLAW SERVICE.—Thou turnest man to destruction.

Choir. m   Cres.   Dim.   m

Thou turn-est man to de-struction, and say-est re-turn, and say-est re-

Dim.   m

Thou turnest man to destruction, Thou turn-est man to de-struction, and say-est re-turn, and say-est re-

turn, re-turn, re-turn, ye chil-dren of men; For a thou-sand years in thy sight are but as

turn, re-turn, re-turn, ye chil-dren of men; For a thou-sand years in thy sight are but as

Cres. Dim. pp   mf

yes-ter-day when it is past, and as a watch in the night, as a watch in the night. So teach us to

Cres. Dim. pp   mf

yes-ter-day when it is past, and as a watch in the night, as a watch in the night. So teach us to

m   Cres.

number our days, that we may apply our hearts unto wisdom, that we may ap-ply our hearts un-to wis-dom.

m   Cres.

number our days, that we may apply our hearts unto wisdom, that we may ap-ply our hearts un-to wis-dom.

Selection 71.

Thou turnest man to destruction, and sayest, return, ye children of men; for a thousand years in thy sight are but as yesterday when it is past, and as a watch in the night.

So teach us to number our days, that we may apply our hearts unto wisdom.

ERDLAW. C. M.

Choir and Congregation.

GEO. F. ROOT.

1. Teach me the meas-ure of my days, 'Thou Mak-er of my frame,

I would sur-vey life's nar-row space, And learn how frail I am.

---

281 WATTS.

1 Teach me the measure of my days,
  Thou Maker of my frame;
  I would survey life's narrow space,
  And learn how frail I am.

2 A span is all that we can boast,
  An inch or two of time!
  Man is but vanity and dust,
  In all his flower and prime.

3 What should I wish, or wait for, then,
  From creatures, earth and dust?
  They make our expectations vain,
  And disappoint our trust.

4 Now I forbid my carnal hope,
  My fond desire recall:
  I give my mortal interest up,
  And make my God my all.

282 ANON.

1 Be merciful to me, O God!
  Be merciful to me;
  For though I sink beneath thy rod,
  Yet do I trust in thee.

2 Thou art my refuge, and I know
  My burden thou dost bear,
  And I would seek, where'er I go,
  To cast on thee my care.

3 Thou knowest, Lord, my flesh how frail,
  Strong though my spirit he;
  Oh, then assist, when foes assail,
  The soul that clings to thee.

4 And, gracious Lord, whate'er befall,
  A thankful heart be mine,—
  A heart that answers to thy call,
  One that is wholly thine.

5 And may I ne'er forget that thou
  Wilt soon return again,
  And those who love thy coming now
  Shall shine in glory then.

283 COWPER.

1 Oh! for a closer walk with God,
  A calm and heavenly frame,—
  A light to shine upon the road
  That leads me to the Lamb!

2 Where is the blessedness I knew
  When first I saw the Lord?
  Where is the soul-refreshing view
  Of Jesus and his word?

3 Return, O holy Dove, return,
  Sweet messenger of rest!
  I hate the sins that made thee mourn,
  And drove thee from my breast.

4 The dearest idol I have known,
  Whate'er that idol be,
  Help me to tear it from thy throne,
  And worship only thee.

5 So shall my walk be close with God,
  Calm and serene my frame;
  So purer light shall mark the road,
  That leads me to the Lamb.

284 STENNETT.

1 With tears of anguish I lament,
  Here, at thy feet, my God,
  My passion, pride, and discontent,
  And vile ingratitude.

2 Sure, never was a heart so base,
  So false as mine has been;
  So faithless to its promises,
  So prone to every sin.

3 How long, dear Savior, shall I feel
  These struggles in my breast?
  When wilt thou bow my stubborn will,
  And give my conscience rest?

4 Break, sovereign grace, oh, break the charm,
  And set the captive free;
  Reveal, almighty God, thine arm,
  And haste to rescue me.

Selection 72.—BOYLSTON SERVICE.—I am the way. Come unto me.

I am the Way, the Truth and the Life; Come, come un-to me. He that com-eth to me shall

nev-er hun-ger, and he that be-liev-eth on me shall nev-er thirst. Come! come! come! the

Spir-it and the Bride say, come, and let him that hear-eth say, come, And who-so-ev-er will,

who-so-ev-er will, let him take the wa-ter of life free-ly. All that the Fa-ther

giv-eth me shall come, shall come to me, and him that cometh to me I will in no wise cast out.

Selection 72.

I am the Way, the Truth and the Life. Come unto me. He that cometh to me shall never hunger, and he that believeth on me shall never thirst.

The Spirit and the Bride say come, and let him that heareth say come. And whosoever will, let him take the water of life freely.

All that my Father giveth me shall come to me, and him that cometh to me I will in no wise cast out.

BOYLSTON. S. M.

DR. L. MASON.

The Spirit, in our hearts, Is whisp'ring "Sinner, come;" The bride, the Church of Christ, proclaims, To all his children, "Come!"

285
ONDERDONK.

1 The Spirit, in our hearts,
Is whispering, "Sinner, come;"
The bride, the Church of Christ, proclaims,
To all his children, "Come!"

2 Let him that heareth say
To all about him, "Come!"
Let him that thirsts for righteousness,
To Christ, the fountain, come!

3 Yes, whosoever will,
Oh! let him freely come,
And freely drink the stream of life;
'T is Jesus bids him come.

4 Lo! Jesus, who invites,
Declares, "I quickly come;"
Lord, even so! we wait thine hour;
O blest Redeemer, come!

286
DOBELL.

1 Now is the accepted time,
Now is the day of grace;
O sinners! come, without delay,
And seek the Savior's face.

2 Now is the accepted time,
The Savior calls to-day;
To-morrow it may be too late;—
Then why should you delay?

3 Now is the accepted time,
The gospel bids you come;
And every promise, in his word,
Declares there yet is room.

4 Lord, draw reluctant souls,
And feast them with thy love;
Then will the angels spread their wings,
And bear the news above.

10

287
C. WESLEY.

1 A charge to keep I have,
A God to glorify,
A never-dying soul to save,
And fit it for the sky.

2 To serve the present age,
My calling to fulfill;
Oh, may it all my powers engage
To do my Master's will.

3 Arm me with jealous care,
As in thy sight to live;
And oh, thy servant, Lord, prepare
A strict account to give.

4 Help me to watch and pray.
And on thyself rely,
Assured, if I my trust betray,
I shall forever die.

288
C. WESLEY.

1 Thou seest my feebleness,
Jesus, be thou my power,—
My help and refuge in distress,
My fortress and my tower.

2 Give me to trust in thee;
Be thou my sure abode:
My horn, and rock, and buckler be,
My Savior, and my God.

3 Myself I can not save,
Myself I can not keep;
But strength in thee I surely have,
Whose eyelids never sleep.

4 My soul to thee alone,
Now, therefore, I commend:
Lord Jesus, love me as thine own,
And love me to the end.

289
MONTGOMERY.

1 Oh! where shall rest be found—
Rest for the weary soul?
'T were vain the ocean depths to sound,
Or pierce to either pole.

2 The world can never give
The bliss for which we sigh:
'Tis not the whole of life to live,
Nor all of death to die.

3 Beyond this vale of tears
There is a life above,
Unmeasured by the flight of years;
And all that life is love.

4 There is a death whose pang
Outlasts the fleeting breath:
Oh, what eternal horrors hang
Around the second death!

5 Lord God of truth and grace!
Teach us that death to shun:
Lest we be banished from thy face,
And evermore undone.

290
MUHLENBERG.

1 Oh, cease, my wandering soul,
On restless wing to roam;
All this wide world, to either pole,
Hath not for thee a home.

2 Behold the ark of God!
Behold the open door!
Oh, haste to gain that dear abode,
And rove, my soul, no more.

3 There safe thou shalt abide,
There sweet shall be thy rest,
And every longing satisfied,
With full salvation blest.

Selection 73.—MIDDLETON SERVICE.—Whosoever will come after me.

G. F. R.

Solo. Recitative.

Who-so-ev-er will come af-ter me, let him de-ny him-self, and take up his cross and fol-low me.

Choir. *Cres.*

He was wound-ed for our trans-gres-sions, he was bruis-ed for our in-i-qui-ties. The

Dim. *Cres.* *Dim.*

chas-tise-ment of our peace was up-on him, and by his stripes we are heal-ed.

Solo.

God for-bid that I should glo-ry, save in the cross of our Lord, of our Lord Je-sus

Christ, of our Lord Je-sus Christ, by whom the world is cru-ci-fied un-to me, and I un-to the world.

Selection 73.

Whosoever will come after me, let him deny himself, and take up his cross and follow me. He was wounded for our transgressions, he was bruised for our iniquities: the chastisement of our peace was upon him, and with his stripes we are healed. God forbid that I should glory, save in the cross of our Lord Jesus Christ, by whom the world is crucified unto me, and I unto the world.

MIDDLETON. 8s & 7s, Double.

Choir and Congregation. *New arrangement.*

1. { In the cross of Christ I glo - ry, Tow-'ring o'er the wrecks of time; }
{ All the light of sa-cred sto - ry Gath - ers round its head sublime. } When the woes of life o'er-take me,

Hopes de-ceive, and fears an - noy, Nev - er shall the cross for-sake me : Lo! it glows with peace and joy.

291 Bowring.

1 In the cross of Christ I glory,
   Towering o'er the wrecks of time;
All the light of sacred story
   Gathers round its head sublime.
When the woes of life o'ertake me,
   Hopes deceive, and fears annoy,
Never shall the cross forsake me :
   Lo! it glows with peace and joy.

2 When the sun of bliss is beaming
   Light and love upon my way,
From the cross the radiance streaming,
   Adds new lustre to the day.
Bane and blessing, pain and pleasure,
   By the cross are sanctified ;
Peace is there, that knows no measure,
   Joys that evermore abide.

292 Miss Havergal.

1 Yes, he knows the way is dreary,
   Knows the weakness of our frame,
Knows that hand and heart are weary ;
   He in all points felt the same.
Look to him, and faith shall brighten,
   Hope shall soar, and faith shall burn :
Peace once more thy heart shall brighten,
   Rise, he calleth thee, return.

293 C. Wesley.

1 Full of trembling expectation,
   Feeling much, and fearing more,
Mighty God of my salvation !
   I thy timely aid implore ;
Suffering Son of Man ! be near me,
   All my sufferings to sustain,
By thy sorer griefs to cheer me,
   By thy more than mortal pain.

2 Call to mind that unknown anguish,
   In thy days of flesh below ;
When thy troubled soul did languish
   Under a whole world of woe ;
When thou didst our curse inherit,
   Groan beneath our guilty load,
Burdened with a wounded spirit,
   Bruised by the wrath of God.

3 By thy most severe temptation,
   In that dark, satanic hour ;
By thy last mysterious passion,
   Screen me from the adverse power !
By thy fainting in the garden,
   By thy bloody sweat, I pray,
Write upon my heart the pardon,
   Take my sins and fears away.

294 Anon.

1 Holy Father, thou hast taught me
   I should live to thee alone ;
Year by year thy hand hath brought me
   On through dangers oft unknown.
When I wandered thou hast found me ;
   When I doubted, sent me light,
Still thine arm has been around me,
   All my paths were in thy sight.

2 In the world will foes assail me,
   Craftier, stronger far than I ;
And the strife may never fail me,
   Well I know, before I die.
Therefore, Lord, I come, believing
   Thou canst give the power I need ;
Through the prayer of faith receiving
   Strength—the Spirit's strength, indeed.

3 I would trust in thy protection,
   Wholly rest upon thine arm ;
Follow wholly thy direction,
   Thou, mine only guard from harm !
Keep me from mine own undoing,
   Help me turn to thee when tried,
Still my footsteps, Father, viewing,
   Keep me ever at thy side !

Selection 74.—ELLESDIE SERVICE.—If any man will come after me.

If an-y man will come af-ter me, let him de-ny him-self, and take up his cross dai-ly,

take up his cross dai-ly and fol-low me. In the world ye shall have trib-u-la-tion, ye shall have tribu-

la-tion. But be of good cheer, I have overcome the world, I have o-ver-come the world. If an-y

man will come af-ter me, let him de-ny himself and take up his cross dai-ly, take up his cross

and fol-low me, let him take up his cross dai-ly

dai-ly   and fol-low me,   and fol-low me.

Selection 74.

If any man will come after me, let him deny himself, and take up his cross daily and follow me.

1 In the world ye shall have tribulation. But be of good cheer, I have overcome the world. If any man will come after me, let him deny himself, and take up his cross daily and follow me.

ELLESDIE.   8s & 7s.   Double.

Choir and Congregation.   New arrangement.

1. Je - sus, I my cross have tak - en, All to leave and fol - low thee; Nak - ed, poor, de-spised, for - sak - en, Thou, from hence, my all shalt be! Per - ish ev - 'ry fond am - bi - tion, All I've sought, or hoped, or known, Yet how rich is my con - di - tion, God and heav'n are still my own!

(For 1st verse see tune.)

295   LYTE.

2 Let the world despise and leave me,
    They have left my Savior, too;
Human hearts and looks deceive me—
    Thou art not, like them, untrue;
Oh! while thou dost smile upon me,
    God of wisdom, love, and might,
Foes may hate, and friends disown me,
    Show thy face, and all is bright.

3 Man may trouble and distress me,
    'T will but drive me to thy breast,
Life with trials hard may press me,
    Heaven will bring me sweeter rest!
Oh! 'tis not in grief to harm me,
    While thy love is left to me;
Oh! 't were not in joy to charm me,
    Were that joy unmixed with thee.

296   LYTE.

1 Know, my soul, thy full salvation,
    Rise o'er sin, and fear, and care;
Joy to find in every station
    Something still to do or bear.
Think what Spirit dwells within thee;
    Think what Father's smiles are thine;
Think that Jesus died to win thee;
    Child of heaven, canst thou repine?

2 Haste thee on from grace to glory,
    Armed by faith, and winged by prayer!
Heaven's eternal day's before thee,
    God's own hand shall guide thee there:
Soon shall close thy earthly mission,
    Soon shall pass thy pilgrim days,
Hope shall change to glad fruition,
    Faith to sight, and prayer to praise.

297   SHIRLEY.

1 Sweet the moments, rich in blessing,
    Which before the cross we spend;
Life, and health, and peace possessing,
    From the sinner's dying Friend.
Truly blessed is this station,
    Low before his cross to lie,
While we see divine compassion,
    Beaming in his gracious eye.

2 Love and grief our hearts dividing,
    With our tears his feet we bathe;
Constant still, in faith abiding,
    Life deriving from his death.
For thy sorrows we adore thee,
    For the pains that wrought our peace,
Gracious Savior! we implore thee
    In our souls thy love increase.

Selection 75.—DANBURY SERVICE.—Simon, son of Jonas, lovest thou me?

G. F. R.

Jesus saith unto Simon Peter, Si - mon, son of Jo - nas, lov - est thou me more than these?

He saith unto him, Yea, Lord; thou know-est that I love thee. He saith unto him, Feed my lambs.

He saith unto him again the sec-ond time, Si - mon, son of Jo - nas, lov - est thou me?

He saith unto him, Yea, Lord; thou know-est that I love thee. He saith unto him, Feed my sheep.

He saith unto him the third time, Si - mon, son of Jo - nas, lov - est thou me?

Peter was grieved because he said unto him the third time, Lov - est thou me? And he said unto him,

Lord, thou know - est all things; thou know-est that I love thee. Jesus saith unto him, Feed my sheep.

Selection 75.

Read words from page 150.

Choir and Congregation.

DANBURY. 7s.

Geo. F. Root.

298 1. Hark, my soul! it is the Lord; 'T is thy Sav - ior, hear his word; Je - sus speaks, and speaks to thee: "Say, poor sin - ner, lov'st thou me?"

2 Mine is an unchanging love,
Higher than the heights above ;
Deeper than the depths beneath,
Free and faithful, strong as death.

3 Lord! it is my chief complaint,
That my love is weak and faint ;
Yet, I love thee and adore ;
Oh, for grace to love thee more.

299 Anon.

1 Savior! teach me day by day,
Love's sweet lesson to obey ;
Sweeter lesson can not be,
Loving him who first loved me.

2 With a child-like heart of love,
At thy bidding may I move ;
Prompt to serve and follow thee,
Loving him who first loved me.

3 Teach me all thy steps to trace,
Strong to follow in thy grace ;
Learning how to love from thee,
Loving him who first loved me.

4 Love in loving finds employ—
In obedience all her joy ;
Ever new that joy will be
Loving him who first loved me.

5 Thus may I rejoice to show
That I feel the love I owe ;
Singing, till thy face I see,
Of his love who first loved me.

300 Scheffler.

1 Earth has nothing sweet or fair,
Lovely forms or beauties rare,
But before my eyes they bring
Christ, of beauty Source and Spring.

2 When the morning paints the skies,
When the golden sunbeams rise,
Then my Savior's form I find
Brightly imaged on my mind.

3 When the star-beams pierce the night,
Oft I think on Jesus' light,
Think how bright that light will be
Shining through eternity.

4 Come, Lord Jesus! and dispel
This dark cloud in which I dwell,
And to me the power impart
To behold thee as thou art.

Selection 75.

Choir and Congregation.

LLOYD. L. M. 6 lines.

Words by Rev. C. Wesley.
Music arr. for this work.

301 1. My Sav-ior, thou thy love to me, In want, in pain, in shame, hast shown, For me, up - on th' ac - curs - ed tree,
2. Oh, that I, like a lit - tle child, May fol - low thee; nor ev - er rest Till sweet-ly thou hast pour'd thy mind

Didst by thy pre-cious death a - tone; Thy death up - on my heart impress, That nothing may it thence e - rase.
And low - ly mind in - to my breast! Oh, may I now, and ev - er be, One spir - it, dear-est Lord, with thee!

Selection 76.—MERIBAH SERVICE.—Let not your heart be troubled.   † † †

Let not your heart be troub-led: ye be-lieve in God, be-lieve al - so in me. In my

Fa - ther's house are man - y man-sions: if it were not so I would have told you. I go to prepare a

place for you. And if I go and pre-pare a place for you, I will come a - gain, I will

Selection 76.

Let not your heart be troubled: ye believe in God, believe also in me.

In my Father's house are many mansions: if it were not so I would have told you.

I go to prepare a place for you.

And if I go to prepare a place for you, I will come again and receive you unto myself, that where I am, there ye may be also.

MERIBAH. C. P. M.

Dr. L. Mason.

Choir and Congregation.

1. When thou, my righteous Judge, shalt come To take thy ransomed people home, Shall I a-mong them stand?

Shall such a worthless worm as I, Who sometimes am a-fraid to die, Be found at thy right hand?

---

302   HUNTINGTON.

1 When thou, my righteous Judge, shalt come
To take thy ransomed people home,
  Shall I among them stand?
Shall such a worthless worm as I,
Who sometimes am afraid to die,
  Be found at thy right hand?

2 I love to meet thy people now,
Before thy feet with them to bow,
  Though vilest of them all;
But, can I bear the piercing thought,
What if my name should be left out,
  When thou for them shalt call?

3 O Lord, prevent it by thy grace,
Be thou my only hiding-place,
  In this the accepted day;
Thy pardoning voice, oh, let me hear,
To still my unbelieving fear,
  Nor let me fall, I pray.

4 Among thy saints let me be found,
Whene'er the archangel's trump shall sound,
  To see thy smiling face;
Then loudest of the throng I'll sing,
While heaven's resounding mansions ring
  With shouts of sovereign grace.

---

303   C. WESLEY.

1 O God! my inmost soul convert,
And deeply on my thoughtful heart
  Eternal things impress:
Give me to feel their solemn weight,
And save me ere it be too late;
  Wake me to righteousness.

2 Before me place, in dread array,
The pomp of that tremendous day,
  When thou with clouds shalt come
To judge the nations at thy bar;
And tell me, Lord! shall I be there
  To meet a joyful doom!

3 Be this my one great business here.—
With holy trembling, holy fear,
  To make my calling sure!
Thine utmost counsel to fulfill,
And suffer all thy righteous will,
  And to the end endure!

4 Then Savior, then my soul receive,
Then bid me in thy presence live,
  And reign with thee above;
Where faith is sweetly lost in sight,
And hope, in full, supreme delight,
  And everlasting love.

---

304   ANSTICE.

1 O Lord, how happy should we be
If we could cast our care on thee,
  If we from self could rest:
And feel at heart that One above
In perfect wisdom, perfect love,
  Is working for the best.

2 Could we but kneel and cast our load
E'en while we pray, upon our God,
  Then rise with lightened cheer;
Sure that the Father who is nigh
To still the famished raven's cry,
  Will hear in that we fear.

3 We can not trust him as we should;
So chafes weak nature's restless mood
  To cast its peace away;
But birds and flowerets round us preach,
All, all the present evil teach
  Sufficient for the day.

4 Lord, make these faithless hearts of ours
Such lessons learn from birds and flowers;
  Make them from self to cease,
Leave all things to a Father's will,
And taste, before him lying still,
  E'en in affliction, peace.

Selection 77.—GREENVILLE SERVICE.—They wandered in the wilderness.

They wan-dered in the wil-der-ness in a sol - i-ta-ry way, in a

sol - i-ta-ry way; They had no cit-y to dwell .. in, Hun-gry and

thirst-y, their soul faint-ed in them, their soul ... faint-ed in them.

Then they cried un-to the Lord, and he de-livered them, then they cried un-to the Lord, and he de-

livered them out of all their dis-tresses. O my God, I trust in thee, Show me thy ways, teach me thy paths.

Selection 77.

They wandered in the wilderness in a solitary way; they had no city to dwell in. Hungry and thirsty, their soul fainted in them.

Then they cried unto the Lord, and he delivered them out of all their distresses. O my God, I trust in thee. Show me thy ways, teach me thy paths.

GREENVILLE. 8s & 7s. 6 lines.

Choir and Congregation.

ROSSEAU.

1. Gen-tly Lord, oh, gen-tly lead us Thro' this lone-ly vale of tears; Thro' the changes thou'st decreed us,

Till our last great change appears. Oh, re-fresh us, oh, re-fresh us, Trav'ling thro' this wil-der-ness.

305
HASTINGS.

1 Gently, Lord, oh, gently lead us
Through this lonely vale of tears;
Thro' the changes thou 'st decreed us,
Till our last great change appears.

Oh, refresh us, oh, refresh us,
Trav'ling through this wilderness.

2 When temptation's darts assail us,
When in devious paths we stray,
Let thy goodness never fail us,
Lead us in thy perfect way.

Oh, refresh us, oh, refresh us,
Trav'ling through this wilderness.

3 In the hour of pain and anguish,
In the hour when death draws near,
Suffer not our hearts to languish,—
Suffer not our souls to fear.

Oh, refresh us, oh, refresh us,
Trav'ling through this wilderness.

4 And, when mortal life is ended,
Bid us on thy bosom rest,
Till, by angel-bands attended,
We awake among the blest.

Oh, refresh us, oh, refresh us,
Trav'ling through this wilderness.

306
WILLIAMS.

1 Guide me, O thou great Jehovah,
Pilgrim through this barren land;
I am weak, but thou art mighty;
Hold me with thy powerful hand;
Bread of heaven, Bread of heaven,
Feed me till I want no more.

2 Open thou the crystal fountain
Whence the healing streams do flow;
Let the fiery, cloudy pillar
Lead me all my journey through;
Strong Deliverer, Strong Deliverer,
Be thou still my Strength and Shield.

3 When I tread the verge of Jordan,
Bid my anxious fears subside;
Death of death! and hell's destruction!
Land me safe on Canaan's side;
Songs of praises, Songs of praises,
I will ever give to thee.

307
EDMESTON.

1 Lead us, heavenly Father, lead us
O'er the world's tempestuous sea;
Guard us, guide us, keep us, feed us,
For we have no help but thee;
Yet possessing Every blessing,
If our God our Father be.

2 Savior, breathe forgiveness o'er us;
All our weakness thou dost know;
Thou didst tread this earth before us;
Thou didst feel its keenest woe;
Lone and dreary, Faint and weary,
Through the desert thou didst go.

3 Spirit of our God, descending,
Fill our hearts with heavenly joy;
Love with every passion blending,
Pleasure that can never cloy;
Thus provided, Pardoned, guided,
Nothing can our peace destroy.

308
KELLY.

1 God of our salvation, hear us;
Bless, oh, bless us, ere we go!
When we join the world, be near us,
Lest we cold and careless grow:
Savior, keep us—Savior, keep us—
Keep us safe from every foe.

2 As our steps are drawing nearer
To our best and lasting home,
May our view of heaven grow clearer,
Hope more bright of joys to come;
And, when dying, And, when dying,
May thy presence cheer the gloom.

Selection 78.—AUTUMN SERVICE.—God so loved the world.

G. F. R.

God so loved the world, loved the world, that he gave his on - ly be - got - ten Son, his

on - ly be - got - ten Son, that who - so - ev - er be - liev - eth in him, who - so - ev - er be-

liev - eth in him should not per - ish, should not per - ish, but have ev - er - last - ing life. For

God so loved the world, loved the world, that he gave his on - ly be - got - ten Son, his
That he gave his Son,

For God so loved the world, that he gave his on - ly Son,

on - ly be - got - ten Son, that who - so - ev - er be - liev - eth in him should have ev - er - last - ing life.
that he who believ - eth should

that who - so - ev - er be - liev - eth in him should

Selection 78.

God so loved the world that he gave his only begotten
Son, that whosoever believeth in him should not perish, | but have everlasting life. **God so loved the world that he**
gave his only begotten Son.

AUTUMN. 8s & 7s. Double.

Choir and Congregation.　　　　　　　　　　　　　　　Scotch Melody.

Love di-vine, all love ex-cell-ing, Joy of heav'n to earth come down, Fix in us thy hum-ble

dwell-ing; All thy faith-ful mer-cies crown; Je-sus! thou art all com-pas-sion, Pure, un-

bound-ed love thou art; Vis-it us with thy sal-va-tion, En-ter ev-'ry trembling heart.

309　　　　　　C. Wesley.

1 Love divine, all love excelling,—
　Joy of heaven, to earth come down!
Fix in us thy humble dwelling,
　All thy faithful mercies crown:
Jesus! thou art all compassion,
　Pure, unbounded love thou art;
Visit us with thy salvation,
　Enter every trembling heart.

2 Breathe, oh, breathe thy loving Spirit
　Into every troubled breast!
Let us all in thee inherit,
　Let us find thy promised rest:
Come, almighty to deliver,
　Let us all thy grace receive!
Speedily return, and never,
　Never more thy temples leave!

3 Finish then thy new creation,
　Pure, unspotted may we be:
Let us see our whole salvation
　Perfectly secured by thee!
Changed from glory into glory,
　Till in heaven we take our place;
Till we cast our crowns before thee,
　Lost in wonder, love, and praise.

310　　　　　　Mant.

1 Lord, thy glory fills the heaven;
　Earth is with its fullness stored;
Unto thee be glory given,
　Holy, holy, holy Lord!
Heaven is still with anthems ringing,
　Earth takes up the angels' cry,
Holy, holy, holy, singing,
　Lord of hosts, thou Lord most high.

2 Ever thus in God's high praises,
　Brethren, let our tongues unite,
While our thoughts his greatness raises,
　And our love his gifts excite:
With his seraph train before him,
　With his holy church below,
Thus unite we to adore him,
　Bid we thus our anthem flow.

3 Lord, thy glory fills the heaven;
　Earth is with its fullness stored;
Unto thee be glory given,
　Holy, holy, holy Lord!
Thus thy glorious name confessing,
　We adopt the angels' cry,
Holy, holy, holy, blessing
　Thee, the Lord our God most high!

311　　　　　　C. Wesley.

1 Come, thou long-expected Jesus,
　Born to set thy people free;
From our fears and sins release us,
　Let us find our rest in thee:
Israel's Strength and Consolation,
　Hope of all the saints thou art;
Dear Desire of every nation,
　Joy of every longing heart.

2 Born, thy people to deliver;
　Born a child, and yet a King;
Born to reign in us forever,
　Now thy precious kingdom bring:
By thine own eternal Spirit,
　Rule in all our hearts alone;
By thine all sufficient merit,
　Raise us to thy glorious throne.

312　　　　　　Anon.

1 Peace of God, which knows no measure,
　Heavenly sunlight of the soul,
Peace beyond all earthly treasure,
　Come, and all our hearts control.
Come, almighty to deliver!
　Naught shall make us, then, afraid;
We will trust in thee forever,
　Thou on whom our hope is stayed.

Selection 79.—MARTYN SERVICE.—Thou art my hiding-place.

Choir. Reverently.   Cres.   mf   p   † † †

Thou art my Hid-ing-place, In thee, O Lord, do I put my trust, yea, in the shad-ow of thy

Dim.   Cres.   Dim.

wings will I make my ref-uge, will I make my ref-uge,   un - til these ca-

m   p

un - til these ca-lam-i-ties be o-ver-past, un-til these ca-lam-i-ties be

lam - - i - ties   be

Somber.   Slower.   Cres.   Dim.

o - ver - past. O my God! O my God! all thy waves and thy bil-lows are gone o-ver me,

O   my   God!   O   my   God!   are   Rit.

all thy waves and thy bil-lows, all thy waves and thy bil-lows are gone o - ver me.

all   thy waves   are

Selection 79.

Thou art my Hiding-place; in thee, O Lord, do I put my trust, yea, in the shadow of thy wings will I make my refuge until these calamities be overpast. O my God, all thy waves and thy billows are gone over me.

MARTYN. 7s.

S. B. MARSH.

Choir and Congregation.

1. Jesus, lover of my soul, Let me to thy bosom fly, While the billows near me roll, While the tempest still is high; Hide me, O my Savior, hide, Till the storm of life is past; Safe into the haven guide, Oh, receive my soul at last!

313

C. WESLEY.

1 Jesus! lover of my soul,
Let me to thy bosom fly
While the billows near me roll,
While the tempest still is high.
Hide me, O my Savior! hide,
Till the storm of life is past;
Safe into the haven guide;
Oh, receive my soul at last!

2 Other refuge have I none;
Hangs my helpless soul on thee;
Leave, ah! leave me not alone,
Still support and comfort me.
All my trust on thee is stayed;
All my help from thee I bring;
Cover my defenceless head
With the shadow of thy wing.

3 Thou, O Christ! art all I want;
More than all in thee I find;
Raise the fallen, cheer the faint,
Heal the sick, and lead the blind.
Just and holy is thy name,
I am all unrighteousness;
Vile and full of sin I am,
Thou art full of truth and grace.

4 Plenteous grace with thee is found,—
Grace to pardon all my sin;
Let the healing streams abound,
Make and keep me pure within;
Thou of life the fountain art,
Freely let me take of thee;
Spring thou up within my heart,
Rise to all eternity.

314

HASTINGS.

1 Jesus, merciful and mild,
Lead me as a helpless child:
On no other arm but thine
Would my weary soul recline;
Thou art ready to forgive,
Thou canst bid the sinner live—
Guide the wanderer, day by day,
In the strait and narrow way.

2 Thou canst fit me by thy grace
For the heavenly dwelling-place;
All thy promises are sure,
Ever shall thy love endure;
Then what more could I desire,
How to greater bliss aspire?
All I need, in thee I see,
Thou art all in all to me.

315

BONAR.

1 Oh, this soul, how dark and blind!
Oh, this foolish, earthly mind!
Oh, this froward, selfish will,
Which refuses to be still!
Oh, these ever-roaming eyes,
Upward that refuse to rise!
Oh, these wayward feet of mine,
Found in every path but thine!

2 Oh, this stubborn, prayerless knee,
Hands so seldom clasped to thee,
Longings of the soul, that go
Like the wild wind, to and fro!
To and fro, without an aim,
Turning idly whence they came,
Bringing in no joy, no bliss,
Only adding weariness!

3 Giver of the heavenly peace!
Bid, oh, bid these tumults cease,
Minister thy holy balm;
Fill me with thy Spirit's calm:
Thou, the Life, the Truth, the Way,
Leave me not in sin to stay;
Bearer of the sinner's guilt,
Lead me, lead me, as thou wilt!

Selection 80.—BETHANY SERVICE.—Though he slay me, yet will I trust in him.

Tho' he slay me, tho' he slay me, yet will I trust in him, yet will I trust in him, he shall

be my sal - va - - tion. Lead me in thy truth and teach me, for thou art the God of

my sal - va - tion, Thou art the God of my sal - va - tion. Yea, though I walk through the

val-ley of the shad-ow, through the val-ley of the shad-ow of death, I will fear no e - vil, for

thou art with me, thy rod and thy staff, they comfort me. Lead me and teach me, lead, oh, lead me.

Selection 80.

Though he slay me, yet will I trust in him, He shall be my salvation.

Lead me in thy truth and teach me, for thou art the God of my salvation.

Yea, though I walk through the valley of the shadow of death, I will fear no evil, for thou art with me, thy rod and thy staff, they comfort me.

Lead me and teach me, lead, oh, lead me.

BETHANY. 6s & 4s.

Choir and Congregation.

Dr. L. MASON.

1. Near-er, my God, to thee, Near-er to thee! E'en tho' it be a cross That rais-eth me;

Still all my song shall be, Near-er, my God, to thee, Near-er, my God, to thee, Near-er to thee!

316 (For 1st verse see tune.)
S. F. ADAMS.

2 Though like the wanderer,
The sun gone down,
Darkness be over me,
My rest a stone,
Yet in my dreams I'd be
Nearer, my God, to thee,
Nearer, my God, to thee,
Nearer to thee!

3 There let the way appear,
Steps unto heaven;
All that thou sendest me,
In mercy given;
Angels to beckon me
Nearer, my God, to thee,
Nearer, my God, to thee,
Nearer to thee!

4 Then, with my waking thoughts
Bright with thy praise,
Out of my stony griefs
Bethel I'll raise;
So by my woes to be
Nearer, my God, to thee,
Nearer, my God, to thee,
Nearer to thee!

5 Or if, on joyful wing
Cleaving the sky,
Sun, moon and stars forgot,
Upward I fly,
Still all my song shall be,
Nearer, my God, to thee,
Nearer, my God, to thee,
Nearer to thee!

317
MRS. BONAR.

1 Fade, fade, each earthly joy;
Jesus is mine!
Break, every tender tie;
Jesus is mine:
Dark is the wilderness;
Earth has no resting-place;
Jesus alone can bless:
Jesus is mine!

2 Tempt not my soul away;
Jesus is mine!
Here would I ever stay;
Jesus is mine:
Perishing things of clay,
Born but for one brief day,
Pass from my heart away;
Jesus is mine!

3 Farewell, ye dreams of night,
Jesus is mine!
Lost in this dawning bright,
Jesus is mine:
All that my soul has tried,
Left but a dismal void;
Jesus has satisfied;
Jesus is mine!

4 Farewell, mortality;
Jesus is mine:
Welcome, eternity;
Jesus is mine:
Welcome, O loved and blest!
Welcome, sweet scenes of rest;
Welcome, my Savior's breast;
Jesus is mine!

318
MRS. PRENTISS.

1 More love to thee, O Christ,
More love to thee!
Hear thou the prayer I make,
On bended knee;
This is my earnest plea,
More love, O Christ, to thee,
More love, O Christ, to thee,
More love to thee!

2 Once earthly joy I craved,
Sought peace and rest;
Now thee alone I seek,
Give what is best;
This all my prayer shall be,
More love, O Christ, to thee,
More love, O Christ, to thee,
More love to thee!

3 Let sorrow do its work,
Send grief and pain;
Sweet are thy messengers,
Sweet their refrain;
When they can sing with me,
More love, O Christ, to thee,
More love, O Christ, to thee,
More love to thee!

4 Then shall my latest breath
Whisper thy praise;
This be the parting cry
My heart shall raise,
This still its prayer shall be,
More love, O Christ, to thee,
More love, O Christ, to thee,
More love to thee!

Selection 81.—OLIVET SERVICE.—He was despised and rejected of men.

Choir. May be sung as a Solo.

Dim. P

G. F. R.

He was de - spis - ed and re - ject - ed of men; a man of sor - rows, and ac-

a man of sor - rows, and ac-

quaint - ed with grief: and we hid, as it were, our fac - es from him: he was de-

spis - ed, and we es - teem - ed him not. Sure - ly, sure - ly he hath borne our griefs,

and car - ried our sor - rows, and the Lord hath laid on him the in - i - qui - ty of us all.

Selection 81.

He is despised and rejected of men, a man of sorrows, and acquainted with grief; and we hid, as it were, our faces from him. He was despised, and we esteemed him not. Surely he hath borne our griefs and carried our sorrows, and the Lord hath laid on him the iniquity of us all.

OLIVET. 6s & 4s.

Choir and Congregation.

Dr. L. Mason.

1. My faith looks up to thee, Thou Lamb of Cal - va - ry, Sav - ior di - vine! Now hear me while I pray, Take all my guilt a - way, Oh, let me from this day Be whol - ly thine!

319 PALMER.

1 My faith looks up to thee,
Thou Lamb of Calvary,
Savior divine!
Now hear me while I pray,
Take all my guilt away,
Oh, let me from this day
Be wholly thine!

2 May thy rich grace impart
Strength to my fainting heart;
My zeal inspire;
As thou hast died for me,
Oh, may my love to thee
Pure, warm, and changeless be,
A living fire.

3 While life's dark maze I tread,
And griefs around me spread,
Be thou my guide;
Bid darkness turn to day,
Wipe sorrow's tears away,
Nor let me ever stray
From thee aside.

4 When ends life's transient dream,
When death's cold, sullen stream
Shall o'er me roll,
Blest Savior! then, in love,
Fear and distrust remove;
Oh, bear me safe above,
A ransomed soul!

320 HASTINGS.

1 Savior, I look to thee,
Be not thou far from me,
'Mid storms that lower:
On me thy care bestow,
Thy loving kindness show,
Thine arms around me throw,
This trying hour.

2 Savior, I look to thee,
Feeble as infancy,
Gird up my heart:
Author of life and light,
Thou hast an arm of might,
Thine is the sovereign right,
Thy strength impart.

3 Savior, I look to thee,
Let me thy fullness see,
Save me from fear;
While at thy cross I kneel,
All my backslidings heal,
And a free pardon seal,
My soul to cheer.

4 Savior, I look to thee,
Thine shall the glory be,
Hearer of prayer:
Thou art my only aid,
On thee my soul is stayed,
Naught can my heart invade,
While thou art near.

321 MRS. HEMANS.

1 Lowly and solemn be
Thy children's cry to thee,
Father divine:
A hymn of suppliant breath,
Owning that life and death
Owning that life and death
Alike are thine.

2 O Father, in that hour,
When earth all succoring power
Shall disavow;
When spear, and shield, and crown,
In faintness are cast down;
In faintness are cast down;
Sustain us, thou.

3 By him who bowed to take
The death-cup for our sake,
The thorn, the rod;
From whom the last dismay,
Was not to pass away;
Was not to pass away;
Aid us, O God.

4 Tremblers beside the grave,
We call on thee to save,
Father divine:
Hear, from our suppliant breath;
Keep us in life and death,
Keep us in life and death,
Thine, only thine.

Selection 82.—ZILPAH SERVICE.—Scarcely for a righteous man will one die.

Choir. p   m   G. F. R.

Scarcely for a righteous man, for a righteous man will one die, yet peradventure for a good man some would

e - ven dare to die. But God commendeth his love to-ward us, in that, while we were yet sinners,

while we were yet sin-ners, Christ died for us, Christ died for us, while we were yet sin-ners, Christ died for us.

ZILPAH. 8s & 7s. Double.

Words by REV. JOHN NEWTON.
Music arr. by GEO. F. ROOT.

Choir and Congregation.

322 1. One there is a-bove all oth-ers, Well deserves the name of Friend; } Which of all our friends to save us,
His is love beyond a brother's, Cost-ly, free, and knows no end; }

2. When he liv'd on earth a - bas-ed, Friend of sin-ners was his name; } Oh, for grace our hearts to soft-en,
Now, a - bove all glo-ry rais-ed, He re-joic-es in the same; }

Could or would have shed his blood? He a-lone has died to save us, Re - con-cil'd in Him to God.
Teach us, Lord, at length to love! We, a - las! for-get too oft-en, What a Friend we have a - bove.

(Sel. 73.   Whosoever will come after me.   Tune, Rockingham, p. 38.)

323　　[L. M.]　　WATTS.

1 When I survey the wondrous cross,
On which the Prince of glory died,
My richest gain I count but loss,
And pour contempt on all my pride.

2 See, from his head, his hands, his feet,
Sorrow and love flow mingled down ;
· Did e'er such love and sorrow meet,
Or thorns compose so rich a crown ?

3 Were the whole realm of nature mine,
That were a present far too small ;
Love so amazing, so divine,
Demands my soul, my life, my all.

(Sel. 74.   If any man will come after me.   Tune, Evan, p. 191.)

324　　[C. M.]　　DOANE.

1 Come, trembling sinner, in whose breast
A thousand thoughts revolve ;
Come, with your guilt and fear oppressed,
And make this last resolve :—

2 " I 'll go to Jesus, though my sins
Like mountains round me close ;
I know his courts, I 'll enter in,
Whatever may oppose.

3 " Prostrate I 'll lie before his throne,
And there my guilt confess ;
I 'll tell him I 'm a wretch outdone,
Without his sovereign grace.

4 " Perhaps he will admit my plea,
Perhaps will hear my prayer ;
But if I perish, I will pray,
And perish only there.

5 " I can but perish if I go ;
I am resolved to try ;
For if I stay away, I know
I must forever die."

(Sel. 72.   I am the way.   Tune, Retreat, p. 170.)

325　　[L. M.]　　COXE.

1 How beauteous were the marks divine,
That in thy meekness used to shine,
That lit thy lonely pathway, trod
In wondrous love, O Son of God !

2 Oh, who like thee, so humbly bore
· The scorn, the scoffs of men, before ?
So meek, forgiving, godlike, high,
So glorious in humility ?

3 Ev'n death which sets the prisoner free,
Was pang, and scoff, and scorn to thee ;
Yet love through all thy torture glowed,
And mercy with thy life-blood flowed.

4 Oh, in thy light be mine to go,
Illuming all my way of woe !
And give me ever on the road
To trace thy footsteps, Son of God.

(Sel. 72.   I am the way.   Tune, Retreat, p. 170.)

326　　[L. M.]　　BOWRING.

1 How sweetly flowed the gospel sound
From lips of gentleness and grace,
When listening thousands gathered round,
And joy and gladness filled the place !

2 From heaven he came, of heaven he spoke,
To heaven he led his followers' way ;
Dark clouds of gloomy night he broke,
Unvailing an immortal day.

3 " Come, wanderers, to my Father's home,
· Come, all ye weary ones, and rest : "
Yes, sacred Teacher, we will come,
Obey thee, love thee, and be blest !

4 Decay then, tenements of dust ;
Pillars of earthly pride, decay :
A nobler mansion waits the just,
And Jesus has prepared the way.

(Sel. 73.   Whosoever will come after me.   Tune, Stephens, p. 179.)

327　　[C. M.]　　DOANE.

1 Thou art the Way : to thee alone
From sin and death we flee ;
And he who would the Father seek,
Must seek him, Lord, by thee.

2 Thou art the Truth : thy word alone
True wisdom can impart ;
Thou only canst instruct the mind,
And purify the heart.

3 Thou art the Life : the rending tomb
Proclaims thy conquering arm ;
And those who put their trust in thee
Nor death nor hell shall harm.

4 Thou art the Way, the Truth, the Life :
Grant us to know that Way ;
That Truth to keep, that Life to win,
Which leads to endless day.

(Sel. 60.   Cast away from you all your transgression.   Tune, Rockingham, p. 39)

328　　[L. M.]　　WATTS.

1 My dear Redeemer, and my Lord,
I read my duty in thy word ;
But in thy life the law appears,
Drawn out in living characters.

2 Such was thy truth, and such thy zeal,
Such deference to thy Father's will,
Such love, and meekness so divine,
I would transcribe and make them mine.

3 Cold mountains and the midnight air
Witnessed the fervor of thy prayer ;
The desert thy temptations knew,
Thy conflict and thy victory too.

4 Be thou my pattern, make me bear
More of thy gracious image here ;
Then God, the Judge, shall own my name
Among the followers of the Lamb.

(Sel. 62.   Come unto me.   Tune, Dennis, p. 62.)

329　　[S. M.]　　WATTS.

1 Is this the kind return,
Are these the thanks we owe,
Thus to abuse eternal love,
Whence all our blessings flow?

2 To what a stubborn frame,
Has sin reduced our mind !
What strange rebellious wretches we,
And God as strangely kind !

3 Turn, turn us, mighty God,
And mould our souls afresh ;
Break, sovereign grace, these hearts of stone,
And give us hearts of flesh.

(Sel. 73.   Whosoever will come after me.   Tune, Rockingham, p. 39.)

330　　[L. M.]　　STEELE.

1 Make us, by thy transforming grace,
Dear Savior, daily more like thee !
Thy fair example may we trace,
To teach us what we ought to be !

2 To do thy heavenly Father's will
Was thy employment and delight ;
Humility and holy zeal
Shone through thy life divinely bright.

3 But ah ! how blind ! how weak we are !
How frail ! how apt to turn aside !
Lord, we depend upon thy care,
And ask thy Spirit for our guide.

Selection 83.—LYRA SERVICE.—Lord, thou hast been our dwelling place.

Choir. Somber.

Lord, thou hast been our dwelling place in all gen-e-ra-tions. Be - fore the mountains were

Before the mountains were brought forth, be-

fore the mountains were

brought forth, were brought forth, or e-ven thou hadst form-ed the earth and the world; From ev-er-last-ing to

fore the mountains were

ev-er-last-ing thou art God, From ev-er-last-ing to ev-er-last-ing thou art God.

LYRA. C. M.

Words by REV. F. W. FABER.
Music by GEO. F. ROOT.

Choir and Congregation.

331
1. How dread are thine e - ter - nal years, O ev - er - last - ing Lord! By
2. Oh, how I fear thee, Liv - ing God, With deep - est, tend - 'rest fears,

pros-trate spir - its day and night In - ces-sant-ly a-dored.
wor - ship thee with trem-bling hope, And pen - i - ten-tial tears.

3 Yet I may love thee, too, O Lord,
   Almighty as thou art;
   For thou hast stooped to ask of me
   The love of my poor heart.

4 No earthly father loves like thee,
   No mother half so mild,
   Bears and forbears, as thou hast done
   With me, thy sinful child.

(Sel 35. My soul is exceeding sorrowful. Tune, Martyn, p. 159: or Benevento, p. 250.)

332 [7s. double.] GRANT.

1 Savior, when in dust to thee,
Low we bow th' adoring knee;
When, repentant, to the skies
Scarce we lift our streaming eyes:
Oh! by all thy pain and woe,
Suffered once for man below,
Bending from thy throne on high,
Hear thy people while they cry.

2 By thy birth and early years,
By thy human griefs and tears,
By thy fasting and distress
In the lonely wilderness:
By thy victory in the hour
Of the subtle tempter's power;
Jesus, look with pitying eye;
Hear thy people while they cry.

3 By thine hour of dark despair,
By thine agony of prayer,
By the purple robe of scorn,
By thy wounds—thy crown of thorn;
By thy cross—thy pangs and cries;
By thy perfect sacrifice;
Jesus, look with pitying eye;
Hear thy people while they cry.

4 By thy deep expiring groan,
By the sealed sepulchral stone,
By thy triumph o'er the grave,
By thy power from death to save;
Mighty God, ascended Lord,
To thy throne in heaven restored,
Savior, Prince, exalted high,
Hear thy people while they cry.

(Sel. 62. Come unto me. Tune, Hendon, p. 178.)

333 [7s.] ANON.

1 Where for safety shall I fly?
Savior, unto thee I cry,
Dangers every-where attend,
Let thine arm my soul defend.

2 Let thy gracious hand impart,
Strength and comfort to my heart,
Ever keep me near to thee,
Till I'm called thy face to see.

3 Oh, that home, eternal, blest,
Where the soul shall find its rest;
Lord till that transporting day,
Onward lead me in thy way.

(Sel. 60. Though he slay me. Tune, Auber, p. 25)

334 [7s. 6 lines] BOWDLER.

1 Lord, before thy throne we bend·
Now to thee our prayers ascend:
Servants to our Master true,
Lo! we yield thee homage due:
Children, to thy throne we fly,
Abba, Father, hear our cry!

2 Low before thee, Lord! we bow,
We are weak—but mighty thou:
Sore distressed, yet suppliant still,
Here we wait thy holy will;
Bound to earth, and rooted here,
Till our Savior God appear.

3 Leave us not beneath the power
Of temptation's darkest hour:
Swift to seal their captives' doom,
See our foes exulting come!
Jesus, Savior! yet be nigh,
Lord of life and victory.

(Sel. 93. If ye endure chastening. Tune, Clarion, p. 111.)

335 [7s. double.] SWAIN.

1 Brethren, while we sojourn here,
Fight we must, but should not fear;
Foes we have, but we've a Friend,
One that loves us to the end:
Forward, then, with courage go;
Long we shall not dwell below;
Soon the joyful news will come,
"Child, your Father calls—come home!"

2 In the way a thousand snares
Lie, to take us unawares;
Satan, with malicious art,
Watches each unguarded part:
But, from Satan's malice free,
Saints shall soon victorious be;
Soon the joyful news will come,
"Child, your Father calls—come home!"

3 But of all the foes we meet,
None so oft mislead our feet,
None betray us into sin
Like the foes that dwell within;
Yet let nothing spoil our peace,
Christ shall also conquer these;
Soon the joyful news will come,
"Child, your Father calls—come home!"

Tune, Olmutz, p. 212.)

336 [S. M.] WATTS.

1 From the first dawning light,
Till the dark evening rise,
For thy salvation, Lord! I wait
With ever-longing eyes.

2 Remember all thy grace,
And lead me in thy truth;
Forgive the sins of riper days,
And follies of my youth.

3 The Lord is just and kind,
The meek shall learn his ways;
And every humble sinner find
The methods of his grace.

Sel. 106. Why art thou cast down. Tune. Keble, p. 14.)

337 [C. M.] LYTE.

1 As pants the hart for cooling streams,
When heated in the chase,
So longs my soul, O God, for thee,
And thy refreshing grace.

2 For thee, my God—the living God,
My thirsty soul doth pine;
Oh, when shall I behold thy face,
Thou Majesty divine!

3 Why restless, why cast down, my soul?
Trust God; who will employ
His aid for thee, and change these sighs
To thankful hymns of joy.

(Tune, Boylston, p. 145.)

338 [S. M.] WATTS.

1 Mine eyes and my desire
Are ever to the Lord;
I love to plead his promises,
And rest upon his word.

2 Lord, turn thee to my soul;
Bring thy salvation near:
When will thy hand release my feet
From sin's destructive snare?

3 When shall the sovereign grace
Of my forgiving God
Restore me from those dangerous ways
My wandering feet have trod?

4 Oh, keep my soul from death,
Nor put my hope to shame!
For I have placed my only trust
In my Redeemer's name.

5 With humble faith I wait
To see thy face again;
Of Israel it shall ne'er be said,
He sought the Lord in vain.

Selection 84.—LABAN SERVICE.—They be many that fight against me.

Choir: or Solo by Tenor or Soprano, the Organ playing accompanying parts.

G. F. R.

They be ma - ny that fight a - gainst me, O thou Most High, Ev - 'ry day they wrest my

words, all their tho'ts are a - gainst me for e - vil; They gath - er them-selves to - geth - er, they

hide them-selves, they mark my steps, they mark my steps when they wait for my soul.

They be ma - ny that fight a - gainst me, they be ma - ny that fight a - gainst me.

Choir and Congregation.

LABAN. S. M.

Words by GEO. HEATH.
Music by Dr. L. MASON.

339   1. My soul, be on thy guard, Ten thou-sand foes a - rise; The hosts of sin are press - ing hard

To draw thee from the skies.

1 My soul, be on thy guard,
   Ten thousand foes arise;
   The hosts of sin are pressing hard
   To draw thee from the skies.

2 Oh, watch, and fight, and pray!
   The battle ne'er give o'er;
   Renew it boldly every day,
   And help divine implore.

3 Ne'er think the victory won,
   Nor once at ease sit down;
   Thy arduous work will not be done
   Till thou obtain thy crown.

4 Fight on, my soul, till death
   Shall bring thee to thy God!
   He'll take thee at thy parting breath
   Up to his blest abode.

MISSIONARY CHANT. L. M.

Choir and Congregation.

ZEUNER.

1. O God, thou art my God a - lone; Ear - ly to thee my soul shall cry,

A pil - grim in a land un-known, A thirst - y land, whose springs are dry.

(Sel. 17. The Lord is good to all. Tune, Missionary Chant.)

340
MONTGOMERY.

1 O God, thou art my God alone;
  Early to thee my soul shall cry,
  A pilgrim in a land unknown,
  A thirsty land, whose springs are dry.

2 Oh, that it were as it hath been,
  When, praying in the holy place,
  Thy power and glory I have seen,
  And marked the footsteps of thy grace!

3 Yet, through this rough and thorny maze,
  I follow hard on thee, my God:
  Thy hand unseen upholds my ways;
  I safely tread where thou hast trod.

4 Better than life itself thy love,
  Dearer than all beside to me:
  For whom have I in heaven above,
  Or what on earth, compared with thee?

(Sel. 66. Blessed are they that mourn. Tune, Missionary Chant.)

341
C. ELVIN.

1 With broken heart and contrite sigh,
  A trembling sinner, Lord, I cry;
  Thy pardoning grace is rich and free;
  O God, be merciful to me!

2 I smite upon my troubled breast,
  With deep and conscious guilt oppressed;
  Christ and his cross my only plea:
  O God, be merciful to me!

3 Far off I stand with tearful eyes,
  Nor dare uplift them to the skies;
  But thou dost all my anguish see:
  O God, be merciful to me!

4 Nor alms, nor deeds, that I have done,
  Can for a single sin atone;
  To Calvary alone I flee:
  O God, be merciful to me!

5 And when redeemed from sin and hell,
  With all the ransomed throng I dwell,
  My raptured song shall ever be,
  God hath been merciful to me!

(Sel. 7. I laid me down and slept. Tune, Missionary Chant.)

342
C. WESLEY.

1 O thou, to whose all-searching sight
  The darkness shineth as the light;
  Search, prove my heart, it pants for thee;
  Oh! burst these bonds, and set it free.

2 If in this darksome wild I stray,
  Be thou my light, be thou my way:
  No foes, no violence I fear,
  While thou, Almighty God, art near.

3 When rising floods my soul o'erflow,
  When sinks my heart in waves of woe,
  Jesus, thy timely aid impart,
  And raise my head, and cheer my heart.

4 Savior, where'er thy steps I see,
  Dauntless, untired, I follow thee;
  Oh! let thy hand support me still,
  And lead me to thy holy hill.

(Sel. 78. God so loved the world. Tune, Missionary Chant.)

343
HOLMES.

1 O Love Divine! that stooped to share
  Our sharpest pang, our bitterest tear,
  On thee we cast each earth-born care,
  We smile at pain while thou art near.

2 Though long the weary way we tread,
  And sorrow crown each lingering year,
  No path we shun, no darkness dread,
  Our hearts still whispering, thou art near.

3 When drooping pleasure turns to grief,
  And trembling faith is changed to fear,
  The murmuring wind, the quivering leaf,
  Shall softly tell us thou art near.

4 On thee we fling our burdening woe,
  O Love Divine, forever dear;
  Content to suffer while we know,
  Living or dying, thou art near!

(Sel 74. If any man will come after me. Tune, Missionary Chant.)

344
WATTS.

1 Stand up, my soul, shake off thy fears,
  And gird the gospel armor on;
  March to the gates of endless joy,
  Where Jesus, thy Great Captain's gone.

2 Hell and thy sins resist thy course;
  But hell and sin are vanquished foes;
  Thy Savior nailed them to the cross,
  And sung the triumph when he rose.

3 Then let my soul march boldly on,—
  Press forward to the heavenly gate;
  There peace and joy eternal reign,
  And glittering robes for conquerors wait.

4 There shall I wear a starry crown,
  And triumph in almighty grace,
  While all the armies of the skies
  Join in my glorious Leader's praise.

Selection 85.—RETREAT SERVICE.—In the time of trouble he shall hide me.

In the time of troub - le, he shall hide me, he shall hide me, he shall hide me in

his pa - vil - ion, in his pa - vil - ion, In the se - cret of his tab - er - na - cle shall he

hide me, In the se - cret of his tab - er - na - cle shall he hide.. me. There re-

main - eth there - fore a rest for the peo - ple of God, for the peo - ple of God, There re-

main - eth there - fore, there re - main - eth there - fore a rest . . . for the peo - ple of God.

Selection 85.

In the time of trouble he shall hide me in his pavilion, | There remaineth therefore a rest for the people of God.
in the secret of his tabernacle, shall he hide me.

RETREAT. L. M.

Choir and Congregation. Dr. T. HASTINGS.

1. From ev-ery storm-y wind that blows, From ev-ery swell-ing tide of woes,

There is a calm, a sure re-treat; 'Tis found be-neath the mer-cy seat.

345 STENNETT.

1 From every stormy wind that blows,
  From every swelling tide of woes,
  There is a calm, a sure retreat ;
  'T is found beneath the mercy-seat.

2 There is a place where Jesus sheds
  The oil of gladness on our heads,—
  A place, than all besides, more sweet ;
  It is the blood-bought mercy-seat.

3 There is a scene where spirits blend,
  Where friend holds fellowship with friend ;
  Though sundered far, by faith they meet
  Around one common mercy-seat.

4 There, there, on eagle wings we soar,
  And sense and sin molest no more,
  And heaven comes down our souls to greet,
  And glory crowns the mercy-seat.

346 ELLIOTT.

1 My God, is any hour so sweet,
  From blush of morn to evening star,
  As that which calls me to thy feet,
  The calm and holy hour of prayer?

2 Blest is the tranquil break of morn,
  And blest the hush of solemn eve,
  When on the wings of prayer up-borne,
  This fair, but transient, world I leave.

3 Then is my strength by thee renewed ;
  Then are my sins by thee forgiven ;
  Then dost thou cheer my solitude,
  With clear and beauteous hopes of heaven.

4 No words can tell what sweet relief,
  There for my every want, I find ;
  What strength for warfare, balm for grief,
  What deep and cheerful peace of mind !

5 Lord, till I reach the blissful shore,
  No privilege so dear shall be,
  As thus my inmost soul to pour
  In faithful filial prayer to thee !

347 COWPER.

1 Jesus, where'er thy people meet,
  There they behold thy mercy-seat ;
  Where'er they seek thee, thou art found,
  And every place is hallowed ground.

2 For thou, within no walls confined,
  Inhabitest the humble mind ;
  Such ever bring thee where they come,
  And going, take thee to their home.

3 Great Shepherd of thy chosen few !
  Thy former mercies here renew ;
  Here to our waiting hearts proclaim
  The sweetness of thy saving name.

348 KELLY.

1 How sweet to leave the world awhile,
  And seek the presence of our Lord !
  Dear Savior ! on thy people smile,
  And come, according to thy word.

2 From busy scenes we now retreat,
  That we may here converse with thee :
  Ah ! Lord ! behold us at thy feet ;
  Let this the "gate of heaven" be.

3 "Chief of ten thousand ! " now appear,
  That we by faith may see thy face :
  Oh ! speak, that we thy voice may hear,
  And let thy presence fill this place.

349 STENNETT.

1 Where two or three, with sweet accord,
  Obedient to their sovereign Lord,
  Meet to recount his acts of grace,
  And offer solemn prayer and praise ;—

2 There will the gracious Savior be,
  To bless the little company ;
  There, to unvail his smiling face,
  And bid his glories fill the place.

3 We meet at thy command, O Lord !
  Relying on thy faithful word ;
  Now send the Spirit from above,
  And fill our hearts with heavenly love.

PRAYER.

Selection 86.—WOODLAND SERVICE.—O thou that hearest prayer.

Arr. by G. F. R.

Choir. O thou, . . . O thou, un - to

O thou that hear - est prayer, O thou . . . that hear - est prayer,

O thou

thee, ... un - to thee, . .

un - to thee shall all flesh come, un - to thee shall all flesh come.

The Lord is nigh un - to all them that call, un - to all them that

The Lord is nigh un - to all that call, un - to all

call up - on him . . in truth.

that call up-on him in truth. O thou that hear - est prayer, un - to thee shall all flesh

Slow and soft. In time. Dim.

come, un - to thee shall all flesh come, un - to thee, un - to thee shall all . . . . flesh come.

Selection 86.

Oh, thou that hearest prayer, unto thee shall all flesh come. | The Lord is nigh unto all them that call upon him, to all that call upon him in truth.

WOODLAND. C. M.

Choir and Congregation.   N. D. GOULD.

1. I love to steal a-while a-way From ev-'ry cum-b'ring care,
And spend the hours of set-ting day In hum-ble, grate-ful prayer.

350   BROWN.

1 I love to steal awhile away
 From every cumbering care,
 And spend the hours of setting day
 In humble, grateful prayer.

2 I love to think on mercies past,
 And future good implore,
 And all my cares and sorrows cast
 On him whom I adore.

3 I love by faith to take a view
 Of brighter scenes in heaven;
 The prospect doth my strength renew,
 While here by tempests driven.

4 Thus, when life's toilsome day is o'er,
 May its departing ray
 Be calm as this impressive hour,
 And lead to endless day.

351   MONTGOMERY.

1 Prayer is the soul's sincere desire,
 Uttered or unexpressed;
 The motion of a hidden fire
 That trembles in the breast.

2 Prayer is the burden of a sigh,
 The falling of a tear,
 The upward glancing of an eye,
 When none but God is near.

3 Prayer is the simplest form of speech
 That infant lips can try;
 Prayer the sublimest strains that reach
 The Majesty on high.

4 Prayer is the Christian's vital breath,
 The Christian's native air:
 His watchword at the gates of death—
 He enters heaven with prayer.

5 Prayer is the contrite sinner's voice,
 Returning from his ways;
 While angels in their songs rejoice,
 And cry—"Behold he prays!"

6 O thou, by whom we come to God—
 The Life, the Truth, the Way;
 The path of prayer thyself has trod,
 Lord! teach us how to pray.

352   HASTINGS.

1 The Savior bids thee watch and pray
 Through life's momentous hour;
 And grants the Spirit's quickening ray
 To those who seek his power.

2 The Savior bids thee watch and pray,
 Maintain a warrior's strife;
 O Christian! hear his voice to-day:
 Obedience is thy life.

3 The Savior bids thee watch and pray,
 For soon the hour will come
 That calls thee from the earth away
 To thy eternal home.

4 The Savior bids thee watch and pray,
 Oh, hearken to his voice,
 And follow where he leads the way,
 To heaven's eternal joys!

(If preferred, Sel. 85. "He shall hide me," and Tune, Erdlaw, p. 143.)

353   STEELE.

1 Dear Father, to thy mercy-seat
 My soul for shelter flies:
 'Tis here I find a safe retreat
 When storms and tempests rise.

2 My cheerful hope can never die,
 If thou, my God, art near;
 Thy grace can raise my comforts high,
 And banish every fear.

3 My great Protector, and my Lord!
 Thy constant aid impart;
 Oh! let thy kind, thy gracious word
 Sustain my trembling heart.

4 Oh! never let my soul remove
 From this divine retreat;
 Still let me trust thy power and love,
 And dwell beneath thy feet.

DENNIS. S. M.

Choir and Congregation.

Arr. by Dr. L. Mason.

1. Jesus, who knows full well The heart of every saint, In-vites us, all our grief to tell, To pray and nev-er faint.

(Sel. 86. O thou that hearest prayer.)

354
NEWTON.

1 Jesus, who knows full well
　The heart of every saint,
Invites us, all our grief to tell,
　To pray and never faint.

2 He bows his gracious ear—
　We never plead in vain ;
Then let us wait till he appear,
　And pray, and pray again.

3 Jesus, the Lord, will hear
　His chosen when they cry ;
Yes, though he may a while forbear,
　He'll help them from on high.

4 Then let us earnest cry,
　And never faint in prayer ;
He sees, he hears, and, from on high,
　Will make our cause his care.

(Sel. 86. O thou that hearest prayer.)

355
C. WESLEY.

1 Jesus, my strength, my hope,
　On thee I cast my care,
With humble confidence look up,
　And know thou hear'st my prayer.

2 Give me on thee to wait,
　Till I can all things do ;
On thee, almighty to create,
　Almighty to renew.

3 I want a godly fear,
　A quick-discerning eye,
That looks to thee when sin is near,
　And sees the tempter fly ;—

4 A spirit still prepared,
　And armed with jealous care,
Forever standing on its guard,
　And watching unto prayer.

(Sel. 86. O thou that hearest prayer.)

356
SIGOURNEY.

1 Where wilt thou put thy trust ?
　In a frail form of clay,
That to its element of dust
　Must soon resolve away.

2 Where wilt thou cast thy care?
　Upon an erring heart,
Which hath its own sore ills to bear,
　And shrinks from sorrow's dart ?

3 No—place thy trust above
　This shadowy realm of night,
In him, whose boundless power and love
　Thy confidence invite.

4 His mercies still endure
　When skies and stars grow dim,
His changeless promise standeth sure,
　Go—cast thy care on him.

Selection 86.—O thou that hearest prayer.

SEYMOUR. 7s.

Choir and Congregation.

Words by NEWTON.
Music from WEBER.

357
1. Come, my soul, thy suit pre-pare, Je-sus loves to an-swer prayer ; He him-self has
2. Lord ! I come to thee for rest, Take pos-ses-sion of my breast ; There, thy sov'reign

bid　thee pray, There-fore will　not say thee nay.
right main-tain, And, with-out　a　ri-val reign.

3 While I am a pilgrim here,
　Let thy love my spirit cheer ;
Be my Guide, my Guard, my Friend,
　Lead me to my journey's end.

4 Show me what I have to do,
　Every hour my strength renew ;
Let me live a life of faith,
　Let me die thy people's death.

Selection 87.—WINDSOR SERVICE.—God is our Refuge and Strength.

God is our Ref - uge, our Ref - uge and Strength. A ver - y pres - ent Help in

time of troub - le, a ver - y pres - ent Help in time, in time of troub - le.

There fore we will not fear, though the earth be re - moved, and though the mount-ains be

car - ried in - to the midst of the sea. God is our Ref - uge, our Ref - uge and Strength.

WINDSOR. C. M.

Choir and Congregation.

Words by Dr. WATTS.
Old Scotch tune.

358 1. O God, our Help in a - ges past, Our Hope for years to come, Our Shel - ter from the

storm - y blast, And our E - ter - nal Home.

2 Before the hills in order stood,
Or earth received her frame,
From everlasting thou art God,
To endless years the same.

3 O God, our Help in ages past,
Our Hope for years to come,
Be thou our Guard while troubles last,
And our Eternal Home.

Selection 88.—FEDERAL ST. SERVICE.—He breathed on them.

He breathed on them, and saith un-to them, Re-ceive ye the Ho-ly Ghost. There is therefore

now no con-dem-na-tion to them which are in Christ Je - sus, who walk not af-ter the

flesh, but af-ter the Spir - - it. For as ma-ny as are led by the

Spir - it of God, they are the sons of God. The Spir-it it-self bear-eth

wit-ness with our spir-it, that we are the chil-dren of God, that we are the children of God.

Selection 88.

He breathed on them, and saith unto them, receive ye the Holy Ghost. There is therefore no condemnation to them that are in Christ Jesus, who walk not after the flesh but after the Spirit. For as many as are led by the Spirit of God, they are the sons of God. The Spirit itself beareth witness with our spirits that we are the children of God.

FEDERAL ST. L. M.

Choir and Congregation.

Words by REV. JOHN WESLEY.
Music by H. K. OLIVER.

Come, gracious Spir - it, heaven-ly Dove, With light and com - fort from a - bove:

Be thou our guardian, thou our guide! O'er ev-'ry thought and step pre-side.

359
BROWNE.

1 Come, gracious Spirit, heavenly Dove,
With light and comfort from above :
Be thou our guardian, thou our guide!
O'er every thought and step preside.

2 To us the light of truth display,
And make us know and choose thy way:
Plant holy fear in every heart,
That we from God may ne'er depart.

3 Lead us to holiness—the road
That we must take to dwell with God;
Lead us to Christ, the living way,
Nor let us from his precepts stray.

4 Lead us to God, our final rest,
To be with him forever blest;
Lead us to heaven, its bliss to share—
Fullness of joy forever there!

360
CASWALL.

1 Come, O Creator, Spirit blest!
And in our souls take up thy rest ;
Come, with thy grace and heavenly aid,
To fill the hearts which thou hast made.

2 Great Comforter! to thee we cry ;
O highest gift of God most high!
O fount of life! O fire of love!
Send sweet anointing from above!

3 Kindle our senses from above,
And make our hearts o'erflow with love;
With patience firm, and virtue high,
The weakness of our flesh supply.

4 Far from us drive the foe we dread,
And grant us thy true peace instead ;
So shall we not, with thee for guide,
Turn from the path of life aside.

361
STEELE.

1 Sure the blest Comforter is nigh,
'T is he sustains my fainting heart ;
Else would my hopes forever die,
And every cheering ray depart.

2 Whene'er, to call the Savior mine,
With ardent wish my heart aspires,—
Can it be less than power divine,
That animates these strong desires ?

3 And, when my cheerful hope can say,
I love my God and taste his grace,—
Lord! is it not thy blissful ray,
That brings this dawn of sacred peace?

4 Let thy good Spirit in my heart
Forever dwell, O God of love!
And light and heavenly peace impart,—
Sweet earnest of the joys above.

362
BEDDOME.

1 Come, blessed Spirit! source of light!
Whose power and grace are unconfined,
Dispel the gloomy shades of night—
The thicker darkness of the mind.

2 To mine illumined eyes, display
The glorious truth thy word reveals;
Cause me to run the heavenly way,
Thy book unfold, and loose the seals.

3 Thine inward teachings make me know
The mysteries of redeeming love,
The vanity of things below,
And excellence of things above.

363
DODDRIDGE.

1 Come, sacred Spirit, from above,
And fill the coldest heart with love :
Oh! turn to flesh the flinty stone,
And let thy sovereign power be known.

2 Speak thou, and from the haughtiest eyes
Shall floods of contrite sorrow rise ;
While all their glowing souls are borne
To seek that grace which now they scorn.

3 Oh! let a holy flock await,
In crowds around thy temple-gate !
Each pressing on with zeal to be
A living sacrifice to thee.

12

Selection 88.—He breathed on them.

HENDON. 7s.

Words by John Stocker.
Music arr. by Dr. Mason.

Choir and Congregation.

364
1. Gra-cious Spir-it, Love di-vine! Let thy light with-in me shine; All my guilt-y fears re-move,
2. Speak thy pard'ning grace to me, Set the bur-dened sin-ner free; Lead me to the Lamb of God,

Fill me with thy heav'n-ly love, Fill me with thy heav'n-ly love.
Wash me in his pre-cious blood, Wash me in his pre-cious blood.

3 Life and peace to me impart,
  Seal salvation on my heart;
  Breathe thyself into my breast,—
  Earnest of immortal rest.

4 Let me never from thee stray,
  Keep me in the narrow way;
  Fill my soul with joy divine,
  Keep me, Lord! forever thine.

365   REED.

1 Holy Ghost! with light divine,
  Shine upon this heart of mine;
  Chase the shades of night away,
  Turn my darkness into day.

2 Holy Ghost! with power divine,
  Cleanse this guilty heart of mine;
  Long hath sin, without control,
  Held dominion o'er my soul.

3 Holy Ghost! with joy divine,
  Cheer this saddened heart of mine;
  Bid my many woes depart,
  Heal my wounded, bleeding heart.

4 Holy Spirit! all-divine,
  Dwell within this heart of mine;
  Cast down every idol-throne,
  Reign supreme —and reign alone.

366   Lyra Cath.

1 Holy Spirit! Lord of light!
  From thy clear, celestial height,
  Come, thou Light of all that live!
  Thy pure, beaming radiance give!

2 Come, thou Father of the poor!
  Come with treasures which endure;
  Thou, of all consolers best,
  Visiting the troubled breast.

3 Thou in toil art comfort sweet;
  Pleasant coolness in the heat;
  Solace in the midst of woe;
  Dost refreshing peace bestow.

4 Light immortal! light divine!
  Visit thou these hearts of thine;
  If thou take thy grace away,
  Nothing pure in man will stay.

5 Give us comfort when we die;
  Give us life with thee on high!
  In thy sevenfold gifts descend;
  Give us joys which never end.

Selection 89.
Choir and Congregation.

RAWSON. 7s & 5s.

Words by Geo. Rawson.
Music arr. for this work.

367
1. Ho-ly Ghost! the In-fi-nite! Shine upon our nature's night With thy blessed inward light, Com-fort-er Divine!
2. Like the dew, thy peace distill; Guide, subdue our wayward will, Things of Christ unfolding still, Comforter Divine!
3. In us "Ab-ba, Fa-ther," cry, Earnest of our bliss on high, Seal of im-mor-tal-i-ty,—Com-fort-er Divine!

We are sinful: cleanse us, Lord; We are faint: thy strength afford; Lost—until by thee restored, Comforter Divine!
In us, for us, in-ter-cede, And, with voiceless groanings, plead Our un-ut-ter-a-ble need, Comforter Divine!
Search for us the depths of God; Bear us up the star-ry road, To the height of thine a-bode, Comforter Divine!

STEPHENS. C. M.

Choir and Congregation. WM. JONES.

1. Come, Ho - ly Spir - it, heav'n - ly Dove! With all thy quick -'ning pow'rs,

Kin - dle a flame of sa - cred love In these cold hearts of ours.

368 [*Sel. 12. Tune, Stephens.*] WATTS.

1 Come, Holy Spirit, heavenly Dove!
  With all thy quickening powers,
  Kindle a flame of sacred love
  In these cold hearts of ours.

2 Look! how we grovel here below,
  Fond of these trifling toys!
  Our souls can neither fly nor go
  To reach eternal joys.

3 In vain we tune our formal songs;
  In vain we strive to rise;
  Hosannas languish on our tongues,
  And our devotion dies.

4 Dear Lord, and shall we ever live
  At this poor, dying rate—
  Our love so faint, so cold to thee,
  And thine to us so great?

5 Come, Holy Spirit, heavenly Dove!
  With all thy quickening powers;
  Come shed abroad a Savior's love,
  And that shall kindle ours.

369 [*Sel. 88. Tune, Stephens.*] TATE.

1 Come, Holy Ghost, Creator, come,
  Inspire these souls of thine;
  Till every heart which thou hast made
  Be filled with grace divine.

2 Thou art the Comforter, the gift
  Of God, and fire of love;
  The everlasting spring of joy,
  And unction from above.

3 Enlighten our dark souls, till they
  Thy sacred love embrace;
  Assist our minds, by nature frail,
  With thy celestial grace.

4 Teach us the Father to confess,
  And Son, from death revived,
  And thee, with both, O Holy Ghost,
  Who art from both derived.

LEIGHTON. S. M.

Choir and Congregation. Words by Rev. JOSEPH HART.
Music by H. W. GREATOREX.

370 1. Come, Ho - ly Spir - it, come! Let thy bright beams a - rise:
Dis - pel the sor - row

2. Re - vive our droop-ing faith, Our doubts and fears re - move,
And kin - dle in our

from our minds, The dark - ness from our eyes.

breasts the flame Of nev - er - dy - ing love.

3 'T is thine to cleanse the heart,
  To sanctify the soul,
  To pour fresh life in every part,
  And new-create the whole.

4 Come, Holy Spirit, come;
  Our minds from bondage free;
  Then shall we know, and praise, and love,
  The Father, Son, and thee.

Selection 89.—GERMANY SERVICE.—Thou wilt keep him in perfect peace.

Thou wilt keep him in per-fect peace, in per-fect peace, whose mind is stayed on thee, . . on

thee, Thou wilt keep him, thou wilt keep him, thou wilt keep him in
Thou wilt keep him in per-fect peace, . . .

per-fect peace, whose mind is stayed . . on thee. Trust ye in the Lord for-ev-er, . .
stayed on

Lord, . . . trust ye for-ev-er, trust ye in the Lord for-ev - er, for in the Lord Je - ho - vah is ev-er-last-ing

strength, is ev - er - last - ing strength. Thou wilt keep him in per-fect peace, whose mind is stay'd on thee.

Thou wilt keep him in perfect peace, whose mind is stayed on thee, whose mind is stayed on thee.

Selection 89.

Thou wilt keep him in perfect peace, whose mind is | Lord Jehovah is everlasting strength. Thou wilt keep him
stayed on thee. Trust ye in the Lord forever, for in the | in perfect peace, whose mind is stayed on thee.

GERMANY. L. M.

BEETHOVEN.

Choir and Congregation.

1. Oh, hap-py day that fixed my choice On thee, my Sav-ior and my God!

Well may this glow-ing heart re - joice, And tell its rap-tures all a - broad.

371
DODDRIDGE.

1 Oh, happy day that fixed my choice
   On thee, my Savior, and my God!
   Well may this glowing heart rejoice,
   And tell its raptures all abroad.

2 Oh, happy bond, that seals my vows
   To him who merits all my love!
   Let cheerful anthems fill his house,
   While to that sacred shrine I move.

3 'T is done; the great transaction's done:
   I am my Lord's, and he is mine;
   He drew me, and I followed on,
   Charmed to confess the voice divine.

4 High heaven, that hears the solemn vow,
   That vow renewed shall daily hear;
   Till, in life's latest hour, I bow
   And bless in death a bond so dear.

372
WTON.

1 Kindred in Christ! for his dear sake
   A hearty welcome here receive;
   May we together now partake
   The joys which only he can give.

2 May he, by whose kind care we meet,
   Send his good Spirit from above;
   Make our communications sweet,
   And cause our hearts to burn with love.

3 Forgotten be each worldly theme,
   When Christians meet together thus;
   We only wish to speak of him,
   Who lived, and died, and reigns, for us.

4 Thus,—as the moments pass away,—
   We'll love, and wonder, and adore;
   And hasten on the glorious day,
   When we shall meet to part no more.

373
REED.

1 Oh, that I could forever dwell,
   Delighted at the Savior's feet;
   Behold the form I love so well,
   And all his tender words repeat.

2 The world shut out from all my soul,
   And heaven brought in with all its bliss,—
   Oh! is there aught, from pole to pole,
   One moment to compare with this?

3 This is the hidden life I prize—
   A life of penitential love;
   When most my follies I despise,
   And raise my highest thoughts above;

4 When all I am I clearly see,
   And freely own, with deepest shame;
   When the Redeemer's love to me
   Kindles within a deathless flame.

374
STEELE.

1 Thou only Sovereign of my heart,
   My Refuge, my almighty Friend—
   And can my soul from thee depart,
   On whom alone my hopes depend?

2 Eternal life thy words impart;
   On these my fainting spirit lives;
   Here sweeter comforts cheer my heart,
   Than all the round of nature gives.

3 Low at thy feet my soul would lie;
   Here safety dwells, and peace divine;
   Still let me live beneath thine eye,
   For life, eternal life, is thine.

375
HEGINBOTHAM.

1 Sweet peace of conscience, heavenly guest,
   Come, fix thy mansion in my breast;
   Dispel my doubts, my fears control,
   And heal the anguish of my soul.

2 Come, smiling hope, and joy sincere,
   Come, make your constant dwelling here;
   Still let your presence cheer my heart,
   Nor sin compel you to depart.

3 O God of hope and peace divine!
   Make thou these secret pleasures mine;
   Forgive my sins, my fears remove,
   And fill my heart with joy and love.

Selection 90.—ARLINGTON SERVICE.—Whosoever therefore shall be ashamed of me.

Choir. Impressively.

Who-so-ev-er there-fore shall be a-shamed of me, and of my words, of

him al-so shall the Son of Man be a-shamed, of him al-so shall the Son of Man be a-

Cres.
Dim.
shamed when he com-eth in the glo-ry of his Fa-ther, of his Fa-ther, and the ho-ly an-gels.

Who-so-ev-er therefore shall be ashamed of me and of my words, of him al-so shall the

Rit.
Son of Man be a-shamed, of him al-so shall the Son of Man be a-shamed.

Selection 90.

Whosoever therefore shall be ashamed of me and of my words, of him also shall the Son of Man be ashamed when | he cometh in the glory of his Father, and the holy angels, of him also shall the Son of Man be ashamed.

ARLINGTON. C. M.   DR. ARNE.

Choir and Congregation.

I'm not a-shamed to own my Lord, Or to de-fend his cause;

Main-tain the hon - or of his word, The glo-ry of his cross.

376 WATTS.

1 I'm not ashamed to own my Lord,
Or to defend his cause;
Maintain the honor of his word,
The glory of his cross.

2 Jesus, my God!—I know his name—
His name is all my trust;
Nor will he put my soul to shame,
Nor let my hopes be lost.

3 Firm as his throne his promise stands,
And he can well secure
What I've committed to his hands,
Till the decisive hour.

377 DODDRIDGE.

1 Do not I love thee, O my Lord?
Behold my heart, and see;
And turn the dearest idol out
That dares to rival thee.

2 Is not thy name melodious still
To mine attentive ear?
Doth not each pulse with pleasure bound,
My Savior's voice to hear?

3 Thou knowest that I love thee, Lord;
But oh! I long to soar
Far from the sphere of mortal joys,
And learn to love thee more.

378 WATTS.

1 Am I a soldier of the cross,
A follower of the Lamb?
And shall I fear to own his cause,
Or blush to speak his name?

2 Must I be carried to the skies
On flowery beds of ease?
While others fought to win the prize,
And sailed through bloody seas?

3 Are there no foes for me to face?
Must I not stem the flood?
Is this vile world a friend to grace,
To help me on to God?

4 Sure I must fight, if I would reign;
Increase my courage, Lord!
I'll bear the toil, endure the pain,
Supported by thy word.

5 Thy saints, in all this glorious war,
Shall conquer, though they die;
They view the triumph from afar,
And seize it with their eye.

6 When that illustrious day shall rise,
And all thy armies shine
In robes of victory through the skies,
The glory shall be thine.

379 ANON.

1 To whom, my Savior, shall I go,
If I depart from thee?
My guide through all this vale of woe,
And more than all to me.

2 The world reject thy gentle reign,
And pay thy death with scorn;
Oh! they could plait thy crown again,
And sharpen every thorn.

3 But I have felt thy dying love
Breathe gently through my heart,
To whisper hope of joys above—
And can we ever part?

4 Ah! no, with thee I'll walk below,
My journey to the grave:
To whom, my Savior, shall I go,
When only thou canst save?

380 STEELE.

1 Dear Savior, let thy glory shine,
And fill thy dwellings here,
Till life, and love, and joy divine
A heaven on earth appear.

2 Then shall our hearts enraptured say,
Come, great Redeemer! come,
And bring the bright, the glorious day,
That calls thy children home.

Selection 91.—STEPHENS SERVICE, No. 2.—Come and hear, all ye that fear God.

Come and hear, all ye that fear God, and I will de-clare what he hath done for my soul. I

cried un - to him with my voice, . . and he was ex - tolled with my tongue.

Bless - ed be God who hath not turn'd a-way my prayer, nor his mer - cy from me, his mer - cy from me.

Come and hear, all ye that fear God, and I will de-clare what he hath done, what he hath done for my soul.

Come and hear, all ye that fear God, and I will de-clare what he hath done, what he hath done for my soul.

Selection 91.

Come and hear, all ye that fear God, and I will declare what he hath done for my soul. I cried unto him with my voice, and he was extolled with my tongue. Blessed be God, who hath not turned away my prayer, nor his mercy from me. Come and hear, all ye that fear God, and I will declare what he hath done for my soul.

STEPHENS. C. M.

Choir and Congregation.

WM. JONES.

1. Sal - va - tion! oh, the joy - ful sound! 'Tis plea - sure to our ears;

A sov - 'reign balm for ev - 'ry wound, A cor - dial for our fears.

381 WATTS.

1 Salvation!—oh, the joyful sound!
'Tis pleasure to our ears;
A sovereign balm for every wound,
A cordial for our fears.

2 Buried in sorrow and in sin,
At hell's dark door we lay;—
But we arise by grace divine,
To see a heavenly day.

3 Salvation!—let the echo fly
The spacious earth around;
While all the armies of the sky
Conspire to raise the sound.

382 NEEDHAM.

1 Oh, how divine, how sweet the joy,
When but one sinner turns,
And, with an humble, broken heart,
His sins and errors mourns.

2 Pleased with the news, the saints below,
In songs their tongues employ;
Beyond the skies the tidings go,
And heaven is filled with joy.

3 Nor angels can their joys contain,
But kindle with new fire;—
"The sinner lost is found," they sing,
And strike the sounding lyre.

383 NEWTON.

1 Amazing grace! how sweet the sound
That saved a wretch like me!
I once was lost, but now am found—
Was blind, but now I see.

2 'Twas grace that taught my heart to fear,
And grace my fears relieved;
How precious did that grace appear,
The hour I first believed.

3 Through many dangers, toils, and snares,
I have already come;
'Tis grace hath brought me safe thus far,
And grace will lead me home.

4 Yes—when this flesh and heart shall fail,
And mortal life shall cease,
I shall possess, within the vail,
A life of joy and peace.

384 WATTS.

1 What shall I render to my God,
For all his kindness shown?
My feet shall visit thine abode,
My songs address thy throne.

2 Among the saints that fill thy house,
My offering shall be paid;
There shall my zeal perform the vows
My soul in anguish made.

3 How much is mercy thy delight,
Thou ever-blessed God!
How dear thy servants in thy sight—
How precious is their blood!

4 How happy all thy servants are!
How great thy grace to me!
My life, which thou hast made thy care,
Lord! I devote to thee.

385 DODDRIDGE.

1 Sing, all ye ransomed of the Lord,
Your great Deliverer sing:
Ye pilgrims, now for Zion bound,
Be joyful in your King.

2 His hand divine shall lead you on,
Through all the blissful road;
Till to the sacred mount you rise,
And see your gracious God.

3 Bright garlands of immortal joy
Shall bloom on every head;
While sorrow, sighing, and distress,
Like shadows, all are fled.

4 March on in your Redeemer's strength;
Pursue his footsteps still;
And let the prospect cheer your eye
While laboring up the hill.

Selection 92.—DOWNS SERVICE.—The Lord is the portion of mine inheritance.

G. F. R.

Selection 92.

The Lord is the portion of mine inheritance, and of my cup. | The lines are fallen unto me in pleasant places: yea, I have a goodly heritage. Thou, O Lord, art my portion.

DOWNS. C. M.

Choir and Congregation.

Dr. L. Mason.

1. Thou art my por - tion, O my God! Soon as I know thy way,

My heart makes haste t' o - bey thy word, And suf - fers no de - lay.

386 WATTS.

1 Thou art my portion, O my God;
   Soon as I know thy way,
   My heart makes haste t' obey thy word,
   And suffers no delay.

2 I choose the path of heavenly truth,
   And glory in my choice;
   Not all the riches of the earth
   Could make me so rejoice.

3 The testimonies of thy grace
   I set before mine eyes;
   Thence I derive my daily strength,
   And there my comfort lies.

4 Now I am thine—forever thine—
   Oh, save thy servant, Lord!
   Thou art my shield, my hiding-place;
   My hope is in thy word.

387 BEDDOME.

1 If God is mine, then present things
   And things to come are mine;
   Yea, Christ, his word, and Spirit too,
   And glory all divine.

2 If he is mine, then from his love
   He every trouble sends;
   All things are working for my good,
   And bliss his rod attends.

3 If he is mine, let friends forsake,
   Let wealth and honor flee;
   Sure be who giveth me himself,
   Is more than these to me.

4 Oh! tell me, Lord, that thou art mine;
   What can I wish beside?
   My soul shall at the fountain live,
   When all the streams are dried.

388 ADDISON.

1 When all thy mercies, O my God!
   My rising soul surveys,
   Transported with the view, I'm lost
   In wonder, love, and praise.

2 Ten thousand thousand precious gifts
   My daily thanks employ;
   Nor is the least a cheerful heart,
   That tastes those gifts with joy.

3 Through every period of my life,
   Thy goodness I'll pursue;
   And after death, in distant worlds,
   The glorious theme renew.

4 Through all eternity, to thee
   A joyful song I'll raise:
   But oh! eternity's too short
   To utter all thy praise!

389 RYLAND.

1 O Lord! I would delight in thee,
   And on thy care depend;
   To thee in every trouble flee,
   My best, my only Friend.

2 When all created streams are dried,
   Thy fullness is the same;
   May I with this be satisfied,
   And glory in thy name.

3 No good in creatures can be found,
   But may be found in thee;
   I must have all things, and abound,
   While thou art God to me.

390 WATTS.

1 Unshaken as the sacred hill,
   And fixed as mountains be,
   Firm as a rock the soul shall rest,
   That leans, O Lord! on thee.

2 Not walls, nor hills, could guard so well,
   Old Salem's happy ground,
   As those eternal arms of love,
   That every saint surround.

3 Deal gently, Lord! with souls sincere,
   And lead them safely on,
   To the bright gates of Paradise,
   Where Christ, their Lord, is gone.

Selection 93.—BOND SERVICE.—If ye endure chastening.

If ye en-dure chast'ning, God dealeth with you as with sons; for whom the Lord lov - eth, he

chas - ten - eth. The Spir- it it - self bear-eth wit - ness with our spir - it, that we are the chil-dren of

God. If ye endure chast'ning, God dealeth with you as with sons; for ye have not received the

spir - it of bond-age a - gain to fear, a - gain to fear, but ye have re-

ceived the spir - it of a - dop - tion, where - by we cry, Ab - ba, Fa - ther.

Selection 93.

If ye endure chastening, God dealeth with you as with sons; for whom the Lord loveth, he chasteneth. The Spirit itself beareth witness with our spirit, that we are | the children of God. For ye have not received the spirit of bondage again to fear, but ye have received the spirit of adoption, whereby we cry, Abba, Father.

BOND. C. M.

Choir and Congregation.   GEO. F. ROOT.

1. My God, my Fa - ther, bliss - ful name! Oh, may I call thee mine?

May I with sweet as - sur - ance claim A por - tion so di - vine.

391   STEELE.

1 My God, my Father, blissful name!
   Oh, may I call thee mine?
   May I with sweet assurance claim
   A portion so divine?

2 Whate'er thy providence denies
   I calmly would resign,
   For thou art good and just and wise:
   Oh, bend my will to thine!

3 Whate'er thy sacred will ordains,
   Oh, give me strength to bear!
   And let me know my Father reigns,
   And trust his tender care.

4 Thy sovereign ways are all unknown
   To my weak, erring sight:
   Yet let my soul adoring own
   That all thy ways are right.

392   LYTE.

1 There is a safe and secret place
   Beneath thy wings divine;
   Reserved for all the heirs of grace:
   Oh, be that refuge mine!

2 The least and feeblest there may bide,
   Uninjured and unawed;
   While thousands fall on every side,
   He rests secure in God.

3 He feeds in pastures large and fair,
   Of love and truth divine;
   O child of God, O glory's heir!
   How rich a lot is thine!

4 A hand almighty to defend,
   An ear for every call,
   An honored life, a peaceful end,
   And heaven to crown it all!

393   WATTS.

1 Why should the children of a King
   Go mourning all their days?
   Great Comforter! descend and bring
   Some tokens of thy grace.

2 Dost thou not dwell in all the saints,
   And seal the heirs of heaven?
   When wilt thou banish my complaints,
   And show my sins forgiven?

3 Assure my conscience of her part
   In the Redeemer's blood;
   And bear thy witness with my heart
   That I am born of God.

4 Thou art the earnest of his love,
   The pledge of joys to come;
   And thy soft wings, celestial Dove!
   Will safe convey me home.

394   C. WESLEY.

1 If thou impart thyself to me,
   No other good I need!
   If thou, the Son, shalt make me free,
   I shall be free indeed.

2 I can not rest till in thy blood
   I full redemption have;
   But thou, through whom I come to God,
   Canst to the utmost save.

3 I, too, with thee, shall walk in white:
   With all thy saints shall prove
   What is the length and breadth and height
   And depth of perfect love.

395   DODDRIDGE.

1 My Father, God! how sweet the sound,
   How tender and how dear!
   Not all the melody of heaven
   Could so delight the ear.

2 Come, sacred Spirit, seal the name
   On my expanding heart;
   And show, that in Jehovah's grace
   I share a filial part.

3 Cheered by a signal so divine,
   Unwavering I believe;
   My spirit Abba, Father! cries,
   Nor can the sign deceive.

Selection 94.—EVAN SERVICE.—A new commandment I give unto you.

A new com-mand-ment I give un-to you, that ye love one an-oth-er, that ye love one an-

oth-er, as I have lov-ed you, as I have lov-ed you, that ye al-so love one an-oth-er.

Be-hold how good and how pleas-ant it is for breth-ren to dwell to-geth-er in

u-ni-ty! Be-hold how good, how good and how pleasant, for breth-ren to dwell in u-ni-ty.

Selection 94.

A new commandment I give unto you, that ye love one another. As I have loved you, that ye also love one another. | Behold, how good and how pleasant it is for brethren to dwell together in unity.

EVAN. C. M.

Arr. by Dr. Mason.

Choir and Congregation.

1. How sweet, how heav'n-ly is the sight, When those who love the Lord

In one an-oth-er's peace de-light, And so ful-fill his word.

---

396 SWAIN.

1 How sweet, how heavenly is the sight,
  When those who love the Lord
In one another's peace delight,
  And so fulfill his word!

2 When each can feel his brother's sigh,
  And with him bear a part!
When sorrow flows from eye to eye,
  And joy from heart to heart!

3 When, free from envy, scorn and pride,
  Our wishes all above,
Each can his brother's failings hide,
  And show a brother's love!

4 Love is the golden chain that binds
  The happy souls above;
And he's an heir of heaven who finds
  His bosom glow with love.

397 BURDER.

1 Come, ye that know and fear the Lord,
  And raise your thoughts above:
Let every heart and voice accord,
  To sing that "God is love."

2 This precious truth his word declares,
  And all his mercies prove;
Jesus, the gift of gifts, appears,
  To show that "God is love."

3 Behold his patience, bearing long
  With those who from him rove;
Till mighty grace their hearts subdues,
  To teach them—"God is love."

4 Oh, may we all, while here below,
  This best of blessings prove;
Till warmer hearts, in brighter worlds,
  Proclaim that "God is love."

398 C. WESLEY.

1 Let saints below in concert sing
  With those to glory gone;
For all the servants of our King
  In earth and heaven are one.

2 One family—we dwell in him—
  One church above, beneath,
Though now divided by the stream,—
  The narrow stream of death;—

3 One army of the living God,
  To his command we bow;
Part of the host have crossed the flood,
  And part are crossing now.

4 Lord Jesus! be our constant guide:
  And, when the word is given,
Bid death's cold flood its waves divide,
  And land us safe in heaven.

399 C. WESLEY.

1 Bless'd be the dear uniting love,
  That will not let us part;
Though here we may far off remove—
  We still are one in heart.

2 Joined in one Spirit to our head,
  Where he appoints, we go;
And still in Jesus' footsteps tread,
  And show his praise below.

3 Partakers of the Savior's grace,
  The same in mind and heart—
Nor joy, nor grief, nor time, nor place,
  Nor life, nor death, can part.

4 But let us hasten to the day
  Which shall our flesh restore,
When death shall all be done away,
  And we shall part no more.

400 MONTGOMERY.

1 Come in, thou blessed of the Lord,
  Stranger nor foe art thou;
We welcome thee with warm accord,
  Our friend, our brother, now.

2 Come with us,—we will do thee good,
  As God to us hath done;
Stand but in him, as those have stood
  Whose faith the victory won.

Selection 95.—VALENTIA SERVICE.--The Lord is my Shepherd.

G. F. R.

The Lord is my Shep-herd; I shall not want. He mak-eth me to lie down in green pas-tures: he

leadeth me, he lead-eth me be-side the still wa-ters, he re-stor-eth my soul, he re-stor-eth my

soul: he lead-eth me in the paths of right-eousness for his name's sake, for his name's sake.

VALENTIA. C. M.

Choir and Congregation.

Words from TATE & BRADY's Coll.
Music from Dr. MASON's arrangement.

401

1. The Lord him-self, the might-y Lord, Vouch-safes to be my guide; The Shep-herd by whose
2. In ten-der grass he makes me feed, And gen-tly there re-pose; Then leads me to cool

con-stant care   My wants are all sup-plied.
shades, and where   Re-fresh-ing wa-ter flows.

3 He does my wandering soul reclaim,
    And, to his endless praise,
  Instruct with humble zeal to walk
    In his most righteous ways.

4 I pass the gloomy vale of death,
    From fear and danger free;
  For there his aiding rod and staff
    Defend and comfort me.

WILLIAMS. C. M. Double.

Choir and Congregation.

Arr. by G. F. R.

I heard the voice of Je - sus say, "Come un - to me and rest;
Lay down, thou wea - ry one, lay down Thy head up-on my breast!" I came to Je-sus as I was,

Wea-ry, and worn, and sad, I found in him a rest - ing-place, And he hath made me glad.

(For 1st verse see tune.)

402
BONAR.

2 I heard the voice of Jesus say,—
"Behold, I freely give
The living water; thirsty one,
Stoop down, and drink, and live!"
I came to Jesus, and I drank
Of that life-giving stream;
My thirst was quenched, my soul revived,
And now I live in him.

3 I heard the voice of Jesus say,—
"I am this dark world's light;
Look unto me, thy morn shall rise
And all thy day be bright!"
I looked to Jesus, and I found
In him my Star, my Sun;
And in that light of life I'll walk,
Till all my journey's done.

(Sel. 95. The Lord is my Shepherd.)

403
WATTS.

1 My Shepherd will supply my need,
Jehovah is his name;
In pastures fresh he makes me feed,
Beside the living stream.
He brings my wandering spirit back,
When I forsake his ways;
And leads me, for his mercy's sake,
In paths of truth and grace.

13

2 When I walk through the shades of death,
Thy presence is my stay;
A word of thy supporting breath
Drives all my fears away.
Thy hand, in sight of all my foes,
Doth still my table spread;
My cup with blessings overflows,
Thine oil anoints my head.

3 The sure provisions of my God
Attend me all my days;
Oh, may thy house be mine abode,
And all my works be praise;
There would I find a settled rest,
While others go and come,—
No more a stranger, or a guest,
But like a child at home.

404
LYNCH.

1 O, where is he that trod the sea,
O, where is he that spake,
And demons from their victims flee,
The dead their slumbers break;
The palsied rise in freedom strong,
The dumb men talk and sing,
And from blind eyes, benighted long,
Bright beams of morning spring.

2 O, where is he that trod the sea,
O, where is he that spake,
And dark waves, rolling heavily,
A glassy smoothness take;
And lepers, whose own flesh has been,
A solitary grave,
See with amaze that they are clean,
And cry, 'Tis he can save.

3 O, where is he that trod the sea,
'Tis only he can save;
To thousands hungering wearily,
A wondrous meal he gave:
Full soon, celestially fed,
Their mystic fare they take;
'T was springtide when he blest the bread,
And harvest when he brake.

4 O, where is he that trod the sea,
My soul, the Lord is here:
Let all thy fears be hushed in thee;
To leap, to look, to hear,
Be thine : thy needs he'll satisfy:
Art thou diseased, or dumb?
Or dost thou in thy hunger cry?
"I come," saith Christ, "I come."

Selection 96.—GORTON SERVICE.—The Lord is my Shepherd.

WM. MASON.

The Lord is my Shep-herd, I shall not want. He mak-eth me to lie down in

green pas-tures, he lead-eth me, he lead-eth me be-side the still wa - ters: he re-

re - stor - eth my

stor-eth, re - stor-eth my soul, he re - stor - eth my soul, he re - stor - - - eth my

he re - stor - eth   re - stor - eth my

soul; he lead-eth me, he lead-eth me in the   in the paths of right-eous-ness, in the

paths . . .

paths . . .

paths of right-eous - ness, for his name's sake, for his name's . . . . . sake.

Selection 96.

The Lord is my Shepherd, I shall not want. He maketh me to lie down in green pastures, he leadeth me beside the | still waters: he restoreth my soul; he leadeth me in the paths of righteousness for his name's sake.

GORTON. S. M.

Choir and Congregation.   Arr. by Dr. L. Mason.

1. While my Re-deem-er's near, My Shep-herd and my Guide,

I bid fare-well to ev-'ry fear, My wants are all sup-plied.

---

405   Steele.

1 While my Redeemer's near,
My Shepherd and my guide,
I bid farewell to every fear,
My wants are all supplied.

2 To ever fragrant meads,
Where rich abundance grows,
His gracious hand indulgent leads,
And guards my sweet repose.

3 Dear Shepherd, if I stray,
My wand'ring feet restore;
To thy fair pastures guide my way,
And let me rove no more.

406   Watts.

1 The Lord my Shepherd is,
I shall be well supplied;
Since he is mine, and I am his,
What can I want beside?

2 He leads me to the place
Where heavenly pasture grows,
Where living waters gently pass,
And full salvation flows.

3 If e'er I go astray,
He doth my soul reclaim;
And guides me in his own right way,
For his most holy name.

---

4 While he affords his aid,
I can not yield to fear;
Tho' I should walk through death's dark shade,
My Shepherd's with me there.

5 In spite of all my foes,
Thou dost my table spread;
My cup with blessings overflows,
And joy exalts my head.

6 The bounties of thy love
Shall crown my future days;
Nor from thy house will I remove,
Nor cease to speak thy praise.

407   C. Wesley.

1 Thou very present Aid
In suffering and distress,
The mind which still on thee is stayed,
Is kept in perfect peace.

2 The soul by faith reclined
On the Redeemer's breast,
'Mid raging storms, exults to find
An everlasting rest.

3 Sorrow and fear are gone,
Whene'er thy face appears;
It stills the sighing orphan's moan,
And dries the widow's tears.

---

4 It hallows every cross;
It sweetly comforts me;
Makes me forget my every loss,
And find my all in thee.

5 Jesus, to whom I fly,
Doth all my wishes fill;
What though created streams are dry?
I have the fountain still.

6 Stripped of each earthly friend,
I find them all in one,
And peace and joy which never end,
And heaven, in Christ, begun.

408   Keble.

1 Blest are the pure in heart,
For they shall see their God;
The secret of the Lord is theirs;
Their soul is Christ's abode.

2 He to the lowly soul
Doth still himself impart,
And for his dwelling, and his throne,
Chooseth the pure in heart.

3 Lord! we thy presence seek;
May ours this blessing be;
Oh, give the pure and lowly heart,—
A temple meet for thee.

Selection 97.—GOLDEN HILL SERVICE.—If ye keep my commandments.

G. F. R.

If ye keep my com-mand-ments ye shall a-bide in my love. I am the vine, ye are the branches.

He that a - bid-eth in me, and I in him, the same bring-eth forth much fruit, the same bringeth forth much

fruit. . . . If ye keep my commandments,

fruit. If ye keep my commandments, ye shall a-bide in my love, ye shall a-bide, shall a-bide in my love.

GOLDEN HILL. S. M.

Words by Dr. DODDRIDGE.
WESTERN TUNE.

Choir and Congregation.

409
1. Dear Sav - ior, we are thine, By ev - er - last - ing bands; Our hearts, our souls, we
2. To thee we still would cleave With ev - er - grow - ing zeal; If mil - lions tempt us

would re - sign En - tire - ly to thy hands,
Christ to leave, Oh, let them ne'er pre - vail!

3 Thy Spirit shall unite
　Our souls to thee, our Head;
　Shall form in us thine image bright,
　And teach thy paths to tread.

4 Since Christ and we are one,
　Why should we doubt or fear?
　If he in heaven has fixed his throne,
　He 'll fix his members there.

(Sel. 103. Fear not, little flock. Tune, Olmutz, p. 212.)

410 [S. M.] GERHARDT.

1 Give to the winds thy fears;
Hope, and be undismayed;
God hears thy sighs and counts thy tears;
God shall lift up thy head.

2 Through waves, and clouds, and storms,
He gently clears thy way;
Wait thou his time; so shall this night
Soon end in joyous day.

3 Far, far above thy thought
His counsel shall appear,
When fully he the work hath wrought,
That caused thy needless fear.

4 What though thou rulest not!
Yet heaven, and earth, and hell
Proclaim, God sitteth on the throne,
And ruleth all things well.

(Sel. 77. They wandered in the wilderness. Tune, Temple, p. 23.)

411 [7s.] JOHNSON.

Onward, Christian, though the region
Where thou art be drear and lone;
God has set a guarded legion
Very near thee; press thou on.

2 Listen, Christian; their hosanna
Rolleth o'er thee: "God is love,"
Write upon thy red-cross banner,
"Upward ever; heaven's above."

3 Be this world the wiser, stronger,
For thy life of pain and peace,
While it needs thee: oh! no longer
Pray thou for thy quick release.

4 Pray thou, Christian, daily rather,
That thou be a faithful son;
By the prayer of Jesus, "Father,
Not my will, but thine, be done."

(Sel. 7. The Lord is good to all. Tune, Autumn, p. 157)

412 [8s. and 7s.] BOWRING.

1 God is love; his mercy brightens
All the path in which we rove;
Bliss he wakes, and woe he lightens;
God is wisdom, God is love.

2 Chance and change are busy ever;
Man decays, and ages move;
But his mercy waneth never;
God is wisdom, God is love.

3 Ev'n the hour that darkest seemeth,
Will his changeless goodness prove;
From the gloom his brightness streameth,
God is wisdom, God is love.

4 He with earthly cares entwineth
Hope and comfort from above:
Everywhere his glory shineth;
God is wisdom, God is love.

(Sel. 77. They wandered in the wilderness. Tune, Dennis, p. 126.)

413 [S. M.] ANON.

1 The people of the Lord
Are on their way to heaven;
There their their great reward;
The prize will there be given.

2 'Tis conflict here below;
'Tis triumph there, and peace:
On earth we wrestle with the foe;
In heaven our conflicts cease.

3 'Tis gloom and darkness here;
'Tis light and joy above;
There all is pure, and all is clear;
There all is peace and love.

4 Then let us joyful sing;
The conflict is not long:
We hope in heaven to praise our King
In one eternal song.

(Sel. 64. They that wait upon the Lord. Tune, Holley, p. 279.)

414 [7s.] LLOYD.

1 Wait, my soul, upon the Lord,
To his gracious promise flee,
Laying hold upon his word,
"As thy days thy strength shall be."

2 If the sorrows of thy case
Seem peculiar still to thee,
God has promised needful grace,
"As thy days thy strength shall be."

3 Days of trial, days of grief,
In succession thou mayst see;
This is still thy sweet relief,
"As thy days thy strength shall be."

4 Rock of Ages, I'm secure,
With thy promise full and free;
Faithful, positive, and sure—
"As thy days thy strength shall be."

(Tune, St. Thomas, p. 51)

415 [S. M.] C. WESLEY.

1 Soldiers of Christ, arise,
And gird your armor on,
Strong in the strength which God supplies,
Through his eternal Son:

2 Strong in the Lord of hosts,
And in his mighty power,
Who in the strength of Jesus trusts,
Is more than conqueror.

3 Stand, then, in his great might,
With all his strength endued,
And take, to arm you for the fight,
The panoply of God:

4 That, having all things done,
And all your conflicts past,
You may o'ercome through Christ alone,
And stand complete at last.

(Sel. 103. Fear not, little flock. Tune, Olmutz, p. 212.)

416 [S. M.] SWAIN.

1 I stand on Zion's mount,
And view my starry crown;
No power on earth my hope can shake,
Nor hell can thrust me down.

2 The lofty hills and towers,
That lift their heads on high,
Shall all be leveled low in dust—
Their very names shall die.

3 The vaulted heavens shall fall,
Built by Jehovah's hands;
But firmer than the heavens, the Rock
Of my salvation stands!

(Sel. 22. Great is the Lord. Tune, Leighton, p. 177.)

417 [S. M.] GALLAGHER.

1 The sun himself shall fade,
The starry worlds shall fall;
Yet through a vast eternity,
Shall God be all in all.

2 Though now his ways are dark,
Concealed from mortal sight,
His counsels are divinely wise,
And all his judgments right.

3 In God my trust shall stand,
While waves of sorrow roll;
In life or death his name shall be
The refuge of my soul.

Selection 98.—BOYLSTON SERVICE, No. 2.—If ye keep my commandments.

G. F. R.

If ye keep my com-mand-ments, ye shall a - bide in my love, ye shall a - bide in my love.

This is my com-mand-ment, this is my com-mand-ment: That ye love one an - oth - er, as

I have lov - ed you, that ye love one an - oth - er, as I have lov - ed you.

BOYLSTON. S. M.

Words by Rev. J. FAWCETT.
Music by Dr. L. MASON.

Choir and Congregation.

418
1. Blest be the tie that binds Our hearts in Chris - tian love: The fel - low-ship of kin - dred minds
2. Be - fore our Fa - ther's throne We pour our ar - dent prayers; Our fears, our hopes, our aims are one,

Is like to that a - bove.
Our com - forts and our cares.

3 We share our mutual woes,
　Our mutual burdens bear;
And often for each other flows
　The sympathizing tear.

4 When we asunder part
　It gives us inward pain;
But we shall still be joined in heart,
　And hope to meet again.

5 This glorious hope revives
　Our courage by the way;
While each in expectation lives,
　And longs to see the day.

6 From sorrow, toil, and pain,
　And sin, we shall be free,
And perfect love and friendship reign
　Through all eternity.

(Sel. 90. Whosoever therefore shall be ashamed
of me. Tune, Rockingham, p 39.)

419   [L. M.]   GRIGG.

1 Jesus! and shall it ever be,
  A mortal man ashamed of thee?
  Ashamed of thee, whom angels praise,
  Whose glories shine through endless days?

2 Ashamed of Jesus! that dear Friend
  On whom my hopes of heaven depend!
  No; when I blush—be this my shame,
  That I no more revere his name.

3 Ashamed of Jesus! yes, I may,
  When I've no guilt to wash away;
  No tear to wipe, no good to crave,
  No fear to quell, no soul to save.

4 Till then—nor is my boasting vain—
  Till then I boast a Savior slain!
  And oh, may this my glory be,
  That Christ is not ashamed of me!

(Sel. 41. And they shall call his name Immanuel. Tune, Bemerton, p. 139; or Bond, p. 73.)

420   [C. M.]   NEWTON.

1 How sweet the name of Jesus sounds
  In a believer's ear!
  It soothes his sorrows, heals his wounds,
  And drives away his fear.

2 It makes the wounded spirit whole,
  And calms the troubled breast;
  'Tis manna to the hungry soul,
  And to the weary, rest.

3 Jesus! my Shepherd, Guardian, Friend,
  My Prophet, Priest, and King;
  My Lord, my Life, my Way, my End,
  Accept the praise I bring.

(Sel. 41. And they shall call his name Immanuel. Tune, Bond, p. 73.)

421   [C. M]   DODDRIDGE.

1 Jesus! I love thy charming name,
  'Tis music to mine ear;
  Fain would I sound it out so loud,
  That earth and heaven should hear.

2 All my capacious powers can wish,
  In thee doth richly meet;
  Not to mine eyes is light so dear,
  Nor friendship half so sweet.

3 Thy grace still dwells upon my heart,
  And sheds its fragrance there;—
  The noblest balm of all its wounds,
  The cordial of its care.

(Sel. 20. I will lift up mine eyes; or Sel. 24. Be
joyful in God. Tune, Stephens, p. 11.)

422   [C. M]   WATTS.

1 My God! the spring of all my joys,
  The life of my delights,
  The glory of my brightest days,
  And comfort of my nights!

2 In darkest shades if he appear,
  My dawning is begun:
  He is my soul's sweet morning star,
  And he my rising sun.

3 The opening heavens around me shine
  With beams of sacred bliss,
  While Jesus shows his love is mine,
  And whispers, I am his!

4 My soul would leave this heavy clay,
  At that transporting word;
  Run up with joy the shining way,
  To meet my dearest Lord.

5 Fearless of hell and ghastly death,
  I'd break through every foe;
  The wings of love and arms of faith
  Should bear me conqueror through.

(Sel. 79. Thou art my hiding place. Tune, Dennis, p. 126.)

423   [S. M.]   LYTE.

1 My spirit on thy care,
  Blest Savior, I recline,
  Thou wilt not leave me to despair,
  For thou art love divine.

2 Whate'er events betide,
  Thy will they all perform;
  Safe in thy breast my head I hide,
  Not fear the coming storm.

3 Let good or ill befall,
  It must be good for me,—
  Secure of having thee in all,
  Of having all in thee.

(Sel. 85. In the time of trouble he shall hide me. Tune, Boylston, p. 145.)

424   [S. M.]   WATTS.

1 My God, my Life, my Love,
  To thee, to thee I call;
  I can not live, if thou remove,
  For thou art all in all.

2 Not all the harps above
  Can make a heavenly place,
  If God his residence remove,
  Or but conceal his face.

3 Nor earth, nor all the sky,
  Can one delight afford—
  No, not a drop of real joy
  Without thy presence, Lord.

4 Thou art the sea of love,
  Where all my pleasures roll;
  The circle where my passions move,
  And centre of my soul.

(Sel. 89. Thou wilt keep him in perfect peace.
Tune, Germany, p. 181.)

(Repeat first half of tune.)

425   [L. M. 6 lines.]   C. WESLEY.

1 Jesus, thou source of calm repose,
  All fullness dwells in thee divine;
  Our strength, to quell the proudest foes;
  Our light, in deepest gloom to shine;
  Thou art our fortress, strength and tower,
  Our trust and portion, evermore.

2 Jesus, our Comforter thou art,
  Our rest in toil, our ease in pain;
  The balm to heal each broken heart,
  In storms our peace, in loss our gain;
  Our joy, beneath the worldling's frown;
  In shame, our glory and our crown;—

3 In want, our plentiful supply;
  In weakness, our almighty power;
  In bonds, our perfect liberty;
  Our refuge in temptation's hour;
  Our comfort, amidst grief and thrall;
  Our life in death; our all in all.

(Tune, Germany, p. 181.)

(Repeat first half of tune.)

426   [L. M. 6 lines]   GRANT.

1 When, streaming from the eastern skies,
  The morning light salutes mine eyes,
  O Sun of righteousness divine,
  On me with beams of mercy shine!
  Oh! chase the clouds of guilt away,
  And turn my darkness into day.

2 When each day's scenes and labors close,
  And wearied nature seeks repose,
  With pardoning mercy richly blest,
  Guard me, my Savior, while I rest;
  And, as each morning sun shall rise,
  Oh, lead me onward to the skies!

Selection 99.—HENDON SERVICE, No. 2.—My sheep hear my voice.

Choir. Andante. Cres. G. F. R.

My sheep hear my voice, and I know them, and they fol-low me; and I give un-to

f *m* *mf*

them e-ter-nal life, I give un-to them e-ter-nal life; and they shall nev-er

Cres. Rall.

per-ish, they shall nev-er per-ish, nei-ther shall an-y pluck them out of my hand.

pp Cres. *p*

My sheep hear my voice, and I know them, and they fol-low me; and I give un-to

m *p* *f* e-ter—nal life.

them e-ter-nal life, and I give un-to them, I give e-ter-nal life.

e-ter—nal life.

Selection 99.

My sheep hear my voice, and I know them, and they follow me; and I give unto them eternal life; and they shall never | perish, neither shall any pluck them out of my hand. My sheep hear my voice, and I know them, and they follow me.

HENDON. 7s.

Choir and Congregation.   Arr. by Dr. L. Mason.

1. To thy pas-tures, fair and large, Heavenly Shepherd, lead thy charge; And my couch with

tend'rest care, 'Mid the spring-ing grass pre - pare, Mid the springing grass pre - pare.

427   HAMMOND.

1 To thy pastures fair and large,
  Heavenly Shepherd, lead thy charge,
  And my couch, with tenderest care,
  'Mid the springing grass prepare.

2 When I faint with summer's heat,
  Thou shalt guide my weary feet,
  To the streams that, still and slow,
  Through the verdant meadows flow.

3 Safe the dreary vale I tread,
  By the shades of death o'erspread,
  With thy rod and staff supplied,
  This my guard—and that my guide.

4 Constant to my latest end,
  Thou my footsteps shalt attend;
  And shalt bid thy hallowed dome
  Yield me an eternal home.

428   HILL.

1 Cast thy burden on the Lord,
  Only lean upon his word;
  Thou wilt soon have cause to bless,
  His unchanging faithfulness.

2 He sustains thee by his hand,
  He enables thee to stand;
  Those, whom Jesus once hath loved,
  From his grace are never moved.

3 Heaven and earth may pass away,
  God's free grace shall not decay;
  He hath promised to fulfill
  All the pleasure of his will.

4 Jesus! guardian of thy flock,
  Be thyself our constant rock!
  Make us by thy powerful hand,
  Firm as Zion's mountain stand.

(For this hymn repeat first half of tune.)

429   AXON.

1 Shepherd, with thy tenderest love,
  Guide me to thy fold above;
  Let me hear thy gentle voice;
  More and more in thee rejoice;
  From thy fullness grace receive,
  Ever in thy Spirit live.

2 Filled by thee my cup o'erflows,
  For thy love no limit knows:
  Guardian angels, ever nigh,
  Lead and draw my soul on high;
  Constant to my latest end,
  Thou my footsteps wilt attend.

3 Jesus, with thy presence blest
  Death is life, and labor rest;
  Guide me while I draw my breath,
  Guard me through the gate of death,
  And at last, oh, let me stand,
  With the sheep at thy right hand.

430   MONTGOMERY.

1 To thy temple we repair—
  Lord, we love to worship there,
  When within the vail we meet
  Thee upon the mercy-seat.

2 While thy glorious name is sung,
  Tune our lips—unloose our tongue;
  Then our joyful souls shall bless
  Thee, the Lord our Righteousness.

3 While thy word is heard with awe,
  While we tremble at thy law,
  Let thy gospel's wondrous love
  Every doubt and fear remove.

4 From thy house when we return,
  Let our hearts within us burn,
  That at evening we may say—
  " We have walked with God to-day."

Selection 100.—PLEYEL'S HYMN SERVICE.—And the ransomed of the Lord shall return.

Selection 100.

And the ransomed of the Lord shall return and come to Zion with songs and everlasting joy upon their heads. They shall obtain joy and gladness, and sorrow and sighing shall flee away. They shall come with songs and everlasting joy upon their heads.

PLEYEL'S HYMN. 7s.

Choir and Congregation.

J. PLEYEL.

1. Chil - dren of the heav'n - ly King, As ye jour - ney, sweet - ly sing;

Sing your Sav - ior's wor - thy praise, Glo - rious in his works and ways.

---

431 CENNICK.

1 Children of the heavenly King,
   As ye journey, sweetly sing;
   Sing your Savior's worthy praise,
   Glorious in his works and ways.

2 Ye are traveling home to God
   In the way the fathers trod;
   They are happy now, and ye
   Soon their happiness shall see.

3 Shout, ye little flock, and blest!
   You on Jesus' throne shall rest;
   There your seat is now prepared;
   There your kingdom and reward.

4 Lord, submissive make us go,
   Gladly leaving all below;
   Only thou our Leader be,
   And we still will follow thee.

432 MADAN.

1 Now begin the heavenly theme,
   Sing aloud in Jesus' name;
   Ye, who his salvation prove,
   Triumph in redeeming love.

2 Ye, who see the Father's grace
   Beaming in the Savior's face,
   As to Canaan on ye move,
   Praise, and bless redeeming love.

3 Mourning souls! dry up your tears;
   Banish all your sinful fears;
   See your guilt and curse remove,—
   Canceled by redeeming love.

4 When his Spirit leads us home,
   When we to his glory come,
   We shall all the fullness prove
   Of the Lord's redeeming love.

433 EVANS.

1 Faint not, Christian! though the road,
   Leading to thy blest abode,
   Darksome be, and dangerous too,
   Christ thy Guide will bring thee through.

2 Faint not, Christian! though the world
   Has its hostile flag unfurled;
   Hold the cross of Jesus fast,
   Thou shalt overcome at last.

3 Faint not, Christian! though within
   There's a heart so prone to sin;
   Christ, the Lord, is over all;
   He'll not suffer thee to fall.

4 Faint not, Christian! Jesus near
   Soon in glory will appear;
   And his love will then bestow
   Power to conquer every foe.

434 MAITLAND.

1 Christian, let your heart be glad!
   March in heavenly armor clad;
   Fight! nor think the battle long;
   Victory soon will tune your song.

2 Let not sorrow dim your eye;
   Soon shall every tear be dry;
   Let not fears your course impede;
   Great your strength, if great your need.

3 Onward then to battle move!
   More than conqu'ror you shall prove;
   Though opposed by many a foe,
   Christian soldier, onward go!

435 ANON.

1 Heavenly Father, sovereign Lord,
   Be thy glorious name adored!
   Lord, thy mercies never fail;
   Hail, celestial goodness, hail!

2 Though unworthy, Lord, thine ear,
   Deign our humble songs to hear;
   Purer praise we hope to bring,
   When around thy throne we sing.

3 While on earth ordained we stay,
   Guide our footsteps in thy way,
   Till we come to dwell with thee,
   Till we all thy glory see.

Selection 101.—NETTLETON SERVICE.—God be merciful unto us, and bless us.

God be mer-ci-ful un-to us, be mer-ci-ful and bless us, and cause his face to shine, to

that thy way may be known, may be known up-on the earth, thy

shine up-on us, that thy way may be known up-on the earth, up-on the earth, thy sav-ing

sav - - ing health a - mong all na - tions.

health a-mong all na-tions, thy sav-ing health a-mong all na-tions. Let the peo-ple praise thee,

let the peo-ple praise thee, let the peo-ple praise thee, O God, let the peo-ple praise thee, O God.

un - to us, . . .

God be mer-ci-ful un - to us, and bless us, and bless us, be mer-ci-ful, and bless . . us.

un - to us, . . .

Selection 101.

God be merciful unto us, and bless us, and cause his face to shine upon us, that thy way may be known upon earth, | thy saving health among all nations. Let the people praise thee, O God, let all the people praise thee.

NETTLETON. 8s & 7s. Double.

Words and Music by Rev. A. NETTLETON.

Choir and Congregation.

436 1. { Come, thou Fount of ev'ry bless-ing, Tune my heart to sing thy grace; }
{ Streams of mercy, nev-er ceas-ing, Call for songs of loud-est praise; } Teach me some me-lodious son-net,
2. { Oh, to grace how great a debt - or Dai-ly I'm con-strain'd to be! }
{ Let thy goodness, like a fet - ter, Bind my wand'ring heart to thee; } Prone to wander, Lord, I feel it;

Sung by flam-ing tongues above; Praise the mount—I'm fix'd up - on it!—Mount of thy re - deem-ing love.
Prone to leave the God I love; Here's my heart, oh, take and seal it; Seal it for thy courts a - bove.

Selection 99.—My sheep hear my voice.

BAVARIA. 8s & 7s. Double.

German.

Choir and Congregation.

1. { Sav-ior, like a Shepherd lead us: Much we need thy ten-der care; }
{ In thy pleas-ant pas-tures feed us, For our use thy fold pre-pare: } We are thine: do thou be-friend us,

Be the guard-ian of our way; Keep thy flock, from sin de - fend us, Seek us when we go a - stray.

437 (First verse in music.)
Miss THRUPP.
2 Thou hast promised to receive us,
Poor and sinful though we be;
Thou hast mercy to relieve us,
Grace to cleanse, and power to free :
Early let us seek thy favor,
Early help us do thy will ;
Holy Lord, our only Savior!
With thy grace our bosom fill.

438 (Sel. 99. My sheep hear my voice.
Tune. Bavaria.) MUHLENBURG.
1 Savior! who thy flock art feeding
With the Shepherd's kindest care,
All the feeble gently leading,
While the lambs thy bosom share ;
Now, these little ones receiving,
Fold them in thy gracious arm ;
There, we know, thy word believing,
Only there secure from harm.

2 Never, from thy pasture roving,
Let them be the lion's prey ;
Let thy tenderness, so loving,
Keep them all life's dangerous way :
Then, within thy fold eternal,
Let them find a resting-place,
Feed in pastures ever vernal,
Drink the rivers of thy grace.

Selection 102.—GOLDWARK SERVICE.—Commit thy way unto the Lord.

Com-mit thy way un-to the Lord, un-to the Lord, Trust al-so in him, trust al-so in
in him,

him. The Lord is good, is good to all, the Lord is good, is good to
The Lord is good, is good to all, . to all, the Lord is good to all, is good

and his ten - - - der mer - - - cies are o - - ver all his works,
all; his ten-der mercies are o - ver all, are o - ver all his works, are o - ver all, are
to all;

o - ver all, his ten - der mer - cies are o - ver all his works, are o - ver all, o - ver

all . . his works. Com-mit thy way un-to the Lord, trust al - so in him, trust al - so in him.

Selection 102.

Commit thy way unto the Lord, trust also in him. The | works. Commit thy way unto the Lord, trust also in
Lord is good to all, and his tender mercies are over all his | him.

GOLDWARE.   7s & 6s.

Words by ANNA L. WARING.
Music from MENDELSSOHN.
Arr. by GEO. F. ROOT.

Choir and Congregation.

439
1. In heav'n-ly love a-bid-ing, No change my heart shall fear, And safe is such con-fid-ing, For
2. Wher-ev-er he may guide me, No want shall turn me back; My Shepherd is be-side me, And

noth-ing chang-es here: The storm may roar with-out me, My heart may low be laid, But
noth-ing can I lack! His wis-dom ev-er wak-eth, His sight is nev-er dim: He

God is round a-bout me, And can I be dis-mayed?
knows the way he tak-eth, And I will walk with him.

3 Green pastures are before me,
   Which yet I have not seen;
Bright skies will soon be o'er me,
   Where darkest clouds have been.
My hope I can not measure;
   My path to life is free;
My Savior has my treasure,
   And he will walk with me.

440   HAWEIS.

1 To thee, my God and Savior!
   My heart exulting sings,
Rejoicing in thy favor,
   Almighty King of kings!
I'll celebrate thy glory,
   With all thy saints above,
And tell the joyful story
   Of thy redeeming love.

2 Soon as the morn, with roses
   Bedecks thy dewy east,
And when the sun reposes
   Upon the ocean's breast,
My voice, in supplication,
   Well-pleased the Lord shall hear:
Oh! grant me thy salvation,
   And to my soul draw near.

441   MONTGOMERY.

1 God is my strong salvation,
   What foe have I to fear?
In darkness and temptation,
   My Light, my Help is near:
Though hosts encamp around me,
   Firm in the fight I stand;
What terror can confound me,
   With God at my right hand?

2 Place on the Lord reliance;
   My soul, with courage wait;
His truth be thine affiance,
   When faint and desolate:
His might thy heart shall strengthen,
   His love thy joy increase;
Mercy thy day shall lengthen;
   The Lord will give thee peace!

442   DAVIS.

1 From every earthly pleasure,
   From every transient joy,
From every mortal treasure
   That soon will fade and die;
No longer these desiring,
   Upward our wishes tend,
To nobler bliss aspiring,
   And joys that never end.

2 What though we are but strangers
   And sojourners below,
And countless snares and dangers
   Surround the path we go?
Though painful and distressing,
   Yet there's a rest above;
And onward still we're pressing,
   To reach that land of love.

Selection 103.—PORTUGUESE HYMN SERVICE.—Fear not, little flock.

Fear not, little flock, for it is your Father's good pleasure to give you the kingdom.

PORTUGUESE HYMN. 11s.

Choir and Congregation.

Romish Melo'y.

1. How firm a foun-da-tion, ye saints of the Lord! Is laid for your faith in his

ex-cel-lent word! What more can he say, than to you he hath said,— To you, who for

ref-uge to Je-sus have fled, To you, who for ref-uge to Je-sus have fled!

---

443   *(For first verse see tune.)*   KIRKHAM.

2 "Fear not, I am with thee, oh, be not dismayed,
  For I am thy God, I will still give thee aid :
  I'll strengthen thee, help thee, and cause thee to stand,
  Upheld by my gracious, omnipotent hand.

3 "When through the deep waters I call thee to go,
  The rivers of sorrow shall not overflow ;
  For I will be with thee thy trials to bless,
  And sanctify to thee thy deepest distress.

4 "Ev'n down to old age all my people shall prove
  My sovereign, eternal, unchangeable love ;
  And then, when gray hairs shall their temples adorn,
  Like lambs they shall still in my bosom be borne."

14

444   ANON.

1 Tho' faint, yet pursuing, we go on our way ;
  The Lord is our Leader, his word is our stay ;
  Though suffering, and sorrow, and trial be near,
  The Lord is our refuge, and whom can we fear?

2 He raiseth the fallen, he cheereth the faint ;
  The weak, and oppressed—he will hear their complaint ;
  The way may be weary, and thorny the road,
  But how can we falter? our help is in God !

3 Though clouds may surround us, our God is our light ;
  Though storms rage around us, our God is our might ;
  So faint, yet pursuing, still onward we come ;
  The Lord is our Leader, and heaven is our home !

Selection 104.—HURSLEY SERVICE.—Thy sun shall no more go down.

Thy sun shall no more, shall no more go down; neither shall thy moon withdraw it-self, for the

Lord shall be thine everlast-ing light, and the days of thy mourning shall be end—ed, for the

Lord the Lord shall be thy light, thine ev—————er-last—ing light.

HURSLEY. L. M.

Words by Rev. JOHN KEBLE.
Music arr. by W. H. MONK.

Choir and Congregation.

445 1. Sun of my soul! thou Sav-ior dear, It is not night if thou be near: Oh, may no earth-born
      2. When soft the dews of kind-ly sleep My wea-ried eye-lids gen-tly steep, Be my last tho't—how

cloud a-rise To hide thee from thy serv-ant's eyes!
sweet to rest For-ev-er on my Sav-ior's breast!

3 Abide with me from morn till eve,
   For without thee I can not live;
   Abide with me when night is nigh,
   For without thee I dare not die.

4 Be near to bless me when I wake,
   Ere thro' the world my way I take;
   Abide with me till in thy love
   I lose myself in heaven above.

Selection 63.

Let us lay aside every weight and the sin that doth so easily beset us, and let us run with patience the race that is set before us, looking unto Jesus, the Author and Finisher of faith.

VINCENT. 11s.

Choir and Congregation.

Arranged for this work.

446 1 Oh, eyes that are wea - ry, and hearts that are sore! Look, look, un - to Je - sus, and sor - row no more!

The light of his coun-te-nance shin - eth so bright That here, as in heav - en, there need be no night.

2 While looking to Jesus my heart can not fear;
I tremble no more when I see Jesus near;
I know that his presence my safeguard will be,
For, "Why are you troubled?" he saith unto me.

3 Still looking to Jesus, oh, may I be found,
When Jordan's dark waters encompass me round:
They bear me away in his presence to be,
To see him still nearer whom always I see.

Selection 103.—Fear not, little flock.

GRAYLOCK. 11s.

Choir and Congregation.

† † †

447 1. The Lord is my Shep-herd, no want shall I know; I feed in green pas-tures, safe-fold - ed I rest;
2. Thro' the valley and shad - ow of death tho' I stray, Since thou art my guar - dian, no e - vil I fear;

He lead - eth my soul where the still wa-ters flow, Re-stores me when wand'ring, re-deems when oppressed.
Thy rod shall de - fend me, thy staff be my stay; No harm can be - fall with my Com - fort - er near.

3 In the midst of affliction my table is spread;
With blessings unmeasured my cup runneth o'er;
With perfume and oil thou anointest my head;
Oh, what shall I ask of thy providence more?

4 Let goodness and mercy, my bountiful God!
Still follow my steps till I meet thee above;
I seek—by the path which my forefathers trod,
Through the land of their sojourn—thy kingdom of love.

Selection 105.—OLMUTZ SERVICE.—By the rivers of Babylon.

Choir. Somber toward grief.   p   Cres.   Dim. G. F. R.

By the riv-ers of Bab-y-lon, there we sat down, we wept, we wept, when we re-mem-bered

in the midst . . . .

Dim.   Cres.   Dim.   Cres.   m

Zi- on, we hang'd our harps up - on the wil - lows, in the midst there-of, we

Cres.   Dim. e rit.

hang'd our harps up - on the wil - lows, in the midst there-of, in the midst there-of.

OLMUTZ. S. M.

Words by Rev. A. M. Toplady.
Music arr. by Dr. Mason.

Choir and Congregation.

448   1. Your harps, ye trem-bling saints, Down from the wil - lows take: Loud to the praise of love di - vine
     2. Tho' in a for - eign land, We are not far from home; And near - er to our house a - bove

Bid ev - 'ry string a - wake.

We ev - 'ry mo-ment come.

3 His grace will to the end
    Stronger and brighter shine;
   Nor present things, nor things to come,
    Shall quench the spark divine.

4 When we in darkness walk,
    Nor feel the heavenly flame,
   Then is the time to trust our God,
    And rest upon his name.

5 Soon shall our doubts and fear
    Subside at his control;
   His loving-kindness shall break thro'
    The midnight of the soul.

6 Blest is the man, O Lord,
    Who stays himself on thee;
   Who waits for thy salvation, Lord,
    Shall thy salvation see.

Choir and Congregation.

SWAIN. S. M. Double.

Words by Rev. H. Bonar.
Music arr. for this work.

449

1. I was a wan-d'ring sheep, I did not love the fold; I did not love my Shepherd's voice,
2. The Shepherd sought his sheep, The Fa - ther sought his child, He fol - low'd me o'er vale and hill,

I would not be con - trolled: I was a way-ward child, I did not love my home.
O'er des - erts waste and wild; He found me nigh to death, Fam-ish'd, and faint, and lone;

I did not love my Fa-ther's voice, I lov'd a - far to roam.
He bound me with the bands of love; He sav'd the wand'ring one.

3 I was a wandering sheep,
I would not be controlled;
But now I love my Shepherd's voice,
I love, I love the fold:
I was a wayward child;
I once preferred to roam;
But now I love my Father's voice,
I love, I love his home.

Choir and Congregation.

NOLAN. 11s & 10s.

Words by Rev. J. Knox.
Music arr. for this work.

450

1. The Lord is my Shep-herd, he makes me re - pose Where the pas-tures in beau - ty are grow - ing,
2. He strengthens my spir - it, he shows me the path Where the arms of his love shall en - fold me;

He leads me a - far from the world and its woes, Where in peace the still wa - ters are flow - ing.
And when I walk thro' the dark val - ley of death, His rod and his staff will up - hold me.

Selection 106.—TRUST SERVICE.—Why art thou cast down?

Quartet. p

Why art thou cast down, O my soul, O my soul? and why art thou dis-qui-et-ed?

Cres. **Slower.** me

why art thou dis-qui-et-ed with-in me? why art thou cast down, O my

why, my soul? m

soul, O my soul? and why art thou dis-qui-et-ed with-in me?

TRUST. 6s. Double.

Words by Dr. T. HASTINGS.
Music arr. by GEO. F. ROOT.

Choir and Congregation.

451
1. Be tranquil, O my soul, Be qui-et, ev-'ry fear! Thy Fa-ther hath con-trol, And he is ev-er near;
2. A Father's chast'ning hand Is lead-ing thee a-long; Nor dis-tant is the land Where swells th'immortal song;

Ne'er of thy lot complain, What-ev-er may be-fall, Sickness, or care, or pain, 'T is well-ap-point-ed all.
Oh, then, my soul, be still! Await high heav'n's decree; Seek but thy Fa-ther's will, It shall be well with thee.

Selection 124.

In my Father's house are many mansions. If it were not so I would have told you. I go to prepare a place for you. And if I go and prepare a place for you, I will come again, and receive you unto myself, that where I am there ye may be also. In my Father's house are many mansions. If it were not so I would have told you.

MANOAH. C. M.

Words by Dr. WATTS,
Arr. by H. W. GREATOREX.

Choir and Congregation.

452
1. When I can read my ti - tle clear To man-sions in the skies, I'll bid fare-
2. Should earth a - gainst my soul en - gage, And fie - ry darts be hurled, Then I can

well to ev - 'ry fear, And wipe my weep-ing eyes.
smile at Sa - tan's rage, And face a frown-ing world.

3 Let cares like a wild deluge come,
   And storms of sorrow fall;
   May I but safely reach my home,
   My God, my heaven, my all!—

4 There I shall bathe my weary soul
   In seas of heavenly rest;
   And not a wave of trouble roll
   Across my peaceful breast.

SILVER ST. S. M.

Words by Dr. DODDRIDGE.
L. SMITH.

Choir and Congregation.

453
1. Grace! 'tis a charm - ing sound! Har - mo - nious to the ear! Heaven with the ech - o
2. Grace first con-trived a way To save re - bel - lious man; And all the steps which

shall re - - sound, And all the earth shall hear.
grace dis - play, Which drew the won - drous plan.

3 Grace led my roving feet
   To tread the heavenly road;
   And new supplies each hour I meet
   While pressing on to God.

4 Grace all the work shall crown,
   Through everlasting days;
   It lays in heaven the topmost stone,
   And well deserves the praise.

(Sel. 93. If ye endure chastening, God dealeth with you as with sons; for whom the Lord loveth he chasteneth. Tune, Silver St.)

454   WATTS.

1 Behold what wondrous grace
   The Father has bestowed
   On sinners of a mortal race,
   To call them sons of God!

2 If in my Father's love
   I share a filial part,
   Send down thy Spirit, like a dove,
   To rest upon my heart.

3 We would no longer lie
   Like slaves beneath the throne;
   Our faith shall Abba, Father! cry,
   And thou the kindred own.

455   [Sel. 93]   ANON.

1 Heirs of unending life,
   While yet we sojourn here,
   Oh, let us our salvation work
   With trembling and with fear.

2 God will support our hearts,
   With might before unknown;
   The work to be performed is ours,
   The strength is all his own.

Selection 62.—Come unto me.

ELLIOTT. 8s & 6s.

Words by C. ELLIOTT.
Music arr. by G. F. ROOT.

Choir and Congregation.

456
1. O Holy Sav - ior! Friend un-seen, Since on thine arm thou bidst me lean, Help me, thro'
2. Blest with this fel - low-ship di - vine, Take what thou wilt, I'll not re - pine: For, as the

out life's chang-ing scene, By faith to cling to thee.
branch - es to the vine, My soul would cling to thee.

3 Though oft I seem to tread alone,
Life's dreary waste, with thorns o'ergrown,
Thy voice of love, in gentlest tone,
Still whispers, "Cling to me!"

4 Tho' faith and hope are often tried,
I ask not, need not, aught beside;
So safe, so calm, so satisfied,
The soul that clings to thee!

Selection 85.—In the time of trouble he shall hide me.

RAFFLES. C. M. Double.

Words by Rev. THOS. RAFFLES.
Music by GEO. F. ROOT.

Choir and Congregation.

457
1. Thou art my hid - ing-place, O Lord! In thee I put my trust;
2. When storms of fierce temptation beat, And fu-rious foes as - sail,

Encour-aged by thy ho - ly word,
My ref - uge is the mer - cy - seat,

A fee - ble child of dust: I have no ar - gu - ment beside, I urge no oth - er plea;
My hope with - in the vail: From strife of tongues, and bit - ter words, My spir - it flies to thee;

And 't is e - nough my Sav - ior died, My Sav - ior died for me!
Joy to my heart the tho't af - fords, My Sav - ior died for me!

3 And when thine awful voice commands
This body to decay,
And life, in its last lingering sands,
Is ebbing fast away;—
Then, though it be in accents weak,
My voice shall call on thee,
And ask for strength in death to speak,
"My Savior died for me."

RETREAT. L. M.

Choir and Congregation.

Dr. T. Hastings.

1. My God, my Fa-ther, while I stray Far from my home, on life's rough way.

Oh, teach me from my heart to say, "Thy will be done, thy will be done!"

458
C. Elliott.

1 My God, my Father, while I stray
Far from my home, on life's rough way,
Oh, teach me from my heart to say,
"Thy will be done, thy will be done!"

2 What though in lonely grief I sigh
For friends beloved no longer nigh,
Submissive still would I reply,
"Thy will be done, thy will be done!"

3 If thou shouldst call me to resign
What most I prize,—it ne'er was mine;
I only yield thee what was thine:
"Thy will be done, thy will be done!"

4 If but my fainting heart be blest
With thy sweet Spirit for its guest,
My God, to thee I leave the rest;
"Thy will be done, thy will be done!"

459
Anon.

1 I can not always trace the way
Where thou, Almighty One, dost move;
But I can always, always say,
That God is love, that God is love.

2 When fear her chilling mantle flings
O'er earth, my soul to heaven above,
As to her native home, upsprings,
For God is love, for God is love.

2 When myst'ry clouds my darken'd path,
I'll check my dread, my doubts reprove;
In this my soul sweet comfort hath,
That God is love, that God is love.

4 Yes, God is love;—a thought like this
Can every gloomy thought remove,
And turn all tears, all woes, to bliss,
For God is love, for God is love.

460
Bryant.

1 Oh, deem not they are blest alone,
Whose lives a peaceful tenor keep;
For God, who pities man, hath shown
A blessing for the eyes that weep.

2 The light of smiles shall fill again
The lids that overflow with tears;
And weary hours of woe and pain
Are promises of happy years.

3 There is a day of sunny rest
For every dark and troubled night;
And grief may bide an evening guest,
But joy shall come with early light.

4 For God has marked each sorrowing day,
And numbered every secret tear,
And heaven's long age of bliss shall pay
For all his children suffer here.

MAITLAND. C. M.

Choir and Congregation.

Western Air.

461 1. Must Je-sus bear the cross a-lone, And all the world go free? No, there's a cross for

ev-'ry one, And there's a cross for me.

2 This consecrated cross I'll bear
Till death shall set me free,
And then go home my crown to wear,
For there's a crown for me.

3 Oh, precious cross! oh, glorious crown!
Oh, resurrection day!
Ye angels, from the stars come down,
And bear my soul away.

Choir and Congregation.

STARLING. S. M.

Words by Rev. A. M. TOPLADY.
Music arr. for this work.

462

1. If, thro' un-ruf-fled seas, Tow'rd heav'n we calm-ly sail, With grate-ful hearts, O
2. But should the sur-ges rise, And rest de-lay to come, Blest be the sor-row—

God, to thee, We'll own the fav-'ring gale.
kind the storm, Which drives us near-er home.

3 Soon shall our doubts and fears
   All yield to thy control:
Thy tender mercies shall illume
   The midnight of the soul.

4 Teach us, in every state,
   To make thy will our own;
And when the joys of sense depart,
   To live by faith alone.

Selection 62.—Come unto me, all ye that labor and are heavy laden, and I will give you rest.

TRUST. 6s. Double.

Choir and Congregation.

Arr. by GEO. F. ROOT.

1. Dear Savior, as thou wilt! Oh, may thy will be mine; In-to thy hand of love I would my all re-sign;

Thro' sor-row, or thro' joy, Conduct me as thine own, And help me still to say, My Lord, thy will be done!

463   SCHMOLKE.

1 Dear Savior, as thou wilt!
   Oh, may thy will be mine;
Into thy hand of love
   I would my all resign;
Through sorrow, or through joy,
   Conduct me as thine own,
And help me still to say,
   My Lord, thy will be done.

2 Dear Savior, as thou wilt!
   Though seen through many a tear,
Let not my star of hope
   Grow dim or disappear:
Since thou on earth hast wept,
   And sorrowed oft alone,
If I must weep with thee,
   My Lord, thy will be done.

3 Dear Savior, as thou wilt!
   All shall be well for me:
Each changing future scene
   I gladly trust with thee:
Straight to my home above
   I travel calmly on,
And sing, in life or death,
   My Lord! thy will be done.

ROCK OF AGES. 7s. 6 lines.

Choir and Congregation.

Words by Rev. A. M. Toplady.
Music by Dr. T. Hastings.

464 1. Rock of A - ges, cleft for me! Let me hide my-self in thee; Let the wa - ter and the blood,

From thy wound-ed side that flow'd, Be of sin the doub-le cure, Cleanse me from its guilt and pow'r.

2 Not the labor of my hands
Can fulfill the law's demands;
Could my zeal no respite know,
Could my tears forever flow,
All for sin could not atone:
Thou must save, and thou alone.

3 Nothing in my hand I bring,
Simply to thy cross I cling;
Naked, come to thee for dress,
Helpless, look to thee for grace;
Vile, I to the fountain fly,
Wash me, Savior, or I die.

4 While I draw this fleeting breath,
When my eyelids close in death;
When I soar to worlds unknown,
See thee on thy judgment-throne;
Rock of Ages, cleft for me!
Let me hide myself in thee.

PLEYEL'S HYMN. 7s.

Choir and Congregation.

Words by J. Montgomery.
Music by Pleyel.

465 1. Peo - ple of the liv - ing God, I have sought the world a - round, Paths of sin and
2. Now to you my spir - it turns— Turns, a fu - gi - tive un - blest; Breth-ren, where your

sor - row trod, Peace and com - fort no - where found
al - tar burns, Oh, re - ceive me in - to rest!

3 Lonely I no longer roam,
Like the cloud, the wind, the wave:
Where you dwell shall be my home,
Where you die shall be my grave;—

4 Mine the God whom you adore,
Your Redeemer shall be mine;
Earth can fill my soul no more,
Every idol I resign.

(Tune, Missionary Chant, p. 231.)

466 [L. M.] WATTS.

1 'T is by the faith of joys to come
We walk through deserts dark as night;
Till we arrive at heaven, our home,
Faith is our guide, and faith our light.

2 The want of sight she well supplies;
She makes the pearly gates appear;
Far into distant worlds she pries,
And brings eternal glories near,

3 Cheerful we tread the desert through,
While faith inspires a heavenly ray;
Though lions roar, and tempests blow,
And rocks and dangers fill the way.

(Tune, Federal St., p. 176.)

467 [L. M.] KEBLE.

1 If on our daily course our mind
Be set, to hallow all we find,
New treasures still, of countless price,
God will provide for sacrifice.

2 Old friends, old scenes, will lovlier be,
As more of heaven in each we see;
Some softening gleam of love and prayer
Shall dawn on every cross and care.

3 The trivial round, the common task,
Will furnish all we ought to ask;—
Room to deny ourselves, a road
To bring us daily nearer God.

4 Only, O Lord, in thy dear love,
Fit us for perfect rest above;
And help us this and every day,
To live more nearly as we pray.

(Tune. Sicily, p. 284, without repeat.)

468 [8s. and 7s.] NEVIN.

1 Always with us, always with us—
Words of cheer and words of love;
Thus the risen Savior whispers,
From his dwelling-place above.

2 With us when we toil in sadness,
Sowing much and reaping none;
Telling us that in the future
Golden harvests shall be won.

3 With us when the storm is sweeping
O'er our pathway dark and drear;
Waking hope within our bosoms,
Stilling every anxious fear.

4 With us in the lonely valley,
When we cross the chilling stream!
Lighting up the steps to glory
With salvation's radiant beam.

Tune, Naomi, p. 141.)

469 [C. M.] FLETCHER.

1 Think gently of the erring one!
And let us not forget,
However darkly stained by sin,
He is our brother yet.

2 Heir of the same inheritance,
Child of the self-same God;
He hath but stumbled in the path;
We have in weakness trod.

3 Forget not thou hast often sinned,
And sinful yet must be:
Deal gently with the erring one,
As God has dealt with thee.

Sel. 27. The Lord is my strength and song.
Tune, Olmutz, p. 212.)

470 [S. M.] MOULTRIE.

1 Rejoice in God alway;
When earth looks heavenly bright,
When joy makes glad the livelong day,
And peace shuts in the night.

2 Rejoice when care and woe
The fainting soul oppress;
When tears at wakeful midnight flow,
And morn brings heaviness.

3 Rejoice in hope and fear;
Rejoice in life and death;
Rejoice when threatening storms are near,
And comfort languisheth.

4 So, though our path is steep,
And many a tempest lowers,
Shall his own peace our spirits keep,
And Christ's dear love be ours.

(Sel. 107. Not every one. Tune, Dennis. p. 126.)

471 [S. M.] DODDRIDGE.

1 Ye servants of the Lord!
Each in his office wait,
Observant of his heavenly word,
And watchful at his gate.

2 Let all your lamps be bright,
And trim the golden flame;
Gird up your loins as in his sight,
For awful is his name.

3 Watch,—'t is your Lord's command;
And while we speak he's near;
Mark the first signal of his hand,
And ready all appear.

4 Oh, happy servant he,
In such a posture found!
He shall his Lord with rapture see,
And be with honor crowned.

(Tune, Hendon, p. 26.)

472 [7s] WARDLAW.

1 Christ, of all my hopes the Ground,
Christ, the Spring of all my joy,
Still in thee let me be found,
Still for thee my powers employ.

2 Fountain of o'erflowing grace!
Freely from thy fullness give;
Till I close my earthly race,
Be it—"Christ for me to live!"

3 Then,—oh, then an entrance give
To the land of cloudless sky;
Having known it "Christ to live,"
Let me know it "gain to die."

(Tune, Olmutz, p. 212.)

473 [S. M.] WATTS.

1 Oh, bless the Lord, my soul!
Let all within me join,
And aid my tongue to bless his name,
Whose favors are divine!

2 Oh, bless the Lord, my soul!
Nor let his mercies lie
Forgotten in unthankfulness,
And without praises die.

3 'T is he forgives thy sins;
'T is he relieves thy pain;
'T is he that heals thy sicknesses,
And makes thee young again.

4 He crowns thy life with love,
When ransomed from the grave:
He, who redeemed my soul from hell,
Hath sovereign power to save.

(Tune, Calderwood, p.41.)

474 [7s. 6 lines.] NEWTON.

1 Quiet, Lord, my froward heart,
Make me teachable and mild,
Upright, simple, free from art,
Make me as a weaned child:
From distrust and envy free,
Pleased with all that pleases thee.

2 What thou shalt to-day provide,
Let me as a child receive;
What to-morrow may betide,
Calmly to thy wisdom leave:
'T is enough that thou wilt care;
Why should I the burden bear?

3 As a little child relies
On a care beyond his own;
Knows he 's neither strong nor wise,
Fears to stir a step alone:—
Let me thus with thee abide,
As my Father, Guard, and Guide.

Selection 107.—ROSEHILL SERVICE, No. 2.--Not every one that saith unto me, Lord.

Choir. *p*

Not ev-'ry one that saith un-to me, Lord! Lord! not ev-'ry one that saith un - to me, Lord! Lord! shall

Cres.   **Dim.**

en - ter in - to the king-dom of heav'n, shall en - ter in - to the king-dom of heav'n; but he that do - eth the

p

will of my Fa-ther, the will of my Fa-ther, which is in heaven. Not ev-'ry one that saith un - to me,

Cres.

Lord! Lord! but he that do -eth the will of my Fa-ther, the will of my Fa-ther, which is in heav'n.

ROSEHILL. L. M.

Words by Dr. WATTS.
Music by J. E. SWEETSER.

Choir and Congregation.

475 1. So let our lips' and lives ex-press The ho - ly gos - pel we pro-fess: So let our works and

vir - tues shine, To prove the doc - trine all di - vine.

2 Thus shall we best proclaim abroad
The honors of our Savior God ;
When his salvation reigns within,
And grace subdues the power of sin.

3 Religion bears our spirits up,
While we expect that blessed hope,—
The bright appearance of the Lord :
And faith stands leaning on his word.

Selection 108.—MENDON SERVICE.—Lift up your eyes and look on the fields.

G. F. R.

Lift up your eyes and look on the fields, for they are white al - read - y to the har - vest; And

he that reap-eth re - ceiv-eth wa - ges, and gath'reth fruits un-to life e - ter - nal, and gath'reth fruits un-to

life e - ter - nal, That both he that soweth and he that reapeth may rejoice, may rejoice to-geth - er, that

both he that sow-eth may re - joice, and he that reap-eth may re - joice, may re-joice, may re-joice to-

geth - er. Lift up your eyes, lift up your eyes, lift up your eyes, and look on the fields.

Selection 108.

Lift up your eyes and look on the fields, for they are white already to the harvest! And he that reapeth receiveth wages, and gathereth fruit unto life eternal, that both he that soweth and he that reapeth may rejoice together. Lift up your eyes and look on the fields, for they are white already to the harvest!

MENDON. L. M.

Choir and Congregation.

Arr. by Dr. L. MASON.

1. Go, la-bor on; spend and be spent,—Thy joy to do the Fa-ther's will;
It is the way the Mas-ter went; Should not the serv-ant tread it still?

476   BONAR.

1 Go, labor on; spend and be spent,—
Thy joy to do the Father's will;
It is the way the Master went;
Should not the servant tread it still?

2 Go, labor on; 't is not for naught;
Thine earthly loss is heavenly gain;
Men heed thee, love thee, praise thee not;
The Master praises,—what are men?

3 Go, labor on; enough, while here,
If he shall praise thee, if he deign
Thy willing heart to mark and cheer:
No toil for him shall be in vain.

4 Toil on, and in thy toil rejoice;
For toil comes rest, for exile, home;
Soon shalt thou hear the Bridegroom's voice,
The midnight peal: "Behold, I come!"

477   BONAR.

1 Go, labor on, while it is day;
The world's dark night is hastening on:
Speed, speed thy work,—cast sloth away!
It is not thus that souls are won.

7 Men die in darkness at your side,
Without a hope to cheer the tomb':
Take up the torch and wave it wide—
The torch that lights time's thickest gloom.

3 Toil on,—faint not; keep watch, and pray!
Be wise the erring soul to win;
Go forth into the world's highway;
Compel the wanderer to come in.

4 Go, labor on; your hands are weak;
Your knees are faint, your soul cast down;
Yet falter not; the prize you seek
Is near,—a kingdom and a crown!

478   GIBBONS.

1 When Jesus dwelt in mortal clay,
What were his works from day to day,
But miracles of power and grace,
That spread salvation through our race?

2 Teach us, O Lord, to keep in view
Thy pattern, and thy steps pursue;
Let alms bestowed, let kindness done,
Be witnessed by each rolling sun.

3 That man may last, but never lives,
Who much receives, but nothing gives;
Whom none can love, whom none can thank,
Creation's blot, creation's blank!

4 But he who marks, from day to day,
In generous acts his radiant way,
Treads the same path his Savior trod,
The path to glory and to God.

479   MONTGOMERY.

1 Jesus! our best beloved Friend,
On thy redeeming name we call;
Jesus! in love to us descend,
Pardon and sanctify us all.

2 Our souls and bodies we resign,
To fear and follow thy commands;
Oh! take our hearts, our hearts are thine,
Accept the service of our hands.

3 Firm, faithful, watching unto prayer,
Our Master's voice will we obey,
Toil in the vineyard here, and bear
The heat and burden of the day.

4 Yet, Lord, for us a resting-place,
In heaven, at thy right hand prepare;
And till we see thee face to face,
Be all our conversation there.

480   MONTGOMERY.

1 Command thy blessing from above,
O God, on all assembled here;
Behold us with a Father's love,
While we look up with filial fear.

2 Command thy blessing, Jesus, Lord!
May we thy true disciples be;
Speak to each heart the mighty word,—
Say to the weakest, Follow me.

Selection 109.—EVAN SERVICE, No. 2.—Beloved, if God so loved us.

Be-lov--ed, if God so lov'd us, we ought al-so to love one an-oth-er, we ought al-so to love one an-

oth-er. Be-lov-ed, be-lov-ed, if God so lov'd us, if God so lov'd us, we ought al-so to love one an-

oth-er. And this commandment have we receiv'd from him: that he who lov-eth God lov-eth his broth-er al-so.

Be-lov-ed, if God so lov'd us, we ought al-so to love one an-oth-er, to love one an-oth-er.

EVAN. C. M.

Words by Dr. DODDRIDGE.
Music arr. by Dr. MASON.

Choir and Congregation.

481 1. Fa-ther of mer-cies, send thy grace, All pow'r-ful from a-bove, To form, in our o-

be-dient souls, The im-age of thy love.

2 Oh, may our sympathizing breasts
  The generous pleasure know,
  Kindly to share in others' joy,
  And weep for others' woe.

3 When the most helpless sons of grief
  In low distress are laid,
  Soft be our hearts their pains to feel,
  And swift our hands to aid.

Sel. 109 Beloved if God so loved us. Tune, (Sel. 109. Beloved if God so loved us. Tune, (Sel. 109. Beloved if God so loved us. Tune,
Evan, p. 224.)   Evan, p. 224.)   Evan, p. 224)

482 [C. M.] WILLIAMS.

1 How shall we show our love to thee,
  Thou living God most high,
  But loving this thy family,
  For which thou deign'dst to die ?

2 If thou for me such love didst bear,
  Shall I not love again ?
  For all are objects of thy care;
  Thy love doth all sustain.

3 If we have love for thee in heaven,
  'T is seen by love on earth:
  Love only, love which God hath given,
  Doth prove our heavenly birth.

4 Whate'er we do, where'er we go,
  Let love our sonship prove:
  Our lives the fire celestial show,
  Our thoughts and words be love.

483 [C. M.] ANON.

1 Scorn not the slightest word or deed,
  Nor deem it void of power;
  There's fruit in each wind-wafted seed,
  That waits its natal hour.

2 A whispered word may touch the heart
  And call it back to life ;
  A look of love bid sin depart,
  And still unholy strife.

3 No act falls fruitless; none can tell
  How vast its power may be,
  Nor what results infolded dwell
  Within it silently.

4 Work on, despair not, bring thy mite,
  Nor care how small it be ;
  God is with all that serve the right,
  The holy, true, and free.

484 [C. M.] DODDRIDGE.

1 Jesus, our Lord, how rich thy grace!
  Thy bounties how complete !
  How shall we count the matchless sum !
  How pay the mighty debt !

2 High on a throne of radiant light
  Dost thou exalted shine;
  What can our poverty bestow,
  When all the worlds are thine ?

3 But thou hast brethren here below,
  The partners of thy grace;
  And wilt confess their humble names,
  Before thy Father's face.

4 In them thou may'st be clothed and fed,
  And visited and cheered ;
  And in their accents of distress,
  Our Savior's voice is heard.

OLMUTZ. S. M.

Choir and Congregation.   Arr. by Dr. MASON.

1. Lab'rers of Christ, a - rise, And gird you for the toil! The dew of promise from the skies Al-ready cheers the soil.

(Sel. 108. Lift up your eyes and look on the Sel 108. Lift up your eyes and look on the Sel 108. Lift up your eyes and look on the
fields)   fields.)   fields.)

485 SIGOURNEY.

1 Laborers of Christ, arise,
  And gird you for the toil!
  The dew of promise from the skies
  Already cheers the soil.

2 Go where the sick recline,
  Where mourning hearts deplore;
  And where the sons of sorrow pine,
  Dispense your hallowed store.

3 Be faith, which looks above,
  With prayer, your constant guest;
  And wrap the Savior's changeless love
  A mantle round your breast.

4 So shall you share the wealth
  That earth may ne'er despoil,
  And the blest gospel's saving health
  Repay your arduous toil.

486 MONTGOMERY.

1 Sow in the morn thy seed:
  At eve hold not thy hand;
  To doubt and fear give thou no heed;
  Broadcast it o'er the land !

2 Beside all waters sow,
  The highway furrows stock,
  Drop it where thorns and thistles grow,
  Scatter it on the rock.

3 The good, the fruitful ground
  Expect not here nor there ;
  O'er hill and dale alike 'tis found;
  Go forth, then, everywhere.

4 Thou canst not tell in vain;
  Cold, heat, and moist, and dry,
  Shall foster and mature the grain
  For garners in the sky.

487 BONAR.

1 Make haste, O man, to live,
  For thou so soon must die;
  Time hurries past thee like the breeze;
  How swift its moments fly !

2 To breathe, and wake, and sleep,
  To smile, to sigh, to grieve,
  To move in idleness through earth—
  This, this is not to live.

3 Make haste, O man, to do
  Whatever must be done;
  Thou hast no time to lose in sloth,
  Thy day will soon be gone.

4 Up, then, with speed, and work;
  Fling ease and self away—
  This is no time for thee to sleep—
  Up, watch, and work, and pray!

15

Selection 110.—STOCKWELL SERVICE, No. 2.—Cast thy bread upon the waters.

G. F. R.

Cast thy bread up-on the wa-ters, cast thy bread up-on the wa-ters, and thou shalt find it

days. Cast thy bread up-on the wa-ters, cast thy bread up-on the wa-ters, and thou shalt

find it af-ter ma-ny days. They that sow in tears shall reap, shall reap in joy. He that goeth forth and

weep-eth, bear-ing pre-cious seed, shall doubtless come a-gain with re-joic-ing, bringing his sheaves with him.

STOCKWELL. 8s & 7s.

Words by Rev. H. F. LYTE.
Music by Rev. D. E. JONES.

488 1. Vain were all our toil and la-bor, Did not God that la-bor bless; Vain, without his grace and

fa-vor, Ev-'ry tal-ent we pos-sess.

2 Vainer still the hope of heaven,
   That on human strength relies;
   But to him shall help be given
   Who in humble faith applies.

3 Seek we, then, the Lord's Anointed;
   He shall grant us peace and rest:
   Ne'er was suppliant disappointed,
   Who thro' Christ his prayer addressed.

(Sel. 110. Tune, Stockwell.)

489
HASTINGS.

1 He that goeth forth with weeping,
  Bearing precious seed in love,
  Never tiring, never sleeping,
  Findeth mercy from above.

2 Soft descend the dews of heaven,
  Bright the rays celestial shine ;
  Precious fruits will thus be given,
  Through an influence all divine.

3 Sow thy seed, be never weary,
  Let no fears thy soul annoy;
  Be the prospect ne'er so dreary,
  Thou shalt reap the fruits of joy.

4 Lo, the scene of verdure brightening,
  See the rising grain appear ;
  Look again ! the fields are whitening,
  For the harvest time is near.

(Sel. 110. Tune, Stockwell.)

490
MRS. HANAFORD.

1 Cast thy bread upon the waters;
  Wildly though the billows roll,
  They but aid thee as thou toilest
  Truth to spread from pole to pole.

2 As the seed, by billows floated,
  To some distant island lone,
  So to human souls benighted,
  That thou flingest may be borne.

3 Cast thy bread upon the waters;
  Why wilt thou still doubting stand ?
  Bounteous shall God send the harvest?
  If thou sow'st with liberal hand.

4 Give then freely of thy substance—
  O'er this cause the Lord doth reign;
  Cast thy bread, and toil with patience,
  Thou shalt labor not in vain.

(Sel. 110. Tune, Stockwell.)

491
HASTINGS.

1 Pilgrims in this vale of sorrow,
  Pressing onward toward the prize,
  Strength and comfort here we borrow
  From the Hand that rules the skies.

2 'Mid these scenes of self-denial,
  We are called the race to run;
  We must meet full many a trial
  Ere the victor's crown is won.

3 Love shall every conflict lighten,
  Hope shall urge us swifter on,
  Faith shall every prospect brighten,
  Till the morn of heaven shall dawn.

4 On the Eternal arm reclining,
  We at length shall win the day;
  All the powers of earth combining,
  Shall not snatch our crown away.

Selection 110.—Cast thy bread upon the waters.

WEBSTER. 8s & 7s. Double.

Words by Rev. B. FRANCIS.
Music arr. for this work.

Choir and Congregation.

492 1. Praise the Sav-ior, all ye na-tions, Praise him, all ye hosts a-bove; Shout with joy-ful
2. With my sub-stance I will hon-or My Re-deem-er and my Lord; Were ten thou-sand

ac-cla-ma-tions, His di-vine, vic-to-rious love. Be his king-dom now pro-mot-ed,
worlds my man-or, All were noth-ing to his word. While the her-alds of sal-va-tion

Let the earth her Mon-arch know; Be my all to him de-vot-ed, To my Lord my all I owe.
His a-bound-ing grace pro-claim, Let his friends of ev-'ry sta-tion Glad-ly join to spread his fame.

Selection 111.—ANVERN SERVICE.—Awake! put on thy strength.

A-wake! a-wake! put on thy strength, O Zi - on; put on thy beau-ti-ful gar-ments, thy

beau - ti - ful gar - ments, O Je - ru - sa - lem, O Je - ru - sa - lem, the ho - ly cit - y.

Solo. Baritone.

From hence - forth there shall no more come in - to thee the un - cir-cum-cised and the un-clean.

Shake thyself from the dust. A-rise, and sit down, O Je - ru - sa - lem; loose thy - self from the

bands of thy neck, O cap - tive daugh-ter of Zi - on, O cap - tive daugh-ter of Zi - on.

Choir.

A-wake! a-wake! put on thy strength, a-wake! a-wake;

Put on thy strength.

Selection 111.

Awake! awake! put on thy strength, O Zion; put on thy beautiful garments, O Jerusalem, the holy city. From henceforth, there shall no more come into thee the uncircumcised and the unclean. Shake thyself from the dust; arise, and sit down, O Jerusalem; loose thyself from the bands of thy neck, O captive daughter of Jerusalem.

Awake! awake! put on thy strength, O Zion: put on thy beautiful garments, O Jerusalem, the holy city.

ANVERN. L. M.

Choir and Congregation.   Arr. by Dr. L. Mason.

1. Tri-umph-ant Zi - on, lift thy head From dust, and dark - ness, and the dead! Tho' hum-bled long, a-wake at length, And gird thee with thy Sav - ior's strength, And gird thee with thy Sav-ior's strength.

493   DODDRIDGE.

1 Triumphant Zion, lift thy head
From dust, and darkness, and the dead;
Though humbled long, awake at length,
And gird thee with thy Savior's strength.

2 Put all thy beauteous garments on,
And let thy various charms be known:
The world thy glories shall confess,
Decked in the robes of righteousness.

3 No more shall foes unclean invade,
And fill thy hallowed walls with dread;
No more shall hell's insulting host,
Their victory and thy sorrows boast.

4 God, from on high, thy groans will hear;
His hand thy ruins shall repair;
Nor will thy watchful monarch come
To guard thee in eternal peace.

494   VOKE.

1 Behold the expected time draw near,
The shades disperse, the dawn appear!
Behold the wilderness assume
The beauteous tints of Eden's bloom!

2 Events with prophecies conspire,
To raise our faith, our zeal to fire:
The ripening fields, already white,
Present a harvest to the sight.

3 The untaught heathen waits to know
The joy the gospel will bestow:
The exiled captive, to receive
The freedom Jesus has to give.

4 Come, let us, with a grateful heart,
In this blest labor share a part;
Our prayers and offerings gladly bring,
To aid the triumphs of our King.

495   MONTGOMERY.

1 From day to day, before our eyes,
Grows and extends the work begun;
When shall new creation rise
O'er every land beneath the sun?

2 When, in the Sabbath of his love,
Shall God from all his labors rest;
And bending from his throne above,
Again pronounce his creatures blest?

3 As sang the morning stars of old,
Shouted the sons of God for joy;
His widening reign while we behold,
Let praise and prayer our tongues employ;

4 Till the redeemed in every clime,
Yea, all that breathe, and move, and live,
To Christ, through every age of time,
The kingdom, power, and glory give.

496   VOKE.

1 Sovereign of worlds! display thy power;
Be this thy Zion's favored hour;
Bid the bright Morning Star arise,
And point the nations to the skies.

2 Set up thy throne where Satan reigns,—
On Afric's shore, on India's plains,
On wilds and continents unknown,—
And make the nations all thine own.

3 Speak! and the world shall hear thy voice;
Speak! and the desert shall rejoice;
Scatter the gloom of heathen night,
And bid all nations hail the light.

497   BEDOME.

1 Ascend thy throne, almighty King,
And spread thy glories all abroad;
Let thine own arm salvation bring,
And be thou known the gracious God.

2 Let millions bow before thy seat,
Let humble mourners seek thy face,
Bring daring rebels to thy feet,
Subdued by thy victorious race.

3 Oh, let the kingdoms of the world
Become the kingdoms of the Lord!
Let saints and angels praise thy name;
Be thou thro' heaven and earth adored.

Selection 112.—MISSIONARY CHANT SERVICE.—Go ye into all the world.

Go ye in-to all the world, and preach the gos-pel to ev-'ry creat-ure!

For the Son of man is come to seek, and save that which was lost, to

seek and save that which was lost. Neither is there sal-va-tion in an-y oth-er.

Solo. Soprano or Tenor.

For there is none oth—er name, there is none oth-er name

giv'n a-mong men, where-by we must be sav—ed.

Choir.

Go ye in-to all the world, go ye in-to all the world, and preach the gos-pel to ev-'ry creat-ure.

Selection 112.

Go ye into all the world, and preach the gospel to every creature. For the Son of man is come to seek and save that which was lost. Neither is there salvation in any other. For there is none other name given among men, whereby we must be saved. Go ye into all the world, and preach the gospel to every creature.

MISSIONARY CHANT. L. M.

Choir and Congregation.   ZEUNER.

1. Ye Chris-tian her - alds, go pro - claim   Sal - va - tion in   Im - man - uel's name;

To dis - tant climes the tid - ings bear,   And plant the Rose of Sha - ron there.

---

498   YORE.

1 Ye Christian heralds! go, proclaim
  Salvation through Immanuel's name;
  To distant climes the tidings bear,
  And plant the Rose of Sharon there.

2 He'll shield you with a wall of fire,
  With flaming zeal your breast inspire,
  Bid raging winds their fury cease,
  And hush the tempest into peace.

3 And when our labors all are o'er,
  Then we shall meet to part no more,—
  Meet with the blood-bought throng, to fall,
  And crown our Jesus—Lord of all!

499   MONTGOMERY.

1 O Spirit of the living God,
  In all thy plentitude of grace,
  Where'er the foot of man hath trod,
  Descend on our apostate race.

2 Give tongues of fire, and hearts of love,
  To preach the reconciling word;
  Give power and unction from above,
  Where'er the joyful sound is heard.

3 Baptize the nations, far and nigh;
  The triumphs of the cross record;
  The name of Jesus glorify,
  Till every kindred call him Lord.

500   WATTS.

1 Jesus shall reign where'er the sun
  Doth his successive journeys run;
  His kingdoms stretch from shore to shore,
  Till moons shall wax and wane no more.

2 For him shall endless prayer be made,
  And praises throng to crown his head;
  His name, like sweet perfume, shall rise
  With every morning sacrifice.

3 People and realms of every tongue
  Dwell on his love with sweetest song;
  And infant voices shall proclaim
  Their early blessings on his name.

4 Let every creature rise, and bring
  Peculiar honors to our King:
  Angels descend with songs again,
  And earth repeat the long amen.

501   WATTS.

1 "Go, preach my gospel," saith the Lord,
  "Bid the whole earth my grace receive,
  He shall be saved that trusts my word;
  And be condemned that won't believe.

2 "I'll make your great commission known,
  And ye shall prove my gospel true,
  By all the works that I have done,
  By all the wonders ye shall do.

3 "Teach all the nations my commands;
  I'm with you till the world shall end;
  All power is vested in my hands;
  I can destroy, and I defend."

4 He spake, and light shone round his head,
  On a bright cloud to heaven he rode;
  They to the farthest nations spread
  The grace of their ascended God.

502   COLLYER.

1 Assembled at thy great command,
  Before thy face, dread King, we stand;
  The voice that marshaled every star,
  Has called thy people from afar.

2 We meet, through distant lands to spread
  The truth for which the martyrs bled;
  Along the line, to either pole,
  The thunder of thy praise to roll.

3 Our prayers assist, accept our praise,
  Our hopes revive, our courage raise;
  Our counsels aid, to each impart
  The single eye, the faithful heart.

4 Forth with thy chosen heralds come,
  Recall the wandering spirits home;
  From Zion's mount send forth the sound,
  To spread the spacious earth around.

Selection 113.—WARWICK SERVICE.—The wilderness and the solitary place shall be glad.

The wil - der - ness and the sol - i - ta - ry place shall be glad . . . in thee, and the

shall be glad in thee, in thee,

des - ert shall re-joice and blossom as the rose, and blos - som as the rose, and the ran-somed of the

Lord shall re-turn, and come to Zi - on with songs, shall come to Zi - on with ev - er-last-ing joy up-

on their heads, upon their heads, with ev - er - last -ing joy up - on their heads. They shall obtain joy and

glad - ness, and sor - row and sigh - ing shall flee a - way, shall flee a - way.

Selection 113.

The wilderness and the solitary place shall be glad in thee, and the desert shall rejoice and blossom as the rose. And the ransomed of the Lord shall return and come to | Zion with songs and everlasting joy upon their heads. They shall obtain joy and gladness, and sorrow and sighing shall flee away.

WARWICK. C. M.

Choir and Congregation. STANLEY.

1. Let Zi - on and her sons re - joice. Be - hold the prom - ised hour!

Her God hath heard her mourn-ing voice, And comes to ex - alt his pow'r.

503 WATTS.

1 Let Zion and her sons rejoice,
  Behold the promised hour!
Her God hath heard her mourning voice,
  And comes to exalt his power.

2 Her dust and ruins that remain
  Are precious in our eyes;
Those ruins shall be built again,
  And all that dust shall rise.

3 The Lord will raise Jerusalem,
  And stand in glory there;
Nations shall bow before his name,
  And kings attend with fear.

4 This shall be known when we are dead,
  And left on long record,
That nations yet unborn may read,
  And trust and praise the Lord.

504 MONTGOMERY.

1 Daughter of Zion! from the dust
  Exalt thy fallen head;
Again in thy Redeemer trust,—
  He calls thee from the dead.

2 Awake, awake, put on thy strength,—
  Thy beautiful array;
The day of freedom dawns at length,—
  The Lord's appointed day.

3 Rebuild thy walls, thy bounds enlarge,
  And send the heralds forth;
Say to the south,—"Give up thy charge,
  And keep not back, O north!"

4 They come! they come! thine exiled bands,
  Where'er they rest or roam,
Have heard thy voice in distant lands,
  And hasten to their home.

5 Thus, though the universe shall burn,
  And God his works destroy,
With songs, thy ransomed shall return,
  And everlasting joy.

505 MONTGOMERY.

1 Spirit of power and might, behold
  A world by sin destroyed!
Creator Spirit, as of old,
  Move on the formless void.

2 Give thou the word: that healing sound
  Shall quell the deadly strife,
And earth again, like Eden crowned,
  Produce the tree of life.

3 If sang the morning stars of joy
  When nature rose to view,
What strains will angel harps employ
  When thou shalt all renew!

4 And if the sons of God rejoice
  To hear a Savior's name,
How will the ransomed raise their voice,
  To whom that Savior came!

5 Lo! every kindred, tongue, and tribe,
  Assembling round the throne,
The new creation shall ascribe
  To sovereign love alone.

506 LOGAN.

1 O city of the Lord! begin
  The universal song:
And let the scattered villages
  The joyful notes prolong.

2 Let Kedar's wilderness afar
  Lift up the lonely voice;
And let the tenants of the rock
  In accent rude rejoice.

3 Oh! from the streams of distant lands
  To our Jehovah sing;
And joyful, from the mountain-tops,
  Shout to the Lord, the King.

4 Let all combined, with one accord,
  The Savior's glories raise,
Till in the earth's remotest bounds
  The nations sound his praise.

Selection 114.—ZION SERVICE.—How lovely the feet of the messengers are.

How love - ly the feet   of the mes - sengers are, How heav'n-ly the tid - ings they bring from afar: How

ear - nest their mes - sage, how charming their voice! Lift up,   oh, ye peo - ple, your hearts, and re-joice; The

watchmen of Zi - on,   re-spons - ive-ly sing, And heav - en re-ech-oes   the prais - es we bring.

How love - - ly the feet   .   .   of the mes - - sen-gers are,   .   .   How

How love - ly the feet,   how love - ly the feet,   how love - ly the feet of the mes-sen-gers are,   How

heav'n - - ly the tid - - - ings they bring   . . .   from a - far.   . . . .   How

heav'n-ly the tid - ings,   heav'n-ly the tid - ings, how heav'n-ly the tid - ings they bring from a - far.   How

love - - ly, how love - - ly, how love - - ly they are.

love - ly they are,   how love - ly they are,   how love - ly, how love - ly they are.

Selection 114.

How lovely the feet of the messengers are. How heavenly the tidings they bring from afar. How earnest their
message, how charming their voice: Lift up, oh, ye people, your hearts, and rejoice. The watchmen of Zion re-
sponsively sing, and heaven re-echoes the praises we
bring.

ZION. 8s 7s & 4s.

Choir and Congregation.   Dr. Thos. Hastings.

1. On the mount-ain's top ap-pear-ing, Lo! the sa-cred her-ald stands!
   Wel-come news to Zi-on bear-ing— Zi-on, long in hos-tile lands: Mourn-ing
cap-tive! God him-self shall loose thy bands; Mourning cap-tive! God him-self shall loose thy bands.

---

507 KELLY.

1 On the mountain's top appearing,
  Lo! the sacred herald stands,
  Welcome news to Zion bearing—
  Zion, long in hostile lands:
    Mourning captive!
  God himself shall loose thy bands.

2 Has thy night been long and mournful?
  Have thy friends unfaithful proved?
  Have thy foes been proud and scornful,
  By thy sighs and tears unmoved?
    Cease thy mourning;
  Zion still is well beloved.

3 God, thy God, will now restore thee;
  He himself appears thy Friend;
  All thy foes shall flee before thee;
  Here their boasts and triumphs end
    Great deliverance
  Zion's King will surely send.

4 Peace and joy shall now attend thee;
  All thy warfare now is past;
  God thy Savior will defend thee;
  Victory is thine at last:
    All thy conflicts
  End in everlasting rest.

508 MONSELL.

1 O'er the distant mountains breaking,
  Comes the reddening dawn of day;
  Rise, my soul, from sleep awaking,
  Rise, and sing, and watch, and pray:
    'T is thy Savior,
  On his bright, returning way.

2 O thou long-expected, weary
  Waits my anxious soul for thee;
  Life is dark, and earth is dreary
  Where thy light I do not see:
    O my Savior,
  When wilt thou return to me?

3 Nearer is my soul's salvation,
  Spent the night, the day at hand;
  Keep me in my lowly station,
  Watching for thee, till I stand,
    O my Savior,
  In thy bright and promised land.

4 With my lamp well-trimmed and burning,
  Swift to hear, and slow to roam,
  Watching for thy glad returning
  To restore me to my home,
    Come, my Savior,
  O my Savior, quickly come.

509 WILLIAMS.

1 O'er the gloomy hills of darkness
  Look, my soul! be still,—and gaze;
  See the promises advancing
  To a glorious day of grace:
    Blessed jubilee!
  Let thy glorious morning dawn.

2 Let the dark, benighted pagan,
  Let the rude barbarian see
  That divine and glorious conquest,
  Once obtained on Calvary:
    Let the gospel
  Loud resound, from pole to pole!

3 Kingdoms wide that sit in darkness—
  Grant them, Lord, the glorious light;
  Now from eastern coast to western
  May the morning chase the night;
    Let redemption,
  Freely purchased, win the day.

4 Fly abroad, thou mighty gospel!
  Win and conquer,—never cease;
  May thy lasting, wide dominions
  Multiply and still increase:
    Sway thy scepter,
  Savior! all the world around.

Selection 115.—HAMDEN SERVICE.—How lovely is Zion.

G. F. R.

How love-ly is Zi-on, how love-ly is Zi-on, how love-ly is Zi-on, cit-y of our God.

Oh, how love-ly, oh, how love-ly, Zi-on, cit-y of our God.

How love-ly is Zi-on, how love-ly is Zi-on, how love-ly is Zi-on, cit-y of our God.

How love-ly is Zi-on, how love-ly is Zi-on, how love-ly is

Joy and peace shall dwell in thee, joy and peace shall dwell in thee, joy and peace shall dwell in thee, joy and peace shall dwell in thee, joy and

Zi-on, how love-ly! Oh, how love-ly, oh, how love-ly is Zi-on, cit-y of our God.

peace shall dwell in thee. How love-ly, how love-ly, how love-ly is Zi-on.

Selection 115.

How lovely is Zion, city of our God. Joy and peace shall dwell in thee.

HAMDEN. 8s 7s & 4s.

Choir and Congregation.

Words by Rev. Thos. Kelly.
Music by Dr. L. Mason.

510

1. Zi - on stands with hills sur-round - ed,— Zi - on, kept by pow'r di - vine; All her foes sha'll be con-
2. Ev-'ry hu - man tie may per - ish; Friend to friend un - faith - ful prove; Mothers cease their own to
3. In the fur - nace God may prove thee, Thence to bring thee forth more bright, But can nev - er cease to

found - ed, Tho' the world in arms com - bine; Hap - py Zi - on, what a fav-ored lot is thine!
cher - ish; Heav'n and earth at last re - move: But no chang - es can at-tend Je - ho-vah's love.
love thee; Thou art pre - cious in his sight; God is with thee, God thine ev - er-last-ing light.

(Sel. 115. Tune, Hamden.)

511 KELLY.

1 See, from Zion's sacred mountain,
Streams of living water flow;
God has opened there a fountain,
That supplies the world below;
They are blessed
Who its sovereign virtues know.

2 Through ten thousand channels flowing,
Streams of mercy find their way:
Life, and health, and joy bestowing,
Waking beauty from decay ;
O ye nations!
Hail the long-expected day.

3 Gladdened by the flowing treasure,
All-enriching as it goes,
Lo! the desert smiles with pleasure
Buds and blossoms as the rose ;
Lo! the desert
Sings for joy where'er it flows.

(Tune, Martyn, p. 159.)

512 [7s.] BURTON.

1 Holy Bible! book divine!
Precious treasure! thou art mine!
Mine to tell me whence I came;
Mine to tell me what I am ;—

---

2 Mine to chide me when I rove ;
Mine to show a Savior's love ;
Mine thou art to guide and guard ;
Mine to punish or reward ;—

3 Mine to comfort in distress,
If the Holy Spirit bless ;
Mine to show, by living faith,
Man can triumph over death ;—

4 Mine to tell of joys to come,
And the rebel sinner's doom ;
Oh, thou holy book divine !
Precious treasure, thou art mine!

(Tune, Nuremburg, p. 53.)

513 [7s.] C. WESLEY.

1 Sons of men, behold from far,
Hail the long-expected Star !
Star of truth that gilds the night,
Guides bewildered men aright.

2 Nations all, remote and near,
Haste, to see your Lord appear ;
Haste, for him your hearts prepare,
Meet him manifested there !

3 There behold the Day-spring rise,
Pouring light on mortal eyes ;
See it chase the shades away,
Shining to the perfect day !

(Tune, Autumn, p. 137; or Faben, p. 245.)

514 [8s and 7s.] CODNER.

1 Lord, I hear of showers of blessing
Thou art scattering full and free;
Showers thy thirsty soul refreshing;
Let some droppings fall on me !
Pass me not, O gracious Father !
Lost and sinful though I be;
Thou might'st curse me, but the rather
Let thy mercy light on me.

2 Have I long in sin been sleeping?
Long been slighting, grieving thee?
Has the world my heart been keeping ?
Oh ! forgive and rescue me !
Pass me not, O mighty Spirit !
Thou canst make the blind to see;
Testify of Jesus' merit,
Speak the word of peace to me.

(Tune, Boylston, p. 108.)

515 [S. M.] BURGESS.

1 The harvest dawn is near,
The year delays not long;
And he who sows with many a tear,
Shall reap with many a song.

2 Sad to his toil he goes,
His seed with weeping leaves;
But he shall come, at twilight's close,
And bring his golden sheaves.

Selection 116.—WEBB SERVICE.—Arise! shine! for thy light is come.   *

A - rise! shine! for thy light   is   come, and the glo - ry   of the Lord   is   ris - en up-

on thee. For be - hold,   the dark-ness shall cov - er   the earth, and gross dark-ness the peo - ple; but the

Lord shall a - rise   up - on thee, and his glo - ry   shall be seen   up - on thee, and his

glo - ry shall be seen   up - on thee; and the gentiles shall come to thy light, . .   to the bright-ness

and kings . . .   to the

of   thy ris - ing. Lift up thine eyes round a-bout   and see! lift up thine eyes, lift up thine eyes.

brightness of thy ris - ing.

Selection 116.

Arise! shine! for thy light is come, and the glory of the Lord is risen upon thee. For, behold, the darkness shall cover the earth, and gross darkness the people, but the Lord shall arise upon thee, and his glory shall be seen upon thee; and the gentiles shall come to thy light, and kings to the brightness of thy rising.

Lift up thine eyes round about thee, and see! Lift up thine eyes.

WEBB. 7s & 6s.

GEO. JAMES WEBB.

Choir and Congregation.

1. The morning light is breaking, The darkness dis-ap-pears; The sons of earth are wak-ing To pen-i-ten-tial tears: Each breeze that sweeps the ocean Brings tidings from a-far, Of nations in com-mo-tion, Prepar'd for Zion's war.

516　　　S. F. SMITH.

1 The morning light is breaking;
　The darkness disappears;
　The sons of earth are waking
　To penitential tears;
　Each breeze that sweeps the ocean
　Brings tidings from afar,
　Of nations in commotion,
　Prepared for Zion's war.

2 See heathen nations bending
　Before the God we love,
　And thousand hearts ascending
　In gratitude above;
　While sinners, now confessing,
　The gospel call obey,
　And seek the Savior's blessing,—
　A nation in a day.

3 Blest river of salvation!
　Pursue thine onward way;
　Flow thou to every nation,
　Nor in thy richness stay:
　Stay not till all the lowly
　Triumphant reach their home;
　Stay not till all the holy
　Proclaim—"The Lord is come!"

517　　　HASTINGS.

1 Now be the gospel banner,
　In every land, unfurled;
　And be the shout,—"Hosanna!"
　Re-echoed through the world;
　Till every isle and nation,
　Till every tribe and tongue,
　Receive the great salvation,
　And join the happy throng.

2 Yes,—thou shalt reign forever,
　O Jesus, King of kings!
　Thy light, thy love, thy favor,
　Each ransomed captive sings:
　The isles for thee are waiting,
　The deserts learn thy praise,
　The hills and valleys greeting,
　The song responsive raise.

518　　　EDMESTON.

1 Roll on, thou mighty ocean;
　And, as thy billows flow,
　Bear messengers of mercy
　To every land below.
　Arise, ye gales, and waft them
　Safe to the destined shore;
　That man may sit in darkness,
　And death's black shade no more.

2 O thou eternal Ruler,
　Who holdest in thine arm
　The tempests of the ocean,
　Protect them from all harm!
　Thy presence, Lord, be with them,
　Wherever they may be;
　Though far from us, who love them,
　Still let them be with thee.

519　　　GOUGH.

1 How beauteous on the mountains,
　The feet of him that brings,
　Like streams from living fountains,
　Good tidings of good things;
　That publisheth salvation,
　And jubilee release,
　To every tribe and nation,
　God's reign of joy and peace.

2 Lift up thy voice, O watchman,
　And shout from Zion's towers
　Thy hallelujah chorus,
　"The victory is ours!"
　The Lord shall build up Zion
　In glory and renown,
　And Jesus, Judah's Lion,
　Shall wear his rightful crown.

Selection 117.—WESLEY SERVICE.—Break forth into joy! Sing together. G. F. R.

Break forth in-to joy! break forth in-to joy! Sing to-geth-er, ye waste plac-es,

ye waste plac-es of Je-ru-sa-lem, ye waste plac-es of Je-ru-sa-lem.

For the Lord hath com-fort-ed his peo-ple, he hath re-deem-ed Je-ru-sa-

lem. Break forth in-to joy! break forth in-to joy! Sing to-geth-er, ye waste plac-es.

WESLEY. 11s & 10s.

Words by Dr. Thos. Hastings.
Music by Dr. L. Mason.

Choir and Congregation.

520 1. Hail to the bright-ness of Zi-on's glad morning! Joy to the lands that in dark-ness have lain!
2. Lo, in the des-ert rich flow-ers are springing; Streams ev-er co-pious are glid-ing a-long;
3. See, from all lands, from the isles of the o-cean, Praise to Je-ho-vah as-cend-ing on high;

Hush'd be the ac-cents of sor-row and mourning; Zi-on in tri-umph be-gins her mild reign.
Loud from the mountain tops ech-oes are ring-ing; Wastes rise in verd-ure, and min-gle in song.
Fallen are the en-gines of war and com-mo-tion; Shouts of sal-va-tion are rend-ing the sky.

The wil - der - ness   and the sol - i - ta - ry place   shall be glad for

The wil - der-ness and the sol - i - ta - ry p'ace shall be glad for

them,   shall be glad   for them, and the des - ert shall re - joice,   and
and shall

them, shall be   glad   for them,   and the des - ert shall   re - joice,   and
and shall

blos-som as   the   rose.   It shall blos - som a - bund-ant-ly, and re - joice, and re-

blos - som as the rose.   It shall blos - som a - bund-ant-ly,   and re - joice, and re-

blos-som as   the

joice, e - ven with joy,   e - ven with joy and sing - ing. It shall blos - som, it shall blos - som.

joice, e - ven with joy,   e - ven with joy and sing - ing. It shall blos - som, it shall blos - som.

16

Selection 117.—Break forth into joy.

Sing "The Wilderness," etc., between 2d and 3d verses of hymn.

PLEYEL'S HYMN. 7s.

Words by Dr. L. Bacon.
Music by Pleyel.

Choir and Congregation.

521 1. Wake the song of ju - bi - lee, Let it ech - o o'er the sea! Now is come the

prom - is'd hour; Je - sus reigns with glo - rious pow'r.

2 All ye nations, join and sing,
Praise your Savior, praise your King;
Let it sound from shore to shore—
"Jesus reigns for evermore!"

3 Hark! the desert lands rejoice;
And the islands join their voice;
Joy! the whole creation sings,—
"Jesus is the King of kings!"

MIDDLETON. 8s & 7s. Double.

Words by Rev. C. Wesley.
Music arranged.

Choir and Congregation.

522 1. Light of those whose dreary dwelling Bor - ders on the shades of death! Rise on us, thy love re-veal-ing,
2. Still we wait for thine ap-pear - ing; Life and joy thy beams im-part, Chas-ing all our fears, and cheering

Dis - si - pate the clouds be - neath: Thou of heav'n and earth Cre a - tor, In our deep - est dark-ness rise,—
Ev - 'ry poor, be - night-ed heart: Come and man - i - fest thy fa - vor To the ran-som'd, help-less race;

Scat-t'ring all the night of na - ture, Pour-ing day up - on our eyes.
Come, thou glo-rious God and Sav - ior! Come, and bring the gos-pel grace.

3 Save us, in thy great compassion,
O thou mild, pacific Prince!
Give the knowledge of salvation,
Give the pardon of our sins;
By thine all-sufficient merit,
Every burdened soul release;
Every weary, wandering spirit
Guide into thy perfect peace.

MISSIONARY HYMN. 7s & 6s.

Choir and Congregation.

Words by Bishop Heber.
Music by Dr. L. Mason.

523 1. From Greenland's i-cy mountains, From India's coral strand, Where Afric's sunny fountains Roll down their golden sand.

From many an ancient river, From many a balm-y plain, They call us to de-liv-er Their land from error's chain.

2 What though the spicy breezes
Blow soft o'er Ceylon's isle;
Though every prospect pleases,
And only man is vile;
In vain with lavish kindness
The gifts of God are strown;
The heathen, in his blindness,
Bows down to wood and stone!

3 Shall we, whose souls are lighted
With wisdom from on high,—
Shall we, to men benighted,
The lamp of life deny?
Salvation, oh, salvation!
The joyful sound proclaim,
Till earth's remotest nation
Has learned Messiah's name.

4 Waft, waft, ye winds, his story,
And you, ye waters, roll,
Till, like a sea of glory,
It spreads from pole to pole;
Till o'er our ransomed nature
The Lamb for sinners slain,
Redeemer, King, Creator,
In bliss returns to reign!

WEBB. 7s & 6s.

Choir and Congregation.

Words by James Montgomery.
Music by G. J. Webb.

524 1. Hail to the Lord's Anointed, Great David's greater Son! Hail in the time ap-point-ed, His reign on earth be-gun!

He comes to break op-pres-sion, To set the cap-tive free, To take away transgression, And rule in e-qui-ty.

2 He comes with succor speedy,
To those who suffer wrong;
To help the poor and needy,
And bid the weak be strong;
To give them songs for sighing,
Their darkness turn to light,
Whose souls, condemned and dying,
Were precious in his sight.

3 He shall come down like showers
Upon the fruitful earth,
And love and joy, like flowers,
Spring in his path to birth:
Before him on the mountains
Shall peace, the herald, go:
And righteousness, in fountains,
From hill and valley flow.

4 For him shall prayer unceasing
And daily vows ascend;
His kingdom still increasing,—
A kingdom without end:
The tide of time shall never
His covenant remove;
His name shall stand forever,—
That name to us is—Love.

Selection 118.—FABEN SERVICE.—Walk about Zion, and go round about her.

Walk a - bout Zi - on, and go round a - bout her, walk a - bout Zi - on, and go round a - bout her, Mark ye well her bul-warks! con - sid - er her pal - a - ces, Mark ye well her bul warks! Tell the tow'rs thereof. The Lord hath chos - en Zi - on, he hath de- sir'd it for his hab - i - ta - tion. Beau - ti - ful for sit - u - a - tion, the joy of the whole earth, the joy of the whole earth is Mount Zi - - on, Mount Zi - on, the cit - y of the great King.

Selection 118.

Walk about Zion, and go round about her! mark ye well her bulwarks! consider her palaces! Tell the towers thereof.

The Lord hath chosen Zion, he hath desired it for his habitation. Beautiful for situation, the joy of the whole earth is Mount Zion,—Mount Zion, the city of the great King.

FABEN. 8s & 7s. **Double.**

Words by NEWTON.
Music by Dr. J. H. WILCOX.

Choir and Congregation.

525
1. Glorious things of thee are spok-en, Zi-on! cit-y of our God! He whose word can ne'er be
2. See, the streams of liv-ing wa-ters, Springing from e-ter-nal love, Well sup-ply thy sons and
3. Round each hab-i-ta-tion hover-ing, See the cloud and fire ap-pear! For a glo-ry and a

brok-en, Formed thee for his own a-bode. On the Rock of A-ges found-ed, What can
daugh-ters, And all fear of want re-move. Who can faint, while such a riv-er Ev-er
cov'r-ing, Show-ing that the Lord is near. He who gives them dai-ly man-na, He who

shake thy sure re-pose? With sal-va-tion's wall surround-ed, Thou may'st smile on all thy foes.
flows their thirst t'assuage? Grace, which like the Lord, the Giv-er, Nev-er fails from age to age.
list-ens when they cry, Let him hear the loud ho-san-na, Ris-ing to his throne on high.

(Between 2d and 3d verses.)

Choir.

The Lord is round a-bout his peo-ple, is round a-bout his peo-ple, In the

mf

(End with tune, 3d verse.)

day-time he al-so led them with a cloud, And all the night with a light of fire.

Selection 86.—God is our Refuge and Strength.

WARD. L. M.

Words by Dr. WATTS.
Music arr. by Dr. L. MASON.

Choir and Congregation.

526 1. God is the ref-uge of his saints, When storms of sharp dis-tress in-vade; Ere we can of-fer

our com-plaints, Be-hold him pres-ent with his aid.

2 Let mountains from their seats be hurled
Down to the deep, and buried there,
Convulsions shake the solid world—
Our faith shall never yield to fear.

3 Zion enjoys her Monarch's love,
Secure against a threatening hour;
Nor can her firm foundation move,
Built on his truth, and armed with power.

Selection 116.—Arise, shine, for thy light is come.

WATCHMAN, TELL US. 7s. Double.

Words by Sir JOHN BOWRING.
Music from FRANZ ABT.

Choir and Congregation.

527 1. Watchman, tell us of the night, What its signs of promise are; Trav'ler, o'er yon mountain's height
2. Watchman, tell us of the night! High-er yet that star as-cends; Trav'ler, bless-ed-ness and light,

See that glo-ry-beaming star! Watchman, does its beauteous ray Aught of joy or hope fore-tell? Trav'ler,
Peace and truth its course portends. Watchman, will its beams a-lone Gild the spot that gave them birth? Trav'ler,

yes; it brings the day, Prom-ised day of Is-ra-el.
a-ges are its own, See, it bursts o'er all the earth.

3 Watchman, tell us of the night,
For the morning seems to dawn.
Trav'ler, darkness takes its flight,
Doubt and terror are withdrawn.
Watchman, let thy wanderings cease;
Hie thee to thy quiet home.
Trav'ler, lo! the Prince of Peace!
Lo! the Son of God is come!

DORRNANOE. 8s & 7s.

Choir and Congregation.   I. B. WOODBURY.

528 1. Take my heart, O Father! take it; Make and keep it all thine own; Let thy Spir - it melt and break it— This proud heart of sin and stone.

2 Father, make me pure and lowly,
　　Fond of peace and far from strife;
　Turning from the paths unholy
　　Of this vain and sinful life.

3 Ever let thy grace surround me;
　　Strengthen me with power divine,
　Till thy cords of love have bound me;
　　Make me to be wholly thine.

EWING. 7s & 6s.

Words translated by Rev. RAY PALMER, D. D.
Music by ALEX. EWING.

Choir and Congregation.

529 1. O Bread to pil-grims giv - en, O Food that an - gels eat, O Man - na sent from heav - en, For heaven-born na-tures meet. Give us, for thee long pin - ing, To eat till rich - ly filled; Till, earth's de-lights re - sign - ing, Our ev - ery wish is stilled.

2. O Wa - ter, life - be - stow - ing, From out the Sav - ior's heart, A fount-ain pure - ly flow - ing, A fount of love thou art. Oh, let us, free - ly tast - ing, Our burn-ing thirst as - suage; Thy sweet-ness, nev - er wast - ing, A - vails from age to age.

3 Jesus, this feast receiving,
　　We thee unseen adore;
　Thy faithful word believing,
　　We take, and doubt no more.
Give us, thou true and loving,
　　On earth to live in thee;
Then, death the veil removing,
　　Thy glorious face to see.

SILOAM. C. M.

Choir and Congregation.   I. B. WOODBURY.

1. By cool Si - lo - am's sha - dy rill, How sweet the lil - y grows;

How sweet the breath, be - neath the hill, Of Sha - ron's dew - y rose.

530   HEBER.

1 By cool Siloam's shady rill
  How sweet the lily grows;
  How sweet the breath, beneath the hill,
  Of Sharon's dewy rose!

2 Lo! such the child whose early feet
  The paths of peace have trod,
  Whose secret heart, with influence sweet,
  Is upward drawn to God.

3 By cool Siloam's shady rill
  The lily must decay;
  The rose, that blooms beneath the hill,
  Must shortly fade away.

4 And soon, too soon, the wintry hour
  Of man's maturer age
  Will shake the soul with sorrow's power,
  And stormy passion's rage.

5 O thou who givest life and breath,
  We seek thy grace alone,
  In childhood, manhood, age, and death,
  To keep us still thine own.

531   WATTS.

1 How large the promise! how divine!
  To Abr'ham and his seed:
  "I'll be a God to thee and thine,
  Supplying all their need."

2 The words of his extensive love
  From age to age endure:
  The Angel of the covenant proves,
  And seals the blessings sure.

3 Jesus the ancient faith confirms,
  To our great fathers given;
  He takes young children to his arms,
  And calls them heirs of heaven.

4 Our God!—how faithful are his ways!
  His love endures the same;
  Nor from the promise of his grace
  Blots out the children's name.

532   DODDRIDGE.

1 O God of Bethel, by whose hand
  Thy people still are fed;
  Who through this weary pilgrimage
  Hast all our fathers led!

2 Our vows, our prayers, we now present,
  Before thy throne of grace;
  God of our fathers! be the God
  Of their succeeding race.

3 Through each perplexing path of life
  Our wandering footsteps guide;
  Give us, each day, our daily bread,
  And raiment fit provide.

4 Oh, spread thy covering wings around,
  Till all our wanderings cease,
  And at our Father's loved abode,
  Our souls arrive in peace.

5 Such blessings from thy gracious hand
  Our humble prayers implore;
  And thou shalt be our chosen God,
  Our portion evermore.

533   DODDRIDGE.

1 See, Israel's gentle Shepherd stands,
  With all engaging charms;
  Hark, how he calls the tender lambs,
  And folds them in his arms!

2 "Permit them to approach," he cries,
  "Nor scorn their humble name;
  For 't was to bless such souls as these
  The Lord of angels came."

3 We bring them, Lord, in thankful hands,
  And yield them up to thee;
  Joyful that we ourselves are thine,
  Thine let our offspring be.

4 Ye little flock, with pleasure hear;
  Ye children, seek his face;
  And fly, with transport, to receive,
  The blessings of his grace.

534   MONTGOMERY.

1 Shepherd of souls, refresh and bless
  Thy chosen pilgrim flock,
  With manna from the wilderness,
  With water from the rock.

2 Be known to us in breaking bread,
  But do not then depart;
  Savior, abide with us and spread
  Thy table in our heart.

3 Oh, sup with us in love divine;
  Thy body and thy blood,
  That living bread, that heavenly wine,
  Be our immortal food.

(Lord's Supper.)

(Tune, Evan, p. 224.)

535 [C. M.] MONTGOMERY.

1 According to thy gracious word,
In meek humility,
This will I do, my dying Lord,
I will remember thee.

2 Thy body, broken for my sake,
My bread from heaven shall be·
Thy testamental cup I take,
And thus remember thee.

3 Remember thee, and all thy pains
And all thy love to me;
Yea, while a breath, a pulse remains,
Will I remember thee.

4 And when these failing lips grow dumb,
And mind and memory flee,
When thou shalt in thy kingdom come,
Then, Lord, remember me!

(Lord's Supper.)

(Tune, Evan, p. 224.)

536 [C. M.] NOEL.

1 If human kindness meets return,
And owns the grateful tie;
If tender thoughts within us burn,
To feel a friend is nigh;—

2 Oh, shall not warmer accents tell
The gratitude we owe
To him, who died our fears to quell—
Who bore our guilt and woe!

3 While yet in anguish he surveyed
Those pangs he would not flee,
What love his latest words displayed,—
"Meet and remember me!"

4 Remember thee—thy death, thy shame,
Our sinful hearts to share!—
O memory! leave no other name
But his recorded there.

(Lord's Supper.)

(Tune, Evan, p. 224.)

537 C. M.] BONAR.

1 Opprest with noon-day's scorching heat,
To yonder cross I flee;
Beneath its shelter take my seat:
No shade like this for me!

2 Beneath that cross clear waters burst—
A fountain sparkling free;
And there I quench my desert thirst:
No spring like this for me!

3 A stranger here, I pitch my tent
Beneath this spreading tree;
Here shall my pilgrim life be spent:
No home like this for me!

4 For burdened ones a resting-place,
Beside that cross I see;
I here cast off my weariness:
No rest like this for me!

(Ministry.)

(Sel. 114. How lovely the feet. Tune, Key of D.)

538 [S. M.] WATTS.

1 How beauteous are their feet
Who stand on Zion's hill!
Who bring salvation on their tongues,
And words of peace reveal.

2 How charming is their voice!
How sweet their tidings are!
"Zion, behold thy Savior King;
He reigns and triumphs here."

3 How happy are our ears,
That hear this joyful sound!
Which kings and prophets waited for,
And sought, but never found.

4 How blessed are our eyes,
That see this heavenly light!
Prophets and kings desired it long,
But died without the sight.

5 The watchmen join their voice,
And tuneful notes employ;
Jerusalem breaks forth in songs,
And deserts learn the joy.

6 The Lord makes bare his arm
Through all the earth abroad;
Let every nation now behold
Their Savior and their God!

(Welcoming a Pastor.)

Sel. 114. How lovely the feet. Tune, Grigg, p. 228.)

539 [L. M.] MONTGOMERY.

1 We bid thee welcome in the name
Of Jesus, our exalted Head;
Come as a servant: so he came,
And we receive thee in his stead.

2 Come as a shepherd; guard and keep
This fold from hell, and earth, and sin;
Nourish the lambs, and feed the sheep,
The wounded heal, the lost bring in.

3 Come as a teacher, sent from God,
Charged his whole counsel to declare;
Left o'er our ranks the prophet's rod,
While we uphold thy hands with prayer.

4 Come as a messenger of peace,
Filled with the Spirit, fired with love!
Live to behold our large increase,
And die to meet us all above.

(For Dedication.)

(Sel. 118. Walk about Zion, without interlude. Tune, St. Anns, in D flat, p. 75.)

540 [C. M.] COXE.

1 Oh, where are kings and empires now
Of old that went and came?
But, Lord, thy church is praying yet,
A thousand years the same.

2 We mark her goodly battlements,
And her foundations strong;
We hear within the solemn voice
Of her unending song.

3 For not like kingdoms of the world
Thy holy church, O God!
Though earthquake shocks are threatening her,
And tempests are abroad;—

4 Unshaken as eternal hills,
Immovable she stands,
A mountain that shall fill the earth,
A house not made by hands.

(For Dedication.)

(Sel. 118. Walk about Zion, without interlude. Tune, St. Anns, in D flat, p. 75.)

541 [C. M.] BRYANT.

1 O thou, whose own vast temple stands,
Built over earth and sea,
Accept the walls that human hands
Have raised to worship thee.

2 Lord, from thine inmost glory send,
Within these courts to bide,
The peace that dwelleth without end,
Serenely by thy side!

3 May erring minds that worship here
Be taught the better way;
And they who mourn, and they who fear,
Be strengthened as they pray.

4 May faith grow firm, and love grow warm,
And pure devotion rise,
While round these hallowed walls the storm
Of earth-born passion dies.

Selection 119.—BENEVENTO SERVICE.—Thou carriest them away. (Close of year.)

Choir. Somber. *p* Cres. *f* G. F. R.

Thou car-riest them a-way, thou car-riest them a-way as with a flood, as with a flood, they

Slow and soft. Duet.

are as a-sleep. In the morn-ing they are like grass which grow-eth up, in the morning it

Cres. *mf* Dim.

flour-ish-eth and grow-eth up, in the evening it is cut down and with-er-eth.

Solo.

Thou turn-est

Choir. *m* *p*

And say-est, re-turn, re-turn, ye children of men, ye chil-dren of men.

man to de-struc-tion.

BENEVENTO. 7s. Double.

Words by Rev. JOHN NEWTON.
Music by S. WEBBE.

Choir and Congregation.

542

1. While with ceaseless course the sun Hasted thro' the former year, Many souls their race have run, Nevermore to meet us here;
2. Thanks for mercies past receive; Pardon for our sins renew; Teach us henceforth how to live, With e-ter-ni-ty in view;

Fixed in an e-ter-nal state, They have done with all below; We a lit-tle longer wait, But how lit-tle, none can know.
Bless thy word to old and young, Fill us with a Savior's love; When our life's short race is run, May we dwell with thee a-bove.

(Tune, Duke St., p. 98.)

543 [L. M. National.]

BACON.

1 O God, beneath thy guiding hand,
Our exiled fathers crossed the sea ;
And when they trod the wintry strand,
With prayer and psalm they worshiped thee.

2 Thou heard'st, well-pleas'd the song, the pray'r;
Thy blessing came ; and still its power
Shall onward through all ages bear
The memory of that holy hour.

3 Laws, freedom, truth, and faith in God
Came with those exiles o'er the waves ;
And where their pilgrim feet have trod,
The God they trusted guards their graves.

4 And here thy name, O God of love,
Their children's children shall adore,
Till these eternal hills remove,
And spring adorns the earth no more.

(Tune, Duke St., p. 98.)

544 [L. M. New Year.]

DOODRIDGE.

1 Great God, we sing that mighty hand,
By which supported still we stand :
The opening year thy mercy shows ;
Let mercy crown it till it close.

2 By day, by night—at home, abroad,
Still we are guarded by our God ;
By his incessant bounty fed,
By his unerring counsel led.

3 With grateful hearts the past we own :
The future—all to us unknown—
We to thy guardian care commit,
And peaceful leave before thy feet.

4 In scenes excited or depressed,
Be thou our joy, and thou our rest ;
Thy goodness all our hopes shall raise,
Adored, through all our changing days.

5 When death shall close our earthly songs,
And seal, in silence, mortal tongues,
Our Helper, God, in whom we trust,
Shall keep our souls and guard our dust.

(Tune, Naomi, p. 141.)

545 [C. M. Close of year.]

WATTS.

1 Thee we adore, eternal Name !
And humbly own to thee
How feeble is our mortal frame,
What dying worms are we !

2 The year rolls round, and steals away
The breath that first it gave ;
Whate'er we do, whate'er we be,
We're traveling to the grave.

3 Great God ! on what a slender thread
Hang everlasting things !
The eternal state of all the dead
Upon life's feeble strings !

4 Infinite joy, or endless woe,
Attends on every breath ;
And yet, how unconcerned we go
Upon the brink of death !

5 Waken, O Lord, our drowsy sense,
To walk this dangerous road !
And if our souls are hurried hence,
May they be found with God.

Tune, Amsterdam, p. 261.

546 [7s. and 6s. Close of year.]

BURTON.

1 Time is winging us away
To our eternal home ;
Life is but a winter's day—
A journey to the tomb ;
Youth and vigor soon will flee,
Blooming beauty lose its charms ;
All that's mortal soon shall be
Enclosed in death's cold arms.

2 Time is winging us away
To our eternal home ;
Life is but a winter's day—
A journey to the tomb ;
But the Christian shall enjoy
Health and beauty, soon, above,
Far beyond the world's alloy,
Secure in Jesus' love.

(Tune, Nuremburg, p. 53.)

547 [7s. Thanksgiving.]

MONTGOMERY.

1 Thank and praise Jehovah's name !
For his mercies, firm and sure,
From eternity the same,
To eternity endure.

2 Let the ransomed thus rejoice,
Gathered out of every land,
As the people of his choice,
Plucked from the destroyer's hand.

3 To a pleasant land he brings,
Where the vine and olive grow,
Where, from flowery hills, the springs
Through luxuriant valleys flow.

4 Oh, that men would praise the Lord
For his goodness to their race ;
For the wonders of his word,
And the riches of his grace !

(Tune, Nuremburg, p. 53.)

548 [7s. Thanksgiving.]

STRONG.

1 Swell the anthem, raise the song ;
Praises to our God belong ;
Saints and angels join to sing
Praises to the heavenly King.

2 Blessings from his liberal hand
Flow around this happy land :
Kept by him, no foes annoy ;
Peace and freedom we enjoy.

3 Here, beneath a virtuous sway,
May we cheerfully obey ;
Never feel oppression's rod,
Ever own and worship God.

(Tune, Temple, p. 23.)

549 [8s. and 7s. double. Reform.]

COKE.

1 We are living, we are dwelling,
In a grand and awful time,
In an age on ages telling,
To be living is sublime !
Hark ! the waking up of nations,
Gog and Magog to the fray !
Hark ! what soundeth ? is creation
Groaning for its latter day ?

2 Worlds are charging, heaven beholding,
Thou hast but an hour to fight ;
Now the blazoned cross unfolding,
On—right onward, for the right !
On ! let all the soul within you
For the truth's sake go abroad !
Strike ! let every nerve and sinew
Tell on ages—tell for God !

(This hymn may be sung to Wilmot, p. 55 ; or to
any 8s. and 7s. tune, by making the last line
of each verse " Far at sea, far, far at sea.")

550 [P. M. Seamen.]

MRS. SIMPSON.

1 Star of peace ! to wanderers weary,
Bright the beams that smile on me,
Cheer the pilot's vision dreary,
Far, far at sea.

2 Star of hope ! gleam on the billow,
Bless the soul that sighs for thee ;
Bless the sailor's lonely pillow,
Far, far at sea.

3 Star of faith ! when winds are mocking
All his toil, he flies to thee ;
Save him on the billows rocking,
Far, far at sea,

4 Star divine ! oh, safely guide him,—
Bring the wanderer home to thee !
Sore temptations long have tried him,
Far, far at sea.

OCCASIONAL.

AMERICA. 6s & 4s.

Choir and Congregation.

Words by Rev. S. F. SMITH.
Music arr. by HENRY CAREY.

551
1. My country, 'tis of thee, Sweet land of lib-er-ty, Of thee I sing: Land where my fathers died! Land of the
2. Let music swell the breeze, And ring from all the trees Sweet freedom's song: Let mortal tongues awake, Let all that

pil-grim's pride! From ev-'ry mountain side Let free-dom ring.
breathe partake, Let rocks their si-lence break, The sound pro-long.

3 Our fathers' God, to thee—
Author of liberty—
To thee we sing;
Long may our land be bright,
With freedom's holy light;
Protect us by thy might,
Great God, our King!

HOMEWARD. 10s & 5s.

Words by Rev. C. WESLEY.

In singing observe the repetition of the words in the 1st verse, and make a similar repetition in 2d and 3d verses.

Choir and Congregation.   Roll round   .   .   Music arr. for this work.

552
1. Come, let us a - new our jour-ney pur-sue, Roll round with the year, And never stand still till the

Roll round

Mas-ter ap-pear, till the Mas-ter ap-pear; His a-dor-a-ble will let us glad-ly ful-fill, And our

tal-ents im-prove, our tal-ents im-prove By the pa-tience of hope and the la-bor of love.

2 Our life is a dream,
Our time, as a stream,
Glides swiftly away,
And the fugitive moment refuses to stay.
The arrow is flown,
The moment is gone,
The millennial year
Rushes on to our view, and eternity's near.

3 Oh, that each in the day
Of his coming might say,
"I have fought my way through,
"I have finished the work thou didst give me to do."
Oh, that each from his Lord
May but hear the glad word,
"Well and faithfully done,
"Enter into thy joy, and receive now thy crown."

553 [L. M.]   FORD.

1 How vain is all beneath the skies!
How transient every earthly bliss!
How slender all the fondest ties,
That bind us to a world like this!

2 The evening cloud, the morning dew,
The withering grass, the fading flower,
Of earthly hopes are emblems true—
The glory of a passing hour!

3 But though earth's fairest blossoms die,
And all beneath the skies is vain,
There is a land, whose confines lie
Beyond the reach of care and pain.

4 Then let the hope of joys to come
Dispel our cares, and chase our fears:
If God be ours, we're traveling home,
Though passing through a vale of tears.

554 [7s. 6 lines.]   MANT.

1 Son of God! to thee I cry:
By the holy mystery
Of thy dwelling here on earth,
By thy pure and holy birth,
Hear, oh, hear my lowly plea!
Manifest thyself to me!

2 Lamb of God! to thee I cry:
By thy bitter agony,
By thy pangs to us unknown,
By thy spirit's parting groan,
Hear, oh, hear my lowly plea:
Manifest thyself to me!

3 Lord of glory, God most high!
Man exalted to the sky!
With thy love my bosom fill,
Prompt me to perform thy will:
Then thy glory I shall see—
Thou wilt bring me home to thee.

555 [7s.]   MANDE.

1 Thine forever! God of love,
Hear us from thy throne above!
Thine forever may we be,
Here, and in eternity!

2 Thine forever! oh, how blest
They who find in thee their rest!
Savior, Guardian, heavenly Friend,
Oh, defend us to the end!

3 Thine forever! Savior, keep
These thy frail and trembling sheep;
Safe alone beneath thy care,
Let us all thy goodness share.

4 Thine forever! thou our Guide,—
All our wants by thee supplied,—
All our sins by thee forgiven,—
Lead us, Lord, from earth to heaven!

556 [C. M.]   WATTS.

1 How sweet and awful is the place,
With Christ within the doors,
While everlasting love displays
The choicest of her stores!

2 While all our hearts, and all our songs,
Join to admire the feast,
Each of us cries, with thankful tongue,—
"Lord, why was I a guest?

3 "Why was I made to hear thy voice,
And enter while there's room,
When thousands make a wretched choice,
And rather starve than come?"

4 'Twas the same love that spread the feast,
That sweetly drew us in;
Else we had still refused to taste,
And perished in our sin.

5 Pity the nations, O our God!
Constrain the earth to come;
Send thy victorious word abroad,
And bring the strangers home.

557 [C. M.]   ANON.

1 Remember thy Creator now,
In these thy youthful days;
He will accept thine earliest vow,
And listen to thy praise.

2 Remember thy Creator now,
Seek him while he is near;
For evil days will come, when thou
Shalt find no comfort here.

3 Remember thy Creator now,
His willing servant be:
Then, when thy head in death shall bow,
He will remember thee.

4 Almighty God! our hearts incline
Thy heavenly voice to hear;
Let all our future days be thine,
Devoted to thy fear.

558 [L. M. 6 lines.]   ANON.

1 At evening time let there be light;
Life's little day draws near its close;
Around me fall the shades of night,
The night of death, the grave's repose
To crown my joys, to end my woes,
At evening time let there be light.

2 At evening time let there be light:
Stormy and dark hath been my day;
Yet rose the morn divinely bright;
Dews, birds, and blossoms cheered the way;
Oh, for one sweet, one parting ray!
At evening time let there be light.

3 At evening time there shall be light!
For God hath spoken; it must be:
Fear, doubt, and anguish take their flight;
His glory now is risen on me;
Mine eyes shall his salvation see:
'T is evening time, and there is light!

559 [S. M.]   WATTS.

1 When overwhelmed with grief,
My heart within me dies,
Helpless, and far from all relief,
To heaven I lift mine eyes.

2 Oh, lead me to the Rock
That's high above my head,
And make the covert of thy wings
My shelter and my shade!

3 Within thy presence, Lord,
Forever I'll abide;
Thou art the tower of my defence,
The refuge where I hide.

4 Thou givest me the lot
Of those that fear thy name;
If endless life be their reward,
I shall possess the same.

560 [C. M.]   ANON.

1 We bless thee for thy peace, O God!
Deep as the soundless sea,
Which falls like sunshine on the road
Of those who trust in thee.

2 We ask not, Father, for repose
Which comes from outward rest,
If we may have within our woes
Thy peace within our breast;—

3 That peace which suffers and is strong,
Trusts where it cannot see,
Deems not the trial way too long,
But leaves the end with thee;—

4 That peace which flows serene and deep—
A river in the soul,
Whose banks a living verdure keep:
God's sunshine o'er the whole!

5 Such, Father, give our hearts such peace,
Whate'er the outward be,
Till all life's discipline shall cease,
And we go home to thee.

Selection 120.—FUNERAL SERVICE.—Blessed are the dead.

Bless-ed are the dead who die in the Lord, bless-ed are the dead who die in the Lord from henceforth.

Yea! saith the spir - it, that they may rest, that they may rest from their la - bors, rest from their la - bors,

and their works do fol - low them, and their works do fol - low them, and their works do fol - low them, do

and their works do fol - low them, do

fol - low them. Bless-ed are the dead who die in the Lord, bless-ed are the dead who die in the Lord.

CHINA. C. M.

Words by Dr. WATTS.
Music by T. SWAN.

Choir and Congregation.

561 1. Why do we mourn de - part - ing friends, Or shake at death's a - larms? 'Tis but the voice that

Je - sus sends To call them to his arms.

2 The graves of all the saints he blessed,
    And softened every bed,
  Where should the dying members rest,
    But with the dying Head.

3 Thence he arose, ascending high,
    And showed our feet the way,
  Up to the Lord we too shall fly,
    At the great rising day.

Selection 120.—Blessed are the dead who die in the Lord.

HEBRON. L. M.

Words by Mrs. MACKAY.
Music by Dr. L. MASON.

Choir and Congregation.

562
1. A - sleep in Je - sus! bless-ed sleep! From which none ev - er wake to weep; A calm and un - dis-
2. A - sleep in Je - sus! oh, how sweet To be for such a slum-ber meet! With ho - ly con - fi-

turb'd re - pose, Un - brok - en by the last of foes.
dence to sing That death, in him, hath lost its sting!

3 Asleep in Jesus! peaceful rest!
Whose waking is supremely blest;
No fear, no woe shall dim the hour
That manifests the Savior's power.

4 Asleep in Jesus! oh, for me
May such a blissful refuge be:
May mine still be this blessed sleep
From which none ever wake to weep.

563 BARBAULD.

1 How blest the righteous when he dies!
When sinks a weary soul to rest;
How mildly beam the closing eyes,
How gently heaves th' expiring breast.

2 So fades a summer cloud away;
So sinks the gale when storms are o'er;
So gently shuts the eye of day;
So dies a wave along the shore.

3 A holy quiet reigns around,
A calm which life nor death destroys;
And naught disturbs that peace profound
Which his unfettered soul enjoys.

Selection 120.—Blessed are the dead who die in the Lord.

OLMUTZ. S. M.

Music arr. by Dr. L. MASON.

Choir and Congregation.

1. "For-ev - er with the Lord!" A-men! so let it be; Life from the dead is in that word; 'Tis immortal - i - ty.

564 MONTGOMERY.

1 "Forever with the Lord!"
Amen! so let it be;
Life from the dead is in that word;
'T is immortality.

2 Here, in the body pent,
Absent from thee I roam;
Yet nightly pitch my moving tent
A day's march nearer home.

3 "Forever with the Lord!"
Father, if 't is thy will,
The promise of thy gracious word
E'en here to me fulfil.

4 So, when my latest breath
Shall rend the veil in twain,
By death I shall escape from death,
And life eternal gain.

565 BETHUNE.

1 It is not death to die—
To leave this weary road,
And, 'mid the brotherhood on high,
To be at home with God.

2 It is not death to close
The eye long dimmed by tears,
And wake, in glorious repose
To spend eternal years.

3 It is not death to bear
The wrench that sets us free [air
From dungeon chain—to breathe the
Of boundless liberty.

4 It is not death to fling
Aside this sinful dust,
And rise, on strong exulting wing,
To live among the just.

5 Jesus, thou Prince of life!
Thy chosen can not die;
Like thee, they conquer in the strife,
To reign with thee on high.

Selection 121.—MT. VERNON SERVICE.—Hark! on that sigh a soul hath gone to rest.

Hark! on that sigh a soul hath gone to rest, a soul hath gone to rest; Sweet was the smile that

bade it burst to life, A heav'n-born beam il - lum'd the dy - ing breast, And gen - tly still'd the last convulsive

strife, the last con-vul - sive strife. Hark! on that sigh a soul hath gone to rest, hath gone to rest.

MT. VERNON. 8s & 7s.

Words by S. F. SMITH.
Music by Dr. L. MASON.

Choir and Congregation.

566 1. Sis-ter, thou wast mild and love - ly, Gen - tle as the sum - mer breeze, Pleas - ant as the

air of eve - ning, When it floats a - mong the trees.

2 Dearest sister, thou hast left us,
    Here thy loss we deeply feel;
    But 't is God that hath bereft us:
    He can all our sorrows heal.

3 Yet again we hope to meet thee,
    When the day of life is fled,
    Then in heaven with joy to greet thee,
    Where no farewell tear is shed.

Selection 132.—SCOTLAND SERVICE.—Thy brother shall rise again.

G. F. R.

Choir. *p*

Thy broth-er shall rise a-gain, shall rise a-gain.   I am the Re-sur-rec-tion, the Re-sur-

rec-tion and the Life; he that be-liev-eth on me, though he were dead, though he were dead, yet shall he

live; and who-so-ev-er liv-eth and be-liev-eth in   me, shall nev-er die, shall nev-er die.

SCOTLAND. 12s.

Words by Bishop HEBER.
Music by J. CLARK.

Choir and Congregation.

567 1. Thou art gone to the grave! but we will not de-plore thee, Tho' sor-rows and dark-ness en-
2. Thou art gone to the grave! but we will not de-plore thee, Since God was thy ran-som, thy

com-pass the tomb; The Sav-ior has pass'd thro' its por-tals be-fore thee, And the lamp of his
Guardian and Guide; He gave thee, he took thee, and he will re-store thee, And death hath no

love is thy guide thro' the gloom, And the lamp of his love is thy guide thro' the gloom.
sting since the Sav-ior hath died,   And death hath no sting since the Sav-ior hath died.

17

Selection 123.—BARTIMEUS SERVICE.—Precious in the sight of the Lord.

Choir.   m   p   m   G. F. R.

Pre - cious in the sight of the Lord is the death of his saints; for tho' the

bod - y die, for tho' the bod - y die, the soul shall live for - ev - er, the soul shall

live for - ev - er.   Let not your heart be troub - led, let not your heart be troub - led.

BARTIMEUS. 8s & 7s.

Choir and Congregation.

Words by Rev. W. B. COLLYER.
Music by DANIEL READ.

568 1. Cease, ye mourn-ers, cease to lan-guish   O'er the grave of those you love;   Pain and death, and
      2. While our si - lent steps are stray-ing   Lone - ly thro' night's deep'ning shade,   Glo - ry's bright - est

night and an-guish,   En - ter not the world a - bove.
beams are play-ing   Round the hap - py Chris - tian's head.

2 Light and peace at once deriving
   From the hand of God most high,
   In his glorious presence living,
   They shall never, never die.

4 Now, ye mourners, cease to languish,
   O'er the grave of those you love;
   Far removed from pain and anguish,
   They are chanting hymns above.

Selection 124.—OAK SERVICE.—In my Father's house are many mansions.

Choir. Reverently.

G. F. R.

In my Fa-ther's house are ma-ny man-sions: if it were not so, I would have

told you. I go to pre-pare a place for you. And if I go and pre-pare a place for

you, I will come a-gain, and re-ceive you, I will come a-gain, and re-ceive you

un-to my-self; that where I am, that where I am, there, there, ye may be al - so.

OAK. 6s & 4s.

Words by Rev. Thos. R. Taylor.
Music by Dr. L. Mason.

Choir and Congregation.

569
1. I'm but a stran-ger here, Heav'n is my home; Earth's but a des-ert drear, Heav'n is my home;
2. What tho' the tem-pests rage, Heav'n is my home; Short is my pil-grim-age, Heav'n is my home;

Dan-ger and sor-row stand Round me on ev-ery hand; Heav'n is my fa-ther-land, Heav'n is my home.
Time's cold and win-try blast Soon will be o-ver-past; I shall reach home at last, Heav'n is my home.

Selection 125.—VARINA SERVICE.—Blessed are they.

Bless-ed, bless-ed are they that do his commandments, that they may have right to the tree of life, that

they may have right to the tree of life, and may en-ter in thro' the gates in-to the cit-y, may

en-ter in thro' the gates in-to the cit-y. They shall hun-ger no more, neither thirst an-y

more; neither shall the sun light on them, nor an-y heat, for the Lamb which is in the

Nor shall the sun light on them,

midst of the throne shall feel them, shall feed them, and shall lead them, shall lead them un-to

fountains of liv-ing wa-ters; and God shall wipe a-way all tears, shall wipe a-way all tears from their eyes.

Selection 125.

Blessed are they that do his commandments, that they may have right to the tree of life, and may enter in through the gates into the city.

They shall hunger no more, neither thirst any more;

neither shall the sun light on them, nor any heat, for the Lamb which is in the midst of the throne shall feed them, and shall lead them unto fountains of living waters; and God shall wipe away all tears from their eyes.

VARINA. C. M. Double.

Choir and Congregation.

Words by Dr. WATTS.
Music arr. by G. F. ROOT.

570
1. There is a land of pure de-light, Where sun's im-mor-tal reign; In-fi-nite day ex-
2. Oh, could we make our doubts re-move, Those gloomy doubts that rise, And view the Ca-naan

cludes the night, And pleas-ures ban-ish pain. There ev-er-last-ing spring a-bides, And
that we love, With un-be-cloud-ed eyes; Could we but climb where Mo-ses stood, And

nev-er-with'ring flow'rs; Death, like a nar-row sea, di-vides This heavenly land from ours.
view the landscape o'er, Not Jordan's stream, nor death's cold flood, Should fright us from the shore.

571
WATTS.

1 Give me the wings of faith, to rise
  Within the vail, and see
  The saints above, how great their joys,
  How bright their glories be.

2 I ask them—whence their victory came?
  They, with united breath,
  Ascribe their conquest to the Lamb,—
  Their triumph to his death.

3 They marked the footsteps he had trod;
  His zeal inspired their breast;
  And following their incarnate God,
  Possess the promised rest.

4 Our glorious Leader claims our praise,
  For his own pattern given,—
  While the long cloud of witnesses
  Show the same path to heaven.

572
DICKSON.

1 O mother dear, Jerusalem,
  When shall I come to thee?
  When shall my sorrows have an end,
  Thy joys when shall I see?

2 Oh, happy harbor of God's saints?
  Oh, sweet and pleasant soil!
  In thee no sorrow can be found,
  Nor grief, nor care, nor toil.

3 No dimly cloud o'ershadows thee,
  Nor gloom, nor darksome night;
  But every soul shines as the sun,
  For God himself gives light.

4 Thy walls are made of precious stone,
  Thy bulwarks diamond-square,
  Thy gates are all of orient pearl—
  O God! if I were there!

573
MONTGOMERY.

1 While thro' this changing world we roam
  From infancy to age,
  Heaven is the Christian pilgrim's home,
  His rest at every stage.

2 Thither, his raptured thought ascends,
  Eternal joys to share;
  There, his adoring spirit bends,
  While here, he kneels in prayer.

3 From earth his freed affections rise,
  To fix on things above,
  Where all his hope of glory lies,
  Where all is perfect love.

4 There, too, may we our treasure place—
  There let our hearts be found;
  That still, where sin abounded, grace
  May more and more abound.

Selection 126.—AMSTERDAM SERVICE.—Eye hath not seen, nor hath ear heard.

Eye hath not seen, nor hath ear heard, nei-ther have en-tered in-to the

heart of man, the things which God hath pre-pared for them that love . . . him.

Thou wilt show me the path of life, in thy pres-ence is fullness of joy, and at thy right hand there are pleasures,

there are plea-sures for ev - ermore, there are pleasures for ev - ermore, there are pleasures for ev - er-more.

Selection 126.

Eye hath not seen, nor hath ear heard, neither have entered into the heart of man, the things which God hath prepared for them that love him.

Thou wilt show me the path of life; in thy presence is fullness of joy, and at thy right hand there are pleasures forevermore.

AMSTERDAM. 7s & 6s.

Words by REV. R. SEAGRAVE.
Music by Dr. NARES.

Choir and Congregation.

574.
1. { Rise, my soul, and stretch thy wings, Thy better portion trace ; }
{ Rise from transitory things, Tow'rd heav'n, thy native place. } Sun and moon and stars decay,
2. { Rivers to the ocean run, Nor stay in all their course: }
{ Fire ascending seeks the sun, Both speed them to their source. } So a soul that's born of God,

Time shall soon this earth remove; Rise, my soul, and haste away, To seats prepared above.
Pants to see his glorious face, Upward tends to his abode, To rest in his embrace.

SHINING SHORE. 8s & 7s.

Words by REV. DAVID NELSON.
Music by GEO. F. ROOT.

Choir and Congregation.

575.
1. My days are gliding swiftly by, And I, a pilgrim stranger, Would not detain them as they fly,
2. We'll gird our loins, my brethren dear, Our heav'nly home discerning; Our absent Lord has left us word,

CHORUS.

Those hours of toil and danger. For oh, we stand on Jordan's strand, Our friends are passing over; And
Let ev'ry lamp be burning.

just before, the Shining Shore We may almost discover.

3 Should coming days be cold and dark,
We need not cease our singing;
That perfect rest naught can molest,
Where golden harps are ringing. *Cho.*

4 Let sorrow's rudest tempests blow,
Each chord on earth to sever; [home,
Our King says, Come, and there's our
Forever, oh, forever! *Cho.*

Selection 126.—Eye hath not seen; or, Sel. 127, In my Father's house.

WOODLAND. C. M. 5 lines.

Choir and Congregation.

Words by Rev. W. B. Tappan.
Music by N. D. Gould.

576.
1. There is an hour of peaceful rest, To mourning wand'rers giv'n; There is a joy for souls distress'd,
2. There is a home for wea-ry souls, By sin and sorrow driv'n—When toss'd on life's tem-pestuous shoals,

A balm for ev-'ry wound-ed breast; 'Tis found a-bove—in heav'n.
Where storms a-rise, and o-cean rolls, And all is drear, but heav'n.

3 There faith lifts up her cheerful eye
   To brighter prospects given;
   And views the tempest passing by,
   The evening shadows quickly fly,
   And all serene—in heaven.

4 There fragrant flow'rs immortal bloom,
   And joys supreme are given;
   There rays divine disperse the gloom;
   Beyond the confines of the tomb
   Appears the dawn of heaven!

Selection 125.—Blessed are they that do his commandments.

PARADISE. P. M.

Choir and Congregation.

Words by Rev. F. W. Faber.
Music by J. Barnby.

577.
1. O Par-a-dise, O Par-a-dise, Who doth not crave for rest? Who would not seek the hap-py land

Where loy-al hearts, and true,

REFRAIN.

Where they that lov'd are blest? Where loy - al hearts, and true, Stand ev - er in the light,

Subdued and reverent.

All rap-ture thro' and thro' In God's most ho - ly sight.

2 O Paradise, O Paradise,
   The world is growing old;
   Who would not be at rest, and free,
   Where love is never cold? *Ref.*

3 O Paradise, O Paradise,
   'Tis weary waiting here;
   Oh, joy to be where Jesus is!
   To feel, to see him near. *Ref.*

REST FOR THE WEARY. 8s & 7s.

Words by Rev. SAMUEL Y. HARMER.
Music by Rev. WM. McDONALD.

Choir and Congregation.

578

1. In the Christian's home in glo-ry, There re-mains a land of rest; There my Savior's gone be-fore me,
2. He is fit-ting up my man-sion, Which e-ter-nal-ly shall stand, For my stay shall not be transient,

To ful-fil my soul's re-quest. There is rest for the wea-ry, There is rest for the wea-ry, There is
In that ho-ly, hap-py land.

Chorus.

rest for the wea-ry, There is rest for you, On the oth-er side of Jor-dan, In the sweet fields of

E-den, Where the tree of life is blooming, There is rest for you.

3 And the grave shall then be conquered,
And the sting of death be lost;
And our bark, all safely anchored,
Never more be tempest-tost. *Cho.*

4 Sing, oh, sing, ye heirs of glory:
Shout your triumph as you go;
Zion's gate will ope before ye,
You shall find an entrance through.
Cho.

(Sel. 125. Blessed are they. Tune, Varina, p. 259.)

579   [C. M.]   ANON.

1 Jerusalem, my happy home,
Name ever dear to me,
When shall my labors have an end
In joy and peace in thee?

2 Oh, when, thou City of my God,
Shall I thy courts ascend,
Where congregations ne'er break up,
And Sabbaths have no end.

3 There happier bowers than Eden's bloom,
Nor sin nor sorrow know;
Blest seats! thro' rude and stormy scenes,
I onward press to you.

4 Why should I shrink at pain and woe?
Or feel at death dismay?
I've Canaan's goodly land in view,
And realms of endless day.

5 Apostles, martyrs, prophets there,
Around my Savior stand;
And soon my friends in Christ below,
Will join the glorious band.

6 Jerusalem, my happy home,
My soul still pants for thee;
Then shall my labors have an end,
When I thy joys shall see.

Selection 127.—EWING SERVICE.—And the city was pure gold.

And the cit-y was pure gold, was pure . . . gold. And the founda-tions of the walls of the

was pure gold.

cit-y were gar-nished with all man-ner of prec-ious stones. And the cit-y had no need of the

sun, nei-ther of the moon to shine in it: for the glo-ry of God did

For the

light-en it, for the glo-ry of God did light-en it, and the Lamb was the light there-

glo-ry of God did light-en it, did light-en it,

of, the glo-ry of God did light-en it, and the Lamb is the light there-of.

Selection 127.

And the city was pure gold. And the foundations of the walls of the city were garnished with all manner of precious stones.

And the city had no need of the sun, neither of the moon to shine in it: for the glory of God did lighten it, and the Lamb is the light thereof.

EWING. 7s & 6s.

Choir and Congregation.

Words by Bishop BERNARD.
Music by Bishop ALEX. EWING.

580
1. Je - ru - sa - lem the gold - en, With milk and hon - ey blest, Beneath thy con - tem - pla - tion
2. They stand, those halls of Zi - on, All ju - bi - lant with song, And bright with many an an - gel,

Sink heart and voice op-pres-ed, I know not, oh, I know not What joys a - wait me there,
And all the mar - tyr throng. There is the throne of Da - vid, And there, from toil re - leased,

What ra - dian - cy of glo - ry, What bliss be - yond com-pare.
The shout of them that tri-umph, The song of them that feast.

3 And they who with their Leader,
Have conquered in the fight,
Forever and forever
Are clad in robes of white.
Oh, land that see'st no sorrow!
Oh, state that fear'st no strife!
Oh, royal land of flowers!
Oh, realm, and home of life!

581
BERNARD.

1 Jerusalem the glorious!
The glory of the elect,—
Oh, dear and future vision
That eager hearts expect!
E'en now by faith I see thee,
E'en here thy walls discern;
To thee my thoughts are kindled,
And strive, and pant, and yearn.

2 With jasper glow thy bulwarks,
Thy streets with emeralds blaze;
The sardius and the topaz
Unite in thee their rays.
Thine ageless walls are bonded
With amethyst unpriced;
The saints build up its fabric,
The corner-stone is Christ.

3 O one, O only Mansion,
O Paradise of joy,
Where tears are ever vanished,
And smiles have no alloy;
The Lamb is all thy splendor,
The Crucified thy praise;
His laud and benediction
Thy ransomed people raise.

582
BERNARD.

1 Brief life is here our portion;
Brief sorrow, short-lived care;
The life that knows no ending,
The tearless life, is there.
Oh, happy retribution,
Short toil, eternal rest;
For mortals and for sinners
A mansion with the blest.

2 And now we fight the battle,
But then shall wear the crown
Of full and everlasting
And passionless renown.
But he whom now we trust in,
Shall then be seen and known;
And they that know and see him,
Shall have him for their own.

3 The morning shall awaken,
The shadows shall decay,
And each true-hearted servant
Shall shine as does the day.
There God our King and portion,
In fullness of his grace,
Shall we behold forever,
And worship face to face.

MT. BLANC. P. M.

Choir and Congregation.

J. J. HUSBAND.

1. We are on our jour-ney home, Where Christ our Lord is gone; We shall meet a-round his throne,

When he makes his people one, In the new, .. In the new .. Je - ru - sa - lem.

In the new Je - ru - sa - lem.

(*For 1st verse, see tune.*)

583

BEECHER.

2 We can see that distant home,
Though clouds rise dark between ;
Faith views the radiant dome,
And a luster flashes keen
From the new Jerusalem.

3 Oh, holy, heavenly home !
Oh, rest eternal there !
When shall the exiles come,
Where they cease from earthly care,
In the new Jerusalem.

4 Our hearts are breaking now
Those mansions fair to see ;
O Lord ! thy heavens bow,
And raise us up with thee
To the new Jerusalem.

Selection 125.—Blessed are they that do his commandments.

BEULAH. 7s. Double.

Choir and Congregation.

Words by JAMES MONTGOMERY.
Music by E. IVES, Jr.

584
1. Who are these in bright ar - ray, This in - nu - mer - a - ble throng, Round the al - tar, night and day,
2. These thro' fiery tri - als trod ; These from great af - flic-tion came ; Now, be - fore the throne of God,

Hymning one tri - umph-ant song ? "Worthy is the Lamb, once slain, Bless-ing, hon-or, glo-ry, power,
Sealed with his al - might-y name, Clad in rai-ment pure and white, Vic - tor-palms in ev-ery hand,

Wis - dom, rich-es to ob - tain, New do - min-ion ev - ery hour."
Thro' their dear Redeemer's might, More than con-quer-ors they stand.

3 Hunger, thirst, disease unknown,
On immortal fruits they feed ;
Them the Lamb, amid the throne,
Shall to living fountains lead.
Joy and gladness banish sighs ;
Perfect love dispel all fears ;
And forever from their eyes
God shall wipe away the tears.

Selection 128.—SOUTHINGTON SERVICE.—The Lord's prayer.

Choir. *p*   G. F. R.

Our Father who art in heaven, Hal-low-ed by thy name, Thy king-dom come, thy will be done on

earth as it is in heaven. Give us this day our dai-ly bread,and for-give our debts, for-give our debts, as

we for-give our debt-ors; And lead us not in-to temp-ta-tion, but de-liv-er us from

Slower.

e-vil, for thine is the kingdom, and the pow'r, and the glo-ry for-ev-er and ev-er. A-men.

SOUTHINGTON. S. M.

Choir and Congregation.   F. W. KING.

1. Our heav'nly Father, hear The pray'r we offer now: Thy name be hallow'd far and near,To thee all na-tions bow.

Where it is not convenient to sing the above prelude, the Lord's prayer may be repeated before singing the hymn.

585   MONTGOMERY.

1 Our Heavenly Father, hear
    The prayer we offer now;
  Thy name be hallowed far and near,
    To thee all nations bow.

2 Thy kingdom come; thy will
    On earth be done in love,
  As saints and seraphim fulfill
    Thy perfect law above.

3 Our daily bread supply,
    While by thy word we live
  The guilt of our iniquity
    Forgive, as we forgive.

4 From dark temptation's power
    Our feeble hearts defend;
  Deliver in the evil hour,
    And guide us to the end.

5 Thine, then, forever he
    Glory and power divine;
  The scepter, throne, and majesty
    Of heaven and earth are thine.

Selection 129.—HEBRON SERVICE.—The Lord is thy keeper.

Choir. *p* — The Lord is thy keep-er: the Lord is thy shade up-on thy right hand. The sun shall not

The Lord is thy keep-er: the Lord is thy shade up-on thy right hand. The sun shall not

smite thee by day, nor the moon by night. The Lord shall pre serve thee from all e - vil: He

smite thee by day, nor the moon by night, The Lord shall pre-serve thee from all e - vil: He

nor the moon, nor the moon by night.

shall pre-serve thy soul. The Lord shall preserve thy go-ing out and thy com-ing in, from

shall pre-serve thy soul. The Lord shall preserve thy go-ing out and thy com-ing in, from

The Lord shall preserve, from this time

this time forth, and e - ven for-ev - er, e - ven for - ev - er-more, e - ven for - ev - er-more.

this time forth, and e - ven for - ev - er, e - ven for - ev - er-more, e - ven for - ev - er - more.

for - ev - er-more.

Selection 129.

The Lord is thy keeper: the Lord is thy shade upon thy right hand. The sun shall not smite thee by day, nor the moon by night. The Lord shall preserve thee from all evil: he shall preserve thy soul. The Lord shall preserve thy going out, and thy coming in, from this time forth, and even forever, even forevermore.

HEBRON. L. M.

Choir and Congregation.

Dr. L. Mason.

1. Thus far the Lord hath led me on, Thus far his pow'r pro-longs my days; And ev-'ry eve-ning shall make known Some fresh me-mo-rial of his grace.

---

586 WATTS.

1 Thus far the Lord has led me on;
  Thus far his power prolongs my days;
  And every evening shall make known
  Some fresh memorial of his grace.

2 Much of my time has run to waste,
  And I, perhaps, am near my home;
  But he forgives my follies past,
  And gives me strength for days to come.

3 I lay my body down to sleep;
  Peace is the pillow for my head;
  While well-appointed angels keep
  Their watchful stations round my bed.

587 WATTS.

1 Lord, thou hast search'd and seen me thro';
  Thine eye commands, with piercing view,
  My rising and my resting hours,
  My heart and flesh, with all their powers.

2 My tho'ts, before they are my own,
  Are to my God distinctly known;
  He knows the words I mean to speak
  Ere from my opening lips they break.

3 Within thy circling power I stand;
  On every side I find thy hand;
  Awake, asleep, at home, abroad,
  I am surrounded still with God.

4 Amazing knowledge, vast and great!
  What large extent! what lofty height!
  My soul, with all the powers I boast,
  Is in the boundless prospect lost.

5 Oh, may these tho'ts possess my breast,
  Where'er I rove, where'er I rest;
  Nor let my weaker passions dare
  Consent to sin, for God is there.

588 STEELE.

1 Lord, how mysterious are thy ways!
  How blind are we! how mean our praise!
  Thy steps, can mortal eyes explore?
  'Tis ours to wonder and adore.

2 Great God! I would not ask to see
  What in my coming life shall be;
  Enough for me if love divine
  At length thro' every cloud shall shine.

3 Are darkness and distress my share?
  Then let me trust thy guardian care;
  If light and bliss attend my days,
  Then let my future hours be praise.

4 Yet this my soul desires to know,
  Be this my only wish below,
  That Christ be mine; this great request
  Grant, bounteous God, and I am blest!

589 ANON.

1 God of my life, to thee belong
  The grateful heart, the joyful song;
  Touched by thy love, each tuneful chord
  Resounds the goodness of the Lord.

2 Yet why, dear Lord, this tender care?
  Why doth thy hand so kindly rear
  A useless cumberer of the ground,
  On which so little fruit is found?

3 Still let the barren fig-tree stand.
  Upheld and fostered by thy hand;
  And let its fruit and verdure be
  A grateful tribute, Lord, to thee.

590 MONTGOMERY.

1 Millions within thy courts have met,
  Millions, this day, before thee bowed;
  Their faces Zion-ward were set,
  Vows with their lips to thee have vowed.

2 From east to west, the sun surveyed,
  From north to south, adoring throngs;
  And still, when evening stretch'd her shade,
  The stars came out to hear their songs.

3 And not a prayer, a tear, a sigh,
  Hath failed this day some suit to gain;
  To those in trouble thou wert nigh;
  No one hath sought thy face in vain.

Selection 130,—TALLIS EVE. HYMN SERVICE.—He that dwelleth.

G. F. R.

Solo. Contralto. *Dim.* *Cres.*

He that dwell-eth in the secret place of the Most High, shall a-bide, shall a - bide un-der the

Dim. *Choir. mf* *Cres.*

shad - ow of th'Almighty. I will say of the Lord, he is my Ref - uge and my Fort - ress, my

f *Dim.* *Alto prominent.*

God, my God, in him will I trust. He that dwelleth in the se-cret place of the Most High, shall a-

Cres. *Dim.* *m*

bide, shall a - bide under the shad - ow of th'Almighty. He will cov - er thee, will cov - er thee with his

Dim. *p* *Rit. e dim.*

feath -ers, and un-der his wings shalt thou trust, un-der his wings, un-der his wings shalt thou trust.

Selection 130.

He that dwelleth in the secret place of the Most High, shall abide under the shadow of the Almighty.

I will say of the Lord, he is my Refuge and my Fortress, | my God, in him will I trust. He will cover thee with his feathers, and under his wings shalt thou trust.

TALLIS EVE. HYMN. L. M.

Words by Bishop KEN.
Music by TALLIS.

Choir and Congregation.

591 1. Glo-ry to thee, my God, this night, For all the bless-ings of the light; Keep me, oh, keep me,

King of kings, 'Be-neath thine own al-might-y wings.

2 Be thou my guardian while I sleep,
Thy watchful station near me keep;
My heart with love celestial fill,
And guard me from th' approach of ill.

3 Teach me to live that I may dread
The grave as little as my bed:
Teach me to die, that so I may
Rise glorious at the judgment-day.

BEAMAN. 8s & 7s. Double.

Words by JAMES MONTGOMERY.
Music arr. for this work.

Choir and Congregation.

592 1. Call Je-ho-vah thy sal-va-tion, Rest be-neath th'Al-might-y's shade; In his se-cret
2. He shall charge his an-gel le-gions Watch and ward o'er thee to keep; Tho' thou walk thro'

hab-i-ta-tion, Dwell, and nev-er be dis-mayed! There no tu-mult can a-larm thee,
hos-tile re-gions, Tho' in des-ert wilds thou sleep. Since, with pure and firm af-fec-tion,

Thou shalt dread no hid-den snare; Guile no vi-o-lence can harm thee, In e-ter-nal safeguard there.
Thou on God hast set thy love, With the wings of his pro-tec-tion He shall shield thee from a-bove.

13

Selection 131.—ROSEDALE SERVICE, No. 2.—He shall give his angels charge over thee.

He shall give his an-gels charge over thee, to keep thee in all thy ways. Thou shalt not be afraid, for the

He shall give his an-gels charge over thee, to keep thee in all thy ways. Thou shalt not be afraid, for the

ter - ror by night, nor for the ar - row that flieth by day, Nor for the pes - tilence that

ter - ror by night, nor for the ar - row that flieth by day, Nor for the pes - tilence that

walk - eth in dark-ness, nor for the de-struc-tion that wast-eth at noonday: he shall give his an-gels

walk - eth in dark-ness, nor for the de-struc-tion that wast-eth at noonday: he shall give his an-gels

charge o - ver thee, to keep thee in all thy ways,   to keep thee in all . . . thy ways.

charge o - ver thee, to keep thee in all thy ways,   to keep thee in all, in all thy ways.

to keep,

Selection 131.

He shall give his angels charge over thee, to keep thee in all thy ways.

Thou shalt not be afraid for the terror by night, nor for the arrow that flieth by day, nor for the pestilence that walketh in darkness, nor for the destruction that wasteth at noonday.

He shall give his angels charge over thee, to keep thee in all thy ways.

ROSEDALE. L. M.

Choir and Congregation.

Words by Mrs. STEELE.
Music by GEO. F. ROOT.

593 1. Great God, to thee my ev'n - ing song With hum-ble grat - i - tude I raise; Oh, let thy mer - cy tune my tongue, And fill my heart with live - ly praise.

2 My days unclouded as they pass,
  And every gentle, rolling hour,
Are monuments of wondrous grace,
  And witness to thy love and power.

3 Let hope in thee mine eyelids close,
  With sleep refresh my feeble frame;
Safe in thy care may I repose,
  And wake with praises to thy name.

BADEA. S. M.

Choir and Congregation.

From a German Choral.

1. Once more before we part, Oh, bless the Savior's name; Let every tongue and every heart Adore and praise the same.

594 HART.

1 Once more before we part,
  Oh, bless the Savior's name;
Let every tongue and every heart
  Adore and praise the same.

2 Lord, in thy grace we came,
  That blessing still impart;
We met in Jesus' sacred name,
  In Jesus' name we part.

3 Still on thy holy word
  Help us to feed and grow,
Still to go on to know the Lord,
  And practise what we know.

4 Now, Lord, before we part,
  Help us to bless thy name;
Let every tongue and every heart
  Adore and praise the same.

595 FITCH.

1 Lord, at this closing hour
  Establish every heart
Upon thy word of truth and power,
  To keep us when we part.

2 Peace to our brethren give;
  Fill all our hearts with love;
In faith and patience may we live,
  And seek our rest above.

3 Through changes, bright or drear,
  We would thy will pursue;
And toil to spread thy kingdom here,
  Till we its glory view.

4 To God, the only wise,
  In every age adored,
Let glory from the church arise
  Through Jesus Christ our Lord!

596 DODDRIDGE.

1 The swift declining day,
  How fast its moments fly!
While evening's broad and gloomy shade
  Gains on the western sky.

2 Ye mortals, mark its pace,
  And use the hours of light;
And know, its Maker can command
  At once eternal night.

3 Give glory to the Lord
  Who rules the whirling sphere;
Submissive at his footstool bow,
  And seek salvation there.

4 Then shall new luster break
  Through death's impending gloom,
And lead you to unchanging light,
  In your celestial home.

Selection 132.—EVAN SERVICE, No. 2.—There shall no evil befall.

There shall no e-vil be-fall thee, nei-ther shall an-y plague come nigh thy dwell-ing, Be-

cause thou hast made the Lord who is my Ref-uge, e-ven the Most High, thy hab-i-ta-tion.

He that trust-eth in the Lord, mer-cy shall com-pass him a-bout. . . .
He that trusteth in the Lord, . .

He that trust-eth in the Lord, in the Lord, mer-cy shall com-pass him a-bout.
in . . . the Lord, . . .

There shall no e-vil be-fall thee, nei-ther shall an-y plague come nigh,
There shall no e-vil, neither shall an-y plague come nigh, come nigh thy dwelling, come
nei-ther shall an-y plague come nigh,

nigh thy dwell-ing, there shall no e-vil befall, no e-vil be-fall, no e-vil be-fall thee.
there shall . . no e-vil be-fall thee.

Selection 132.

There shall no evil befall thee, neither shall any plague come nigh thy dwelling, because thou hast made the Lord who is my Refuge, even the Most High, thy habitation.

He that trusteth in the Lord, mercy shall compass him about. There shall no evil befall thee, neither shall any plague come nigh thy dwelling.

EVAN. C. M.

Words by J. Addison.
Music arr. by Dr. Mason.

Choir and Congregation.

597

1. How are thy ser-vants blest, O Lord! How sure is their de-fence; E - ter-nal wis-dom
2. In midst of dan-gers, fears, and deaths, Thy good-ness we'll a - dore; We'll praise thee for thy
3. Our life, while thou pre-serv'st that life, Thy sac - ri - fice shall be; And death, when death shall

is their guide, Their help, om - ni - po - tence.
mer-cies past, And hum - bly hope for more.
be our lot, Shall join our souls to thee.

598

Anon.

1 In mercy, Lord, remember me,
　Through all the hours of night,
　And grant to me most graciously
　The safeguard of thy might.

2 With cheerful heart I close my eyes,
　Since thou wilt not remove,
　Oh, in the morning let me rise
　Rejoicing in thy love.

VESPERS. 8s & 7s.

Words by Miss Auber.
Music arr. from Flotow.

Choir and Congregation.

599

1. Vain-ly thro' night's wea-ry hours, Keep we watch, lest foes a - larm; Vain our bul-warks,
2. Vain were all our toil and la - bor, Did not God that la - bor bless; Vain, without his

and our tow - ers, But for God's pro-tect - ing arm.
grace and fa - vor, Ev - ery tal - ent we pos-sess.

3 Vainer still the hope of heaven,
　That on human strength relies;
　But to him shall help be given,
　Who in humble faith applies.

4 Seek we, then, the Lord's Anointed;
　He will grant us peace and rest;
　Ne'er was suppliant disappointed,
　Who thro' Christ his prayer addressed.

600

Robbins.

1 Lo, the day of rest declineth,
　Gather fast the shades of night;
　May the Sun which ever shineth,
　Fill our souls with heavenly light.

2 While, thine ear of love addressing,
　Thus our parting hymn we sing,
　Father, grant thine evening blessing,
　Fold us safe beneath thy wing.

601

Bickersteth.

1 Heavenly Shepherd, guide us, feed us,
　Through our pilgrimage below,
　And beside the waters lead us,
　Where thy flock rejoicing go.

2 Lord, thy guardian presence ever,
　Meekly bending, we implore;
　We have found thee, and would never,
　Never wander from thee more.

Invocation.

Newton.

1 May the grace of Christ our Savior,
　And the Father's boundless love,
　With the Holy Spirit's favor,
　Rest upon us from above.

2 Thus may we abide in union
　With each other and the Lord;
　And possess, in sweet communion,
　Joys which earth can not afford.

Selection 133.—HOLLEY SERVICE.—Thou from whom we never part.

G. F. R.

Thou from whom we nev-er part, Thou whose love is ev-'ry-where, Thou who

Thou from whom we nev-er part, Thou whose love is ev-'ry-where, Thou who

see - est ev-'ry heart, List-en to our ev'n-ing prayer.

see-est ev-'ry heart, oh, list-en, list-en to our ev'n-ing prayer.

Fill our hearts, O Lord, with love, Love un-fail-ing, full and free, Love that no a-larm can

Love that ev-er rests on thee, that ev-er

move, Love that ev-er rests on thee, Love that rests,

rests . . . . on thee,

that ev-er rests on thee, Oh, list our ev'n-ing prayer, oh, list our ev'n-ing prayer.

Selection 133.

Thou from whom we never part, Thou whose love is ev-ery-where, Thou who seest every heart, Listen to our evening prayer.

Fill our hearts, O Lord, with love, Love unfailing, full and free, Love that no alarm can move, Love that ever rests on thee. Oh, list our evening prayer.

HOLLEY. 7s.

Choir and Congregation.

Geo. Hews.

1. Soft - ly now the light of day Fades up - on my sight a - way;

Free from care, from la - bor free, Lord, I would com - mune with thee.

602 Doane.

1 Softly now the light of day
  Fades upon my sight away;
  Free from care, from labor free,
  Lord, I would commune with thee.

2 Thou, whose all-pervading eye
  Naught escapes without, within,
  Pardon each infirmity,
  Open fault and secret sin.

3 Soon, for me, the light of day
  Shall forever pass away;
  Then, from sin and sorrow free,
  Take me, Lord, to dwell with thee.

603 Newton.

1 Now may he who from the dead
  Brought the Shepherd of the sheep,
  Jesus Christ, our King and Head,
  All our souls in safety keep.

2 May he teach us to fulfill
  What is pleasing in his sight;
  Make us perfect in his will,
  And preserve us day and night!

3 To that great Redeemer's praise,
  Who the cov'nant sealed with blood,
  Let our hearts and voices raise
  Loud thanksgivings to our God.

604 S. F. Smith.

1 Softly fades the twilight ray
  Of the holy Sabbath day;
  Gently as life's setting sun,
  When the Christian's course is run.

2 Night her solemn mantle spreads
  O'er the earth as daylight fades;
  All things tell of calm repose,
  At the holy Sabbath's close.

3 Peace is on the world abroad;
  'Tis the holy peace of God—
  Symbol of the peace within,
  When the spirit rests from sin.

4 Still the Spirit lingers near,
  Where the evening worshipper
  Seeks communion with the skies,
  Pressing onward to the prize.

605 Montgomery.

1 For the mercies of the day,
  For this rest upon our way,
  Thanks to thee alone be given,
  Lord of earth and King of heaven.

2 Cold our services have been,
  Mingled every prayer with sin;
  But thou canst and wilt forgive;
  By thy grace alone we live.

3 While this thorny path we tread,
  May thy love our footsteps lead;
  When our journey here is past,
  May we rest with thee at last.

4 Let these earthly Sabbaths prove
  Foretastes of our joys above;
  While their steps thy children bend
  To the rest which knows no end.

606 Ambrose.

1 Ere the waning light decay,
  God of all, to thee we pray,
  Thee thy healthful grace to send,
  Thee to guard us and defend.

2 Guard from dreams that may affright;
  Guard from terrors of the night;
  Guard from foes, without, within;
  Outward danger, inward sin.

3 Mindful of our only stay,
  Duly thus to thee we pray,
  Duly thus to thee we raise
  Trophies of our grateful praise.

4 Hear the prayer, almighty King;
  Hear thy praises while we sing,
  Hymning with thy heavenly host,
  Father, Son, and Holy Ghost.

Selection 134.—EVENTIDE SERVICE.—Abide with us.

Solo. *m*   *mf* *p*   Dim. †††

A - bide with us, a - bide with us, for it is t'ward even-ing, and the day is far

Cres. Dim. *p*

spent, it is t'ward even-ing, and the day is far spent. A - bide with us, a - bide with us;

m Dim. *m* Dim. Rit. Choir. *p* Cres. Dim e rit.

for it is t'ward even-ing, and the day is far spent. And he went in to tar-ry with them.

And he went in to tar-ry with them.

EVENTIDE. 10s.

Choir and Congregation.

Words by Rev. H. F. LYTE.
Music by W. H. MONK.

607
1. A - bide with me, fast falls the e - ven - tide; The darkness deep - ens, Lord, with me a - bide;
2. Swift to its close ebbs out life's lit - tle day; Earth's joys grow dim, its glo-ries pass a - way;
3. I need thy pres - ence ev-ery pass-ing hour, What but thy grace can foil the tempter's power?

When oth - er help - ers fail, and comforts flee, Help of the helpless, oh, a - bide with me.
Change and de - cay in all a-round I see; O thou who changest not, a - bide with me.
Who like thy-self my guide and stay can be? Thro' cloud and sunshine, Lord, a - bide with me.

Selection 134.—Abide with us, for it is toward evening.

TEMPLE. 8s & 7s. Double.

Choir and Congregation.

Words by Mrs. C. S. Smith.
Arr. from Flotow.

608
1. Tar-ry with me, O my Sav-ior! For the day is pass-ing by; See! the shades of
2. Fee-ble, trem-bling, fainting, dy-ing, Lord, I cast my-self on thee; Tar-ry with me

evening gath-er, And the night is draw-ing nigh. Deep-er, deep-er grow the shadows, Pal-er
thro' the darkness; While I sleep, still watch by me. Tar-ry with me, O my Sav-ior! Lay my

now the glow-ing west, Swift the night of death ad-vances; Shall it be the night of rest?
head up-on thy breast Till the morning; then a-wake me—Morn-ing of e-ter-nal rest!

BOYLSTON. S. M.

Dr. L. Mason.

1. One sweetly solemn thought Comes to me o'er and o'er,—Nearer my home, to-day, am I, Than e'er I've been before.

609
Carey.

1 One sweetly solemn thought
Comes to me o'er and o'er,—
Nearer my home, to-day, am I,
Than e'er I've been before.

2 Nearer my Father's house,
Where many mansions be;
Nearer to-day the great white throne;
Nearer the crystal sea.

3 Nearer the bound of life,
Where burdens are laid down;
Nearer to leave the heavy cross;
Nearer to gain the crown.

4 But, lying dark between,
Winding down through the night,
There rolls the deep and unknown stream
That leads at last to light.

5 Ev'n now, perchance, my feet
Are slipping on the brink,
And I, to-day, am nearer home,—
Nearer than now I think.

6 Father, perfect my trust!
Strengthen my power of faith!
Nor let me stand, at last, alone
Upon the shore of death.

Selection 135.—STOCKWELL SERVICE, No. 1.—The day is far spent.

G. F. R.

The day is far spent, and the night's com-ing on, The hours that are num - bered, for-ev - er are

gone, Their rec - ord is closed with the last fad - ing light, Oh, seek we our Sav-ior's rich

bless - ing to - night. Their rec - ord is closed with the last fad - ing light, Their rec - ord is

closed with the last fad - ing light, Oh, seek we our Sav - ior's rich bless - ing to - night.

STOCKWELL. 8s & 7s.

Words by J. EDMESTEN.
Music by Rev. D. E. JONES.

610

1. Sav-ior, breathe an even-ing bless - ing, Ere re - pose our spir - its seal; Sin and want we come con-

fess - ing, Thou canst save and thou canst heal.

2 Though destruction walk around us,
　Though the arrows near us fly,
Angel guards from thee surround us,
　We are safe if thou art night.

3 Though the night be dark and dreary,
　Darkness can not hide from thee;
Thou art he who, never weary,
　Watcheth where thy people be.

Selection 136,—SEYMOUR SERVICE, No. 2.—I will both lay me down in peace and sleep.

G. F. R.

I will both lay me down in peace and sleep, For thou, Lord, for thou, Lord, on-ly mak-est

me to dwell in safe-ty. I will both lay me down in peace . . .

I will both lay me down . . will lay me down in

. . and sleep, and sleep; For thou, Lord, on-ly mak-est me to dwell in safe-ty.

peace and sleep, and sleep; For thou, Lord, on-ly mak-est me to dwell in safe-ty.

SEYMOUR. 7s.

Choir and Congregation.   Music from WEBER.

611 1. Safe, O Lord, if thou art near, Though the night be dark and drear; Safe, if we may

on-ly see That thou wilt our Guar-dian be.

2 Harmless shall the arrow fly,
  If thy mighty hand is nigh;
  Vain temptation's wily snare,
  If we trust our Father's care.

3 Dwelling in the midst of foes,
  In thine arms may we repose;
  And when life's short day is past,
  Rest with thee in heaven at last.

Selection 137.—SICILY SERVICE.—The Lord bless thee and keep thee.

The Lord bless thee and keep thee, the Lord make his face shine up - on thee, the Lord be gra-cious

un - to thee, be gra-cious un - to thee. The Lord lift up his coun-tenance up - on thee, and

give thee peace. The Lord lift up his countenance up - on thee, and give thee peace, and give thee peace.

SICILY. 8s & 7s. 6 lines.

Words by Rev. W. Shirley.
Melody Sicilian.

Choir and Congregation.

612 1. Lord, dis - miss us with thy bless-ing, Fill our hearts with joy and peace; { Let us each, thy
         { Oh, re - fresh us,

love pos - sess-ing, Tri - umph in re - deem-ing grace; }
oh, re - fresh us, Trav'l-ing through this wil - der - ness. }

2 Thanks we give and adoration,
  For the Gospel's joyful sound;
May the fruits of thy salvation
  In our hearts and lives abound :
May thy presence, may thy presence
  With us evermore be found.

RESPONSIVE SERVICES.

Selection 138.—God is greatly to be feared.

Ps. lxxxix : 7-18.

Minister.

1. God is greatly to be feared in the assembly of the saints, and to be had in reverence of all them that are round about him.

Choir and Congregation.

O Lord God of Hosts, who is a strong lord } like un-to thee, Or to thy faithfulness round a-bout thee.

Minister.

2. Thou rulest the raging of the sea; when the waves thereof arise thou stillest them.

Choir and Congregation.

Thou hast broken Rahab in pieces as } one that is slain. { Thou hast scat-tered thine } enemies with thy strong arm.

Minister.

3. The heavens are thine, the earth also is thine; as for the world and the fulness thereof, thou hast founded them.

Choir and Congregation.

The north and the south thou hast cre- } a-ted them. Tabor and Hermon shall re-joice in thy name.

Minister.

4. Thou hast a mighty arm, strong is thy hand, and high is thy right hand.

Choir and Congregation.

Justice and judgment are the habitation } of thy throne. Mercy and truth shall go before thy face.

Minister.

5. Blessed is the people that know the joyful sound; they shall walk, O Lord, in the light of thy countenance.

Choir and Congregation.

In thy name shall they re-joice all the day, And in thy righteousness shall they be exalt-ed.

Minister.

6. For thou art the glory of their strength, and in thy favor our horn shall be exalted.

Choir and Congregation.

For the Lord is our refuge, And the Holy One of Israel is our King. A-men.

289

Selection 139.—Lord, who shall abide in thy tabernacle?

Ps. xv : 1-4.

Minister.

1. Lord, who shall abide in thy tabernacle? who shall dwell in thy holy hill?

Choir and Congregation.

He that walketh uprightly and worketh righteousness, And speaketh the truth in his heart.

Minister.

2. He that backbiteth not with his tongue, nor doeth evil to his neighbor, nor taketh up a reproach against his neighbor.

Choir and Congregation.

In whose eyes a vile person is contemned, But he hon'reth them that fear the Lord.

Ps. lxxxiv : 4-12.

Minister.

3. Blessed are they that dwell in thy house; they will be still praising thee.

Choir and Congregation.

Blessed is the man whose strength is in thee, In whose heart are the ways of them.

Minister.

4. Who passing through the valley of Baca make it a well; the rain also filleth the pools.

Choir and Congregation.

They go from strength to strength; Every one of them in Zion ap-peareth be-fore God.

Minister.

5. O Lord God of Hosts, hear my prayer. Give ear, O God of Jacob.

Choir and Congregation.

Behold, O God, our shield, And look upon the face of thine An-ointed.

Minister.

6. For a day in thy courts is better than a thousand.

Choir and Congregation.

I had rather be a doorkeeper in the house of my God Than to dwell in the tents of wickedness.

Minister.

7. The Lord God is a sun and shield. The Lord will give grace and glory. No good thing will he withold from them that walk uprightly.

Choir and Congregation.

O Lord of Hosts, Blessed is the man that trusteth in thee. A - men.

Selection 140.—Blessed be the Lord God of Israel.

Luke i: 68-75.

Minister.

1. Blessed be the Lord God of Israel, for he hath visited and redeemed his people.

Choir and Congregation.   Arranged.

And hath raised up a horn of sal-va-tion for us   In the house of his servant Da-vid.

Minister.

2. As he spake by the mouth of the holy prophets which have been since the world began.

Choir and Congregation.

That we should be saved from our en-e-mies, And from the hand of all that hate us.

Minister.

3. To perform the mercy promised to our fathers, and to remember his holy covenant; the oath which he sware to our father Abraham.

Choir and Congregation.

That he would grant }
us that we being de- } hand of our enemies, {
livered out of the

Might serve him
without fear, in ho- } all the days of our life.
liness and right-
eousness before him

1st Kings viii.

Minister.

4. Blessed be the Lord that hath given rest unto his people according to all he promised.

Choir and Congregation.

There hath not }
failed one word of } his good promise, {
Which he prom- }
ised by the } hand of Mo-ses his servant.

Minister.

5. The Lord our God be with us as he was with our fathers.

Choir and Congregation.

Let him not leave us,   nor for-sake us, That he may in - cline our hearts unto him.

Minister.

6. And let the words wherewith we have made supplication before the Lord, be nigh unto the Lord our God, day and night.

Choir and Congregation.

That he may maintain the cause of his servant, And the cause of his people Israel at all times.

Minister.

7. That all the people of the earth may know that the Lord is God, and there is none else.

Choir and Congregation.

Let our heart therefore }
be perfect with the } Lord our God, {
To walk in his }
statutes and to } keep his commandments. A-men

Selection 141,—I will extol thee, my God, O King.

Ps. cxlv.

Choir and Congregation.   Old Chant.

Minister.
1. I will extol thee, my God, O King, and I will bless thy name forever and ever.

Every day will I bless thee, And I will praise thy name for-ev-er and ev-er.

Minister.
2. One generation shall praise thy works to another, and shall declare thy mighty acts.

Choir and Congregation.

I will speak of the glorious hon-or of thy ma-jes-ty, And of thy wondrous works.

Minister.
3. And men shall speak of the might of thy terrible acts, and I will declare thy greatness.

Choir and Congregation.

{ They shall abundantly / utter the memory of } thy great goodness, And shall sing of thy righteous-ness.

Minister.
4. The Lord is gracious and full of compassion, slow to anger and great in mercy.

Choir and Congregation.

The Lord is good to all, And his mercies are o-ver all his works.

Minister.
5. All thy works shall praise thee, O Lord, and thy saints shall bless thee.

Choir and Congregation.

They shall speak of the glory of thy kingdom, And talk of thy power.

Minister.
6. To make known to the sons of men his mighty acts, and the glorious majesty of his kingdom.

Choir and Congregation.

Thy kingdom is an ever-last-ing king-dom, { And thy dominion / endureth through- } out all gen-er-ations.

Minister.
7. The Lord upholdeth all that fall, and raiseth up all the bowed down.

Choir and Congregation.

The eyes of all wait up-on thee, And thou givest them their meat in due sea-son.

Minister.

8. Thou openest thine hand and satisfiest the desire of every living thing.

Choir and Congregation.

The Lord is righteous in all his ways And ho-ly in all his works.

Minister.

9. The Lord is nigh unto all them that call upon him, to all that call upon him in truth.

Choir and Congregation.

He will fulfill the desire of } them that fear him: He also will hear their cry, and will save them.

Minister.

10. The Lord preserveth all them that love him, but all the wicked will he destroy.

Choir and Congregation.

My mouth shall speak the } praise of the Lord: { And let all flesh bless his holy name for- } ev-er and ev-er. A-men.

Selection 142.—God be merciful unto us, and bless us.

Ps. lxvii.

Minister.

1. God be merciful unto us, and bless us; and cause his face to shine upon us.

Choir and Congregation.

Arranged.

That thy way may be known up-on earth; Thy saving health a-mong all nations.

Minister.

2. Let the people praise thee, O God; let all the people praise thee.

Choir and Congregation.

O let the nations be glad and } sing for joy: { For thou shalt judge the people righteously, and govern the } nations up-on earth.

Minister.

3. Let the people praise thee, O God; let all the people praise thee.

Choir and Congregation.

Then shall the earth yield her increase: And God, even our own God, shall bless us.

Minister.

4. God shall bless us; and all the ends of the earth shall fear him.

Choir and Congregation.

God shall bless us: And all the ends of the earth shall fear him. A-men.

19

Selection 143.—The earth is the Lord's.

Ps. xxiv.

A ranged.

Choir and Congregation.

Minister.

1. The earth is the Lord's, and the fullness thereof; the world, and they that dwell therein.

For he hath founded it up - on the seas, And established it up - on the floods.

Choir and Congregation.

Minister.

2. Who shall ascend into the hill of the Lord, or who shall stand in his holy place?

{ He that hath clean hands, and a } pure heart, { Who hath not lifted up his soul unto vanity, nor } sworn de - ceit - ful - ly.

Choir and Congregation.

Minister.

3. He shall receive the blessing from the Lord, and righteousness from the God of his salvation.

This is the generation of them that seek him, That seek thy face, O Ja - cob.

Choir and Congregation.

Minister.

4. Lift up your heads, O ye gates, and be ye lifted up, ye everlasting doors.

And the King of glo - ry shall come in.

Choir and Congregation.

Minister.

5. Who is this King of glory?

The Lord strong and might - y; The Lord might - y in bat - tle.

Choir and Congregation.

Minister.

6. Lift up your heads, O ye gates; even lift them up, ye everlasting doors.

And the King of glo - ry shall come in.

Choir and Congregation.

Minister.

7. Who is this King of glory?

The Lord of hosts, He is the King of glo - ry. A - men.

Selection 144.—I will praise thee, O Lord.

Ps. ix. 1-14.

Minister.

1. I will praise thee, O Lord, with my whole heart; I will show forth all thy marvelous works.

Choir and Congregation. *Arranged.*

I will be glad and rejoice in thee: I will sing praise to thy name, O thou most high.

Minister.

2. When mine enemies are turned back, they shall fall and perish at thy presence.

Choir and Congregation.

For thou hast maintained my right and my cause; Thou satest in the throne judging right.

Minister.

3. Thou hast rebuked the heathen, thou hast destroyed the wicked, thou hast put out their name forever and ever.

Choir and Congregation.

{ O thou enemy, destructions are come to a per- } petual end : { And thou hast destroyed cities; their re- - - } membrance is perished with them.

Minister.

4. But the Lord shall endure forever: he hath prepared his throne for judgment.

Choir and Congregation.

{ And he shall judge the world in } righteous-ness, He shall minister to the people in upright-ness.

Minister.

5. The Lord also will be a Refuge for the oppressed, a Refuge in time of trouble.

Choir and Congregation.

{ And they that know thy name will put their } trust in thee : { For thou Lord hast not for- } sak-en them that seek thee.

Minister.

6. Sing praises to the Lord, which dwelleth in Zion : declare among the people his doings.

Choir and Congregation.

{ When he maketh inquisition for blood he re- } membereth them : He forgetteth not the cry of the humble.

Minister.

7. Have mercy upon me, O Lord ; consider my trouble which I suffer from them that hate me.

Choir and Congregation.

{ That I may show forth all thy praise in the gates of the } daughter of Zi-on : { I will re- joice in } thy sal-va-tion. A-men.

Selection 145.—I will bless the Lord at all times.

Ps. xxxiv.

Minister.

1. I will bless the Lord at all times; his praise shall continually be in my mouth.

Choir and Congregation.

My soul shall make her boast in the Lord; The humble shall hear thereof and be glad.

Minister.

2. Oh, magnify the Lord with me; and let us exalt his name together.

Choir and Congregation.

I sought the Lord and he heard me, And de-liv-ered me from all my fears.

Minister.

3. They looked unto him and were lightened, and their faces were not ashamed.

Choir and Congregation.

This poor man cried, and the Lord heard him, And saved him out of all his troubles.

Minister.

4. The angel of the Lord encampeth round about them that fear him, and delivereth them.

Choir and Congregation.

Oh, taste and see that the Lord is good; Blessed is the man that trust-eth in him.

Minister.

5. Oh, fear the Lord, ye his saints, for there is no want to them that fear him.

Choir and Congregation.

{ The young lions do lack and } suf-fer hun-ger, { But they that seek the } Lord shall not want any good thing.

Minister.

6. Oh, come ye children, hearken unto me, I will teach you the fear of the Lord.

Choir and Congregation.

What man is he that de-sir-eth life, And loveth many days that he may see good.

Minister.

7. Keep thy tongue from evil, and thy lips from speaking guile.

Choir and Congregation.

Depart from evil and do good; Seek peace and pur-sue it.

Minister.

8. The eyes of the Lord are upon the righteous, and his ears are open unto their cry.

Choir and Congregation.

{ The face of the } { Lord is against } them that do e - vil, To cut off the remembrance of them from the earth.

Minister.

9. The righteous cry, and the Lord heareth and delivereth them out of all their troubles.

Choir and Congregation.

{ The Lord is nigh unto } { them that are of a } broken heart, And saveth such as be of a contrite spir - it.

Minister.

10. Many are the afflictions of the righteous, but the Lord delivereth him out of them all.

Choir and Congregation.

He keepeth all his bones; Not one of them is bro - ken.

Minister.

11. Evil shall slay the wicked, and they that hate the righteous shall be desolate.

Choir and Congregation.

{ The Lord re- } { deemeth the } soul of his servants. { And none of them } { that trust in } him shall be des-o-late. A-men.

Selection 146.—Show us thy mercy, O Lord.

From Dan. ix.

Minister.

1. O Lord, the great and dreadful God, keeping the covenant and mercy to them that love him, and to them that keep his commandments. We have sinned, and have committed iniquity, and have done wickedly, and have rebelled, even by departing from thy precepts and from thy judgments.

Choir and Congregation.

Show us thy mer - cy, O Lord, And grant us thy sal - va - tion.

Minister.

2. O Lord, righteousness belongeth unto thee; but unto us confusion of face, as at this day, because we have sinned against thee.

Choir and Congregation. *(Chant as above.)*

Show us thy mercy, O | Lord, ‖ And | grant us thy sal- | vation.

Minister.

3. To the Lord our God belong mercies and forgiveness, though we have rebelled against him: neither have we obeyed the voice of the Lord our God, to walk in his laws, which he has set before us.

Choir and Congregation. *(Chant as above.)*

Show us thy mercy, O | Lord, ‖ And | grant us thy sal- | vation.

Minister.

4. Now therefore, O our God, hear the prayer of thy servants, and their supplications, and cause thy face to shine upon thy sanctuary that is desolate, for the Lord's sake.

Choir and Congregation.

Show us thy mer - cy, O Lord, And grant us thy sal - va - tion. A - men.

Selection 147.—Give ear to my words, O Lord.

Ps. v. 1-11.

Minister.

1. Give ear to my words, O Lord; consider my meditation.

Choir and Congregation. †††

Hearken unto the voice of my cry, my King, and my God, For unto thee do I pray.

Minister.

2. My voice shalt thou hear in the morning, O Lord; in the morning will I direct my prayer unto thee, and will look up.

Choir and Congregation.

{ For thou art not a God that hath pleasure in . . . } wick-ed-ness, Neither shall e-vil dwell with thee.

Minister.

3. The foolish shall not stand in thy sight; thou hatest all workers of iniquity.

Choir and Congregation.

{ Thou shalt destroy } them that speak falsehood; { The Lord will abhor the } bloody and deceitful man.

Minister.

4. But as for me I will come into thy house in the multitude of thy mercy, and in thy fear will I worship toward thy holy temple.

Choir and Congregation.

{ Lead me, O Lord, in thy righteousness be- } cause of mine en-emies; Make thy way straight before my face.

Minister.

5. For there is no faithfulness in their mouth; their inward part is very wickedness.

Choir and Congregation.

Their throat is an o-pen se-pul-chre; They flat-ter with their tongue.

Minister.

6. Destroy thou them, O God, let them fall by their own counsels.

Choir and Congregation.

Cast them out in the multitude of their transgressions, For they have rebelled against thee.

Minister.

7. But let all them that put their trust in thee rejoice. Let them ever shout for joy because thou defendest them.

Choir and Congregation.

Let them also that love thy name Be joyful in thee, Be joyful in thee. A-men.

Selection 148.—For his mercy endureth forever.

(The connection between reading and response should here be so close as to make the music almost continuous.)

Choir and Congregation. 1st.

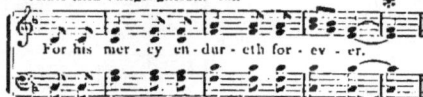

For his mer - cy en-dur - eth for - ev - er.

Choir and Congregation. 2d.

For his mer - cy en-dur - eth for - ev - er.

From Ps. cxxxvi.

Minister.
1. O give thanks unto the Lord ; for he is good :

Minister.
2. O give thanks unto the God of gods :

Minister.
3. O give thanks to the Lord of lords :

Minister.
4. To him who alone doeth great wonders :

Minister.
5. To him that by wisdom made the heavens :

Minister.
6. To him that stretched out the earth above the waters.

Minister.
7. To him that made great lights :

Minister.
8. The sun to rule by day :

Minister.
9. The moon and stars to rule by night :

Minister.
10. To him that smote Egypt in their first-born :

Minister.
11. And brought out Israel from among them :

Minister.
12. With a strong hand, and with a stretched out arm :

Minister.
13. To him which led his people through the wilderness.

Minister.
14. To him which smote great kings :

Minister.
15. And gave their land for a heritage :

Minister.
16. Even an heritage unto Israel his servant :

Minister.
17. Who remembered us in our low estate :

Minister.
18. And hath redeemed us from our enemies :

Minister.
19. Who giveth food to all flesh :

Minister.
20. O give thanks unto the God of heaven :

Choir and Cong. 1st.
For his | mercy en- | dureth for- | ever.

Choir and Cong. 2d.
For his | mercy en- | dureth for- | ever.

Choir and Cong. 1st.
For his | mercy en- | dureth for- | ever.

Choir and Cong. 2d.
For his | mercy en- | dureth for- | ever.

Choir and Cong. 1st.
For his | mercy en- | dureth for- | ever.

Choir and Cong. 2d.
For his | mercy en- | dureth for- | ever.

Choir and Cong. 1st.
For his | mercy en- | dureth for- | ever.

Choir and Cong. 2d.
For his | mercy en- | dureth for- | ever.

Choir and Cong. 1st.
For his | mercy en- | dureth for- | ever.

Choir and Cong. 2d.
For his | mercy en- | dureth for- | ever.

Choir and Cong. 1st.
For his | mercy en- | dureth for- | ever.

Choir and Cong. 2d.
For his | mercy en- | dureth for- | ever.

Choir and Cong. 1st.
For his | mercy en- | dureth for- | ever.

Choir and Cong. 2d.
For his | mercy en- | dureth for- | ever.

Choir and Cong. 1st.
For his | mercy en- | dureth for- | ever.

Choir and Cong. 2d.
For his | mercy en- | dureth for- | ever.

A-men.

Selection 149.—The Lord is my light and my salvation.

Ps. xxvii.

Minister.

1. The Lord is my light and my salvation: whom shall I fear.

Choir and Congregation.

The Lord is the strength of my life: Of whom shall I be a-fraid.

Minister.

2. Though a host should encamp against me, my heart shall not fear.

Choir and Congregation.

Though wars should rise a-gainst me: In this will I be con fi-dent.

Minister.

3. One thing have I desired of the Lord, that will I seek after: that I may dwell in the house of the Lord all the days of my life.

Choir and Congregation.

To behold the beau-ty of the Lord, And to in - quire in his tem-ple.

Minister.

4. In the time of trouble he shall hide me in his pavilion.

Choir and Congregation.

In the se - cret of his ta-ber-na-cle shall he hide me.

Minister.

5. Therefore will I offer in his tabernacle sacrifices of joy.

Choir and Congregation.

I will sing: Yea, I will sing prais-es un - to the Lord.

Minister.

6. Hear, O Lord, when I cry with my voice. Have mercy also upon me, and answer me.

Choir and Congregation.

When thou saidst, Seek ye my face, My heart said unto thee, thy face, Lord, will I seek.

Minister.

7. Hide not thy face far from me: put not away thy servant in anger.

Choir and Congregation.

Thou hast been my help: Leave me not, neither forsake me, O God of my sal-va tion.

Choir and Congregation.

Minister.
8. When my father and mother forsake me, then the Lord will take me up.

Teach me thy way, O Lord, And lead me in a plain path be-cause of mine en - e-mies.

Minister.
9. Deliver me not over unto the will of mine enemies.

Choir and Congregation.

For false witnesses are ris-en up a-gainst me, And such as breathe out cru - el - ty.

Minister.
10. I had fainted unless I had believed to see the goodness of the Lord in the land of the living. Wait on the Lord.

Choir and Congregation.

Be of good courage and he shall strengthen thy heart. Wait, I say, on the Lord. A-men.

Selection 150.—Bless the Lord, O my soul.

From Ps. cxlv.

Minister.
1. The Lord upholdeth all that fall, and raiseth up all those that be bowed down.

Choir and Congregation. 1st.   Arranged.

Bless the Lord, O my soul: And all that is within me bless his ho - ly name.

Minister.
2. The eyes of all wait upon thee; and thou givest them their meat in due season.

Choir and Congregation. 2d.

Bless the Lord, O my soul: And for - get not all his ben - e - fits.

Minister.
3. Thou openest thine hand, and satisfiest the desire of every living thing.
Choir and Congregation. (Chant 1st, as above.)
Bless the Lord, | O my soul: ‖ And all that is within me | bless his | holy | name.‖
Minister.
4. The Lord is righteous in all his ways, and holy in all his works.
Choir and Congregation. (Chant 2d, as above.)
Bless the Lord, | O my | soul: ‖ And for | get not | all his | benefits.‖
Minister.
5. The Lord is nigh unto all them that call upon him, to all that call upon him in truth.
Choir and Congregation. (Chant 1st, as above.)
Bless the Lord, | O my | soul: ‖ And all that is within me | bless his | holy | name.‖
Minister.
6. He will fulfill the desire of them that fear him: he also will hear their cry, and will save them.
Choir and Congregation. (Chant 2d, as above.)
Bless the Lord, | O my | soul: ‖ And for | get not | all his | benefits.‖
Minister.
7. The Lord preserveth all them that love him: but all the wicked will he destroy.
Choir and Congregation. (Chant 1st, as above.)
Bless the Lord, | O my | soul: ‖ And all that is within me | bless his | holy | name.‖
Minister.
8. My mouth shall speak the praise of the Lord: and let all flesh bless his holy name forever and ever.
Choir and Congregation. (Chant 2d, as above.)
Bless the Lord, | O my | soul: ‖ For | ever and | ever. A | men.‖

Selection 151.—Rejoice in the Lord, O ye righteous.

From Ps. xxxiii.

Minister.

1. Rejoice in the Lord, O ye righteous, for praise is comely for the upright.

Choir and Congregation.

Praise the Lord with the harp; Sing unto him with the psaltery and an instrument of ten strings.

Minister.

2. Sing unto him a new song; play skillfully with a loud noise.

Choir and Congregation.

For the word of the Lord is right, And all his works are done in truth.

Minister.

3. By the word of the Lord were the heavens made, and all the host of them by the breath of his mouth.

Choir and Congregation.

He gathereth the waters of the sea together as a heap; He layeth up the depth in store-houses.

Minister.

4. Let all the earth fear the Lord; let all the inhabitants of the world stand in awe of him.

Choir and Congregation.

For he spake, and it was done; He commanded, and it stood fast.

Minister.

5. The Lord looketh from heaven; he beholdeth all the sons of men.

Choir and Congregation.

From the place of his habitation he looketh upon all the inhabitants of the earth. He fashioneth their hearts alike; he considereth all their works.

Minister.

6. Behold the eye of the Lord is upon them that fear him, upon them that hope in his mercy.

Choir and Congregation.

To deliver their soul from death, And to keep them alive in famine.

Minister.

7. Our soul waiteth for the Lord; he is our help and our shield.

Choir and Congregation.

For our hearts shall rejoice in him, Because we have trusted in his holy name. A-men.

Selection 152.—Great and marvelous are thy works.

From Rev. xv.
Minister.

1. Great and marvelous are thy works, Lord God Almighty. Just and true are thy ways, thou King of saints.

Choir and Congregation.

G. J. W.

Who shall not fear thee, O Lord, and glori-fy thy name: For thou a-lone art ho-ly.

Minister.

2. Salvation and glory and honor and power unto the Lord our God, for true and righteous are his judgments.

Choir and Congregation.

Praise our God, all ye his servants, And ye that fear him, both small and great.

Ps. xcv. 1-6.
Minister.

3. O, come let us sing unto the Lord. Let us make a joyful noise to the Rock of our salvation.

Choir and Congregation.

Let us come before his presence with } thanksgiv-ing, And make a joyful noise un-to him with psalms.

Minister.

4. For the Lord is a great God, and a great King above all gods.

Choir and Congregation.

In his hand are the deep places of the earth: The strength of the hills is his al-so.

Minister.

5. The sea is his, and he made it, and his hands formed the dry land.

Choir and Congregation.

O come, let us worship and bow down: Let us kneel be-fore the Lord our Mak-er.

Ps. iv : 8.
Minister.

6. Holy, holy, holy Lord God Almighty, which was and is and is to come.

Choir and Congregation.

Thou art worthy, O Lord, to receive glory and } honor and power: { For thou hast created all things, and for thy pleasure they } are and were cre-a-ted.

Ps. lxxxvi : 9, 10.
Minister.

7. All nations whom thou hast made shall come and worship before thee, O Lord, and shall glorify thy name.

Choir and Congregation.

For thou art great and doest wondrous things: Thou art God a-lone. A-men.

Selection 153,—Bless the Lord, O my soul.

Ps. ciii.

Old Chant.

Minister.

1 Bless the Lord, O my soul, and all that is within me bless his holy name.

Choir and Congregation.

Bless the Lord, O my soul And for - get - not all his ben - e - fits.

Minister.

2. Who forgiveth all thine iniquities, who healeth all thy diseases.

Choir and Congregation.

Who redeemeth thy life from destruction, { Who crowneth thee with loving } kindness and tender mercies.

Minister.

3. Who satisfieth thy mouth with good things so that thy youth is renewed like the eagle's.

Choir and Congregation.

The Lord executeth right-eous-ness, And judgment for all that are oppressed.

Minister.

4. He made known his ways unto Moses, his acts unto the children of Israel.

Choir and Congregation.

The Lord is merciful and gra - cious, Slow to an-ger and plenteous in mer-cy.

Minister.

5. He will not always chide, neither will he keep his an-ger forever.

Choir and Congregation.

He hath not dealt with us after our sins, Nor rewarded us ac-cording to our in-i-quities.

Minister.

6. For as the heaven is high above the earth, so great is his mercy toward them that fear him.

Choir and Congregation.

As far as the east is from the west, So far hath he re - moved our transgressions from us.

Minister.

7. Like as a father pitieth his children, so the Lord pitieth them that fear him.

Choir and Congregation.

For he know-eth our frame: He re - membereth that we are dust.

Minister.

8. As for man his days are as grass, as a flower of the field so he flourisheth.

Choir and Congregation.

For the wind passeth over it and it is gone: And the place there-of shall know it no more.

Minister.

9. But the mercy of the Lord is from everlasting to everlasting upon them that fear him, and his righteousness unto children's children.

Choir and Congregation.

To such as keep his covenant, And to those that remember his commandments to do them.

Minister.

10. The Lord hath prepared his throne in the heavens, and his kingdom ruleth over all.

Choir and Congregation.

Bless the Lord, ye his angels, that ex-} cel in strength: { That do his {commandments, } hearkening to the voice of his word.

Minister.

11. Bless ye the Lord, all ye his hosts, ye ministers of his that do his pleasure.

Choir and Congregation.

Bless the Lord, all his works in all places of his dominion. Bless the Lord, O my soul. A-men.

Selection 154.—Give ear, O Shepherd of Israel.

From Ps. lxxx.

Minister.

1. Give ear, O Shepherd of Israel, thou that leadest Joseph like a flock; thou that dwellest between the cheru- bims, shine forth. Before Ephraim and Benjamin and Manasseh, stir up thy strength, and come and save us.

Choir and Congregation.

Turn us again, O God, and cause thy face to shine: And we shall be saved.

Minister.

2. O Lord God of hosts, how long wilt thou be angry against the prayer of thy people?

Thou feedest them with the bread of tears; and givest them tears to drink in great measure. Thou makest us a strife unto our neighbors: and our enemies laugh among themselves.

Choir and Congregation. *(Chant as above.)*

Turn us again, O God of hosts, and | cause thy face to | shine: | And | we | shall be | saved. |

Minister.

3. Return, we beseech thee, O God of hosts: look down from heaven, and behold, and visit this vine; and the vineyard which thy right hand hath planted, and the branch that thou madest strong for thyself.

It is burned with fire, it is cut down: they perish at the rebuke of thy countenance. Let thy hand be upon the man of thy right hand, upon the son of man whom thou madest strong for thyself. So will we not go back from thee: quicken us, and we will call upon thy name.

Choir and Congregation. *(Chant as above.)*

Turn us again, O Lord God of hosts, | cause thy face to | shine: | And | we | shall be | saved. |

Selection 155.—O sing unto the Lord a new song.

From Ps. xcvi.

Minister.

1. O sing unto the Lord a new song: sing unto the Lord, all the earth.

Choir and Congregation.

Sing unto the Lord, bless his name: Show forth his sal - vation from day to day.

Minister.

2. Declare his glories among the heathen; his wonders among all people.

Choir and Congregation.

For the Lord is great and greatly to be prais-ed: He is to be feared a-bove all gods.

Minister.

3. For all the gods of the nations are idols, but the Lord made the heavens.

Choir and Congregation.

Honor and majesty are be-fore him: Strength and beauty are in his sanctu - a - ry.

Minister.

4. Give unto the Lord, oh, ye kindreds of the people: give unto the Lord glory and strength.

Choir and Congregation.

Give unto the Lord } the glory due un- } to his name: Bring an offering and come in - to his courts.

Minister.

5. O worship the Lord in the beauty of holiness: fear before him, all the earth.

Choir and Congregation.

He shall judge the world with right-eous-ness: And the peo-ple with his truth.

From Ps. cxviii.

Minister.

6. O give thanks unto the Lord, for he is good; for his mercy is forever.

Choir and Congregation.

Let Is - rael now say: That his mer - cy is for - ev - er.

Minister.

7. Let the house of Aaron say that his mercy is for-ever.

Choir and Congregation.

Let them now that fear the Lord say: That his mer - cy is for - ev - er.

Minister.

8. I called upon the Lord in distress. The Lord answered me in a large place.

Choir and Congregation.

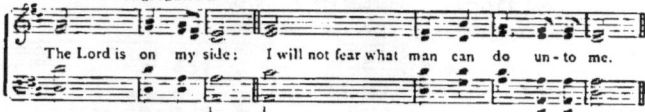

The Lord is on my side: I will not fear what man can do un-to me.

Minister.

9. It is better to trust in the Lord than to put confidence in man. It is better to trust in the Lord than to put confidence in princes.

Choir and Congregation.

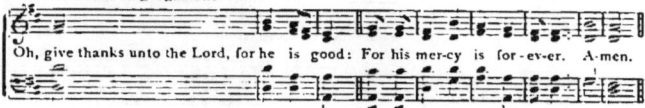

Oh, give thanks unto the Lord, for he is good: For his mer-cy is for-ev-er. A-men.

.Selection 156.—God is our Refuge and Strength.

Minister. Ps. xlvi.

1. God is our Refuge and Strength, a very present help in trouble. Therefore will not we fear, though the earth be removed, and tho' the mountains be carried into the midst of the sea.

Choir and Congregation.   TALLIS.

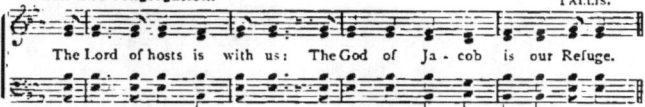

The Lord of hosts is with us: The God of Ja - cob is our Refuge.

Minister.

2. Though the waters thereof roar and be troubled, though the mountains shake with the swelling thereof.

Choir and Congregation. (Chant as above.)

The | Lord of hosts is | with us: The | God of Jacob | is our Refuge.

Minister.

3. There is a river, the streams whereof shall make glad the city of God, the holy place of the tabernacles of the Most High.

Choir and Congregation. (Chant as above.)

The | Lord of hosts is | with us: The | God of Jacob | is our Refuge.

Minister.

4. God is in the midst of her; she shall not be moved: God shall help her, and that right early.

Choir and Congregation. (Chant as above.)

The | Lord of hosts is | with us: The | God of Jacob | is our Refuge.

Minister.

5. The heathen raged, the kingdoms were moved: He uttered his voice, the earth melted.

Choir and Congregation. (Chant as above.)

The | Lord of hosts is | with us: The | God of Jacob | is our Refuge.

Minister.

6. Come, behold the works of the Lord, what desolations he hath made in the earth.

Choir and Congregation. (Chant as above.)

The | Lord of hosts is | with us: The | God of Jacob | is our Refuge.

Minister.

7. He maketh wars to cease unto the end of the earth; he breaketh the bow, and cutteth the spear in sunder; he burneth the chariot in the fire.

Choir and Congregation. (Chant as above.)

The | Lord of hosts is | with us: The | God of Jacob | is our Refuge.

Minister.

8. Be still, and know that I am God: I will be exalted among the heathen, I will be exalted in the earth.

Choir and Congregation.

The Lord of hosts is with us: The God of Ja - cob is our Refuge. A-men.

Selection 157.—Thy testimonies are wonderful.

Ps. cxix : 129-134.

G. J. W.

Minister.

1. Thy testimonies are wonderful, therefore doth my soul keep them.

Choir and Congregation.

The entrance of thy words giv-eth light : It giveth under-stand-ing to the simple.

Minister.

2. I opened my mouth and panted, for I longed for thy commandments.

Choir and Congregation.

Look thou upon me and be merciful } un-to me : As thou usest to do unto those that love thy name.

Minister.

3. Order my steps in thy word, and let not any iniquity have dominion over me.

Choir and Congregation.

Deliver me from the op-pres-sion of men : So will I keep thy precepts.

Ps. cxix : 143-152.

Minister.

4. Trouble and anguish have taken hold on me. Yet thy commandments are my delight.

Choir and Congregation.

The righteousness of thy testimonies is } ev-er-last-ing : Give me under-stand-ing and I shall live.

Minister.

5. I cried with my whole heart : hear me, O Lord ; I will keep thy statutes.

Choir and Congregation.

I cried unto thee : save me, And I shall keep thy tes-ti-monies.

Minister.

6. Hear my voice, according to thy loving kindness. O Lord, quicken me according to thy judgment.

Choir and Congregation.

They draw nigh that follow af-ter mis chief : They are far from thy law.

Minister.

7. Thou art near, O Lord, and all thy commandments are truth.

Choir and Congregation.

Concerning thy testimonies I have } known of old : That thou hast found-ed them for-ev-er. A-men.

Selection 158.—Teach me, O Lord, the way of thy statutes.

Ps. cxiv. 33-40.

Arranged.

Minister.

1. Teach me, O Lord, the way of thy statutes, and I shall keep it unto the end.

Choir and Congregation.

{ Give me understand- ing, and I shall } keep thy law; { Yea, I shall ob- } serve it with my whole heart.

Minister.

2. Make me to go in the path of thy commandments, for therein do I delight.

Choir and Congregation.

Incline my heart unto thy tes - ti mo-nies, And not to cov-et-ous-ness.

Minister.

3. Turn away mine eyes from beholding vanity, and quicken thou me in thy way.

Choir and Congregation.

Stablish thy word un - to thy servant Who is devot - ed to thy fear.

Minister.

4. Turn away my reproach which I fear, for thy judgments are good.

Choir and Congregation.

Behold I have longed af - ter thy precepts; Quicken me in thy righteousness.

Minister.

5 Thy hands have made me and fashioned me. Give me understanding, that I may learn thy commandments.

Choir and Congregation.

{ They that fear thee will be } glad when they see me, { Because I have } hoped in thy word.

Minister.

6. I know, O Lord, that thy judgments are right, and that thou in faithfulness hast afflicted me.

Choir and Congregation.

{ Let, I pray thee, thy merciful kindness } be-fore my comfort, { According to thy } word un-to thy servant.

Minister.

7. Let thy tender mercies come unto me that I may live, for thy law is my delight.

Choir and Congregation.

{ Let the proud be a-shamed, for they dealt perversely with me with- } out a cause. { But I will } med-i-tate in thy precepts. A-men.

20

Selection 159.—The Lord reigneth.

Choir and Congregation.

Ps. xciii.

Minister.

1. The Lord reigneth! he is clothed with majesty.

The Lord is clothed with strength wherewith he hath girded himself: The world also is stablished that it can-not be moved.

Choir and Congregation.

Minister.

2. Thy throne is established of old; thou art from everlasting.

The floods have lifted up, O Lord, the floods have lifted up their voice: The floods lift up their waves.

Choir and Congregation.

Minister.

3. The Lord on high is mightier than the noise of many waters; yea, than the mighty waves of the sea.

Thy testimonies are ver-y sure: Holiness becometh thine house, O Lord, for-ev-er.

Choir and Congregation.

Ps. c.

Minister.

4. Make a joyful noise unto the Lord, all ye lands. Serve the Lord with gladness; come before his presence with singing.

Know ye that the Lord he is good: It is he that hath made us and not we ourselves: We are his people and the sheep of his pasture.

Choir and Congregation.

Minister.

5. Enter into his gates with thanksgiving, and into his courts with praise. Be thankful unto him and bless his name.

For the Lord is good; his mercy is ev-er-last-ing: And his truth endureth to all generations.

Choir and Congregation.

Ps. viii.

Minister.

6. O Lord our Lord! how excellent is thy name in all the earth, who hast set thy glory above the heavens.

Out of the mouths of babes and sucklings hast thou ordained strength be- cause of thine enemies: { *That thou mightest still the* } enemy and the avenger.

Minister.

7. When I consider the heavens the work of thy fingers, the moon and the stars which thou hast ordained, what is man that thou art mindful of him, and the son of man that thou visitest him.

Choir and Congregation.

For thou hast made him a little lower than the angels: Thou hast crown-ed him with glory and honor.

Minister.

8. Thou madest him to have dominion over the works of thy hands. Thou hast put all things under his feet.

Choir and Congregation.

All sheep and ox-en: Yea, and the beasts of the field.

Minister.

9. The fowl of the air and the fish of the sea, and whatsoever passeth through the paths of the seas.

Choir and Congregation.

O Lord our Lord! How excellent is thy name in all the earth. A-men.

Selection 160.—Ho! every one that thirsteth.

From Isa. lv.

Minister.

1. Ho, every one that thirsteth, come ye to the waters, and he that hath no money, come ye, buy, and eat; yea, come, buy wine and milk without money and without price.

Choir and Congregation.

Seek ye the Lord while he may be found, call ye up-on him while he is near

Minister.

2. Wherefore do you spend money for that which is not bread? and your labor for that which satisfieth not? Hearken unto me, and eat ye that which is good, and let your soul delight itself in fatness.

Choir and Congregation. (*Chant as above.*)

Minister.

3. Incline your ear, and come unto me: hear, and your soul shall live; and I will make an everlasting covenant with you, even the sure mercies of David.

Choir and Congregation.

Let the wick-ed for-sake his way, and the un-righteous man his thoughts:

and let him re-turn un-to the Lord, and he will have mer-cy up-on him. A-men

Selection 161.—Hear my prayer, O Lord.

Ps. cxliii.

Minister.

1. Hear my prayer, O Lord, give ear to my supplication. In thy faithfulness answer me, and in thy righteousness.

Choir and Congregation.

And enter not into judgment . . with thy servant, For in thy sight shall no man . . living be jus-ti-fied.

Minister.

2. For the enemy hath persecuted my soul; he hath smitten my life down to the ground.

Choir and Congregation.

He hath made me to dwell in dark-ness, As those that have been long dead.

Minister.

3. Therefore is my spirit overwhelmed within me; my heart within me is desolate.

Choir and Congregation.

I stretch forth my hands unto thee; My soul thirsteth after thee, as a thirst-y land.

Minister.

4. Hear me speedily, O Lord, my spirit faileth. Hide not thy face from me, lest I be like them that go down to the pit.

Choir and Congregation.

Cause me to hear thy loving kindness in the morning, For in thee do I trust.

Minister.

5. Cause me to know the way wherein I should walk, for I lift up my soul unto thee.

Choir and Congregation.

Deliver me, O Lord, from mine en-e-mies; I flee un-to thee to hide me.

From Ps. xxxvi.

Minister.

6. How excellent is thy loving kindness, O God! therefore the children of men put their trust under the shadow of thy wings.

Choir and Congregation.

They shall be abund-antly satisfied with the fatness of thy house, And thou shalt make them drink of the river of thy pleasures.

Minister.

7. For with thee is the fountain of life; in thy light shall we see light.

Choir and Congregation.

Oh, continue thy loving kindness unto them that know thee, And thy right-eousness to the upright in heart. A-men.

Selection 162.—Behold, the Lord's hand is not shortened.

From various Scriptures.

G. F. R.

Choir and Congregation.

Minister.

1. Behold the Lord's hand is not shortened that it can not save, neither his ear heavy that it can not hear.

But your iniquities have separated between } you and your God: { And your sins have hid his } face from you that he will not hear.

Choir and Congregation.

Minister.

2. Wash you, make you clean. Put away the evil of your doings from before mine eyes.

Let the wicked forsake his way, And the un-right-eous man his thoughts.

Choir and Congregation.

Minister.

3. And let him return unto the Lord, and he will have mercy upon him.

And to our God, For he will a-bund-ant-ly par-don.

Choir and Congregation.

Minister.

4. As I live, saith the Lord God, I have no pleasure in the death of the wicked, but that the wicked turn from his way and live.

Turn ye, turn ye from your e-vil ways: For why will ye die, O house of Is-ra-el.

Choir and Congregation.

Minister.

5. Come unto me, all ye that labor and are heavy laden, and I will give you rest.

Take my yoke upon you and learn of me, for I am meek and } lowly in heart: And ye shall find rest un-to your souls.

Choir and Congregation.

Minister.

6. And the Spirit and the Bride say, Come; and let him that heareth say, Come.

And let him that is a-thirst come: { And whosoever will, let him take the } water of life freely. A-men.

Selection 163.—Blessed is the man.

Ps. i: 1-5.

Minister.
1. Blessed is the man that walketh not in the counsel of the ungodly, nor standeth in the way of sinners, nor sitteth in the seat of the scornful.

Choir and Congregation.

{ But his delight is in the } law of the Lord; And in his law doth he meditate day and night.

Minister.
2. And he shall be like a tree planted by the rivers of water, that bringeth forth his fruit in his season.

Choir and Congregation.

His leaf also shall not wither; And whatso-ev-er he do-eth shall pros-per.

Minister.
3. The ungodly are not so, but are like the chaff which the wind driveth away.

Choir and Congregation.

{ Therefore the un-godly shall not } stand in the judgment; { Nor sinners in the congre- } gation of the righteous.

Ps. cxlvi: 5-10.

Minister.
4. Happy is he that hath the Lord of Jacob for his help, whose hope is in the Lord his God.

Choir and Congregation.

Who made heav'n and earth; The sea, and all that is there-in.

Minister.
5. Which executeth judgment for the oppressed; which giveth food to the hungry.

Choir and Congregation.

The Lord loos-eth the pris-on-ers; The Lord o-pen-eth the eyes of the blind.

Minister.
6. The Lord raiseth up them that are bowed down; the Lord loveth the righteous.

Choir and Congregation.

The Lord pre-serv-eth the stran-gers; He relieveth the fa-ther-less and wid-ow.

Minister.
7. The Lord shall reign forever, even thy God, O Zion, unto all generations.

Choir and Congregation.

Oh, give thanks un-to the Lord, For his mer-cy en-dur-eth for-ev-er. A-men.

Selection 164.—Have mercy upon me, O God.

From Ps. li.

Minister.

1. Have mercy upon me, O God, according to thy loving kindness; according unto the multitude of thy tender mercies, blot out my transgressions.

Choir and Congregation.

Wash me thoroughly from mine in - i - qui-ty, And cleanse me from my sin.

Minister.

2. For I acknowledge my transgressions, and my sin is ever before me.

Choir and Congregation.

Against thee, thee only, have I sinned, And done this e - vil in thy sight;
That thou mightest be justified when thou speakest, And be clear when thou judgest.

Minister.

3. Create in me a clean heart, O God, and renew a right spirit within me.

Choir and Congregation.

Cast me not a-way from thy pres-ence, And take not thy Ho - ly Spir - it from me.

Minister.

4. Restore unto me the joy of thy salvation, and uphold me with thy free spirit.

Choir and Congregation.

Then will I teach trans-gressors thy ways: And sinners shall be con-verted un - to thee.

Minister.

5. Deliver me from blood-guiltiness, O God, thou God of my salvation, and my tongue shall sing aloud of thy righteousness.

Choir and Congregation.

O Lord, open thou my lips, And my mouth shall show forth thy praise.

Minister.

6. For thou desirest not sacrifice, else would I give it: thou delightest not in burnt offerings.

Choir and Congregation.

The sacrifices of God are a broken spir-it: { A broken and a contrite heart, O } God, thou wilt not despise.

Selection 165.—The heavens declare the glory of God.

Ps. xix.

Minister.

1. The heavens declare the glory of God, and the firmament showeth his handiwork.

Choir and Congregation. †††

Day unto day ut-ter-eth speech, And night un-to night showeth knowledge.

Minister.

2. There is no speech nor language where their voice is not heard.

Choir and Congregation.

Their line is gone out through all the earth, And their words to the end of the world.

Minister.

3. In them hath he set a tabernacle for the sun, which is as a bridegroom coming out of his chamber, and rejoiceth as a strong man to run a race.

Choir and Congregation.

{ His going forth is from the heaven and his circuit unto the } ends of it, { And there is nothing } hid from the heat thereof.

Minister.

4. The law of the Lord is perfect, converting the soul.

Choir and Congregation.

The testimony of the Lord is sure, Making wise the simple.

Minister.

5. The statutes of the Lord are right, rejoicing the heart.

Choir and Congregation.

The commandment of the Lord is pure, En-light-'ning the eyes.

Minister.

6. The fear of the Lord is clean, enduring forever.

Choir and Congregation.

The judgments of the Lord are true, And right-eous al-to-geth-er.

Minister.

7. More to be desired are they than gold, yea, than much fine gold.

Choir and Congregation.

Sweeter al-so than hon-ey And the hon-ey-comb.

Minister.

S. Moreover, by them is thy servant warned, and in keeping of them there is great reward.

Choir and Congregation.

Who can under - stand his er-rors: Cleanse thou me from se - cret faults.

Minister.

9. Keep back thy servant also from presumptuous sins, let them not have dominion over me.

Choir and Congregation.

Then shall I be upright, And I shall be in - nocent from the great transgres-sion.

Minister.

10. Let the words of my mouth, and the meditations of my heart,

Choir and Congregation.

Be ac - ceptable in thy sight, O Lord, my strength and my Re-deemer.   A - men.

Selection 166.—Turn ye, oh, turn ye, for why will ye die?

From Ezek. xviii.

Minister.

1. When a righteous man turneth away from his righteousness, and committeth iniquity, and dieth in them; for his iniquity that he hath done shall he die.

Choir and Congregation.

Turn ye, oh, turn ye, for why will ye die?

Minister.

2. Again, when a wicked man turneth away from his wickedness that he hath committed, and doeth that which is lawful and right, he shall save his soul alive.

Choir and Congregation. *(Chant as above.)*

Turn ye, oh, | turn ye, for | why will ye | die?

Minister.

3. Because he considereth, and turneth away from all his transgressions that he hath committed, he shall surely live, he shall not die.

Choir and Congregation. *(Chant as above.)*

Turn ye, oh, | turn ye, for | why will ye | die?

Minister.

4. Therefore I will judge you, O house of Israel, every one according to his ways, saith the Lord God. Repent, and turn yourselves from all your transgressions; so iniquity shall not be your ruin.

Choir and Congregation. *(Chant as above.)*

Turn ye, oh, | turn ye, for | why will ye | die?

Minister.

5. Cast away from you all your transgressions, whereby ye have transgressed; and make you a new heart and a new spirit: for why will ye die, O house of Israel?

Choir and Congregation. *(Chant as above.)*

Turn ye, oh, | turn ye, for | why will ye | die?

Minister.

6. For I have no pleasure in the death of him that dieth, saith the Lord God; wherefore turn yourselves, and live ye.

Choir and Congregation.

Turn ye, oh, turn ye, for why will ye die? Why will ye die, O house of Is - ra - el?

Selection 167.—O give thanks unto the Lord.

From Ps. cvii.

Minister.

1. O give thanks unto the Lord, for he is good: for his mercy endureth forever. Let the redeemed of the Lord say so, whom he hath redeemed from the hand of the enemy; and gathered them out of the lands, from the east, and from the west, from the north, and from the south. They wandered in the wilderness in a solitary way; they found no city to dwell in. Hungry and thirsty, their soul fainted in them.

Then they cried unto the Lord in their trouble, and he delivered them out of their distresses. And he led them forth by the right way, that they might go to a city of habitation.

Choir and Congregation.

Oh, that men would praise the Lord for his goodness: And for his wonderful works to the chil-dren of men!

For he satisfieth the long-ing soul: And filleth the hun-gry soul with good-ness.

Minister.

2. Such as sit in darkness and in the shadow of death, being bound in affliction and iron; because they rebelled against the word of God, and contemned the counsel of the Most High.

Therefore he brought down their heart with labor; they fell down, and there was none to help. Then they cried unto the Lord in their trouble, and he saved them out of their distresses. He brought them out of darkness and the shadow of death, and break their bands in sunder.

Choir and Congregation.

Oh, that men would praise the Lord for his goodness: And for his wonderful works to the chil-dren of men!

For he hath broken the gates of brass: And cut the bars of i-ron in sun-der.

Minister.

3. Fools because of their transgression, and because of their iniquities, are afflicted. Their soul abhorreth all manner of meat; and they draw near unto the gates of death. Then they cry unto the Lord in their trouble, and he saveth them out of their distresses. He sent his word, and healed them, and delivered them from their destructions.

Choir and Congregation.

Oh, that men would praise the Lord for his goodness: And for his wonderful works to the chil-dren of men!

And let them sacrifice the sacrifices of thanksgiv - ing: And de - clare his works with re - joic - ing.

Minister.

4. They that go down to the sea in ships, that do business in great waters; these see the works of the Lord, and his wonders in the deep. For he commandeth, and raiseth the stormy wind, which lifteth up the waves thereof. They mount up to the heaven, they go down again to the depths: their soul is melted because of trouble. They reel to and fro, and stagger like a drunken man, and are at their wit's end. Then they cry unto the Lord in their trouble, and he bringeth them out of their distresses. He maketh the storm a calm, so that the waves thereof are still. Then are they glad because they be quiet; so he bringeth them unto their desired haven.

Choir and Congregation.

Oh, that men would praise the Lord for his goodness: And for his wonderful works to the chil-dren of men!

Let them exalt him also in the congregation of the people: And praise him in the as-sembly of the elders. A-men.

Selection 168.—And the Lord shall be King.

Minister. Zech. xiv: 9.

1. And the Lord shall be King over all the earth: in that day shall there be one Lord, and his name One.

Choir and Congregation.

For the earth shall be full of the knowledge of the Lord, as the wa - ters cov - er the sea.

Minister. Isa. xi: 6-9.

2. The wolf also shall dwell with the lamb, and the leopard shall lie down with the kid; and the calf and the young lion and the fatling together; and a little child shall lead them. And the cow and the bear shall feed; their young ones shall lie down together: and the lion shall eat straw like the ox.

Choir and Congregation. (Chant as above.)

For the | earth shall be | full of the | knowledge of the | Lord, as the | waters | cover the | sea.

Minister.

3. And the sucking child shall play on the hole of the asp, and the weaned child shall put his hand on the cocka-trice's den. They shall not hurt nor destroy in all my holy mountain.

A-men.

Choir and Congregation. (Chant as above.)

For the | earth shall be | full of the | knowledge of the | Lord, as the | waters | cover the | sea.

Selection 169.—Lord God of Israel.

TALLIS.

From 1 Kings viii.

Minister.

1. Lord God of Israel, there is no God like thee in heaven above or on earth beneath.

Choir and Congregation.

That keepest covenant and mercy with thy servants, That walk before thee with all their heart.

Minister.

2. Who hast kept with thy servant David, that thou didst promise him.

Choir and Congregation.

Thou spakest al - so with thy mouth, And hast ful-filled it with thine own hand.

Minister.

3. Behold, the heaven of heavens cannot contain thee; how much less this house that we have builded.

Choir and Congregation.

{ Yet have thou re-
{ spect unto the } prayer of thy servants, And to their supplication, O Lord our God.

Minister.

4. Hearken unto the cry and to the prayer which thy servant prayeth before thee this day.

Choir and Congregation.

{ That thine eyes may
be opened toward } night and day, { Even toward the place
of which thou hast } name shall be there.
{ this house . . } { said, My . . }

Minister.

5. Hearken thou to the supplication of thy servants and of thy people Israel, which they shall make in this place.

Choir and Congregation.

Hear thou in heaven thy dwell-ing place, And when thou hear-est for - give.

Minister.

6. Now, therefore, O Lord God, arise into thy resting-place, thou, and the ark of thy strength.

Choir and Congregation.

Let thy priests, O Lord God, be clothed with salvation, And let thy saints rejoice in goodness.

Ps. cxxxii. 13-14.

Minister.

7. For the Lord hath chosen Zion; he hath desired it for his habitation.

Choir and Congregation.

This is my rest for - ev - er, Here will I dwell, saith the Lord. A - men

Selection 170.—Bow down thine ear, O Lord.

Ps. lxxxvi. 1-12.

Minister.
1. Bow down thine ear, O Lord; hear me, for I am poor and needy.

Choir and Congregation.

Preserve my soul for I am ho-ly, O thou my God, save thy servant that trusteth in thee.

Minister.
2. Be merciful unto me, O Lord, for I cry unto thee daily.

Choir and Congregation.

Rejoice the soul of thy servant, For unto thee, O Lord, do I lift up my soul.

Minister.
3. For thou Lord art good and ready to forgive, and plenteous in mercy unto all them that call upon thee.

Choir and Congregation.

Give ear, O Lord, un-to my prayer, And attend to the voice of my suppli-ca'i ns.

Minister.
4. In the day of my trouble I will call upon thee, for thou wilt answer me.

Choir and Congregation.

Among the gods there is none like unto thee, O Lord, Neither are there any works like un-to thy works.

Minister.
5. All nations whom thou hast made shall come and worship before thee, O Lord, and shall glorify thy name.

Choir and Congregation.

For thou art great and doest won-drous things, Thou art God a-lone.

Minister.
6. Teach me thy way, O Lord; I will walk in thy truth. Unite my heart to fear thy name.

Choir and Congregation.

I will praise thee, O Lord my God, with all my heart, And I will glorify thy name for-ev-er-more. A-men.

Selection 171.—The Ten Commandments.

Minister.
And God spake all these words, saying:

I.
Thou shalt have no other Gods before me.

Choir and Congregation.   *Arranged.*

Ho-ly, ho-ly, ho-ly Lord God Almighty: Who was, and who is, and who is to come.

Minister.
Thou shalt not make unto thee any graven image, or any likeness of anything that is in heaven above, or that is in the earth beneath, or that is in the water under the earth; thou shalt not bow down thyself to them, nor serve them; for I the Lord thy God am a jealous God, visiting the in-iquity of the fathers upon the children unto the third and fourth generation of them that hate me; and showing mercy unto thousands of them that love me, and keep my commandments.

Choir and Congregation. *(Chant as above.)*

Holy, | holy, | holy | Lord God Al-| mighty: Who was, and who | is, and who | is to | come.

Minister.

III.
Thou shalt not take the name of the Lord thy God in vain; for the Lord will not hold him guiltless that taketh his name in vain.

Choir and Congregation.

Who will not fear thee, O Lord, and glo-ri-fy thy name? For thou alone art ho-ly.

Minister.
Remember the Sabbath day to keep it holy. Six days shalt thou labor and do all thy work; but the seventh day is the Sabbath of the Lord thy God: in it thou shalt not do any work, thou, nor thy son, nor thy daughter, nor thy man-servant, nor thy maid-servant, nor thy cattle, nor thy

IV.
stranger that is within thy gates; for in six days the Lord made heaven and earth, the sea, and all that in them is, and rested the seventh day: wherefore the Lord blessed the Sabbath day, and hallowed it.

Choir and Congregation.

This is the day which the Lord hath made: We will re-joice and be glad in it.

Minister.

V.
Honor thy father and thy mother, that thy days may be long upon the land which the Lord thy God giveth thee.

Choir and Congregation.

Thy hands have made me and fashion'd me; Make me to understand, that I may learn thy commandments.

Minister.

VI.
Thou shalt not kill.

Choir and Congregation.

With the merciful, thou wilt show thyself mer-ci-ful: With an upright man thou wilt show thyself upright.

Minister.

VII.
Thou shalt not commit adultery.

Choir and Congregation.

Blessed are the pure in heart, For they shall see God.

Minister. **VIII.**
Thou shalt not steal.

Choir and Congregation. *(Chant as above.)*

Order my steps | in thy | word, And let not any iniquity have do-| minion | over | me.

Minister. IX.

Thou shalt not bear false witness against thy neighbor.

Choir and Congregation.

I have chosen the way of truth: Thy judgments have I laid be-fore me.

Minister. X.

Thou shalt not covet thy neighbor's house, thou shalt not covet thy neighbor's wife, nor his man-servant, nor his maid-servant, nor his ox, nor his ass, nor any thing that is thy neighbor's.

Choir and Congregation.

Incline our hearts to thy tes-ti-mo-nies: And not to cov-et-eous-ness.

Minister.

And these words, which I command thee this day, shall be in thine heart; and thou shalt teach them diligently unto thy children, and shalt talk of them when thou sittest in thine house, and when thou walkest by the way, and when thou liest down, and when thou risest up.

Choir and Congregation.

All that the Lord hath spo-ken, We will do and hear. A-men.

Selection 172.—The Law of Love.

Minister. And Jesus said: I.

The first of all the commandments is, Hear, O Israel, the Lord our God is one Lord: And thou shalt love the Lord thy God with all thy heart, and with all thy mind, and with all thy strength.

Choir and Congregation. J. P. S.

With my whole heart have I sought thee; Oh, let me not wander from thy commandments.

Minister. II.

And the second is like unto it: Thou shalt love thy neighbor as thyself. On these two commandments hang all the Law and the Prophets.

Choir and Congregation.

Teach me, O Lord, the way of thy statutes; And I shall keep it un-to the end.

Minister. III.

A new commandment I give unto you: That ye love one another. As I have loved you, that ye also love one another. By this will all men know that ye are my disciples, if ye have love one to another.

Choir and Congregation.

Search me, O God, and know my heart; Try me, and know..my thoughts; And see if there be any wicked way in me; And lead me in the way everlast-ing.

Minister. IV.

Therefore all things whatsoever ye would that men should do to you, do ye even so to them: for this is the Law and the Prophets.

Choir and Congregation.

The law was given by Moses; Grace and truth came by Je-sus Christ. And of his fullness have we all re-ceived; And grace for grace. A-men.

Selection 173.—The Ten Blessings.

G. F. R.

Minister.
And seeing the multitudes, he went up into a mountain; and when he had sat down, his disciples came unto him. And he opened his mouth, and taught them, saying:

I.

Blessed are the poor in spirit: for theirs is the kingdom of heaven.

Choir and Congregation.

The Lord is nigh unto them that are of a { broken heart: And saveth such as be of a contrite spirit.

Minister.

II.

Blessed are they that mourn: for they shall be comforted.

Choir and Congregation.

This is my comfort in my af-flic-tion: For thy word hath quicken'd me.

Minister.

III.

Blessed are the meek: for they shall inherit the earth.

Choir and Congregation.

The meek will he guide in judgment: And the meek will he teach his way.

Minister.

IV.

Blessed are they that do hunger and thirst after righteousness: for they shall be filled.

Choir and Congregation.

He shall receive the blessing from the Lord: { And righteousness from the } God of his sal vation.

Minister.

V.

Blessed are the merciful: for they shall obtain mercy.

Choir and Congregation.

He that trusteth in the Lord: Mercy shall com-pass him a-bout.

Minister.

VI.

Blessed are the pure in heart: for they shall see God.

Choir and Congregation.

Create in me a clean heart, O God: And renew a right spirit with-in me.

Minister.

VII.

Blessed are the peacemakers: for they shall be called the children of God.

Choir and Congregation.

Behold, how good and how pleasant it is { For brethren to dwell to- } gether in u-ni ty.

Minister.

VIII.

Blessed are they that are persecuted for righteousness' sake: for theirs is the kingdom of heaven.

Minister. **IX.**

Blessed are ye when they shall revile you, and persecute you, and shall say all manner of evil against you falsely, for my sake.

Minister. **X.**

Rejoice, and be exceeding glad, for great is your reward in heaven: for so persecuted they the prophets who were before you.

Choir and Congregation.

The salvation of the righteous is of the Lord: He is their strength in the time of trouble.

Choir and Congregation.

The angel of the Lord encampeth Around them that fear him: and de-liv'reth them.

Choir and Congregation.

{ Blessed be the } God of Is-ra-el: { From everlast- } lasting. A-men and A-men.
{ Lord, the } { ing to ever- }

Selection 174.—The Seven Promises.

Minister. Behold, I come quickly: and my reward is with me, to give every man according as his work shall be. I am Alpha and Omega, the Beginning and the End, the First and the Last.

I.

To him that overcometh will I give to eat of the Tree of Life, which is in the midst of the Paradise of God.

Choir and Congregation.

He that hath an ear, let him hear What the Spir-it saith un-to the churches.

Minister. **II.**

He that overcometh, shall not be hurt of the second death.

Choir and Congregation. (Chant as above.)

He that hath an ear, let him | hear: What the | Spirit saith un- | to the | churches.‖

Minister.

To him that overcometh, will I give to eat of the hidden manna; and will give him a white stone; and in the stone a new name written, which no man knoweth saving he that receiveth it.

Choir and Congregation. (Chant as above.) **III.**

He that hath an ear, let him | hear: What the | Spirit saith un- | to the | churches.‖

Minister. **IV.**

He that overcometh, and keepeth my works unto the end, to him will I give power over the nations: and he shall rule them with a rod of iron; as the vessels of a potter shall they be broken to shivers: even as I received of my Father. And I will give him the morning star.

Choir and Congregation. (Chant as above.)

He that hath an ear, let him | hear: What the | Spirit saith un- | to the | churches.‖

Minister. **V.**

He that overcometh, the same shall be clothed in white raiment; and I will not blot out his name out of the book of life; but I will confess his name before my Father, and before his angels.

Choir and Congregation. (Chant as above.)

He that hath an ear, let him | hear: What the | Spirit saith un- | to the | churches.‖

Minister. **VI.**

Him that overcometh will I make a pillar in the temple of my God, and he shall go no more out: and I will write upon him the name of my God, and the name of the city of my God, New Jerusalem, which cometh down out of heaven from my God, and my new name.

Choir and Congregation. (Chant as above.)

He that hath an ear, let him | hear: What the | Spirit saith un- | to the | churches.‖

Minister. **VII.**

To him that overcometh will I grant to sit with me in my throne, even as I also overcame, and am set down with my Father in his throne.

A men.

Choir and Congregation. (Chant as above.)

He that hath an ear, let him | hear: What the | Spirit saith un- | to the | churches.‖

21

Selection 175.—Sound an alarm in my holy mountain.

Joel ii : 1.
Minister.

1. Sound an alarm in my holy mountain, let all the inhabitants of the land tremble; for the day of the Lord cometh, it is nigh at hand.

Choir and Congregation.   Isa. lviii : 11.   G. F. R.

(Cry aloud, spare not, lift thy) voice like a trumpet, (Show my people their transgression and the) house of Jacob their sin.

Isa. iii : 10, 11.
Minister.

2. Say ye to the righteous that it shall be well with him; for they shall eat the fruit of their doings.

Choir and Congregation.

Woe unto the wicked! it shall be ill with him, For the reward of his hands shall be given him.

Ps. cxxxiv.
Minister.

3. Behold, bless ye the Lord, all ye servants of the Lord, which by night stand in the house of the Lord.

Choir and Congregation.

(Lift up your hands in the sanctuary and) bless the Lord. (The Lord that made heaven and earth) bless thee out of Zi-on.

Isa. lii : 7.
Minister.

4. How beautiful upon the mountains are the feet of him that bringeth good tidings that publisheth peace.

Choir and Congregation.

(That bringeth good tidings of good, that) publisheth sal-va-tion. That saith unto Zion, Thy God reign - eth.

Minister.

5. Thy watchmen shall lift up the voice, with the voice together shall they sing.

Choir and Congregation.

For they shall see eye to eye, When the Lord shall bring a - gain Zi - on.

Minister.

6. Break forth into joy, sing together ye waste places of Jerusalem, for the Lord hath comforted his people, he hath redeemed Jerusalem.

Choir and Congregation.

(The Lord hath made bare his arm in the eyes of) all the nations, (And all the ends of the earth shall see the sal-) vation of our God. A-men.

Selection 176.—In the beginning was the Word. (The Incarnation.)

Various Scriptures.

Minister.

1. In the beginning was the Word, and the Word was with God, and the Word was God; and the Word was made flesh and dwelt among us.

Choir and Congregation.

Thou, O Lord, art our Father, our Redeemer: Thy name is from ev - er - last-ing.

Minister.

2. And there were in the same country shepherds abiding in the field, keeping watch over their flocks by night; and, lo, the angel of the Lord came upon them, and the glory of the Lord shone round about them; and they were sore afraid.

Choir and Congregation.

Arise, shine, for thy light is come: And the glory of the Lord is ris - en up - on thee.

Minister.

3. And the angel said unto them, Fear not; for, behold, I bring you good tidings of great joy, which shall be to all people.

Choir and Congregation.

How beautiful up - on the mountains Are the feet of him that bring - eth good tid - ings: That pub - lish-eth peace: That bring - eth good tid-ings of good.

Minister.

4. For unto you is born this day in the city of David, a Savior which is Christ the Lord; and this shall be a sign unto you; ye shall find the babe wrapped in swaddling clothes, lying in a manger.

Choir and Congregation.

Unto us a Child is born; Unto us a Son is given: And his name shall be called Won - der - ful, Coun - sel-lor, the might - y God, the Ev - er - last - ing Fa - ther, the Prince of Peace.

Minister.

5. And suddenly there was with the angel a multitude of the heavenly host, praising God and saying, "Glory to God in the highest, on earth peace, good will toward men."

Choir and Congregation.

Glory to God in the high - est: On earth peace, good will toward men.

Selection 177.—Behold, I stand at the door. (The Altar of God.)

(Various Scriptures.)

G. J. W.

Minister.

1. Behold, I stand at the door and knock; if any man hear my voice and open the door, I will come in to him and sup with him, and he with me.

Choir and Congregation.

I will go unto the al-tar of God, Unto God my ex-ceed-ing joy.

Lead me in thy truth and teach me, For thou art the God of my sal-va-tion.

Minister.

2. If thou bring thy gift to the altar, and there remember that thy brother hath aught against thee, leave there thy gift before the altar and go thy way. First be reconciled to thy brother, and then come and offer thy gift.

Choir and Congregation.

Search me, O God, and know my heart, Try me, and know my thoughts.

And see if there be any wicked way in me, And lead me in the way ev-er-last-ing.

Minister.

3. A new commandment I give unto you, that ye love one another. As I have loved you, that ye also love one another

Choir and Congregation.

I will wash my hands in in-no-cen-cy, So I will compass thine al-tar, O Lord.

That I may publish with the voice of thanks-giv-ing, And tell of a'l thy won-drous works.

Minister.

4. I am the Good Shepherd,
and know my sheep and am
known of mine, and I lay
down my life for the sheep.

Choir and Congregation.

Thou preparest a ta-ble be - fore me, In the pres-ence of mine en-e-mies.

Thou anointest my head with oil, My cup run - neth o - ver.

Minister.

5. I am the Bread of Life.
He that cometh to me shall
never hunger, and he that
believeth on me shall never
thirst.

Choir and Congregation.

What shall I render un-to the Lord For all his ben - e - fits to-ward me.

I will take the cup of sal - va - tion, And call upon the name of the Lord.

Minister.

6. I am the Living Bread
which came down from
heaven. If any one eat of
this Bread he shall live forever, and the bread that I
will give is my flesh, which
I will give for the life of the
world.

Choir and Congregation.

Unto him that lov - ed us, And washed us from our sins in his own blood,

And has made us kings and priests unto God and his Father, To him be glory and dominion for-ev-er and ev-er. A-men.

Selection 178.—I am the Resurrection and the Life. (The Resurrection.)

(Various Scriptures.)

Arranged.

Minister.

1. I am the Resurrection and the Life; he that believeth in me, though he were dead, yet he shall live, and whosoever liveth and believeth in me shall never die.

Choir and Congregation.

The Lord is my Light and my Sal - va - tion, Whom shall I fear?

The Lord is the Strength of my life, Of whom shall I be a - fraid?

Minister.

2. The angel of the Lord descended from heaven, and came and rolled back the stone from the door, and sat upon it; his countenance was like lightning and his raiment white as snow.

Choir and Congregation.

They cried unto the Lord in their troubles, And he saved them out of their dis-tresses. He brought them out of the darkness and the shadow of death, And brake their bands in sunder.

Minister.

3. And the angel said unto the woman, Fear not, for I know that ye seek Jesus who was crucified. He is not here, he is risen as he said.

Choir and Congregation.

For thou wilt not leave my soul in hell. Neither wilt thou suffer thy Holy One to see cor - ruption. Thou wilt show me the path of life. In thy presence is fullness of joy.

Minister.

4. Fear not! I am he that liveth and was dead, and lo! I am alive for evermore, Amen, and have the keys of death and hell.

Choir and Congregation.

Worthy is the Lamb that was slain, To receive power and rich - es and

wis-dom and strength, And hon - or and glo - ry and bless - ing, For - ev - er and ev - er.

Minister.

5. I am the Alpha and the Omega, the Beginning and the End, saith the Lord; who is, and who was, and who is to come, the Almighty.

Choir and Congregation.

The kingdoms of this world are be - come The kingdom of our Lord and

of his Christ. And he shall reign for - ev - er, King of kings, and Lord of lords. A - men.

Selection 179.—If a man love me. (The Holy Spirit.)

(Various Scriptures.)

Minister.

1. If a man love me he will keep my words, and my Father will love him, and we will come to him and make our abode with him.

Choir and Congregation.

Arranged.

Thou art gone up on high, Thou hast led cap - tiv - i - ty

cap - tive. Thou hast received gifts for men, That the Lord God might dwell a - mong them.

Minister.

2. Behold I send the promise of my Father upon you, but tarry ye in the city of Jerusalem until ye be endued with power from on high.

Choir and Congregation.

And suddenly there came a sound from heaven, As of a rush-ing might-y wind.

And there appeared unto them tongues as of fire, And it sat up - on each of them.

Minister.

3. The wind bloweth where it listeth and thou hearest the sound thereof, but canst not tell whence it cometh nor whither it goeth; so is every one that is born of the Spirit.

Choir and Congregation.

Thou sendest forth thy Spir - it, They are cre - a - ted.

And thou renewest the face of the earth, The glory of the Lord shall en - dure for - ev - er.

Minister.

4. The Comforter, which is the Holy Ghost, whom the Father will send in my name, he shall teach you all things, and bring all things to your remembrance whatsoever I have said unto you.

Choir and Congregation.

And the Spirit of the Lord shall rest up - on him; The Spirit of wisdom and un - der-

stand - ing; The Spirit of coun-sel and of might; The Spirit of knowledge and the fear of the Lord.

Minister.

5. I will not leave you comfortless. I will come to you; because I live ye shall live also; at that day shall ye know that I am in my Father and ye in Me and I in you.

Choir and Congregation.

He that hath an ear, let him hear What the Spir - it saith un - to the

church - es. And lo! I am with you al - ways, Even unto the end of the world. A - men.

ADDITIONAL · HYMNS.

Appropriate preludes may be found for many of these additional hymns and tunes, when desired. In selecting them, it will usually be best to have preludes and tunes agree in subjects and keys, but, throughout the book, modulations may take place between preludes and tunes of different keys, for the sake of connecting agreeing subjects. See Preface.

P. P. B.   **WHEN JESUS COMES.**   P. P. BLISS, by per.

"Unto them that look for him shall he appear the second time, without sin, unto salvation."—HEB. 9: 28.

613.

1. { Down life's dark vale we wander, Till Jesus comes :   We watch, and wait, and won-der, Till Je-sus comes. }
   { Oh, let my lamp be burning When Jesus comes :   For him my soul be yearning When Je-sus comes. }

2. { No more heart-pangs nor sadness When Jesus comes ;   All peace, and joy, and gladness When Jesus comes ; }
   { All doubts and fears will vanish When Jesus comes;   All gloom his face will ban-ish When Jesus comes. }

CHORUS.

All joy his lov'd ones bringing When Je-sus comes ; All praise thro' heav-en ring-ing When Je-sus comes;

All beau-ty bright and ver-nal When Je-sus comes; All glo-ry, grand, e-ter-nal, When Je-sus comes.

THY WILL BE DONE.

(Sing the first "Thy Will be Done" to end with.)   Dr. L. MASON.

614.

1. "Thy will be done!" { In devious way the hurrying stream of } life may run; { Yet still our grateful hearts shall say, } "Thy will be done!"

2. "Thy will be done!" { If o'er us shine a gladdening and a } pros-p'rous sun, { This pray'r will make it more divine— } "Thy will be done!"

3. "Thy will be done!" { Though shrouded o'er our } path with gloom { One comfort—one is ours :—to breathe, while we adore, } "Thy will be done!'

(329)

JOHN CALVIN.   **CALVIN'S HYMN.**   GEO. F. ROOT.

615 1. I greet thee, who my sure Re-deem-er art, My on-ly trust, and Sav-ior of my heart!

Who so much toil and woe, And pain didst un-der-go For my poor worth-less sake; We

pray thee from our hearts, All i-dle griefs and smarts, And foolish cares to take, And foolish cares to take.

2 Thou art the true and perfect gentleness,
No harshness hast thou, and no bitterness;
Make us to taste and prove, Make us adore and love
  The sweet grace found in thee;
With longing to abide Ever at thy dear side,
||: In thy sweet unity. :||

3 Poor, banished exiles, wretched sons of Eve,
Full of all sorrows, unto thee we grieve,
To thee we bring our sighs, Our groanings and our cries,
  Thy pity, Lord, we crave;
We take the sinner's place, And pray thee, of thy grace,
||: To pardon and to save. :||

WHO IS HE?   Words and Music by Rev. B. R. HANBY, by per.

616
1. Who is he in yon-der stall, At whose feet the shepherds fall?
2. Who is he in yon-der cot, Bend-ing to his toil-some lot?
3. Who is he who stands and weeps At the grave where Laz'rus sleeps?
4. Who is he in deep dis-tress, Fast-ing in the wil-der-ness?
5. Lo! at mid-night, who is he Prays in dark Geth-sem-a-ne?
6. Who is he in Calv'ry's throes Asks for bless-ings on his foes?
7. Who is he that from the grave Comes to heal, and help, and save?
8. Who is he that on yon throne Rules the world of light a-lone?

'Tis the Lord, oh, wondrous

sto-ry, 'Tis the Lord, the King of glo-ry, At his feet we hum-bly fall, Crown him, crown him Lord of all.

I NEED THEE EVERY HOUR.

Mrs. Annie S. Hawks. "Without me ye can do nothing."—John xv: 5. Rev. R. Lowry, by per.

617
1. I need thee ev-ery hour, Most gra-cious Lord; No ten-der voice like thine Can peace af-ford.
2. I need thee ev-ery hour, Stay thou near by; Tempta-tions lose their power When thou art nigh.

Refrain.
I need thee, oh, I need thee, Ev-ery hour I need thee; Oh, bless me now, my Sav-ior, I come to thee!

3 I need thee every hour
In joy or pain ;
Come quickly and abide,
Or life is vain. *Ref.*

4 I need thee every hour,
Teach me thy will;
And thy rich promises
In me fulfill. *Ref.*

5 I need thee every hour,
Most Holy One ;
Oh, make me thine indeed,
Thou blessed Son. *Ref.*

WHERE HAST THOU BUILT THINE HOUSE?

G. F. R. Matt. vii: 24. Geo. F. Root.

618
1. Where hast thou built thine house, Thy soul's e-ter-nal dwell-ing? Is it up-on the sands of sin, 'Mid

Chorus.
floods and tem-pests swell-ing? Oh, build up-on the Rock, The on-ly sure foun-da-tion; On

Christ a-lone, the Cor-ner-stone, The Rock of our sal-va-tion.

2 What wilt thou do when storms
Upon thy house are beating ?
When, from beneath, the treach'rous sands
That held thee, are retreating ? *Cho.*

3 Wait not until the floods
With final shock appalling,
Shall come, and thou canst never save
Thy ruined house from falling. *Cho.*

WONDERFUL WORDS OF LIFE.

P. P. B.

"The words that I speak unto you they are Spirit and they are Life."—JOHN VI: 63.

P. P. BLISS.

Moderato.

619
1. Sing them o - ver a - gain to me, Won-der - ful words of Life. Let me more of their
2. Christ the bless - ed One gives to all Won-der - ful words of Life. Sin - ner, list to the
3. Sweet-ly ech - o the gos - pel call, Won-der - ful words of Life. Of - fer par - don and

beau - ty see, Won-der-ful words of Life. Words of Life and beauty, Teach me faith and du - ty.
lov - ing call, Won-der-ful words of Life. All so free-ly giv - en, Woo-ing us to heav-en.
peace to all, Won-der-ful words of Life. Je - sus, on - ly Sav - ior, Sanc - ti - fy for - ev - er,

Chorus.

Beau-ti-ful words, won-der-ful words, Wonderful words of life; . . Beau-ti-ful words, won-der-ful words, Wonderful words of life.

OH, TOUCH THE HEM OF HIS GARMENT.

G. F. R.

MATT. IX: 20.

GEO. F. ROOT.

620
1. She on - ly touched the hem of his gar-ment As to his side she stole, A - mid the crowd that
2. She came in fear, all trembling be - fore him, She knew her Lord had come, She felt that from him
3. He turned with "daughter, be of good com-fort, Thy faith hath made thee whole," And peace that pass-eth

gath-ered a - round him, And straightway she was whole.
vir - tue had healed her, The might - y deed was done. Oh, touch the hem of his gar - ment, And
all un - der-stand-ing, With glad-ness filled her soul.

Chorus.

thou, too, shalt be free; His sav - ing pow'r this ver - y hour Shall give new life to thee.

WHY DO YOU WAIT?

G. F. R.

"Behold, now is the accepted time."—2d Cor. 6: 2.

Geo. F. Root.

621
1. Why do you wait, dear broth-er, Oh, why do you tar-ry so long? Your Sav-ior in mer-cy would
2. What do you hope for, broth-er, To gain by a fur-ther de-lay? There's no one to save but this

Chorus.

give you A place in his sanc-ti-fied throng. Why not? why not? why not come to him
Sav-ior, There's no oth-er way but his way.

now? Why not? why not? Why not come to him now?

3 Do you not feel, dear brother,
His Spirit now striving within?
Oh, why not accept his salvation,
And throw off this burden of sin? *Cho.*

4 Linger no longer, brother,
The harvest is passing away,
Your Savior is waiting to bless you,
There's danger and death in delay. *Cho.*

REMEMBER ME, O MIGHTY ONE!

"Lord, remember me, when thou comest into thy kingdom."—Luke 33: 42.

Music arr. by G. F. Root.

With earnest expression.

622
1. When storms around are sweeping, When lone my watch I'm keeping, 'Mid fires of e-vil fall-ing, 'Mid
2. When walking on life's o-cean, Con-trol its rag-ing mo-tion; When from its dangers shrinking, When
3. When weight of sin op-press-es, When dark despair dis-tress-es, All through the life that's mortal, And

Chorus.

tempters voic-es call-ing,
in its dread deeps sinking,   Re-mem-ber me, O Mighty One! Re-mem-ber me, O Mighty One!
when I pass death's portal,

He Leadeth Me.

Rev. Jos. H. Gilmore.   " He leadeth me by the still waters."—Psalm xxiii : 2.   Wm. B. Bradbury, by per.

623 1. He lead-eth me! oh, bless-ed thought! Oh, words with heavenly com-fort fraught; Whate'er I do, wher-e'er I be, Still 'tis God's hand that lead-eth me.

Refrain.

He lead-eth me! He lead-eth me! By his own hand he lead-eth me; His faith-ful follower I would be, For by his hand he lead-eth me.

2 Sometimes 'mid scenes of deepest gloom,
Sometimes where Eden's bowers bloom,
By waters still, o'er troubled sea—
Still 'tis his hand that leadeth me.
Ref.

3 Lord, I would clasp thy hand in mine,
Nor ever murmur or repine—
Content, whatever lot I see,
Since 'tis my God that leadeth me.
Ref.

4 And when my task on earth is done,
When, by thy grace, the victory's won,
E'en death's cold wave I will not flee,
Since God through Jordan leadeth me.
Ref.

We Are Watching, We Are Waiting.

W. O. Cushing.   G. F. Root.

624 1. We are watch-ing, we are wait-ing For the bright pro-phet-ic day, When the shad-ows, wea-ry shadows, From the world shall roll a-way.

Chorus.

We are watching, we are wait-ing For the

dawn-ing of the morn-ing; We are watching, we are wait-ing For the gold-en spires of day;

Lo, he comes, see the King draw near, Zi-on, shout, the Lord is here.

2 We are watching, we are waiting
For the star that brings the day,
When the night of sin shall vanish,
And the shadows melt away. *Cho.*

3 We are watching, we are waiting
For the beauteous King of day;
For the chiefest of ten thousand,
For the Light, the Truth, the Way.
Cho.

SAFE HOME.

Rev. J. F. NEALE.   Music arranged for this work.

625 1. Safe home, safe home in port! Rent cordage, shattered deck, Torn sails, pro-vi-sions short, And
2. The prize, the prize se-cure! The war-rior near-ly fell; Bare all he could en-dure, And
3. No more the foe can harm; No more of leaguered camp, And cry of night a-larm, And

on-ly not a wreck; But oh, the joy up-on the shore, To tell our voy-age per-ils o'er!
bare not al-ways well; But he may smile at troubles gone, Who sets the vic-tor-gar-land on;
need of read-y lamp; And yet how near-ly had he failed—How near-ly had that foe pre-vailed.

But oh, the joy up-on the shore, To tell our voy-age per-ils o'er!
But he may smile at troubles gone, Who sets the victor-garland on.
And yet how near-ly had he failed—How nearly had that foe prevailed!

4 The exile is at home!
Oh, nights and days of tears;
Oh, longings not to roam,
Oh, sins, and doubts, and fears;
‖: What matter now this bitter
fray,
The King has wiped those tears
away. :‖

MY PRAYER.

P. P. B.

"Be ye therefore perfect."—MATT. v : 8.

P. P. Bliss, by per.

626
1. More ho - li - ness give me, More strivings with-in ;   More patience in suff-'ring, More sorrow for sin ;
2. More grat - i - tude give me, More trust in the Lord ;   More pride in his glo - ry, More hope in his word ;
3. More pu - ri - ty give me, More strength to o'er-come; More freedom from earth-stains, More longings for home;

More faith in my Sav - ior, More sense of his care ;   More joy in his serv-ice, More purpose in prayer.
More tears for his sor-rows, More pain at his grief;   More meekness in tri - al, More praise for re - lief.
More fit for the kingdom, More used would I be ;   More bless-ed and ho - ly, More, Sav - ior, *like thee.*

WHITER THAN SNOW.

JAMES NICHOLSON.

"Wash me, and I shall be whiter than snow."—PS. LI : 7.

WM. G. FISCHER, by per.

627
1. Lord Je - sus, I long to be per-fect - ly whole ;   I want thee for - ev - er to live in my soul ;
2. Lord Je - sus, look down from thy throne in the skies, And help me to make a complete sac - ri - fice ;
3. Lord Je - sus, thou se - est I pa-tient - ly wait ; Come now, and within me a new heart cre-ate.

Break down ev - 'ry i - dol, cast out ev - 'ry foe ; Now wash me, and I shall be whit - er than snow.
I give up my - self, and what-ev-er I know ; Now wash me, and I shall be whit - er than snow.
To those who have sought thee, thou never saidst No ; Now wash me, and I shall be whit - er than snow.

Chorus.

Whit - er than snow, yes, whit - er than snow ; Now wash me, and I shall be whit - er than snow.

I WILL SEEK MY FATHER.

PAULINA.

Music arr. by F. W. ROOT.

628

1. When the morn is bright and fair, When sweet songsters charm the air, I will lift my voice in prayer,
2. In the sol-i-tude a-part, In the wil-der-ness or mart, Oh! my sore-ly tempt-ed heart,

I will seek my Fa-ther; Lest my feet should go a-stray From his pure and per-fect way;
I will seek my Fa-ther; In the dark-ness as the day, He shall be my Guide and Stay;

Lest I grieve him as I may, I will seek my Fa-ther.
I will lean on him al-way, I will seek my Fa-ther.

3 When the evening sun is red,
  When each blossom droops its head,
  Kneeling low beside my bed,
    I will seek my Father;
  That I slumber in his care,
  Shielded from each harmful snare,
  And for life or death prepare,
    I will seek my Father.

THE STILL SMALL VOICE.

Softly.

Words and Music. *

629

1. While the Gospel sound is heard, The still small voice is calling; With sal-va-tion's blessed word, The

m Chorus.

dews of heaven are fall-ing. Hear and heed this voice, my bro-ther; 'Tis thy Sav-ior's,

and no other, Soft-ly say-ing, Come! Soft-ly say-ing, Come!

2 He is calling at thy heart;
    Oh, list and thou wilt hear him!
  He would now his grace impart,
    To bring thy spirit near him. *Chorus.*

3 Ever, ever calling thee,
    This still small voice so tender;
  How he would thy soul set free,
    If thou wouldst but surrender. *Cho.*

22

OH, TO BE NOTHING.

" Neither is he that planteth anything, neither he that watereth."—1 Cor. III : 7.

Georgiana M. Taylor.   R. Geo. Halls. Arr. by P. P. Bliss, by per.

630
1. Oh, to be nothing, noth - ing, On - ly to lie at his feet, .. A broken and emptied ves - sel,
2. Oh, to be nothing, noth - ing, On - ly as led by his hand; . A mes-sen-ger at his gate - way,

Cho. *Oh, to be noth-ing, noth - ing, On - ly to lie at his feet, .. A broken and emptied ves - sel,*

Fine.

For the Mas-ter's use made meet. Emptied that he might fill me, As forth to his serv-ice I go;
On - ly waiting for his com-mand. On - ly an instrument read - y, His prais-es to sound at his will;

For the Mas-ter's use made meet.

D. C. Chorus.

Broken, that so un - hindered, His life thro' me might flow.
Wil-ing, should he not require me, In silence to wait on him still. ..

3 Oh, to be nothing, nothing,
Painful the humbling may be,
Yet low in the dust I'd lay me,
That the world might my Savior see.
Rather be nothing, nothing,
To him let their voices be raised,
He is the Fountain of blessing,
He only is meet to be praised. *Cho.*

NO OTHER NAME.

P. P. B.   " Neither is there salvation in any other."—Acts IV : 12.   P. P. Bliss, by per.

631
1. One of - fer of sal - va - tion To all the world make known; The on - ly sure foun-

Chorus.

da - tion Is Christ, the Cor - ner - Stone. No oth - er name is giv - en, No oth - er way is known,

'Tis Je - sus Christ, the First and Last, He saves, and he a - lone.

2 One only door of heaven
Stands open wide to-day,
One sacrifice is given,
'Tis Christ, the living way. *Cho.*

3 My only song and story
Is—Jesus died for me;
My only hope of glory,
The Cross of Calvary. *Cho.*

SWEET HOUR OF PRAYER.

Rev. W. W. Walford.   "Evening, and morning, and at noon will I pray."—Psalm lv : 17.   Wm. B. Bradbury, by per.

632 1. Sweet hour of pray'r! sweet hour of pray'r! That calls me from a world of care, And bids me at my Father's throne
D.C. And oft escaped the tempter's snare, By thy return, sweet hour of pray'r, And oft escaped the tempter's snare,

Fine.

Make all my wants and wish-es known. In sea-sons of distress and grief, My soul has oft-en found re-lief;
By thy return, sweet hour of prayer.

D.C.

2 Sweet hour of prayer! sweet hour of prayer!
Thy wings shall my petition bear
To him whose truth and faithfulness
Engage the waiting soul to bless.
And since he bids me seek his face,
Believe his word, and trust his grace,
||: I'll cast on him my every care.
And wait for thee, sweet hour of prayer! :||

3 Sweet hour of prayer! sweet hour of prayer!
May I thy consolation share,
Till, from Mount Pisgah's lofty height,
I view my home, and take my flight;
This robe of flesh I'll drop, and rise
To seize the everlasting prize;
||: And shout, while passing through the air,
Farewell, farewell, sweet hour of prayer! :||

WATCH AND PRAY.

Charlotte Elliott.   G. F. Root.

633 1. Christian, seek not yet re-pose, Cast thy dreams of ease a-way; Thou art in the midst of foes:

2. Gird thy heavenly ar-mor on, Wear it ev-er, night and day; Ambushed lies the e-vil one:

Refrain.

Watch and pray, Watch and pray.

Watch and pray, Watch and pray, Watch and pray.

Watch, Watch, oh, Watch and pray.

3 Hear the victors who o'ercame,
Still they mark each warrior's way;
All with warning voice exclaim:
Watch and pray.

4 Hear, above all, hear thy Lord,
Him thou lovest to obey;
Hide within thy heart his word:
Watch and pray.

5 Watch, as if on that alone
Hung the issue of the day;
Pray that help may be sent down:
Watch and pray.

ALONG THE RIVER OF TIME.

Geo. F. Root.

Moderato.

634

1. A - long the Riv - er of Time we glide, A - long the Riv - er, a - long the Riv - er, The
2. A - long the Riv - er of Time we glide, A - long the Riv - er, a - long the Riv - er, A
3. A - long the Riv - er of Time we glide, A - long the Riv - er, a - long the Riv - er, Our

swift - ly flow - ing, re - sist - less tide, The swift - ly flow - ing, the swift - ly flow - ing, And
thou - sand dan - gers its cur - rents hide, A thou - sand dan - gers, a thou - sand dan - gers, On
Sav - ior on - ly our bark can guide, Our Sav - ior on - ly, our Sav - ior on - ly, But

soon, ah soon, the end we'll see, Yes, soon 'twill come, and we shall be Float - ing, Float - ing,
ev - ery hand the rocks we see, Oh, dreadful thought! a wreck to be, Float - ing, Float - ing,
with him we se - cure may be, No fear, no doubt, but joy to be Float - ing, Float - ing,

Out on the sea of e - ter - ni - ty! Floating, Floating, Out on the sea of e - ter - ni - ty!

THE PATH IS DARK.

Single voice.

Chorus.

635

1. The path is dark, I can not see, Oh, where, where shall I go? Thy word is a lamp un - to my feet, and a light un - to my path.
2. I seek the way, the heav'nly way, Oh, where, where shall I go? I am the Way, the Truth, the Life, the Way, the Truth, the Life.
3. The toil of life is hard and long, Oh, where, where shall I rest? Come unto me all ye that la - bor, and I will give you rest.
4. Oh, can there be a place for me When life here shall be o'er? I go to prepare a place for you, to prepare a place for you.

SHALL WE GATHER AT THE RIVER.

"And he showed me a pure river of water of life, clear as crystal, proceeding out of the throne of God and of the Lamb."—Rev. xxii: 1.

Rev. Robert Lowry, by per.

Moderato.

636
1. Shall we gath-er at the riv-er, Where bright angel feet have trod; With its crys-tal tide for-ev-er
2. On the mar-gin of the riv-er, Wash-ing up its sil-ver spray, We will walk and worship ev-er,

Chorus.

p

Flow-ing by the throne of God? Yes, we'll gather at the riv-er, The beau-ti-ful, the beau-ti-ful riv-er—
All the hap-py, gold-en day.

Gather with the saints at the riv-er That flows by the throne of God.

3 Ere we reach the shining river,
Lay we every burden down;
Grace our spirits will deliver,
And provide a robe and crown. *Cho.*

4 At the smiling of the river,
Mirror of the Savior's face,
Saints whom death will never sever,
Lift their songs of saving grace. *Cho.*

THEY ARE GATH'RING, SLOWLY GATH'RING.

Words and Music † † †

637
1. They are gath'ring, slow-ly gath'ring In the fair and fade-less land, And the number grow-eth larg-er

Chorus.

Wait-ing for us on the strand. Then re-joice for all the dear ones Who have reached the happy shore;

One by one we'll join their number When our pil-grim-age is o'er.

2 They are going, slowly going,
One by one they disappear,
Kindred, friends, and little children,
To our stricken hearts so dear. *Cho.*

3 They with angel guards are near us,
As we walk life's toilsome way,
Bearing messages of mercy,
Watching lest our feet should stray.
Cho.

DYKES. 11s & 10s.

Bishop HEBER.   Rev. J. B. DYKES.

638
1. Ho-ly, ho-ly, ho - ly! Lord God Almight - y! Ear-ly in the morning our song shall rise to
2. Ho-ly, ho-ly, ho - ly! all the saints a-dore thee, Casting down their golden crowns around the glassy

thee;   Ho-ly, ho-ly, ho - ly! mer - ci-ful and might-y! Fa-ther all glo - rious, endless praise to thee.
sea;   Cher-u-bim and Seraphim falling down before thee, Which wert, and art, and ev - er-more shalt be.

3 Holy, holy, holy! though the darkness hide thee,
Though the eye of sinful man thy glory may not see,
Only thou art holy; there is none beside thee,
Perfect in power, in love, and purity.

4 Holy, holy, holy! Lord God Almighty!
All thy works shall praise thy name in earth, and sky, and
Holy, holy, holy! merciful and mighty!   [sea;
Father all-glorious, endless praise to thee.

IMMANUEL'S LAND.

ANNIE R. COUSIN.   C. M. WYMAN.

639
1. The sands of time are sink - ing, The dawn of heav-en breaks, The sum-mer morn I've sighed for,
2. I've wrestled on toward heav-en, 'Gainst storm and wind and tide, Now, like a wea - ry trav-'ler

The fair, sweet morn a-wakes. Dark, dark hath been the mid-night, But day-spring is at hand,
That lean - eth on his guide, A - mid the shades of even-ing, While sinks life's ling'ring sand,

And glo - ry, glo - ry dwell-eth In Im-man - uel's land.
I hail the glo - ry dawn-ing From Im-man - uel's land.

3 Deep waters crossed life's pathway,
The hedge of thorns was sharp;
Now these lie all behind me—
O! for a well tuned harp!
O! to join hallelujah
With yon triumphant band!
Who sing where glory dwelleth
In Immanuel's land.

THE HALF WAS NEVER TOLD.

P. P. B.

"Behold, the half was not told."—KINGS x : 7.

P. P. BLISS, by per.

640

1. Re-peat the sto-ry o'er and o'er, Of grace so full and free; I love to hear it more and more,
2. Of peace I on-ly knew the name, Nor found my soul its rest, Un - til the sweet-voiced angel came

Chorus.
The half . . was nev-er told,

Since grace has res-cued me. The half was nev - er told, The half was nev-er told,
To soothe my wea - ry breast. nev-er told, nev-er told.

The half . . was never to'd.

1. Of grace divine, so won-der-ful, The half was nev - er told!
2. Of peace, etc. never told.
3. Of joy, etc.
4. Of love, etc.

3 My highest place is lying low
At my Redeemer's feet;
No real *joy* in life I know,
But in his service sweet.

4 And, oh! what rapture will it be,
With all the host above,
To sing through all eternity
The wonders of his *love*.

MEET ME.

"I will come to you."—JOHN XIV : 18.   "Lo, I am with you."—MATT. XXVIII : 20.

DR. J. W. CORSON.

Music written for this work.

641

1. Je - sus, by faith be known, Thy love be-stow; Bless, from thy loft-y throne, My home be - low;
2. Come, and with ac-cents mild, Calm need-less fears; Still ev - 'ry tem-pest wild, Stay thou my tears;

Meet me and claim thine own, Oft in the clos - et lone, Oft in the clos - et lone, Thy mer - cy show.
Let me be rec - on-ciled, On - ly thy lov-ing child, On - ly thy lov - ing child, Thro' com-ing years.

3 Meet "two or three," in prayer,
As thou hast said;
Or, in thy temples fair,
Be thou the Head;
Meet me with throngs that there,
|: Anthems and praises share : |
With sainted dead.

4 Come to my bed of pain,
Night-watches keep;
Life-giving peace maintain
In anguish deep;
Quiet my fevered brain,
|: Let not my trust be vain, : |
Lull me to sleep.

5 On to the brighter land,
Gladden my way;
Savior, with gentle hand,
Be thou my stay;
Lead to the angel-band,
|: Let me with loved-ones stand, : |
In fadeless day.

KNOCKING, KNOCKING, WHO IS THERE.

Mrs. H. B. Stowe, arr.   "Behold, I stand at the door and knock."—Rev. iii: 10.   Geo. F. Root.

642
1. Knocking, knocking, who is there? Waiting, waiting, oh, how fair! 'Tis a Pilgrim, strange and kingly,
2. Knocking, knocking, still he's there, Waiting, waiting, wondrous fair; But the door is hard to o - pen,
3. Knocking, knocking—what, still there? Waiting, waiting, grand and fair; Yes, the pierced hand still knocketh,

Nev - er such was seen be - fore; Ah! my soul, for such a won - der, Wilt thou not un - do the door?
For the weeds and i - vy vine, With their dark and clinging ten - drils, Ev - er round the hinges twine.
And be-neath the crowned hair Beam the pa - tient eyes so ten - der, Of thy Sav - ior, wait-ing there.

LOOK AND LIVE.

P. P. B.   "Look unto me and be ye saved, all the ends of the earth."   P. P. Bliss.

643
1. Look to Je-sus, wea-ry one, Look and live, look and live; Look at what the Lord has done, Look to him and live.
2. Tho' unworthy, vile, unclean, Look and live, look and live; Look a - way from self and sin, Look to him and live.
3. Tho' you've wander'd far away, Look and live, look and live; Harden not your heart to-day, Look to him and live.

See him lift - ed on the tree, Look and live, look and live; Hear him say, "Look unto me," Look to him and live.
Long by Satan's pow'r enslaved, Look and live, look and live; Look to me, ye shall be saved, Look to him and live.
'Tis thy Father calls thee home, Look and live, look and live; Who-so-ev - er will may come, Look to him and live.

Chorus.

Look to Je-sus, weary one, Look and live, look and live; Look at what the Lord has done, Look to him and live.

In the Silent Midnight Watches.

Rev. A. C. Coxe, D. D.

Geo. F. Root.

644
1. In the si-lent midnight watches, List—thy bosom's door! How it knocketh, knocketh, knocketh,
2. Death comes down with reckless footsteps To the hall and hut; Think you death will tar-ry knocking,

Knock-eth ev-er-more! Say not 'tis thy puls-es beat-ing, 'Tis thy heart of sin;
When the door is shut? Je-sus wait-eth, wait-eth, wait-eth, But the door is fast;

'Tis thy Sav-ior knocks and cri-eth, "Rise, and let me in!"
Grieved, a-way thy Sav-ior go-eth, Death breaks in at last.

3 Then 'tis time to stand entreating
Christ to let thee in;
At the gate of heaven beating,
Wailing for thy sin.
Nay, alas! thou guilty creature!
Hast thou, then, forgot?
Jesus waited long to know thee,
Now he knows thee not!

Almost Persuaded.

P. P. B.

"Almost thou persuadest me to be a Christian."—ACTS XXVI: 28.

P. P. Bliss, by per.

645
1. "Al-most per-suad-ed" now to be-lieve; "Al-most per-suad-ed" Christ to re-ceive.
2. "Al-most per-suad-ed," come, come to-day; "Al-most per-suad-ed" turn not a-way.
3. "Al-most per-suad-ed," har-vest is past; "Al-most per-suad-ed," doom comes at last!

Seems now some soul to say, "Go, spir-it, go thy way, Some more con-ven-ient day On thee I'll call."
Je-sus invites you here, An-gels are ling'ring near, Prayers rise from hearts so dear, O wand'rer, come.
"Almost" can not a-vail; "Almost" is sure to fail! Sad, sad that bit-ter wail—"Al-most, but lost!"

BEHOLD THE BRIDEGROOM COMETH.

"And five of them were wise."

Words and Music by Geo. F. Root.

Duet, or Semi-Chorus.

646
1. Our lamps are trimm'd and burning, Our robes are white and clean, We've tarried for the Bridegroom, Oh,
2. Go forth, go forth to meet him, The way is o-pen now, All light-ed with the glo-ry That

may we en-ter in? We know we've nothing worthy That we can call our own—The light, the oil, the
streameth from his brow. Ac-cept the in-vi-ta-tion Be-yond deserv-ing, kind; Make no de-lay, but

Chorus.

robes we wear, Are all from him a-lone. Be-hold, the Bridegroom com-eth! And all may en-ter in,
take your lamps And joy e-ter-nal, find.

Whose lamps are trimm'd and burning, Whose robes are white and clean.

3 We see the marriage splendor
Within the open door;
We know that those who enter
Are blest for evermore.
We see he is more lovely
Than all the sons of men,
But still we know the door once shut,
Will never ope again. *Cho.*

LORD, THY WORD ABIDETH.

G. F. R.

Moderato.

647
1. Lord, thy word a-bid-eth, And our footsteps guideth! Who its truth be-liev-eth, Light and joy re-ceiv-eth.
2. When our foes are near us, Then thy word doth cheer us, Word of con-so-la-tion, Message of sal-va-tion
3. When the storms are o'er us, And dark clouds be-fore us, Then its light di-rect-eth, And our way pro-tect-eth.
4. Who can tell the pleasure, Who re-count the treasure By thy word im-part-ed To the sim-ple hearted.

ETERNITY!

Ellen H. Gates.   "Remember how short my time is."—Ps. lxxxix: 47.   P. P. Bliss, by per.

648

1. Oh, the clanging bells of Time! Night and day they nev-er cease; We are wearied with their chime,
2. Oh, the clanging bells of Time! How their changes rise and fall, But in un-der-tone sublime,
3. Oh, the clanging bells of Time! To their voi-ces, loud and low, In a long, un-rest-ing line

For they do not bring us peace; And we hush our breath to hear, And we strain our eyes to see
Sounding clear-ly through them all, Is a voice that must be heard, As our mo-ments on-ward flee,
We are march-ing to and fro; And we yearn for sight or sound, Of the life that is to be,

Rit.   Rall.

If thy shores are drawing near,— E-ter-ni-ty! E-ter-ni-ty!
And it speaketh aye one word,— E-ter-ni-ty! E-ter-ni-ty!
For thy breath doth wrap us round,— E-ter-ni-ty! E-ter-ni-ty!

4 Oh, the clanging bells of Time !
   Soon their notes will all be dumb,
And in joy and peace sublime,
   We shall feel the silence come ;
And our souls their thirst will s'ake,
   And our eyes the King will see,
When thy glorious morn shall break,—
   Eternity! Eternity!

COME TO THE SAVIOR.

G. F. R.   "Come unto me."   Geo. F. Root.

649

1. Come to the Savior, make no delay, Here in his word he's shown us the way; Here in our midst he's standing to-day,

Chorus.

Ten-der-ly say-ing, "Come." Joyful, joy-ful will the meet-ing be, When from sin our hearts are pure and free,

And we shall gath-er, Sav-ior, with thee, In our e-ter-nal home.

2 "Suffer the children !" oh, hear his voice ;
  Let every heart leap forth and rejoice.
  And let us freely make him our choice ;
   Do not delay, but come. Cho.

3 Think once again, he's with us to-day;
  Heed now his blest commands and obey;
  Hear now his accents tenderly say,
   "Will you, my children, Come ?" Cho.

ADDITIONAL HYMNS.

ONWARD, CHRISTIAN SOLDIERS.

S. BARING GOULD. "The Lord will do wonders among you." Arranged by G. F. R.

650
1. On - ward, Chris-tian sol - diers, Marching as to war, With the Cross of
2. Crowns and thrones may per - ish, Kingdoms rise and wane, But the Church of
3. On - ward, then, ye faith - ful, Join our hap-py throng, Blend with ours your

1. On - ward, Chris-tian sol - diers, Marching, marching as to war, With the Cross, the Cross of
2. Crowns and thrones may fall and per - ish, Kingdoms rise and wane, But the Church, the Church of
3. On - ward, then, ye faith - ful, Join our hap-py, hap - py throng, Blend with ours, with ours your

Je - sus Go - ing on be - fore; Christ, the roy - al Mas - ter, Leads a - gainst the foe;
Je - sus Con-stant will re - main; Gates of hell can nev - er 'Gainst that Church prevail;
voic - es In the tri - umph song; Glo - ry, laud and hon - or, Un - to Christ the King;

Je - sus, Go - ing, go - ing on be - fore.
Je - sus, Constant, con-stant will re - main.
voic-es, In the tri - umph, tri - umph song.

For-ward in - to bat - tle, See, his ban-ners go. On - ward, Christian sol - diers,
We have Christ's own prom - ise, And that can - not fail. On - ward, etc.
This, thro' count-less a - ges, Men and an-gels sing. On - ward, etc.

On - ward, Christian sol-diers, Marching

March-ing as to war, With the Cross of Je - sus Go - ing on be - fore.

march-ing as to war, With the Cross, the Cross of Je - sus, Go-ing, go - ing on be - fore.

NOT HERE, FOR HE IS RISEN.

Mrs. M. B. C. SLADE. G. F. ROOT.

651
1. Ver - y ear - ly in the morn, Came the Ma-rys weeping, Bringing spices rare and sweet, Has-ten-ing with

Chorus.

lov - ing feet, Where their Lord was sleep - ing. Not here, not here, the Loved One dear! Not here, for he is

ris - en. Broke the seal and passed a-way From the si - lent pris - on.

2 Very early in the morn,
  Joyful tidings giving,
  Two, in shining garments, said,
  "Seek him not among the dead,
  But among the living. *Cho.*

3 Very early in the morn,
  Sad, our lost ones seeking;
  Love's sweet incense when we bring,
  May the shining angels sing,
  To our spirits speaking. *Cho.*

THERE IS NO NIGHT THERE.

G. F. R.   *"And the Lamb is the light thereof."*   G. F. ROOT.

652
1. Oh, the hills are sweet and the wa - ters clear, And the meadows green thro' the whole glad year,
2. On the shin-ing waves of the crys-tal sea, Ev - er rests the light in its pur - i - ty,
3. Yes, a - bove all heaven, on his glo-rious throne, Does the Lamb of God send his radiance down,
4. When the night of sin, and its e - vil fires, Fill the poor soul here with its dread de - sires,

And a - bove them all is a radiance rare, From the Sun of heav'n; there is no night there.
And the streets and spires of the cit - y fair In its splen-dor glow! there is no night there.
And the an - gel bands in the gold-en air, Breathe e - ter - nal joy; there is no night there.
Let us strug - gle on thro' the lu - rid glare, To our home a - bove; there is no night there.

Refrain.

There is no night there, There is no night there, For the Lamb is the light, And there's no night there

ANNIVERSARY SONG.

Mrs. M. B. C. SLADE.

653 1. { O Lord, thy servants, gath-ered here, U-nit-ed voic-es raise, }
{ To fill the hour that ends the year, With songs of prayer and praise. }
We'll work while day shall last,

We'll work till set of sun; .. We'll work till harvest's past and gone, When thou wilt say, "Well done!"

2 From vineyards of our Lord and King,
From fair white harvest fields,
The fruits and garnered sheaves we bring,
That our blessed labor yields. *Cho.*

3 We thank thee that the dews divine
Of grace, so full and free,
Have fallen on each tender vine
We're training up to thee. *Cho.*

4 So now we seek thy blessing here,
Our covenant renew,
And joyful start another year,
Our Master's will to do. *Cho.*

RING THE BELLS OF HEAVEN.

"There is joy in the presence of the angels of God over one sinner that repenteth."—LUKE XV: 10.

Rev. W. O. CUSHING.   GEO. F. ROOT.

654 1. { Ring the bells of heav-en! there is joy to-day, For a soul re-turn-ing from the wild; }
{ See! the Fa-ther meets him out up-on the way, Wel-com-ing his wea-ry, wand'ring child. }

Chorus.

Glo-ry! glo-ry! how the an-gels sing; Glo-ry! glo-ry! how the loud harps ring; 'Tis the ransomed ar-my,

like a mighty sea, Pealing forth the anthem of the free.

2 Ring the bells of heaven! there is joy to-day,
For the wanderer now is reconciled;
Yes, a soul is rescued from his sinful way,
And is born anew a ransomed child. *Cho.*

3 Ring the bells of heaven! spread the feast to-day,
Angels, swell the glad triumphant strain;
Tell the joyful tidings! bear it far away!
For a precious soul is born again. *Cho.*

JEWELS.

"And they shall be mine, saith the Lord of hosts, in that day when I make up my jewels."—MALACHI III: 17.

Rev. W. O. CUSHING.   GEO. F. ROOT.

655 1. When he com-eth, when he com-eth To make up his jew-els, All his jew-els, precious

Chorus.

jew-els, His loved and his own. Like the stars of the morn-ing His bright crown a-dorn-ing,

They shall shine in their beau-ty, Bright gems for his crown.

2 He will gather, he will gather
The gems for his kingdom;
All the pure ones, all the bright ones,
His loved and his own. *Cho.*

3 All his children, all his children,
Who love their Redeemer,
Are the jewels, precious jewels,
His loved and his own. *Cho.*

THE TRUMPET WILL SOUND IN THE MORNING.

Characteristic of the Freedmen's Spirituals.   Words and Music by GEO. F. ROOT.

656 1. Oh, we must be read-y by night, For the trum-pet will sound in the morning; We must work while 'tis
2. Be sure that your ar-mor is strong, For the trum-pet will sound in the morning; Nev-er mind tho' the
3. Yes, on till we draw the last breath, For the trum-pet will sound in the morning; E-ven sing at the

Chorus.

call-ed the light, For the trumpet will sound in the morn-ing. Oh, the glo-ry shines up there, Ev-ery
bat-tle be long, For the trumpet will sound in the morn-ing.
riv-er of death, For the trumpet will sound in the morn-ing.

hill and vale a-dorning; Then press right on with all your might, For the trumpet will sound in the morning.

WHAT A FRIEND WE HAVE IN JESUS.

"There is a Friend that sticketh closer than a brother."—PROV. XVIII: 24.

Rev. H. BONAR.
CHARLES C. CONVERSE, by per.

657

1. What a Friend we have in Je - sus, All our sins and griefs to bear; What a priv - i - lege to car - ry
2. Have we tri - als and tempt-a-tions? Is there trouble an - y-where? We should never be dis-cour-aged,

Ev - ery thing to God in prayer. Oh, what peace we oft - en for - feit, Oh, what needless pain we bear—
Take it to the Lord in prayer. Can we find a Friend so faithful, Who will all our sor-rows share?

All be-cause we do not car - ry Ev - ery thing to God in prayer.
Je - sus knows our ev - ery weakness, Take it to the Lord in prayer.

3 Are we weak and heavy laden,
Cumbered with a load of care?
Precious Savior, still our refuge,—
Take it to the Lord in prayer.
Do thy friends despise, forsake thee?
Take it to the Lord in prayer;
In his arms he'll take and shield thee,
Thou wilt find a solace there.

WATCH! SENTINEL, WATCH!

G. F. R.   "I have set watchmen upon thy walls, O Zion."   *

Earnestly.

658

1. Sen - ti - nel, be thou watch-ful, And guard the for-tress well! Guard it from foes that
2. Sen - ti - nel, art thou fear - ful, Up - on the wall a - lone? When from the shad - ows,
3. Sen - ti - nel, art thou wea - ry? The strug - gle, is it long? Cheer up, for soon shall

lurk a - round, And from th'as-saults of hell. Call on thy might - y Mas - ter, His
dark and deep, Sin's fier - y darts are thrown. Put on thy heaven-ly ar - mor, Thy
come to thee The vic - tor's tri - umph song. Soon shall thy Cap - tain call thee To

heaven-ly prom-ise claim, "Ye shall be more than con-quer-ors Who bat-tle in my name."
shield of faith and prayer, Call to thy Sav-ior ev-er near, To hold and keep thee there.
lay thine ar-mor down, Soon shall the glad ex-change be made, Earth's cross for heav-en's crown.

Refrain.

Watch! sen-ti-nel, watch! Pray! sen-ti-nel, pray! Fight! sen-ti-nel, fight! In thy great Redeemer's name.

THE BEACON LIGHT.

E. E. REXFORD.   G. F. R.

659

1. { We are sail-ing o'er an o-cean, To a far and foreign shore, And the waves are dashing round us, And we
     But we look above the billows, In the darkness of the night, And we see the steady gleaming (*Omit.*

2. { Tho' the skies are dark a-bove us, And the waves are dashing high, Let us look toward the beacon, We shall
     'Tis the light of God's great mercy, And he holds it up in view, As a guide-star to his children, (*Omit.*

Chorus.

hear the breakers roar; Of our changeless beacon light. Oh, the light is flashing brightly From a calm and stormless
reach it by and by;   Ev-er sure, and ev-er true.

shore, Where we hope to cast our anchor, When our voy-ag-ing is o'er.

3 He will keep it ever burning,
   From the light-house of his love,
And it always shines the brightest
   When the skies are dark above;
If we keep our eyes upon it,
   And we steer our course aright,
We shall reach the harbor safely,
   By the blessed beacon light. *Cho.*

23

SWEET BY-AND-BY.

"The ransomed of the Lord shall return and come to Zion with songs and everlasting joy upon their heads."—ISA. xxxv : 10.

S. FILLMORE BENNETT.　　　　　　　　　　　　　　　　　　　　JOS. P. WEBSTER, by per.

660 1. There's a land that is fair-er than day, And by faith we can see it a-far; For the

Fa-ther waits o-ver the way, To pre-pare us a dwelling place there. In the sweet by-and-

Chorus.

In the sweet

by, We shall meet on that beau-ti-ful shore, In the sweet by-and-

by-and-by, by-and-by, by-and-by,

by, We shall meet on that beau-ti-ful shore.

by-and-by,

2 We shall sing on that beautiful shore
The melodious songs of the blest,
And our spirits shall sorrow no more,
Not a sigh for the blessing of rest.
　　　　　　　　　　Chorus.

3 To our bountiful Father above,
We will offer our tribute of praise,
For the glorious gift of his love,
And the blessings that hallow our
　　　　　　　　　　[days. *Chorus.*

WHERE ARE THE REAPERS?

E. E. REXFORD.　　"I will say to the reapers, Gather the wheat into my barn."—MATT. xiii : 30.　　GEO. F. ROOT.

661 1. Oh, where are the reap-ers that gar-ner in The sheaves of the good from the fields of sin?
2. Go out in the by-ways and search them all; The wheat may be there, tho' the weeds are tall;

With sick-les of truth must the work be done, And no one may rest till the "harv-est home."
Then search in the high-way, and pass none by But gath-er from all for the home on high.

Chorus.

Where are the reapers! Oh! who will come And share in the glory of the "harvest home?" Oh! who will help us to

gar - ner   in   The sheaves of good from the fields of sin?

3 The fields are rip'ning, and far and wide
  The world now is waiting the harvest tide:
  But reapers are few, and the work is great,
  And much will be lost should the harvest wait.
                                    Chorus.

4 So come with your sickles, ye sons of men,
  And gather together the golden grain:
  Toil on till the Lord of the harvest come,
  Then share ye his joy in the "harvest home."
                                    Chorus.

"WHOSOEVER WILL."

"Whosoever will, let him take the water of life freely."—REV. XXII : 17.

Words and Music by P. P. BLISS, by per.

Joyfully.

662 1. "Whoso-ev - er hear-eth," shout, shout the sound! Send the bless-ed   tid - ings   all   the world a - round;

Spread the joy - ful news wherev - er man is found: "Whoso-ev - er   will, may come." "Who-so-ev - er   will,

Chorus.

who-so - ev - er   will." Send the proc-la-ma-tion o - ver vale   and hill;   'Tis   a   lov-ing Fa - ther

calls the wand'rer home: "Whoso-ev - er   will, may come."

2 Whosoever cometh, heed not delay,
  Now the door is open, enter while you may;
  Jesus is the true, the only Living Way:
    "Whosoever will, may come."

3 "Whosoever will," the promise secure;
  "Whosoever will," forever must endure;
  "Whosoever will," 'tis life for evermore:
    "Whosoever will, may come."

FLEE, AS A BIRD, TO YOUR MOUNTAIN.

Mrs. Dana.   Arr. by Geo. F. Root, by permission of Messrs. O. Ditson & Co.

663 1. Flee, as a bird, to your mount - ain, Thou, who art weary of sin; . . Go to the clear flowing fount - ain,
2. He will pro-tect thee for-ev - er, Wipe every fall - ing tear; . . He will forsake thee, oh, nev - er,

Where you may wash and be clean ; Fly, for th'avenger is near thee, Call, and the Savior will hear thee,
Shel - tered so ten-der-ly there ; Haste then, the hours are fly - ing, Spend not the moments in sigh - ing,

Un poco rit.

He on his bos-om will bear . . thee, Thou who art weary of sin, Oh, thou who art wea-ry of sin.
Cease from your sorrow and cry - ing, The Savior will wipe every tear, The Sav-ior will wipe ev-ery tear.

THOS. MOORE.   COME, YE DISCONSOLATE.   S. WEBBE.

664 1. Come, ye dis - con - so - late, where'er ye lan-guish, Come to the mer - cy-seat, fer - vent-ly kneel ;
2. Joy of the des - o - late, light of the stray-ing, Hope of the pen - i - tent, fade - less and pure ;

Here bring your wounded hearts, here tell your an-guish ; Earth has no sor-row that heav'n can not heal.
Here speaks the Com - fort - er, ten - der - ly say - ing, Earth has no sor-row that heav'n can not cure.

WHAT SHALL THE HARVEST BE.

"Whatsoever a man soweth that shall he also reap."—GAL. VI: 7.   P. P. BLISS, by per.

Andantino.

665 1. Sowing the seed by the dawnlight fair, Sowing the seed in the noontide glare, Sowing the seed in the fading light,
2. Sowing the seed by the wayside high, Sowing the seed on the rocks to die, Sowing the seed where the thorns will spoil,

Sow-ing the seed in the solemn night, Oh, what shall the harvest be? Oh, what shall the harvest be?
Sow-ing the seed in the fer-tile soil, Oh, what shall the harvest be? Oh, what shall the harvest be?

Sown . . . in the dark - ness or sown . . . in the light, . . Sown . . in our

Chorus.

Sown in the darkness or sown in the light, Sown in the darkness or sown in the light, Sown in our weakness or

weak - ness or sown . . . in our might, . . . Gath - ered in time . . or e-

sown in our might, Sown in our weakness or sown in our might, Gathered in time or e-ter-ni-ty,

ter - ni - ty, . . Sure, . . . ah sure, . . will the har - vest be.

Gathered in time or e-ter-ni-ty, Sure, yes, sure will the har-vest be, will the har-vest, the har-vest be.

3 Sowing the seed of a lingering pain,
Sowing the seed of a maddened brain,
Sowing the seed of a tarnished name,
Sowing the seed of eternal shame—
‖: Ah, sure will the harvest be! :‖ *Cho.*

4 Sowing the seed with an aching heart,
Sowing the seed while the tear-drops start,
Sowing in hope till the reapers come,
Gladly to gather the harvest home.
‖: Oh, what shall the harvest be? :‖ *Cho.*

HE IS THE LORD.

"I, even I, am the Lord, and beside me there is no Savior."—ISA. 43: 11,

G. F. R.   G. F. ROOT.

666 1. He is the Lord our Sav - ior, There is no God be - side; The Fa - ther in Him, He the Son On

whom our hopes a - bide: The Spir-it thence pro-ceed-eth from Fa-ther and from Son, For - ev - er blessed

Trin-i-ty, All glorious Three in One.

2 'T was He who came to save us,
From heaven's eternal throne;
'Twas He, our God, who on the earth
Was "with us" as the Son.
He took our human nature,—
Was tempted like as we,
Till, from the grave, with glory crown'd,
He rose in majesty.

3 And now, this wondrous Savior
Is God of earth and heaven;
In him the Father dwelleth still,
To him all power is given;
His Spirit still descendeth
To witness with our own:—
That we may see, in heaven's own
That He is God alone. [light,

DOXOLOGIES.

(For Doxology in Long Meter, see p. 5.)

C. M.

To Father, Son, and Holy Ghost—
One God, whom we adore,
Be glory as it was, is now,
And shall be evermore.

S. M.

THE Father, and the Son,
And Spirit we adore;
We praise, we bless, we worship thee,
One God for evermore.

8s & 7s.

PRAISES evermore be given,
By the countless ransomed host,
To the mighty God of heaven,—
Father, Son, and Holy Ghost.

For 8s & 7s Double, add the following:

Praise the fountain of salvation,
Him by whom our spirits live;
Undivided adoration
To the one Jehovah give.

7s. 6 lines.

PRAISE the name of God most High;
Praise Him, all below the sky;
Praise Him, all ye heavenly host;
Father, Son, and Holy Ghost!
As through countless ages past,
Evermore his praise shall last.

8s, 7s & 4s.

GREAT Jehovah, we adore thee,
Father, Son, and Spirit, One;
Joined in wisdom, power, and glory
On thine everlasting throne:
Endless praises
To Jehovah, Three in One!

H. M.

O GOD! the Father, Son,
And Spirit,—thee we bless;
To thee, Most High, alone
Our worship we address.

Lord, thou hast been
All worlds before,
And evermore
Shalt be. Amen!

7s & 6s.

To thee be praise forever,
Thou glorious King of kings;
Thy wondrous love and favor
Each ransomed spirit sings.
We'll celebrate thy glory
With all thy saints above,
And shout the joyful story
Of thy redeeming love.

6s & 4s.

To GOD—the Father, Son,
And Spirit—Three in One,
All praise be given!
Crown him in every song;
To him your hearts belong;
Let all his praise prolong—
On earth—in heaven.

ADDITIONAL SELECTIONS.

Selection 180.—Trust we in Jehovah's keeping.

(Downs, Key of E Flat, p 187, Hy. 390; Goldwark, p. 207, Hymns 433 and 441; Hillsdale, p. 41, Hy. 76, may follow this Prelude. Other combinations may be made beside those here indicated.)

Trio. Men's voices.   G. F. R.

Trust we in Je - ho - vah's keep-ing, Hope we in his might-y power, God a - bove will ne'er for-

Trust we in Je - ho - vah's keep-ing, Hope we in his might-y power, God a - bove will ne'er for-

sake us, He our Rock, our Strength, our Tower.   **Soprano Solo.** Yes, trust we Je - ho - vah, yes, hope in hi- power,

sake us, He our Rock, our Strength, our Tower.

Soprano Solo.

He is our Rock, our Strength, our Tower.   Yes, trust we Je - ho - vah's keep-ing, Yes,

Trio. Men's voices.

Trust we in Je - ho - vah's keeping, Hope we

hope in his might-y power,   He our Rock, our Strength, our Tower.

in his might-y power, God a - bove will ne'er for - sake us, He our Rock, our Strength, our Tower.

(363)

Selection 181.—Blessed be the name of the Lord forever.

(Silver St., p. 49—Hymns 94, 95 and 98; Wilmot, p. 55, and Hymns on that page; Lenox, p. 57, and Hymns; Addison, p. 64, and Hymns.)

Andante. Solo. Baritone.   G. F. R.

Bless-ed be the name of the Lord for-ev-er. Bless-ed be the name of the Lord . . .

Choir.

The name of the

Bless-ed be the name of the Lord for-ev-er, for wis-dom and might are his. . . .

Choir. *p*

Lord.   are his. Oh!

Fine.

Bless-ed be the name of the Lord for-ev-er, for wis-dom and might are his, are his.

Solo.

He revealeth the deep and secret things, He knoweth what is in the darkness, and the light, and the light, and the

Selection 182.—Rest, spirit, rest.

(Hymns on pp. 254, 255, and 257, singing the tunes in the Key of A flat.)

Arr. from ROOKE.

Solo. Soprano.

Rest, spirit, rest; Thou art fled To realms of endless day; In heav-en blest, By warbling choirs of

ser-aphs led; In heaven blest, Rest, spirit, rest. Rest, rest, rest, spirit, rest, In heaven

Rest, rest, rest, spirit, rest, In heaven

Rest, rest, rest,

b'est, Rest, rest, spirit, rest. Soar, spirit, soar, . . . spir-it, soar, In heaven blest, . . . spir-it,

Solo. Soprano.

Soprano & Alto.

blest, Rest, rest, spirit, rest. Soar, spirit, soar, soar, spirit, soar, In heaven blest,

Tenor & Bass.

rest.

rest, rest, rest, spir-it, rest, In heav-en blest, rest, rest, spir-it, rest.

soar, spir-it, soar, spir-it, soar; Rest, sp'r-it, rest, rest, rest, blest spir-it, rest.

Selection 183.—Out of the depths.

(Naomi, p. 141, Hymns 276 and 279; Come, ye Disconsolate, p. 356; Christmas, p. 129, Hymn 253.)

Out . . of the depths have I cried un-to thee, have I cried un - to thee, un-to

thee, O Lord. . Lord, hear my voice, O hear my voice. Let thine ears be at-

ten-tive to the voice, to the voice of my sup - pli - ca - tions. If thou, Lord, shouldst

mark in-i - - - qui-ties, O Lord, who shall stand? O Lord, who shall stand?

But there is for-give-ness with thee, for-give-ness, for-give-ness, that thou may-est be fear - - ed.

Selection 184.—Oh, give thanks unto the Lord.

(Rockingham, p. 39, and hymns on that page; Chesterfield, p. 43, Hy. 82; St. Thomas, p. 51, Hy. 99; also pages 61, 11 and 13.)

From ROSSINI.

Oh, give thanks un-to the Lord; Make known his deeds a - mong the

peo - ple. Glo - ry ye in his ho - ly name; Give thanks, give thanks for-

ev - er-more. Sing un-to him, sing psalms un-to him; Talk ye of all his

won-drous works. Glo - ry ye in his ho - ly name, Re - joice in

him for ev - er-more, Rejoice for ev - er-more, Rejoice for ev - er-more.

Selection 185.—Bow down thine ear, O Lord.

(Rosehill, p. 31; Hendon, p. 26; Temple, p. 27.)

Arr. from ROSSINI.

Solo. (Bass or Baritone.)

1. Bow down thine ear, O Lord, O Lord, and hear thou me, ... For

dai - ly I will call, .. O Lord, will call on thee.

Choir.

For dai - ly I will call, O Lord, will call on thee, O Lord, on thee.

For dai - ly I will call, O Lord, will call on thee, O Lord, on thee.

Solo. (Alto or Soprano.)

2. Be gra - cious, Lord, to me, Be gra - cious, Lord, to me, ... For

dai - ly I will call, . . O Lord, will call on thee.

Choir.

For dai - ly I will call, O Lord, will call on thee, O Lord, on

For dai - ly I will call, O Lord, will call on thee, O Lord, on

Key of F major.

thee, And I will thank thee, Lord, will thank thee, O my God, And I will praise thy name, O

thee, And I will thank thee, Lord, will thank thee, O my God, And I will praise thy name, O

Lord, for ev - er - more. Thy name, O Lord, Thy name, O Lord.

will praise thy name, O Lord, will praise thy name, O Lord,

Lord, for ev - er - more. Thy name, O Lord, Thy name, O Lord.

Selection 186.—But the Lord is mindful of his own.

(Pleyel's Hymn, p. 203, Hy. 431; Stephens, p. 185, Hy. 385, and others.)

MENDELSSOHN.

Solo.

But the Lord is mindful of his own, he re - mem-bers his chil - dren; But the Lord is

Cres.   *mf*   *Dim.*   *p* *Cres.* *Dim.*

mind.ul of his own, the Lord re - mem-bers his chil - dren, re - mem - - bers his

Somber.   *f*

chil - dren. Bow down be-fore him, ye might - y, for the Lord is near us;

m   *f* *p Cres.* *Dim.* *p*

Bow down be-fore him, ye might - y, for the Lord is near .. us. But the

Cres.   *Cres.* *f*   *p Cres.* *Dim.*

Lord is mindful of his own, he re - mem-bers his chil - dren, re - mem - bers his chil - dren.

Selection 187.—Come unto him.

(Ellesdie, p. 145, Hymn 295; Autumn, p. 157, Hymn 309; Missionary Chant, p. 169, Hymns 341 and 343.)

Andante.   HANDEL.

Come un - to him, all ye that la - bor; come un - to him, ye that are heav-y la - den, and

First time.   Second time.

he will give you rest.   he will give you rest.   Take his yoke upon you and

learn of him, for he is meek and low-ly of heart, and ye shall find rest, and ye shall find rest un-

to your souls.   Take his yoke up-on you and learn of him, for he is meek and

low - ly of heart, and ye shall find rest, and ye shall find rest un-to your souls.

Selection 188.—If with all your hearts.

(Lanesboro', p. 17, Hy. 24 ; Boylston, p. 145, Hy. 285 ; Retreat, p. 171, Hy. 315)   MENDELSSOHN.

"If with all your hearts ye tru-ly seek me, ye shall ev-er sure-ly find me." Thus saith our God. "If with all your hearts ye tru-ly seek me, ye shall ev-er sure-ly find me." Thus saith our God, thus saith our God. Oh, that I knew where I might find him, that I might even come before his presence;

Oh, that I knew where I might find him, that I might ev-en come be-fore his pre-ence,

come be-fore his pres-ence: Oh, that I knew where I might find

him. "If with all your hearts ye tru-ly seek me, ye shall ev-er sure-ly

find me." Thus saith our God. "Ye shall ev-er sure-ly find me." Thus saith our God.

24

Selection 189.—I know that my Redeemer liveth.

(Ariel, p. 97, Hy. 184 ; Olivet, p. 163, Hy. 319 ; Goldwark, p. 207, Hy. 439 and 440.)

HANDEL.

I know that my Re - deem - er liv - eth, and that he shall stand ... at the

lat - ter day ... up-on the earth.

I know that my Re-deem - er liv - eth, and that he shall stand ... at the

lat - ter day up-on the earth, ... up-on the earth.

And tho' worms de-stroy this bod-y,   Yet in my

flesh shall I see God, yet in my flesh shall I see God. I know that my Re-deem-er liveth,

and tho' worms de - stroy this bod-y, yet in my flesh shall I see God, For now is Christ ris-en

from the dead, the first fruits of them that sleep, ...

. . . of them that sleep, the first . . fruits of them that sleep.

For now is Christ ris-en, for now is Christ ris-en from the dead, the first fruits of them that sleep.

Adagio.

Selection 190.—Oh, rest in the Lord.

(Boylston, p. 145, Hy. 290. Also if "Oh, where shall rest be found" were sung first, "Oh, rest in the Lord" would follow appropriately.

MENDELSSOHN.

Solo. Andantino.

Oh, rest in the Lord; wait pa-tient-ly for him, and he shall give thee thy heart's de-

sires; Oh, rest in the Lord, wait pa-tient-ly for him, and he shall give thee thy heart's de-

sires, and he shall give thee thy heart's de-sires. Commit thy way un-to him, and trust in

him; commit thy way un-to him, and trust in him, and fret not thy-self because of e-vil do - ers. Oh, rest in the Lord, wait patiently for him, wait patiently for him; Oh, rest in the

Lord, wait patiently for him, and he shall give thee thy heart's de - sires, and he shall

give thee thy heart's de - sires, and he shall give thee thy heart's de-sires. Oh, rest in the

Lord, Oh, rest in the Lord, and wait, ... wait pa - tient - ly for him.

Selection 191.—All thy works shall praise thee, O Lord.

[St. Ann's, p. 45, Hys. 85, 88 and 89; Hillsdale, p. 33, and hymns, by transposing tune to Key of D.]

Choir. Allegro con Spirito.   FREDERIC W. ROOT.

All thy works shall praise thee, O Lord, and thy saints shall bless thee; All thy works shall praise thee, O Lord,

All thy works shall praise thee, O Lord, and thy saints shall bless thee; All thy works shall praise thee, O Lord,

ff (Great Org.)

and thy saints shall bless thee.

Alto Solo.

and thy saints shall bless thee. They shall speak of the glo-ry of thy kingdom, and talk . . of thy power.

(Sw., with reeds.)

Solo.   **Cres.**   *f*   *p* **Quartet.**

They shall speak of the glo-ry of thy kingdom, They shall speak of the glo-ry of thy kingdom, and and talk, . . .

p

They shall speak of the glo-ry of thy kingdom, and

and talk . . .

Cres.

(Full Sw.)   *f*   *p*

Dim.　　　　　　　　　ff Full Choir.

talk of thy power.　　　All thy works shall praise thee, O Lord, and thy saints shall bless thee;

talk of thy power.　　　All thy works shall praise thee, O Lord, and thy saints shall bless thee;

Dim.　　　ff

(Great Org.)

All thy works shall praise thee, O Lord, and thy saints shall bless thee.

All thy works shall praise thee, O Lord, and thy saints shall bless thee.

Solo.

To make known to the sons of men his mighty acts.

(Sw.)

Soprano Solo.

Thy kingdom is an ev - er - last - ing king-dom,

and the glo-rious maj-es - ty of his kingdom.

Quartet.   Cres.   Dim.   Cres.

And thy do - min - ion en - dur - eth   throughout all gen - er - a - tions,

And thy do - min - ion en - dur - eth   through-

Cres.   Sempre rall.   f   Dim.

(Full Sw.)   Sempre rall.

ff Full Choir.

All thy works shall praise thee, O Lord, and thy saints shall bless thee;

out all gen - er - a - tions. All thy works shall praise thee, O Lord, and thy saints shall bless thee;

Cres.   ff

ff   (Great Org.)

Meno moto.

All thy works shall praise thee, O Lord, and thy saints shall bless . . . thee. . .

All thy works shall praise thee, O Lord, and thy saints shall bless . . . thee. . .

Meno moto.

SELECTIONS.

INDEX OF SUBJECTS.—General Division.

SPECIAL HYMNS & SELECTIONS.

The figures here refer to numbers of Hymns and Selections.

Ab'ba Father, 395, 454, 295; sel. 93.
Abiding, 607, 415.
Accepted time, 273, 621, 629, 631, 645, 652, 656, 663, 665; sel. 59.
Access to God, 315–348, 667, 663.
Activity, 175–192, 410–417, 643, 424–448, 553, 311, 376, 358, 583, 385, 471, 592, 515, 231, 254, 219, 234, 79, 31, 633, 650, 656, 648, 641.
Adoption, 452–455, 391, 393, 395; sel. 93.
Advent, 136–148, 613, 616; sel. 176.
Advocate. See Mediator.
Afflictions, 454–463, 540, 321, 343, 451, 558, 559, 641, 644, 622, 625, 635, 657, 664; sel. 146, 154, 183.
Almost Christian, 615, 621, 215.
Angels, 411, 592, 443.
Anniversary songs, 653.
Ascension, 153–155, 254, 82, 651.
Ashamed of Jesus, 376, 419; sel. 90.
Asleep in Jesus, 562.
Assurance:—
Expressed, 416, 419–411, 615.
Prayed for, 315, 319, 393.
Urged, 448, 431, 446, 443, 311, 385.
Atonement, 205–240, 285–289, 461, 113, 432, 245, 329, 511, 381, 664, 624, 270. See *Additional Hymns*, p. 329.
Attributes of God, 51–61, 60–77, 83–93, 103–131, 273–275, 560–588, 1, 3, 5, 32, 65, 164, 167, 634, 624, 382, 384, 388, 397, 412, 597, 603.
Benevolence (Human), 175–492.
Bible, 189–297, 512, 619, 647.
Brotherly love, 481, 372, 418, 457, 391, 398, 396, 400.
Burial. See *Death* and *Heaven*.
A brother, 567.
A child, 624, 655.
A sister, 566.
A pastor, 567.
A friend, 561.
Calmness, 277, 276, 474.
Calvary, 150–153, 537, 616.
Captain of salvation, 186, 341, 650.
Cares, 428, 211, 446.
Character (of Christ), 325–328, 163, 179.
Charity. See *Brotherly love*.
Cheerfulness, 368, 439. See *Joy*.
Children, 557, 437, 458, 530–533.
Childlike spirit, 474, 614, 617, 621.
Close of worship, 305–308, 84, 277.
Comforter. See *Holy Spirit*.
Communion of Christians:—
With each other. See *Fellowship*.

With God, 345–358, 503, 480, 25, 435, 150, 186, 373, 11, 36.
Communion of saints, 398, 31, 228.
Completeness in Christ, 187.
Confession. See *Repentance* and *Conflict*.
Confidence, 439, 391; sel. 189.
Conflicts, 218–344, 357, 374, 514.
Conformity to Christ, 325–330, 138, 163, 179, 257.
Privileges, 387–395, 375, 452–455, 402, 403, 407, 560.
Church:—
Afflicted, 524.
Beloved of God, 95, 540, 525, 511, 25.
Institutions of, 539, 511, 510, 518, 558.
Ordinances of, 524–547, 400, 534–557, 436–438, 371, 297, 298, 461, 165.
Missions and progress of, 493–527, 311, 544.
Triumph of, 493, 527, 516.
Unity of, 393, 510.
Uniting with. See *Lord's Supper*.
Conscience, 375.
Consecration:—
Of possessions, 323.
Of self to God, 242–248, 255–259, 323, 479, 555, 227, 311, 217, 280, 288, 290, 302, 303, 282, 626, 627, 630.
Consistency, 175, 472.
Consolations. See *Afflictions*.
Constancy, 433, 311, 414.
Contentment, 350, 471.
Conversion. See *Regeneration*.
Conviction. See *Law*.
Corner Stone, 631.
Courage, 410–417, 431–424, 439–448, 219–253, 241, 34, 79, 186, 311, 376, 378, 383, 385, 428, 515, 592, 291, 658, 650, 631.
Covenant, 443, 531; sel. 119, 146, 169.
Creation, 94, 127.
Cross:—
Bearing, 461, 205, 433, 230, 378.
Glorying in, 291, 172, 297, 537.
Salvation by, 321.
Crucifixion, 149, 153, 323.
Death, 561–568, 608, 609, 553.
Decrees of God, 88, 555.
Dedication:—
Of church. See *Sanctuary*.
Of self to God. See *Consecration*.
Delay of repentance, 231, 238, 286, 212, 216.
Dependence:—
On Providence, 586, 50.
On grace, 383, 428, 294, 453, 288.
Depravity. See *Lost state of man*.
Desire of nations, 311.
Despondency. See *Conflict and Encouragement*.
Devotion. See *Consecration* or *Prayer*.

Diligence. See *Activity*.
Divinity (of Christ), 159–187, 110, 616, 666.
Doubt. See *Conflict and Encouragement*.
Doxologies, pages 5, 358, and 277.
Duties, 475–492, 339.
Earnestness. See *Activity*.
Earnest of the spirit, 364, 393.
Election. See *Decrees*.
Encouragements, 371–473, 240 253, 34, 79, 241, 294, 344, 315, 592, 186, 376, 378, 553, 385, 428, 515, 592, 291.
Energy. See *Activity*.
Eternity, 564, 634, 648.
Evening, 44, 586, 591, 596, 602, 610, 359, 593.
Exaltation of Christ, 154–188, 19, 55, 82, 110, 113, 120, 121, 291.
Example:—
Of Christ, 325–330, 163, 179, 472.
Of Christians, 475.
Faintheartedness, 410–417, 428–431, 438–448, 34, 79, 241, 249, 250, 253, 291, 314, 376, 378, 383, 385, 515, 592.
Faith. See *Confidence* and *Trust*.
Gift of God, 259.
Instrument in justification, 304, 222.
Power of, 250, 466.
Prayer for, 279, 456, 37.
Faithfulness of God, 88, 126, 376, 448, 416, 428.
Fall of man. See *Lost state of man*.
Family, 396, 532.
Fasting. See *Afflictions*.
Father, God, our. See *God*.
Fearfulness. See *Conflict and Encouragements*.
Fellowship, 372, 418, 487, 399, 398, 396, 400. See *Brotherly love*.
Fidelity, 257, 295, 467, 479.
Forbearance:—
Divine, 586.
Christian, 179, 469, 277.
Forgiveness:—
Of sin, 60, 217. See *Repentance*.
Of injuries, 469, 179.
Formality, 250, 368, 278.
Funeral. See *Burial* and *Death*.
Friend, Christ our, 322, 657.
Friends in heaven, 575, 569, 31.
Future punishment, 223, 259.
Gentleness, 469.
Gethsemane, 149.
Glory of God. See *God*.
Glorying in the cross. See *Cross*.
God, of—
Being, 56–135, 190.
Benevolence, 118, 72, 473.
Compassion, 208–211. See *Additional Hymns*, p. 329.
Condescension, 173, 58.
Eternity, 92, 358, 73, 3.
Faithfulness, 88, 126, 376, 448, 416, 428.

Father, 58, 124, 451, 295, 454.
Forbearance, 586, 221, 231. See "*Calls*," p. 113.
Glory, 75, 66, 72, 73, 118.
Goodness, 118, 72, 473.
Grace, 54, 453, 383.
Holiness, 127, 310, 28.
Infinity, 588, 272, 274, 92.
Jehovah, 32, 84.
Justice, sel. 155, 152, 161.
Love, 54, 387, 262, 112, 29, 322, 173, 158, 640, 361, 399.
Majesty, 61, 86, 603, 110.
Mercy, 225, 226, 102; sel. 2, 15, 17, 148. See "*Calls*," p. 113.
Mystery, 588, 254, 272, 92.
Omnipotence, 65, 91, 273, 110, 343.
Omnipresence, 131, 124, 271, 343.
Omniscience, 587, 271, 277, 60, 274.
Patience. See *God's Forbearance*.
Pity. See *God's Compassion*.
Providence, 122, 378, 597, 274.
Savior, 83, 183, 440, 666.
Sovereignty, 88, 550.
Supremacy, 73, 88, 119, 86.
Trinity, 119, 658.
Truth, 88, 442, 98, 3, 109.
Unchangeableness, 5, 109, 92, 53, 417, 416, 439, 441.
Unsearchableness, 588, 272, 274.
Wisdom, 60, 412, 56, 274.
Gospel. See *Atonement* and *Way of salvation*.
Grace, 383, 54, 453.
Graces, Christian, 466–475, 276–279, 50, 408, 355, 356.
Gratitude, 50, 473, 52, 53, 588.
Grave, 561–568.
Grieving the Holy Spirit. See *Holy Spirit*.
Growth in grace, 328, 411, 574, 187, 475.
Guidance, Divine, 596, 601, 263, 439, 444.
Happiness, 429–442, 432, 429, 371.
Harvest, 103.
Hearing the word, 84.
Heart:—
Change of. See *Regeneration*.
Deceitfulness of, 284. See *Striving for*, p. 127.
Searching of, 284. See *Striving for*, p. 127.
Surrender of, 257, 342. See *Striving for*, p. 127.
Heaven, 636, 637, 639, 643, 660, 569–581.
Christ there, 564. See *Praise to the Risen Lord*, p. 82.
Friends there, 31, 575, 569, 657.
Home there, 563, 625, 652, 660.
Rest there, 578, 639, 652, 660; sel. 182.
Hell, 259, 223.

381

ALPHABETICAL INDEX OF TUNES.

For many titles of ".Additional Hymns," see first lines.

METRICAL INDEX OF TUNES.

www.ingramcontent.com/pod-product-compliance
Lightning Source LLC
Chambersburg PA
CBHW030904270326
41929CB00008B/562

* 9 7 8 3 3 3 7 2 9 6 5 3 7 *